391
.009
075
Ken

Kennett, Frances.
  The collector's book of fashion / Frances Kennett ;
American editor, Judith Straeten. -- 1st American ed. -
- New York : Crown, c1983.
  256 p. : ill. (some col.) : 28 cm.

Includes index.
Bibliography: p. 250-251.
03327299   LC:82014821   ISBN:0517548607

1. Fashion - History - 20th century. 2. Fashion -
History - 20th century - Collectors and collecting. 3.
                    (SEE NEXT CARD)

THE COLLECTOR'S BOOK OF
FASHION

THE COLLECTOR'S BOOK OF
FASHION

FRANCES KENNETT

American Editor JUDITH STRAETEN

Crown Publishers, Inc
New York

This book is dedicated to my sister, Greta Verdin, always the epitome of style and beauty, and to Chloë, Laura, and Jesse, my other small collection.

Published in the United States by Crown Publishers, Inc., One Park Avenue, New York, New York 10016.

Printed in The Netherlands.

Library of Congress Cataloging in Publication Data

Kennett, Frances.
    The collector's book of fashion.

    Bibliography: p.
    Includes index.
    1. Fashion – Collectors and collecting.
2. Fashion – History – 20th century – Collectors and collecting. 3. Dress accessories – History – 20th century – Collectors and collecting. I. Title.
NK4704.K45 1983 391'.009'04075   82-14821

ISBN 0-517-54860-7

First American Edition.

Produced by Bettina Tayleur Limited
1 Newburgh Street, London W1V 1LH.
Text set by Rowland Phototypesetting Ltd, Bury St Edmunds.
Printed and bound in The Netherlands by de Lange/van Leer b.v., Deventer.
Designed by Leslie & Lorraine Gerry.
Editor: Caroline Eardley.
Picture research: Annette Brown & Philippa Lewis.

Title page: A shaded mauve ostrich feather fan c 1900.

CONTENTS

INTRODUCTION

If there is one single quality that marks the true collector, it is imagination. A labour of love for the objects themselves, the act of collecting encourages and develops a feeling for the tastes and styles of other eras as well as our own. But add imagination to this feeling and the collector is truly in touch with a different age.

The spirit of collecting was best summed up for me by Robert Pusilo, a distinguished New York theatre and film costume designer who was responsible for the lovingly authentic dressing of the film *Hester Street*. He owns thousands of garments, some of which he hires out for film and television work, an activity that finances his collecting habit. His favourite pieces are not couture items, of which he has a few. Instead he showed me a recent acquisition that holds tremendous appeal for him as a genuinely dedicated collector. It was an old brown cotton workdress from the 1910s. The sleeves were faded and grey; the collar had wrinkled and fallen back. This neat dress must have started out in the wardrobe of a schoolmistress or as the morning dress of a housewife of modest means. In time, as could be seen from a glance at the hard-worked elbows, it had passed to the maid. Rummaging in his numerous boxes, Mr Pusilo produced a small brown shawl and folded it around the limp shoulders of the dress. Immediately, a personality and an era were evoked in the juxtaposition of these two shabby objects.

Collecting things that inspire you with this kind of sensitivity to the past is a hobby that enriches the mind and can eventually provide a lasting documentary of both your own taste and your perspective in time. The fashion you would choose now to extract from the last five decades will be vastly different from what will be collected from the same period in fifty years' time. The very act of collecting is an expression of your personality and a significant way of responding to the style of the present. As Mr Pusilo said, 'I am interested in collecting clothes that help me to understand or grasp at another aesthetic of beauty.' It is equally true to say that our own aesthetic as collectors helps to define us.

The people I have met during my researches for this book have all gained a true regard and appreciation for the atmospheres of other ages through the study of their fashions, and in the process have learned a great deal about social history. To open a velvet-lined box and lift out an exquisite wedding fan, or to examine the glamorous complexity of an embroidered jacket by Schiaparelli, puts you in touch with standards of beauty and elegance which are part of a way of life that no longer exists. Any object that stirs the imagination in this way is worth preserving. My aim in writing this book is to help those who have the taste for collecting to gain a vast amount of enjoyment through using their talents in this most varied, colourful and idiosyncratic of fields.

Collecting fashion can offer different satisfactions to different people. For some, it will mean the acquisition of objects of beauty, rarity and high value that will continue to appreciate in worth over the years, bringing both aesthetic pleasure and financial reward. To such collectors, the main attraction is the work of the French couturiers, whose output has now begun to gain esteem and prices comparable with those in the world of picture and antique dealing. Beginners may decide that stylish examples of ready-to-wear clothes offer another kind of satisfaction and interest – particularly if they do not have large financial resources at their disposal. Ready-to-wear can be fascinating, varied, and valuable to document. Even good-quality ready-to-wear from the 1920s to the 1940s may sell quite expensively, and the prices for other periods can only follow suit. The collector can be sure that any well preserved pieces will increase in value as the years go by, particularly if they have labels and details of their origin attached.

Other collectors of fashion will be happier to confine their activities to a single aspect – perhaps lace, fans, buttons or hatpins. Here there may be a far greater choice to be had for a significantly smaller outlay, and the collection will be easier to store. But beware – the smaller items are not always cheap. Fans can reach four-figure sums at auction, and some hatpins in a recent sale in London each fetched several thousand pounds. At the other extreme, many specialist books consider twentieth-century buttons to be valueless except as curiosities, while twentieth-century fans are scarcely given a mention in many collector's manuals. Modern lace, too, is hardly deemed collectable by anyone who can afford to delight in the splendours of hand-made European pieces from the seventeenth and eighteenth centuries; but even so, some modern lace, if well preserved and cherished, will double or treble the buyer's investment within a few years.

I have divided the space in this book fairly equally between ready-to-wear clothes and general fashion history on the one hand, and the work of the great couturiers, and accessory makers on the other. It would be both foolish and financially ruinous for the aspiring collector with limited resources to attempt to concentrate on, say, 1930s couturiers from Schiaparelli to Vionnet. For garments and accessories from before about 1940, the individual is competing in the market with museums, which may have large budgets available for building up their holdings, and with the leading private collectors, who may be very rich indeed. In America, there is further competition from the flourishing business in 'wearables', as opposed to 'collectables'; this caters for the woman who – perhaps for a gallery opening – would rather spend $2,000 on a Poiret velvet cape in not quite good enough condition for a major museum than $3,000 in Saks Fifth Avenue for the latest high-fashion outfit. In a world where money counts, the Poiret cape gives individuality and says, 'I could have gone to Saks, but I really prefer to wear this because it is so beautiful.' Quite apart from being a totally acceptable, indeed rather smart way of saving money, this is, I suppose, not an unsuitable end for a Poiret cape. Its last wearer is just as appreciative of its exotic splendour as the first would have been, just as elegant and moneyed, and just as interested in her own style and its effect on her audience as any one of Poiret's original clients.

Haute couture, then, will be largely beyond the reach of the novice collector. Still, much of the romance in collecting comes from the hope of finding some exquisite couture dress languishing unrecognized in an attic or junk shop – a possibility for which this book will help to prepare you. It still does happen: every collector I have ever met has at some point stumbled across some magnificent piece for next to nothing. And all collectors agree that, once you have spread the word that you are collecting something, examples seem to come to you. People are sympathetic and responsive, as if collectors were the victims of some rare disease and needed to be helped or indulged from time to time. Many collectors have told me of receiving donations, from out of the blue, of second- or third-hand cast-offs that have turned out to be interesting and worthwhile acquisitions. With a little practice, you will develop an instinct and be constantly on the hunt. Cora Ginsburg, the major collector and dealer in New York, goes into small-town bars and restaurants and asks the customers, 'Know anybody around here who's got any trunks?' A question like that is bound to yield some interesting results.

The fashions of the twentieth century provide the collector with the more fleeting reward of owning unusual, or even unique, items that are a pleasure to wear, even if only for a joke. Amateur collectors need not concern themselves with the purist attitudes of museums about this. The idea of wearing old clothes is total anathema to costume curators and conservationists. Their argument is that the supply of antique garments is constantly dwindling; that a valuable part of our heritage is disappearing because of maltreatment – such as the buying and wearing of second-hand clothes by incorrigibles. There are, of course, times when this is a legitimate argument. Exquisite Edwardian lace dresses in good condition are certainly hard to find on both sides of the Atlantic, and it is a shame that some of the best that remain are purchased by expensive shops which ruthlessly cut and alter them, possibly for wearing just once by some wealthy young lady on her wedding day.

Other dresses that might well have withstood careful storage or display in clean air under subdued lighting are ruined by renewed contact with body warmth, sweat and the pollutants of modern city air. There is an appalling story of a beautiful turn-of-the-century satin ball dress that was thoughtlessly cut about for a wedding. It stood up to the fitting sessions and the alterations, but on the day of the wedding itself the accumulated mishandling made it rip right down the back. Exposure to light can make the dyes in an old dress oxidize and literally shred the material to pieces.

On the other hand, there is no shortage of black rayon day dresses from the 1940s, a decade in which ready-to-wear clothes became commonplace. Synthetics such as rayon are in any case more enduring than natural fibres.

There seems every reason to wear a stunning 1940s dress, which can be infinitely more flattering than many of the products of current fashion. It is perfectly sensible to enjoy wearing a favourite dress for a while, treating it with care and respect, and then perhaps, after careful cleaning, to restore it to a collection. Leading authorities have followed this course. Mrs Doris Langley Moore frequently wore garments from her collection, her life's work, which now forms the basis for the Museum of Costume in Bath. On one occasion when I interviewed her she was wearing a 1940s cocktail dress in green grosgrain with gold beading and embroidery around the hem. It was beautiful and in perfect condition, a delight both to wear and to look at.

Your judgement and care in these matters is a reflection of your sense of responsibility as a collector. If you learn to recognize the intrinsic merit of old clothes and accessories, you will simultaneously acquire a respect for the finer pieces and a more familiar affection for the less rare items.

To some extent, price will indicate the importance of a garment and the kind of treatment it should receive, though a considerable number of women would pay thousands for a Fortuny dress and then wear it. This is sacrilege: a Fortuny that has been worn again and again can never be successfully re-pleated. One contemporary artist encases elegantly swathed garments in neat Plexiglass boxes that can be hung on a wall to be displayed like any other valued work of art. I consider this to be a much more suitable end for a Fortuny; I would sooner live with it on the wall than destroy the fabric irrevocably by wearing it.

To highlight the range of possibilities open to the collector, this book does not restrict itself to the work of the great couturiers but also deals with accessories and offers a wide survey of the developments in ready-to-wear clothes in America, England and, to a lesser extent, mainland Europe. A collection of favourite examples of everyday wear might not have much immediate financial value, but it could prove a very worthwhile starting point for a beginner. There are many possible themes that could provide a natural limit to spending – and to the clutter that a costume collection will always bring. I can best illustrate this point by mentioning a few themes among the many discussed in the rest of this book. These include evening wear through the century; the uses of a particular fabric across the changing decades; hats, buttons and other accessories linked by a colour theme; the products of specific areas, such as the sportswear of California or the changing output of Nottingham lace manufacturing. By starting on such a theme as an experiment, the beginner can learn the business of acquiring and develop the habit of research. A limited theme not only imposes discipline but also provides a focus for your efforts.

On the financial aspect of collecting, this book aims only to encourage an awareness of the current state of the market. Even so, it cannot hope to be entirely reliable, as prices can fluctuate alarmingly over as little as six months – a single major auction with some unexpectedly high bids can change a large number of valuations overnight.

This should not prevent you from discovering that there is a fairly obvious scale of values put on clothes and accessories by the salerooms and dealers, from which you should be able to gain some idea of the way in which the market is currently operating. It seems hardly necessary to state that, in general, the older a garment is the more it will cost. However, the excitement of collecting fashion is that this rule is open to very many exceptions.

The amount that a dress will fetch in the saleroom is never entirely predictable. The timid private collector will be among a crowd of museum buyers, specialist dealers, dedicated and often wealthy collectors, and professionals such as theatre or film costume designers with big budgets at their disposal. They will all be looking for different things. The museum representative will be aiming to fill gaps in his collection, and may thus pass over other good buys because his budget will not stretch beyond his specific requirements. The big collector will be equally systematic but is more likely to succumb to a whim and buy an Edwardian walking dress to add to a collection that already contains six of them, but none in that particular, special colour. The costume designer will be attracted by style, colour, flair or even an unusually textured fabric or interesting trimming that catches his eye as something that can be used in a design scheme. Sometimes, as a result, an article will reach a much higher price in the bidding than a knowledgeable observer would have expected. Yet the private collector could be lucky; a big museum buyer does not appear, or a wealthy collector goes down with 'flu, and the chance is there.

Another point about salerooms is that the auctioneer is paid a commission for his services. It therefore makes no sense for him to put up really cheap items because they will yield insufficient commission for the time taken to sell them. One way around this problem is for the saleroom to group undistinguished things into 'lots'. Linens, laces, camisoles, hats and even dresses may be sold in this way. You therefore need to attend the viewings which salerooms usually hold before any sale, examine the articles carefully and check the lots to see which are really worth a bid. Here the individual collector may be faced with a dilemma. If you want one 1920s camisole, what would you do with another nine? A single camisole in a store might cost half as much as the entire lot in the saleroom, but it could, even so, be more sensible and economical to buy the former. At least, you are spared the time-consuming chore of viewing, and you do not end up with things you do not really want.

But you should always remember that single items do, sometimes surprisingly, go for ridiculously low prices at auction. It is certainly worth taking the trouble of attending a few sales to get the feel of the bidding and to see the variation in prices that always happens. A sound piece of advice was given to me by one of the auctioneers at Christie's in London. She has observed that many members of the public are scared by the speed at which bidding takes place in a saleroom; they feel that if they once put up a hand they will never get it down in time to avoid being trapped into paying more than they intended. Salerooms will usually indicate what each lot is expected to fetch, but you should also mark your catalogue with your own top price for anything you particularly like. If you see that the bidding is not reaching the estimated level and that the object is still below your personal price ceiling, you can then try to bid. Marking your catalogue beforehand will make your bidding more controlled, less dangerously impulsive.

As an inexperienced collector, you may face certain risks in the saleroom, but you can do much worse elsewhere. In Britain, there are jumble sales and charity shops. There are also flea markets, Saturday markets, old junk shops that may sometimes have a box of clothes or accessories tucked away in a corner, and more formal antique shops that deal in lace, buttons and perhaps the odd hat or velvet cloak. Junk shops outside London offer distinct possibilities of rewarding finds, but charity shops tend to put a fairly high price on anything that is obviously old, attractive and in good condition: silver mesh bags, strings of glass beads, and so on. In America, the situation is different and rather more extreme. Out-of-town junk shops are again good places to look, but the 'thrift' shops are all too knowing about the second-hand market. They will often price an unusual acquisition much too high, so that the unwary collector ends up paying two or three times the amount he or she would pay in a saleroom or to a reputable dealer.

Small shops that specialize in lace, fans, buttons or old clothes are likely to charge more than is comfortable for many collectors. After all, the dealers have had to sift through the salerooms, to spend hours waiting to bid, to travel widely, searching out trunkloads of interesting old clothes, and to present them clean and well pressed in premises on which they have to pay the overheads. Of course their prices will be high. Any method you choose for building your collection will have its advantages and disadvantages: the more adventurous you are in your sources, the more time you are likely to spend on fruitless quests. The specialist shop may be expensive, but it will have attractive merchandise and, with any luck, the owner will give you the benefit of his or her experience and generally help you to build up an appreciation of your chosen subject. The worst owners will lie about the true nature and scarcity of items in their stock and charge you extortionate prices.

There are, however, many amateur organizations that will help you to learn more about collecting fashion. Many are listed in the final section of this book, as are all museums and collections which have substantial holdings of twentieth-century fashion. They can provide examples for you to study and may be able to give useful advice and help with identification. There is no doubt that collecting takes time; if you can invest that in your chosen area, you will have a great advantage.

Perhaps the greatest attraction of fashion for the collector is that the individual does really stand a good chance of being able to develop an eye for what is valuable for a collection and what is undistinguished. Collecting paintings, say, or silver, requires a great deal of background knowledge and considerable financial investment. Fashion is one of the few areas in which the collector can do well with a reasonable amount of time for research and self-education and a comparatively small outlay of money.

Enthusiasm, patience and a desire to learn are vital attributes for the successful collector, in addition to enough courage or madness to spend a little money on something genuinely liked. Cultivating individual taste and selectivity is the most important preparation for forming a good collection – and fashion allows almost unlimited scope.

*An Edwardian beauty, Miss
Carroll McComas, in 1905.*

THE FIRST DECADE

The 1900s represent the end of the era when ladies were ladies, when romance and mystery were the predominant characteristics of female attire. The Edwardian era became a watershed between the formality of the nineteenth century and the liberating experimentalism of the following twenty years. In some senses it is true to say that the decade was more in the hands of the corsetière than in those of the couturier. The very silhouette of the age shows how the contemporary aesthetic demanded a figure of quite distorted but supremely womanly and other-worldly beauty. The wasp waist, generous 'mono' bust with no cleavage and the high-piled hair all suggested a servitude to strict rules of fashion (and by implication a servitude to men), and it was this celebration of fantasy-womanhood that the new century would slowly abandon. Women were meant to be admired – and to be daringly and deliciously undressed in the imagination. All those buttons and ribbons were so inviting. This was the age of the petticoat, the glimpsed ankle, the unresisting stays, the glory of lace and lacings.

For the collector, the period offers a host of delights, from exquisite undergarments to the prettiest beaded or braided jackets, fine feather stoles, kid gloves, camisoles, buttoned bodices and fringed shawls. This was still a time when all women had clothes made for them. They had to lay out a considerable sum of money for a new outfit because the garments were very substantially made, and involved a great deal of material and decoration. Clothes were habitually made over, handed down, stored and passed on as heirlooms in a way that was not continued in subsequent decades. So it is still possible to find some delightful Edwardian fragments and build up a truly nostalgic, historically valuable collection.

The basic clothing of the decade varied little from 1900 to 1908 or 1909, when the Ballet Russe and Poiret were launched on the Parisian scene. These final years belong stylistically to the next decade, and will be included in the following chapter. The dress of what we term the Edwardian era, leading up to the close of the decade, consisted typically of a high-necked blouse, usually made either in the newly popular Swiss material 'broderie anglaise' decorated all over with eyelet holes in floweret shapes, or in voile, or pintucked linen or cotton, worn in winter over a flared or gored full-length skirt in fine wool or serge, and in summer over a similar skirt made from a lighter-weight fabric. Mansfield and Cunnington, authors of *Handbook of English Costume in the 20th Century 1900–1950*, list the various

The 'S'-bend silhouette of the Edwardian era: a Spring coat and skirt complete with lacy blouse and chiffony sunshade.

A typical Charles Dana Gibson illustration, showing the becoming emphasis on curves and curls, from Everyday People, *1904.*

Top right *A glorious array of Edwardian lacy splendours from* Chic Parisien *published in April 1905. Note the variety of frills and flounces in the skirts.*

The ideal, plump but stylized figure of the period: a lace evening gown designed by Redmayne, 1900, from an illustration in The Queen.

pretty names by which the skirts were known: the 'waterfall', which had tucks around the hips, the 'mermaid', which, as the name suggests, fitted closely over the hips and thighs and flared out from the knees at the back; and the 'sunray', a pleated circular skirt. Various skirts were made with several gored sections, the effect of such cutting on the cross and seaming being to emphasize the downward flow of the skirt, and subtly suggest the form of the legs beneath. By one device or another, every curve of a woman's body was hinted at, or exaggerated, while the wearer pushed out her bust and her bottom to complete the idealized, 'S'-bend silhouette. The embodiment of this ideal was drawn by Charles Dana Gibson, the American illustrator, and was universally known as the 'Gibson Girl'. Her other day-time outfit might well be a shirtwaist dress, with the same shapes as the skirt and blouse, made up in a light-weight lace, satin or cotton lawn. A one-piece dress with no waist seam, fitted bodice and flared skirt ('Princess' line) was another possibility.

It was in evening wear, however, that Edwardian clothes really came into their own. Rich, sumptuous fabrics, with shine, texture and a thousand rich shades and colour combinations were made up into dresses of a deep décolletage, boned and so tightly waisted that the accompanying generosity of bust and hips seems totally fantastic. Wide sprays of feathers, elaborate, dish-shaped hats, and piles of hair, mounted over false pads in the 'Pompadour' style, all complemented the grandeur of the attire.

Fashionable Paris was in its heyday during the 1900s. The clothing was so elaborate that the touch of a couturier was distinctive and necessarily in demand. The most distinguished houses of the time were those of Worth – then in the hands of Gaston, younger son of the great Charles Worth, possibly the first great couturier of France – and Jacques Doucet, who was renowned for the refinement of his taste. A number of women made a tremendous success for themselves in a field where, later, it was the men who reigned. The Great Universal Exhibition of 1900, held in Paris, had a huge fashion section which was presided over by Madame Paquin (wife of a banker, who no doubt helped with her finances). She was the first couturière to open houses abroad, which she did in London, Madrid and Buenos Aires. The Callot Soeurs and Madame Cheruit are other women

A leading designer of the period was Madame Paquin who created this beautifully decorated coat and skirt in 1907, made of blue face cloth with silk braid trimming.

Sumptuous and solid: three designs from the house of Worth. **Above, left** Curiously modern decoration on a bolero-style jacket (1901). **Above, top right** An evening coat showing the love of rich trimming for which the house was justifiably famous (1905–06). **Above, lower right** A Worth ball gown accompanied by all the appropriate accessories – ermine, feathers and bag (1907–8).

who contributed significantly and successfully to Edwardian couture; their clothes are now solely museum pieces, and are very expensive to acquire.

Of equal importance was the work of Redfern, an English tailor who had started in London but soon moved to Paris, and produced the most striking versions of the 'tailleur', or tailored walking-suit, which was another typical outfit of the period. This suit had been popular in England in the 1890s, and Elizabeth Ewing suggests in her *History of Twentieth Century Fashion* that the idea was born during the yachting season at Cowes, as a female version of the man's sporting outfit considered appropriate for such social occasions. Whatever its origins, its acceptability was sealed when Charles Poynter left the London house of Redfern in 1881 to set up a similar establishment in Paris, and launched the tailleur in France. From that date it rivalled the more overtly feminine outfits of Worth and Doucet, and became some slight symbol of emancipation for independent, career-minded women of the time. These suits now seem wonderfully feminine, with their hip-hugging skirts, flowing, heavy hems and nipped-waisted jackets, often complemented by a peplum-cut flare over the hips. A rival in fame as the originator of the tailleur is Charles Creed, another Englishman, who ran a successful tailoring business in London and opened a second establishment in Paris in 1850. He was invited to make a tailored suit, a copy of his client's own, by the Duke of Alba for his wife. The outfit caused a fashion sensation, and soon the tailored walking-suit was ordered from Creed by such distinguished customers as the Queen of Italy, the Infanta of Spain, a Russian duchess and a number of Edwardian theatrical beauties, from Madame Rejane to Gaby Deslys. The reasons for the tailleur's success were that it was immensely practical, it was very flattering in its line, and it was able to be slightly altered in its effect by the choice of blouse worn with it – and the blouses of this period are exquisite in their variety, fabric and workmanship. Even the advertisements from the newly founded big stores of the time show a high standard of detail and decoration on their houses. In 1904 Swan and Edgar of London offered a 'stylish crêpe de Chine slip, prettily made, with Hairpin work, and smart Lace motifs, in Cream, Sky, Pink, Emerald, Turquoise, Navy and Black'. Another shows a 'pretty Accordion-pleated Nun's Veiling Shirt, trimmed Lace Insertion and Hairpin work, in Cream, Sky, Pink, Navy and Black, with Ecru Lace'.

In America, the ready-to-wear industry had started up several decades in advance of England; 'waists', which was the name given to the blouses worn with a tailored suit, or more simply with a dark skirt, were featured in many of the mail-order catalogues issued in the 1890s by such giant concerns as Sears, Roebuck; Marshall Field; and Montgomery Ward: they ranged in price from 50c for a simple cotton shirt to $150 for one in hand-made silk. The blouses were produced in tenement-building sweat-shops, where piece-workers, several to a room, endlessly repeated one part of the manufacturing operation, such as pin-tucking, sleeve insertion or collar mounting, before passing on bundles of the semi-finished garments to the

Exquisite eyelet embroidery, an Edwardian favourite, for a dress designed by Redfern, illustrated in Les Modes, *Paris, 1908.*

next group of workers in this early version of the production-line system. In 1909 the waist-makers went on strike in New York. As Sandra Ley describes it, in *Fashion for Everyone*, 'The strike involved about 20,000 workers and was extremely bitter and violent. It started in November and lasted until February of 1910. The strikers, many of them young women, were beaten and arrested. They not only had to endure the beatings, but starvation and extreme cold as well. They finally won a settlement . . . the fifty-two hour week was considered the greatest gain as a result of the strike.'

In London, the new ready-to-wear business in blouses and underwear was enjoying a boom. In 1899 George Givan from Belfast came to New Bond Street with a fine selection of Irish linen goods. From Paris came Jean Dellière in 1906 to establish the White House, also in New Bond Street, where it trades to this day. Other famous names from this period are the Irish Linen Company and Leighton & Joseph, both also of New Bond Street.

Blouses were not, of course, the only article sold by the little shops, the stores, or the mail-order houses of America. 'Whites' in general were in great demand. This term describes all the articles of clothing made from linen, cotton, lawn or lace, needing to be laundered, and worn underneath the elaborate day dresses or walking-suits of the time. Alison Adburgham in

Early ready-to-wear: an advertisement for blouses from Stagg & Mantles of Leicester Square, London. The plaid version in silk cost 45s 9d, while the model in front, also in silk, cost 24s 9d. Note the hats – a paradise feather for the mink toque, and bunches of wood violets for the white felt sailor hat. The Gentlewoman, November 1904.

Shops and Shopping quotes a typical £100 trousseau from Debenham & Freebody's, London, and mentions that most of the items were 'convent made' – hand stitched, in all probability. The date of this list is 1912, but it would be a good indication of an Edwardian lady's expectations:

	£	s	d
6 chemises, cambric or batiste, trimmed lace or hand embroidery, at 10/6	3	3	0
6 linen chemises, hand embroidered and ribbon, at 18/9	5	12	6
3 evening chemises, fine lawn, trimmed lace and ribbon, at 18/9	2	16	3
6 nightdresses, cambric or nainsook, trimmed embroidery, at 15/9	4	14	6
6 nightdresses, trimmed lace, at 21/9	6	10	6
6 pairs knickers, trimmed hand embroidery or lace, at 15/9	4	14	6
6 linen knickers, trimmed hand embroidery and ribbon, at 18/9	5	12	6
3 knickers, trimmed lace and ribbon, at 21/9	3	5	3
1 crêpe de chine evening petticoat trimmed lace, etc.	3	5	0
1 coloured satin petticoat	1	1	9
3 white petticoats, embroidered flounces, at 12/9	1	18	3
2 white petticoats, trimmed hand embroidery at 18/9	1	17	6
2 white petticoats, trimmed lace and ribbon, at 25/6	2	11	0
6 camisoles hand embroidered or lace, at 8/11	2	13	6
3 linen camisoles, trimmed hand embroidery and ribbon, at 14/9	2	4	3
3 camisoles, trimmed lace and ribbon, at 16/9	2	10	3
3 dozen diaper towels, at 18/9	2	16	3
4 crêpe de santé petticoats, trimmed lace, at 14/9	2	19	0
4 cream Japanese silk petticoats, at 14/9	2	19	0
1 pair Milanese silk knickers		18	9
4 Indian gauze combinations, at 14/9	2	19	0
3 fancy gauze combinations, at 18/9	2	16	3
1 pair Milanese combinations, for evening wear	1	15	3
1 silk dressing gown	2	9	6
1 muslin dressing gown, trimmed lace	1	9	6
1 tea-gown	4	4	0
1 flannel gown	2	9	6
1 silk dressing jacket	1	9	6
1 muslin dressing jacket		18	9
2 boudoir caps, at 18/9	1	17	6
1 nightdress sachet	1	1	9
1 dozen fancy bordered handkerchiefs		12	6
1 dozen fancy cambric handkerchiefs		15	0
1 pair spun woven knickers	1	7	6

'Useful Ivory Jap blouse slip' with Torchon lace insertions – ready-to-wear of intricate workmanship.

Other advertisements indicate both the elaborate workmanship and the universality of certain materials, such as French lace, or Irish crochet work. (Most of the Edwardian dresses currently to be seen in New York, and most of the trousseaux made there for the wealthy, were made of Irish lace: Francesca Bianco, of the Bridal Salon at Saks Fifth Avenue, confirms that at the turn of the century Ireland was a major source of lace, and that any self-respecting or affluent lady of society would naturally acquire her best

Left *A typical dressmaker's salon or atelier photographed in Berlin, 1910.*

Right *An extravagant blouse in fine black net over chiffon, embellished with sequins, from Woollands Bros., London 1904.*

whites and laces from Ireland or France, either through importation or while on her own foreign travels.

A description from an advertisement for D. H. Evans in an issue of the *Queen*, a British magazine, of 1905 gives some idea of the elaborate workmanship which was expected in even standard ready-to-wear lines at the time: 'Prominent in the group will be found the latest *robe de nuit* cut in a round décolleté and with elbow sleeves. This is trimmed with Torchon lace, and beautifully made. Another dainty nightrobe is Irish hand made, exquisitely tucked and adorned with real Torchon . . .'

One of the reasons for such standards having been expected of ready-made items was that the Edwardian lady herself still had the time to spend on finishing her own things with a fine degree of detail and workmanship. The *Queen* at this period included a section entitled 'The Work Table', in which patterns for crochet, lace and home-made buttons were explained in detail. Sometimes, however, the Edwardian lady would make her fine cotton blouse at home, and then take it to an atelier to have the finishing embroidery added to it. Magazines of the time also give the impression that some of the snobbery about handwork applied then exactly as it does today: the *Queen* makes an editorial comment about some wonderful 'hand made washing buttons' for linen 'made by dairy maids on a Polish estate' – not a far cry from the charitably run workshops of the Third World today that produce knits, ponchos and woven cloths for those seeking the 'ethnic' look.

A comparison may be made with a notice of a 'summer white sale' which appeared in a 1905 catalogue put out by Wanamakers, one of America's earliest department stores, based in New York with branches in Phila-delphia and Paris. Included in the bargain offers were shirtwaist suits, wrappers, waists, dressing-sacques, caps and aprons, neckwear, coloured petticoats, white petticoats, chemises, nightgowns, drawers, corset covers, corset and dress improvers, besides children's wear and household linens. The standard underwear for the period on both sides of the Atlantic consisted of the following: first would come a chemise, worn next to the skin, with a little drawstring ribbon round the neck, or a satin ribbon threaded through the edging over the bustline, depending how high the neckline came; over that came the tight corseting which created the extraordinary silhouette of curving, full bosom, flat stomach, arched back and prominent derrière: over that was worn the camisole, either sleeved or sleeveless, trimmed elaborately with lace and forming a bodice beneath the outer clothing. (These of course are now immensely popular in the antique

Below *The corset that made the statuesque curves possible: the 'Bon Ton' from Peter Robinson Ltd, Oxford Street, 1910.*

Above, top *A lovely Edwardian style-setter, encased in lace: Miss Eva Moore, and* **below** *Mrs Lily Langtry in grand pose with the ubiquitous Edwardian corsage and pearls.*

Above, right *Grand Edwardiana: upswept hair, pearl chokers, frills, fans and beaded tassles. Femina et La Mode 1904.*

market; they sell from $15 upwards in New York, in shops such as Victoria Falls, and even Bloomingdales.) Below the waist came the 'drawers' – knee-length knickers – followed by a flannel petticoat, several cotton petticoats, and probably a silk underskirt as a smooth underlining for the dress. Another popular item was a taffeta petticoat which made a rich rustling noise as the wearer walked; this came between the cotton petticoats and the silk underskirt; the sound of a dress rustling over the combination of taffeta and silk sounded expensive. Alison Adburgham describes it in *Shops and Shopping* as 'the psychology of the mink-lined raincoat'.

If day dresses and underwear seem elaborate, they are modest in comparison with the stunning effect of the Edwardian lady out for the evening. Dress clothes reached a height of richness and complication which they were never to see again. Decoration was everything in the Edwardian era, as this description from an issue of the *Lady* of 1902 serves to show: 'Garnitures of pearls, groups of tinsel butterflies or dragonflies and *choux* [rosettes] of velvet or satin, edged with pearly or coral beads, are favourite adornments. White lace robes are encrusted with appliqués of black lace, and black lace robes with the heavier type of Venicepoint in cream or ecru'.

Evening clothes were as richly decorated as the most elaborate fantasy of a theatrical costume; the link was obvious, for the Edwardian era marks the high point of theatre as an influence on fashion – or at least, the ideal of beauty was set by the tastes and innovations of the stars of the theatre. Women such as Eva Moore, Lily Langtry, Sarah Bernhardt and Maxine Elliot set the fashion of the moment. *Vogue* magazine notes for instance that the dancer Florence Walton, who was partnered by her husband Maurice, favoured the silver and gold dresses made for her by Callot Soeurs: when she went to New York they would send her a dress a week. Ruby Miller recalled in her memoirs how, during Ascot week, 'we Gaiety Girls led the fashions, trailing the lawns wearing gorgeous creations of crêpe de Chine, chiffon or lace over petticoats of rustling silk edged with hundreds of yards of fine Valenciennes lace threaded with narrow velvet ribbon. Every stitch sewn by hand and no couturier of repute would have dreamed of copying a model gown'. It seems no coincidence that the two great reformers to emerge at the end of the decade should be people who had close links with the theatre, and often designed for it: Lucile, Lady Duff-Gordon, in England, and Paul Poiret in Paris (both are discussed in the following chapter.)

There was something 'stagey' and theatrical about the styles and manners of the Edwardian lady; before donning her lavish attire, she would relax in the misnomered 'tea gown'. (This was worn not in the afternoons, as one might expect, for tea time was the hour for the 'bridge frock', another elaborate day-time construction worn with a matching 'bridge coat' or an elegant version of a 'waist' or shirt blouse.) The tea gown was put on in the early part of the evening, before the rigorous performance of adorning the body with full evening dress began. It was considered permissible to dine at home in a tea gown, which is not surprising when we consider the beauty and seductiveness of these creations. They were generally made of voile and lace, or of silk, or of the finest wools, and usually had lace decoration. Quite often the dress was cut in one piece, with no waist seam, to fall negligently from a yoke or from the shoulderline. Over-blouses or wraps of lace would accompany these dresses; the edge of the shawl might be decorated with satin ribbons, pompons or lace frills; the dress itself could have inserts of lace running down the front, or lace frills attached to the skirt.

The informal line of these dresses may have been precursor to the loose shape that Poiret created in the decade that followed; they were present in the work of Mariano Fortuny, the Spanish designer in Italy who produced Grecian-style, flowing robes with minute pleats. His work is discussed in the following chapter also, but perhaps the suggestion for his creations lay in the idea of relaxed individuality which the Edwardian society lady allowed herself to manifest discreetly at home in her romantic and beautiful tea gowns.

The wardrobe described above was that of a wealthy woman who could afford to buy her underwear in Bond Street and her dresses from Paris or New

Cinq heures chez Paquin, 1907, *a painting by Henri Gerveux, showing the hustle and bustle at a popular couturier.*

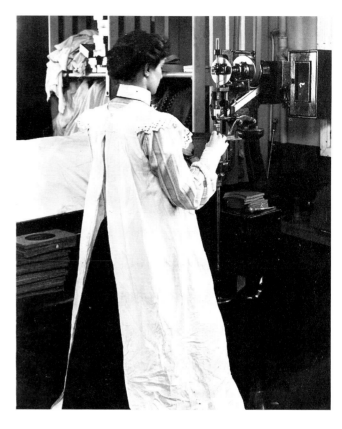

York. But the first decade saw also the beginnings of independence, and with it a genuine move in the styling of fashion to take account of a more practical, realistic attitude to a woman's place in the world. The success of the 'waist' owes a great deal to its popularity with working women; the new stenographer, schoolmistress or shop-girl felt suitably attired in a practical serge skirt or simple, tailor-made suit, but her femininity was still allowed its expression in the delicacy and primness of the 'waist'. This became standard 'uniform' for the working girl, of whom there were many in the big cities of America, in London and in Paris.

An interesting collector's piece from these early days is the 'Prairie dress', a long-sleeved calico or gingham design with a frilled hem, sold through the catalogue companies Sears, Roebuck and Montgomery Ward. The style is also found in home-made versions, which for collectors are even more interesting. It is still possible to find the catalogue versions in dealers' shops for about $160, according to the *Fashion Encyclopedia* by Catherine Houck.

A second influence on more middle-class young women was the growing interest in sport. As early as the 1890s, the so-called 'New Woman' had come into being, madly bicycling about; the Rational Dress Society, formed in England in 1883 and receiving the support of such distinguished aesthetes as Oscar Wilde, had tried to do away with such impracticalities as bustles and petticoats. Their alternatives were unfortunately not particularly appealing, but the idea was bruited that women should wear clothes which combined attraction with a little more simplicity. In the midst of the splendours of the Edwardian era, the appearance of the tailor-made and the shirtwaist suggested a new practicality and plainness, which was in keeping with the adventurousness of so many 'New Women' of the time. Sports, golf, croquet, cricket, hockey, skating and fishing were now considered acceptable pastimes for energetic young women, although one wonders at female agility in so many petticoats.

Day-time fashions could be copied by the rising middle-class woman, even if evening wear were too elaborate to undertake at home. Serge skirts would be made with the help of the newly invented dressmaking pattern, which had first appeared in America in the late nineteenth century (*Harper's Bazaar* offered paper patterns to subscribers in a special supplement from the late 1860s). A contemporary magazine gives suggestions for the fabrics a home dressmaker might use for a simple dress: 'As far as the fabric itself is concerned, any of the soft-falling materials of the hour are equally suitable, crêpe de Chine, silk voile, or canvas, being particularly pretty, while a fine soft cashmere or even a nun's veiling may on occasions be successfully employed.'

Women's magazines such as the *Delineator* in America and the *Lady* in London helped to spread the word about the fashionable Parisiennes. Perhaps the influence of stage actresses and singers was significant, as they were often not women from high society, even if they ended up there through advantageous marriages. The 1900s adhered to a strict orthodoxy in dress, but there were a great many rumblings and revolutions under the surface. Behind the romance of the white lace blouse lies the poverty of the 'waist-maker' who went on strike in the winter freeze of New York. Behind those petticoats and the efficient slim skirt, a *petite bourgeoise* struggles to learn typing and make ends meet. The message slowly but surely communicated to an avid magazine reader of the day was that a 'New Life' could be obtained. Liberation was at hand.

Above *An unusual yet practical hand-knit jersey, the 'Kit-Kat' from Debenham & Freebody, London 1904 – 'suitable for Travelling and Country wear, Golf, Hockey, etc. . . . hand-knitted by Swiss peasantry.'*

Above, left *Yachting and motoring clothes for the emerging, active twentieth-century woman. Les Modes 1908.*

THE TEENS

Far right *A typical simple tunic, banded at the bust, from an illustration by George Barbier, in* Costume Parisiens, *1912.*

Right *Design by Leon Bakst for the costume of Potiphar's wife in Strauss's ballet,* La Legende de Joseph, *in the Ballet Russe season of 1914: pattern on pattern and eastern forms were rapidly absorbed into contemporary fashions.*

Far right *A theatre coat entitled 'Blanc et Noir' for an illustration in* Gazette du Bon Ton *1914; the design is by Redfern, the English tailor who had moved into couture work in Paris a decade before.*

Right *Design for a chapter opening from the* Gazette du Bon Ton *1914, revealing a certain ambivalence about free-flowing clothing: during the 1910s the ankles suffered constriction rather than the waist.*

The years from 1908 to 1919 heralded a complete break with the past. A series of changes began in women's fashion which reflected both a different aesthetic and a real alteration in the status of women. These are years filled with contradictions in terms of dress.

The dominant artistic influence of the decade was that of the Ballet Russe, which arrived in Paris in 1909 with its director Serge Diaghilev. The Ballet's subsequent seasons were wildly popular. The colours and lines inspired by the exotic Oriental costume designs of Léon Bakst for the company seized the imagination of the fashion world and were the major source of ideas until well into the 1920s. The shift, which is so commonly associated with the following decade, can be found in the 1910s too, and existed side by side with more elaborate, full-skirted dresses until at least 1925. During the 1910s, while skirts crept up a few inches from the ground, and the line of the typical dress became that of a simple tunic, banded under the bust, there was also a contradictory movement towards restriction. The seductive and artificial 'S'-bend silhouette of the Edwardian era, when tight corsetry more or less remoulded the female figure, certainly relaxed into a new liberty. But where the waist and hips were freed, the legs suddenly became restricted in a series of fantastical notions, such as the 'hobble' skirt and the 'trotteur'. Skirts were straight, or even tapering inwards, or were draped round the ankles in a hampering effect. Pleats or slits served only to emphasize the lack of freedom of movement. The contradiction between this style and the burgeoning suffragette movement was underlined by the following comment in the London *Times* Weekly Edition in 1914: 'Man cannot imagine a woman, dressed as women have seen fit to dress for the last few years, being competent to take any serious or worthy part in the work of the world. He cannot believe in a woman being capable of efficient, vigorous or independent action when hampered by the skirt of the period.' Further contradic-

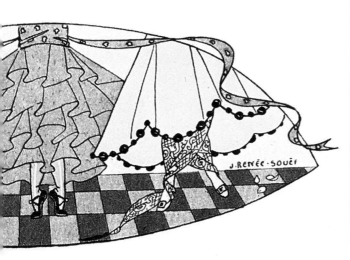

New mannish suits and swashbuckling hats replaced the frills and lace of the 1900s (fashion plate by Helen Robertson, 1912). **Below** *Advertisement for Paul Poiret's licence operation in America, Vogue 1916.*

tions rose between day and evening wear: throughout the decade, the tendency was for day clothes to become increasingly practical and mannish, or directly sporty in look and style, while evening clothes became lusciously 'fancy dress', with all kinds of variations on the Eastern theme, from harem trousers to 'minaret'-shaped dresses with overskirts, all bound with furs, braids, glittering beads and the ubiquitous long strings of brightly coloured costume baubles.

If the Ballet Russe served as the main source of inspiration, there was one man who dominated the period in his wholehearted transformation of the Ballet's theatrical style into high Parisian elegance. This was Paul Poiret. In his own words, Poiret admitted, 'Yes, I freed the bust, but I shackled the legs . . .', referring to the essential underpinning garment which he launched in 1908. This was a new, straight-line corset that did away with the 'S'-bend and started high under the bust (making a separate, figure-supporting brassière a new and important feature of a woman's wardrobe), and descended almost to the knee, creating a slim-hipped, loose-waisted shape, but inhibiting easy sitting and walking. Gradually, the corset was modified so that it became more comfortable and less restricting, leading the trend towards the totally freed figure of the 1920s.

However uncomfortable this garment may seem to us now, it was a complete departure from the elaborate corsetry of the previous decade, and created an exciting new atmosphere in the way that women presented themselves, moved, danced or paraded in the streets. Poiret described the source of his inspiration as classical, although the feeling of his designs is far removed from the 'Empire' style of the Napoleonic era, which had been similarly derived. Poiret's look was more natural, more liberating and less romantic: 'While studying sculptures of ancient times, I learned to use one point of support – the shoulders, where before it had been the waist . . . Fabrics flowed from this ideal point like water from a fountain and draped the body in a way that was entirely natural. . . From now on the breasts will no longer be "worn".' Although Poiret claimed that he owed nothing to Bakst, and was already designing clothes in the most striking reds, oranges and purples before the Ballet Russe arrived in Paris, the Ballet must undoubtedly have urged on the general popularity of these designs and outlandish colours in the circles of high society.

Poiret had also learnt much about the other main artistic influences of the time from his employer, the couturier Jacques Doucet. In private life Doucet formed a splendid collection of works of the early Impressionist painters, of French eighteenth-century art, and also of African sculpture, which was to be a great source of inspiration for shapes and for jewellery over the next two decades. (It is often noted that the international society of the 1910s and 1920s was much less racially prejudiced than later generations: African art, African painting, the black and gorgeous figure of Josephine Baker dancing in Parisian night-clubs, the elegance of jazz band leaders newly arrived from America – the Original Dixieland Jazz Band played to packed houses in London as early as 1919 – all added to a fascination with black culture.) Doucet's clothes were much more restrained than his pupil's, with a refinement which was of another order – more wearable, less dramatic, but

Top left *A good selection of ready-to-wear underpinnings which gave the new straight line and flattened the bust: from Harrods, 1919.*

Below, left La Cape Ecossaise – *theatrical styling, evoking the mood of the 1910s, with turbans and bold fabric designs.* Gazette du Bon Ton, *April 1914.*

Copies of Paris gowns were also available in New York, like this one designed by Jenny, available from Bendels.

27

very appealing. After his training there, Poiret, a Parisian bourgeois by upbringing, moved to the house of Worth, but clearly found the traditional approach of this great designer not to his liking.

In 1904 Poiret opened his own salon, and with his inimitable gift for publicity soon had Paris at his feet. He threw elaborate parties at his house, publicized his own work magnificently, and before long had the society ladies and actresses of the day clamouring for his clashing-coloured, loose-fitting robes. In 1906 he designed a lovely 'robe de minute', a simple, two-piece tunic, which was as far removed from the waist-cinched, petticoat-laden fashions of a few years before as anything that could be imagined. In 1909 he created a standing-out overskirt to his tunic style, known as the 'lampshade' line, and followed it in the same year with his most famous look, the hobble skirt. In 1910 Paris saw Nijinsky, painted black, writhing around the stage in the role of a slave in *Schéhérazade*. Bakst's golden yellows, with swirling circles of purple and orange, and the glittering of gold and silver, confirmed the trend launched by Poiret and secured his supremacy until the end of the decade. One of his most famous designs of 1912 was called 'Sorbet', a 'lampshade' tunic over a long, black, satin skirt; one shoulder was in white satin, the other in black, and the embroidery with pistachio, pink and mauve 'caviare' beads sizzled with 'sherbert' colours.

The soft pastels of Doucet rapidly appeared out of place, and other designers soon joined Poiret in the quest for the rich, exotic and lavish.

Left *A typically gorgeous Callot Soeurs beaded evening dress, a combination of silk brocade, chiffon, lace and jet beaded decoration, 1913.*

Above, right *All the leading names of the decade: left to right, suits by Paquin, Lanvin, Doueillet, and Paquin again – illustrated by Valentine Gross, who also sketched the* Ballet Russe *at the time.* Gazette du Bon Ton *1915.*

Callot Soeurs, two sisters, made exquisite lace blouses and richly beaded party dresses; they were responsible for an enduring vogue for silver and gold lamé in evening dresses. Lanvin and Vionnet both began their careers in this decade (although their work is more fully discussed in the following chapter): Jeanne Lanvin's 'robe de style' was first introduced in 1915, but remained popular throughout the 1920s. A waisted, full-skirted dress, it ran counter to the currently popular looks but was a favourite alternative. Madeleine Vionnet opened her doors in 1912, and her slithery, bias-cut dresses stayed equally popular until the mid-1930s. She, too, favoured the shine of satin and the luxury of crêpe de chine for her dresses. Doeuillet, Worth, Redfern, Idare and Molyneux were other couturiers of the period who produced inventive and distinctive fashions.

Gabrielle Chanel's impact on this decade was most significant in the new ideas about fabric and acceptable style, both of which she changed considerably. Before the First World War, in the first years of the decade, she worked from a small establishment in the rue Cambon in Paris, but in 1914 she moved to Deauville, where the everyday clothes of the local fishermen inspired her to design casual, practical clothes for women – slightly adapted fisherman's-knit sweaters, 'matelot' dresses with pretty, wide, white collars, and a more feminine version of a pea-jacket for sporting occasions. But perhaps the greatest of all her early ideas, and one which had a tremendous impact on the 'eye' of the fashionable lady of the time, was her introduction

of jersey cloth as a smart, acceptable fabric. Her new ensemble, known as a 'dressmaker suit', consisted of a simple, straight skirt with a cardigan – a straight, loose jacket, often made without a collar or with soft-falling revers. A matching blouse completed the outfit, which quite overtook the tailored suit at the time, and has continued as a fashion shape for decades since. Chanel was also one of the first to use synthetic fabrics, and in 1915 showed dresses made of rayon. At first, the fabric did not gain acceptance owing to its rather harsh, rough texture, but after manufacturing improvements it became marketable as 'artificial silk'.

The contrast between the changes made in day wear towards a more realistic but chic look and the continuing excesses of evening wear was sharply defined during the 1910s. One of the leading English couturières of this age was renowned for the splendours of her evening wear, which hardly differed from the contemporary stage designs. Lucile, Lady Duff-Gordon, was one of the few outstanding couturières outside Paris to create exciting styles, and dominated her London salon with such force of personality that buying clothes from her was more of an event than a mere purchase. During the First World War, Lucile added to the dramatic image of her designs by working in the USA for Ziegfeld, among others, creating clothes for the famous 'Follies'. She counted that other sensation of the age, Irene Castle, among her clients. Irene was the wife and dancing partner of Vernon Castle, and a fashion-maker in the truest sense of the word. Her figure and her taste influenced even more women than the work of the great couturiers. A catalogue for a recent exhibition in New York, 'American Women of Style', makes the following comment:

Whatever Irene Castle did was instant fashion. When she cut her hair short, the 'Castle Bob' made headlines: she tied a narrow strip of velvet, sewn with tiny pearls, across her brow, and created the 'headache band'. Her simple, light, floating 'Castle frocks' became the thing to wear, and

Like her sister, the sensational novelist Elinor Glyn, Lucile was a good self-publicist, as the consciously English wording of her New York salon advertisement suggests. Vogue, *September 1919.*

Above, centre *A dramatic Lucile creation for Irene Castle: a dance dress with a bodice of pale blue silk satin and a hooped skirt of chartreuse silk chiffon trimmed with flower garlands, designed for* Watch Your Step *in 1914.*

Above, left *Irene Castle, a tremendous influence on fashion, in dancing pose.*

when she replaced corsets and billowing petticoats with bloomers and a little slip – the easier to dance in – American women delightedly adopted the new lingerie.

Lucile was in many respects the London equivalent of Paul Poiret: she also laid claim to the invention of a 'new line' corset, and loved to use fabrics with splashy designs, or decorated with large, floppy flowers or strings of beads. It is often said that her designs, like those of Poiret, are the work of an artist rather than of a dressmaker, because their effect came from the combination of colours – purple with pink, for example – or an act of decoration, rather than from the cut or shaping of the garment itself.

The 1910s were years when the work of actual artists – illustrators such as Lepape, Barbier, Paul Iribe and Etienne Drian – was highly influential. The styles of the period are best conveyed by the artistic interpretation of them made by these illustrators. In fact, a curious reversal had taken place in 1908: in the early years of the century, photography had been making significant advances as a way of conveying the fashion of the couturiers to the rest of the world; in 1908 Paul Iribe published a small booklet entitled *Les Robes de Paul Poiret* – a wonderful publicity stunt – which was followed three years later by Georges Lepape's *Les Choses de Paul Poiret*. Both works serve to show how women were reduced in their style to a two-dimensional, decorated, romantic image. Ladies in purple or scarlet recline against cushions in colours of the same hue, the wall or window behind enlivened by some complementary wisp of chiffon or lightly dotted fabric. Pattern on pattern, colour on colour, with an all-pervading mood of exoticism and Orientalism, was the look that designers sought to explore.

The collector might well consider making a wonderfully worthwhile

Below, below, right & far right *Trouser outfits drawn by Georges Lepape from the famous volume,* Les Choses de Paul Poiret. *These were fairly extreme designs for the time (1911) but point to the increasing desire for physical liberty in women's clothing.*

'La Joueuse de Théorbe', another theatre coat illustrated by George Barbier of a model by Paquin: fur trims complemented the stiffness of rich brocades for evening wear. (1914).

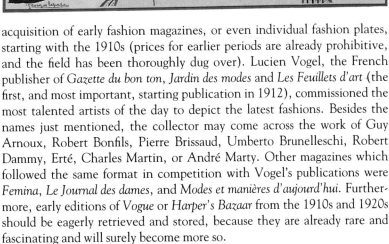

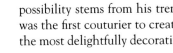

Very French: a pretty Eastern turban set against a formal garden. Another design from Les Choses de Paul Poiret, 1911.

acquisition of early fashion magazines, or even individual fashion plates, starting with the 1910s (prices for earlier periods are already prohibitive, and the field has been thoroughly dug over). Lucien Vogel, the French publisher of *Gazette du bon ton*, *Jardin des modes* and *Les Feuillets d'art* (the first, and most important, starting publication in 1912), commissioned the most talented artists of the day to depict the latest fashions. Besides the names just mentioned, the collector may come across the work of Guy Arnoux, Robert Bonfils, Pierre Brissaud, Umberto Brunelleschi, Robert Dammy, Erté, Charles Martin, or André Marty. Other magazines which followed the same format in competition with Vogel's publications were *Femina*, *Le Journal des dames*, and *Modes et manières d'aujourd'hui*. Further-more, early editions of *Vogue* or *Harper's Bazaar* from the 1910s and 1920s should be eagerly retrieved and stored, because they are already rare and fascinating and will surely become more so.

A further innovation from Paul Poiret which provides another collecting possibility stems from his tremendous activity in applied art forms. Poiret was the first couturier to create his own perfumes, which were packaged in the most delightfully decorative bottles. His perfume company, founded in

Left *A lovely design, revealing a strong French Empire influence, from* Gazette du Bon Ton *1914.*

1911, was named after his eldest daughter, Rosine. Among the items produced by the company were some exquisite paper advertising fans (see my chapter on Fans). In the same year, Poiret set up a second enterprise run by a team of talented young female designers who all worked together under the name of his second daughter, Martine. In 1912 Poiret opened a shop in Paris where the fashionable could buy embroideries, curtaining, fabrics, wallpaper, painted screens, rugs and all manner of other items in a distinctive 'Poiret' image, rather similar in idea to the look created by Laura Ashley today. These fabrics and designs are an excellent example of the way in which the work of a couturier can influence looks, colour, line and the eye of the beholder, in a far-reaching way. Through his boutiques (a second soon opened in London) and through his use of artists, Poiret really did change modern taste.

For example, the current style of fashion illustration may have been responsible for the acceptance of certain new ideas which could be portrayed more attractively, and less provocatively, by the artist than by the camera – or indeed by the reality of a mannequin or model. A good case in point was the décolletage of day wear. From the mid-decade onwards, there was a gradual descent in the front from the high-boned 'choker' style so commonly associated with the Edwardian look of previous years: Poiret (although Lucile also lays claim to the invention) produced a very modest vee-necked dress, which produced a sensation at the time. Slight 'bâteau' shapes were also brought in. On paper, these could be depicted without the slightest hint of sexual revelation: the body beneath remained flat and unexposed. The effect was to accustom the eye to a new line, and make its general adoption easier. 'Fill-ins', that is, slips of linen or voile worn inside the vee neckline, were common at the time. Peter Pan collars set low, with a lining, were also fashionable. By 1913 a very attractive variation was devised where the vee-neck dress was made as a cross-over, with a turned-down collar, and a fill-in fichu or handkerchief beneath.

As we shall see a little later, the new simplicity of day-time dress contributed to the 'democratization' of fashion. Paul Poiret had little notion, when he toured the USA with his personal troupe of mannequins towards the end of the decade, that the simplicity and 'liberty' of his own designs, together with the innovative work of Chanel, would be crucial in helping the ready-to-wear industry of that country to set itself up in rivalry to the fame of Paris. A complicated tailleur à la Worth would be impossible to copy; a jersey suit or a simply gathered shift dress in a bright print was infinitely easier. Poiret was alert to the dangers of piracy, and attempted, on his later tour of the USA in 1922, to ask large store owners to pay him some sort of 'royalty' or licence fee for dresses which were clearly derived from his own designs. He even suggested making a range of 'models' specifically for the American market, but he found no one to collaborate with his schemes. There is no doubt that Poiret, Chanel and other couturiers lost much of the kind of revenue by which their descendants, such as Cardin and Dior, have made millions, that is, in the sale of licences, 'limited editions', and so on.

The Chambre Syndicale did what it could to protect the French industry

A modest vee-neck dress worn at the races at Longchamps, a contrast to the high choker necklines of the previous decade.

43

44

during these innovative years from the depradations of foreigners. From 1911 the Chambre set up regular, well organized group showings by the leading couturiers of Paris for visiting American (and to a much lesser extent British) mass-market buyers. On looking at American fashion magazines up until about 1910, we find virtually no reference to any store's making up-to-the-minute, home-grown fashion garments: almost all the clothes shown for a chic, upper-class audience are imported French models, being re-sold by the large downtown stores. During the 1910s, however, it became more possible for the store buyers to purchase one model in Paris and use it to make the next best thing to couture copies. These copies would be kept tucked away for showing only to favoured clients, and were seldom made with a store label inside. Only the quality of the finish, and possibly such features as the quality of cloth in the lining, or the luxury of the trimming, distinguish them from a French couture garment. Some of the stores advertising copies of French clothes at this period include Bonwit Teller, who put on sale a copy of a Paquin dress for $75; Lord & Taylor, whose numerous versions retailed at about $40, and Wanamakers, whose prices varied from $30 to $50. Gimbel Brothers, Bergdorf Goodman and Saks Fifth Avenue were also active in the business, although at first their notices made it always a little difficult to establish whether they were selling 'imports', 'adaptations', or downright copies. This was an area of fashion retailing that was to remain grey for some time to come.

Not all fashion commentators found slavish copying of French fashions to their liking. In *Ready-Made Miracle: The American Story of Fashion for the Millions* (1967), Jessica Daves quotes Mr Edward Bok, who in 1913 edited *Ladies' Home Journal* and produced a famous diatribe against these perverse Continental influences:

> During the past five years Paris dressmakers have shown a steady degeneration of their waning art in the so-called Paris styles which they have sent over here. No French woman of the slightest refinement wears these styles. They are the hallmark of the Paris Boulevards . . . creations of disordered minds of French dressmakers who have lost all sense of art and decency, have become pure commercialists, and, laughing in their sleeves at the American women, are making damned fools of [them].'

The new décolletage and the 'dressmaker' suit were objects of Bok's attack: presumably the very hint of informality and practicality suggested a licentious unbending that some middle-class Americans found alarming.

However, there were signs in the everyday wear of more middle-class women that new leisure activities, and innovations like the motor car, were having as much effect on clothing as the inspirations of the couturiers. Golfing and tennis were both by now considered quite suitable pursuits for women; other activities seem amazingly strenuous when one considers the weight of clothing still found necessary: yachting, ice-skating, hunting, cycling, and so on. Alison Adburgham's classic study *Shops and Shopping* cites Thomas Burberry of London as one of the pioneers in altering traditional sports clothes for the newly active woman: the 'Free-Stroke Coat' is one which carries immense appeal in its name, with its 'patent Pivot Sleeve and Adaptable Skirt'. Another favourite was the Norfolk jacket,

Left An advertisement from Lord & Taylor of Fifth Avenue, New York, revealing their 'interpretations' of Paris models: copying was never mentioned! (October 1919).
***Below, left** A suit of which Mr Edward Bok would approve: and French-made! Costumes Parisiens 1912.*

Below A German design 'Ayesha' from Berliner Mode 1915, giving some idea of how uniform European styles were at the time.

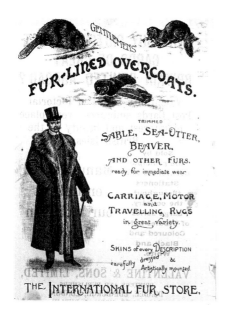

Furs of all kinds for trimmings became very popular. An advertisement for men's coats, 1900. **Above, right** *A typical skating outfit, loaded with furs – photographed in 1910 at Cock Marsh, near Bourne End, suggesting that such luxury was fairly widespread, not confined to the rich capital-city few.*

possibly worn with a Harrods 'Rideasy Skirt', which was divided at the back so that a pleat would fall on each side of the saddle.

Even more revolutionary was the attire devised for travelling in the new and immensely popular motor car. Breezy ladies had to wear a tussore silk dustproof veil in a great swathe over a not-too-large flat hat; alternatively, hoods with mica masks were pulled up over goggles with scarves and fur-lined leather or cloth coats. Sometimes tweeds were lined with camel fleece, vicuña, Irish frieze, squirrel, marmot or mink; it really was a bitterly cold experience to beat along at thirty miles an hour in an open car. As Burberry's commented:

> Automobilism and the demand amongst its votaries for cold-excluding, warmth-holding, rain resisting and dust-proof clothing is bound to lead eventually, and in extreme cases, to the use of fur. But English gentlemen do not take kindly to the *Continental monstrosities* in the shape of horse-skin, sheepskin, wolfskin, and other variations of coats which have the hair, wool and fur outside. The more distinguished form is to use the fur simply as a lining, the outside presenting the appearance of ordinary travelling ulsters.

This comment on taste held true for women's fashions as well as it did for men. 'Ulsters' – good-quality tweed topcoats – were always only trimmed with fur.

Skating, on the other hand, was a much less rigorous cold-weather activity, and by the end of the decade some charming Russian-style outfits could be seen – a knee-length tunic over a close-fitting skirt, with the traditional tight-fitting sleeves, the extremities trimmed with fur. Bloomers or knickerbockers were not seen at this period, although quite extraordinary new clothes enjoyed a brief vogue – such as black serge knickers with a chamois-leather seat for cycling!

In the summer, women's sporting fashions became a little more charming and less aggressively functional. Yachting or river dresses were made with 'matelot' collars, or with nautical ribbon trims. The hems stopped at the ankle to avoid grass and mud stains. In America, attractive 'tub dresses' were offered for younger girls, and were much favoured for playing tennis and other ball games. As their name suggests, they were simple, chemise-like dresses in very pretty cotton lawn or linen fabrics, with lace trim, and could be washed out without fuss at home.

One American manufacturer, Peter Thomson, developed a line of everyday-wear middy blouses and skirts for girls up through college age. Of nice practical fabrics such as crash, duck and linen, they were at the time (from about the 1890s to the end of the 1910s) so common that they were referred to by their wearers as 'Peter Thomsons'. Like all sportswear, they are hard to find today.

Jackets and capes completed the fashionable, sporty, everyday look. Throughout the decade, jackets became progressively looser and less tailored. By the end of the period, the jacket was virtually shapeless, with little padding at the shoulders and a loosely tied belt at the waist or round the hips. While fur was considered *de trop* for a coat, a fur jacket was less 'gross', and all kinds of skins – Persian lamb, beaver, musquash, pony, astrakhan and so on – were acceptable. Capes and shawls remained popular through the decade, either trimmed with fur or decorated with frogging or other braid.

The First World War at first had little effect on women's fashion, certainly not as much as might have been expected from a practical point of view. Women continued to wear their clothes long, and went about their war work, such as nursing, in full-length serge skirts, covering up with long, bulky jackets. Ironically, one of the effects of the war was to provide a great boost for the sale of Parisian fashion in America, because most of Europe was unable to afford Paris prices. America's ready-to-wear industry,

This First World War poster shows how the cumbersome female fashions had to be tied down and protected for practical war work. (1916).

Left *A set of furs 'the ideal Christmas gift' – but note the fragile pair of shoes, hardly suitable for winter weather.*

Right This suit is typical of the bulky, rather unattractive fashions sported during World War I (1915).

just getting off the ground with the establishment of a number of major stores, and a growing mail-order industry, was set back by this return to Europe; but, even so, it was already much further ahead technically than that of Europe. A major reason for this was the sheer size and volume of trade in America. Women living miles away from major cities wanted to buy clothes, and could not always travel to the cities to purchase them. The mail-order industry began as early as the 1880s, and was well under way by the outbreak of the First World War. Siegel Cooper Co, in their catalogue, noted at this time that a woman could write from anywhere in America to obtain 'an imported style. . . created by the famous house of Paquin of Paris.'

In 1911, Lane Bryant, another big catalogue company, was advertising 'lingerie dresses', 'for promenade or casino, for hottest evenings and for Sunday dress; their necessary place in every wardrobe is indeed well-known'. These pretty styles were, as the name suggests, slim, light-weight chemises in lawn, cotton or silk. Sports clothes – the veils, goggles, gloves and other accessories of the lady driver (or driving companion at least) and the simple tennis dresses described previously – were equally easy to sell by mail order.

A Mrs Katherine Busbey went so far as to say in *Home Life in America*, in 1910, that it was much easier for middle-class women to dress well, better and cheaper in America than abroad: 'The ready-made, plain walking-suit in the American shop for $20, $30 and $40 is comparatively better cut and better designed than those for the same price in European markets.' This was undoubtedly true. As Sandra Ley has pointed out in her history of the American industry, the very fact that garment workers in Chicago could go on strike in 1913 indicates that there was already a sizeable ready-to-wear industry. Not only cotton day dresses, in a simple shirtwaist style, but also a number of silk 'afternoon dresses' were being manufactured in large quantities. Chanel's influence on the American ready-to-wear industry was enormous, because her loose, sporty styles suited American taste and could be so easily copied by the mass-market manufacturers. A further boost to the industry was given by the introduction of her innovatory jerseys and the acceptability she gave to synthetics.

In mainland Europe and England, the ready-to-wear industry barely got under way until the end of the First World War. A combination of factors influenced its growth. Firstly, although fashions did not change radically until well into the 1920s, there was a move among working women during the war to cast off the long, straight skirt under the long tunic top which was the main 'line' of the decade, and to wear an elongated tunic dress for active duties, although the garment remained thick, bulky, uncomfortable and rather clumsy. It was certainly one of the least flattering of styles to be seen for some time. But the style was more easily copied by ready-to-wear manufacturers, and the end of the decade saw a growth of simple, wrapover, shirt-type dresses. A similar change occurred with the replacement of tailored blouses, firstly by looser, plainer shapes, with raglan sleeves or turned-down collars, and then by the introduction of knitwear, *à la* Chanel. From 1916 it became quite common to see hand-crocheted jumpers worn

An unusual Parisian hand-knitted suit of rust-coloured silk, a new fashion largely helped by the simpler creations of Chanel, from 1916 onwards.

loosely over skirts, with a belt tied round the hips. The chief innovation was the lack of openings and fastenings: the jumpers were voluminous enough to be pulled down over the head and adjusted with a sash or belt. For the collector, this change in development is very useful. When examining a dress from the 1910s, it may be possible to see that it was shop-bought but altered by a skilful local dressmaker to fit a particular client. Alternatively, a loose, indefinite but machine-finished shape may help to date an early ready-to-wear garment. It was not until these changes became acceptable in fashion that the ready-to-wear industry managed to get a start in England and on the Continent; before that, styles were so elaborate that they were difficult to make in large numbers, and no one would have been seen in anything less than a carefully cut and individually fitted garment that spoke of a dressmaker at work rather than an off-the-peg purchase. Shops simply could not compete with that standard of fit and finish. But the war, with its regimenting demand for uniforms, helped the industry on to its feet: pattern-cutting machinery was improved, and workers became organized for the first time. It is significant that the British Tailors' and Garment Workers' Union was set up only in 1915; the American equivalent, the International Ladies' Garment Workers Union, was founded in 1900.

The end of the war, however, brought irrevocable changes for women. The most important of these was the right to vote – in England in 1918 and in the USA in 1920. The following decade was to see an explosion in fashion which transformed women, and allowed the spread of 'fashion dressing' to filter down through society in an even more pronounced way than it had during the 1910s.

Left Made-to-order (halfway to ready-to-wear) became better styled as fashions became simpler in line. A Harrods advertisement, 1919. **Below** *a stylish militaristic design (based on a Prussian officer's uniform) from Berlin, 1915.*

HARRODS   INEXPENSIVE   AND   CHARMING   FROCKS

I.F. HELEN. Dainty Evening Frock, in Georgette, with draped bodice and tunic skirt. Belt of contrasting coloured ribbon, fastened with posy of flowers. For wear over white or coloured slip. Black, jade, maize, lilac, and cherry. 79/6

I.F. WESTON. Restaurant Frock. Attractively designed in crepe de chine, with tunic of Georgette embroidered in a self or contrasting shade. Black, navy, and newest shades in mole, ivory, pink, and champagne. £5 10 0

I.F. WALDORF. Semi Evening Frock, in Georgette, with panel front and belt trimmed with oxidised lace. Lined throughout with silk. Black, navy, and the loveliest of tones of mole, grey, sky, and pink. 5 Gns.

I.F. RITZ. Smart Evening Frock, in silk net. The tunic skirt is drawn into the hem with narrow silver lace. Waistband of blue and silver brocade, finished with large bow of net at back. Lined throughout silk. Black, maize, and grey. 5½ Gns.

Owing to the fragile nature of these Frocks they cannot be sent on approval or exchange. Patterns of materials and shades will be sent on application to Harrods Inexpensive Frock Department.

THE TWENTIES

Jumper and culottes, a very practical and new golfing outfit typical of between-the-wars styling. Jardin des Modes *1928.*

Above right *Shapes begin to slim towards the garçonne look: winter fashions from* Femina, *November 1921.*

Gazette du Bon Ton *summer dresses for 1920.*

The most interesting paradox in the fashions of the 1920s is that women were able to achieve practical, revolutionary freedom of movement in dress at a time when an atmosphere of frivolity ruled the day. When we compare the photographs of First World War heroines labouring in heavy, ankle-length, serge skirts and tight-fitting jackets, with those, taken a mere five years later, of women in short jersey dresses ending at the knee, casually stuffing their hands into jumper pockets, the contrast could hardly be more extreme. The change is dramatic proof, if ever any were needed, that fashion is affected not solely or even principally by necessity, but by mood.

During the war years, dresses and jackets had become gradually less fitted and easier to wear; but they remained essentially bulky, unattractive garments. By the end of the decade, however, a new mood of gaiety and a desire for glamour inspired Parisian couturiers to slim down their lines and create a completely new silhouette. It began tentatively in 1920 with a loose, tubular dress, reaching to mid-shin and softly belted approximately at the level of the natural waist; but by 1924 the well-known 'flapper' or '*garçonne*' look was established, with a flat-chested, waistless, no-curve slip of a dress, just covering the knee. (It is a common error in stage versions of dresses of this period to make them end at mid-thigh, like the mini of the 1960s. These dresses were never, in the 1920s, so short.)

It is also an irony that the one couturier who had done so much to give individual expression to women in their dress, in colour, shape and originality of decoration, should have faded so rapidly from the scene. Paul Poiret never adjusted his styles to the tastes of the 1920s, although many of his ideas made the new shapes possible. 'Natural form' clothes, turban hats, see-through chiffons and voiles had all formed part of his look, and were now stock-in-trade for a new decade of fashion. But other designers suddenly took command of the stage – a metaphor that applies in a

A good example of high-quality ready-to-wear, made possible by the gradual simplifying of cut and line: 'Fleurs de France', an organdie dress, available from The White House in Bond Street in the early 1920s.

Right Designs by Russian artist, Sonia Delauney, who worked in Paris alongside her modernist-painter husband, Robert. She was a chief source of colour inspiration to couturiers such as Schiaparelli and Patou. (1922–23).

The new vogue for monochrome textures and surface interest created by the movies: Louise Brooks in The Canary Murder Case *(1929).*

particular way to the work of the couturiers of this time, for they all had close links with the world of theatre, and the most important new influence on the world of fashion: film. The 1920s were the first decade when women in the streets not only looked to Paris for inspiration, but also had their fantasies played out on the screen. The looks of Clara Bow, Gloria Swanson and Pola Negri captivated women and set up new ideals of romantic beauty and unreal splendour.

Fashion magazines of the period show the collector at once that the pace of life had suddenly accelerated. The flickering movements of the film, the new concentration in artistic fields on the wonders of machinery, the sudden internationalism that made all things American, African, Eastern easily accessible as design resources, leave the observer dazzled by the energy and variety of it all. The best summary of the colours and shapes of the time is found in the exhibited material of the famous Decorative Arts Exhibition held in Paris in 1925. It is a significant landmark in the history of design because it was the first time that the applied arts had been deemed worthy of a massive show. Modernism, the beauty of mass-made objects, the potential in plastics, concrete and other such substances, attracted a new generation of designers. One couple, Robert and Sonia Delaunay, seem to summarize the artistic feeling of the 1920s. Robert Delaunay glorified the Eiffel Tower in modernist paintings that shimmered with light and movement, seeing in metal and the products of machine industry the prospect of a glorious new world. Sonia, his Russian wife, painted abstract, luminously bright canvases, and simple shapes of curves, triangles and squares, which inspired such couturiers as Patou and Schiaparelli. Along with Chanel and Vionnet, these couturiers formed the taste of the period.

If colours had changed from the soft, muted tones of the Edwardian era, the change in shape was even more remarkable. The 'S'-bend ladies of the 1900s and 1910s were suddenly usurped by a race of flat-chested, bobbed and shingle-headed girls who rushed about in sports cars and played a fierce game

Left *Sports clothes from Berlin, 1922 – skiing was increasingly popular in Europe from the 1920s onwards.*

Right *A typically skilful dress by Madeleine Vionnet, 1928.*

Centre *The famous* trompe l'oeil *handknitted sweater that launched Elsa Schiaparelli's career in Paris. (1928).*

of tennis instead of trailing a fan. A fascinating American study of aesthetics and fashion by Anne Hollander, entitled *Seeing Through Clothes*, provides an evocative summary of the new style of woman in the cinema in the 1920s:

> Silent film naturally tended toward stylization of gesture even in realistic drama; and women's clothing worn in the silent movies corresponded not only to such stylized behavior but also to the new abstract and reduced mode of dress . . . These were different from those of the theater; they had to depend on black and white cinematography, and they had to be easily read without colour and in silent motion.

Miss Hollander lays over-emphasis on the colourlessness of the decade to make a point about the link between cinema and the new female image, but her writing evokes very well the movement and modernity in the way women dressed in the 1920s. But a fact that the films of the age bring out better than the magazines or fashion plates of the time is that these *garçonnes* were just as amply endowed as any average cross-section of women in any other era.

The beauty of couture clothes of the time was caught in the atmosphere of slimness, of the sporty, rangy, angular beauty that they conveyed, whatever the true dimension of the body beneath. Madeleine Vionnet's clothes most epitomize this skill. She specialized in bias-cut silky or crêpe dresses that flowed over the body, touching the best spots and leaving the rest unmentioned. But her simplest shapes have a great deal of structure on the inside: bands of grosgrain support soft crêpe de chine; all manner of clever underpinnings at the waist give an apparently fluid dress a firm structure. Fashion historians label her 'the architect among dressmakers', and her background provides some explanation for her consummate skill. After early marriage and divorce, she went to London, where she worked for Kate Reilly of Bond Street. She returned to Paris where she joined the houses of Callot Soeurs and then Doucet, eventually opening her own couture house just before the outbreak of war. She did not succeed in getting a firm establishment operating until 1919 but, once recognized, she remained a leading figure in the Parisian scene until her retirement in 1939. (The house continued to operate, following her style, under the directorship of her two protégées who worked under the joint name of Mad Carpentier.)

The details of her life simply serve to show, as they do for Schiaparelli, that Madeleine Vionnet was a woman of strong independence, with a hard-working, professional attitude to her creations. Perhaps the women she dressed were more fortunate, financially or emotionally, than she was herself, but they benefited from the strength of her vision of womanhood. Her clothes are essentially more feminine than Schiaparelli's, more subdued and subtle in their appeal. It seems significant that Vionnet liked to make models of her clothes on 'quarter scale figurines, thus assuring the model-in-the-round essential to her predominantly asymmetrical cut', as Madge Garland has described it. Perhaps the exquisite femininity of her slithering, shining, bias-cut dresses was the fantasy of her imagination, so different from the struggle of her real life, and realized in an age of freedom and frivolity for her patrons.

Imagination was given even fuller rein in the début of France's most

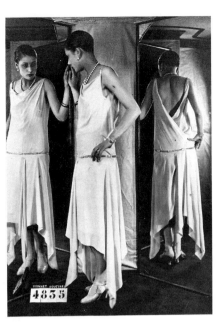

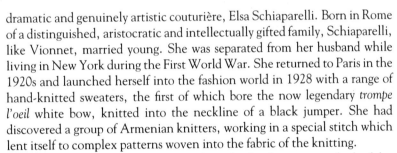

dramatic and genuinely artistic couturière, Elsa Schiaparelli. Born in Rome of a distinguished, aristocratic and intellectually gifted family, Schiaparelli, like Vionnet, married young. She was separated from her husband while living in New York during the First World War. She returned to Paris in the 1920s and launched herself into the fashion world in 1928 with a range of hand-knitted sweaters, the first of which bore the now legendary *trompe l'oeil* white bow, knitted into the neckline of a black jumper. She had discovered a group of Armenian knitters, working in a special stitch which lent itself to complex patterns woven into the fabric of the knitting.

Although Schiaparelli broke away from the familiar *garçonne* look of the 1920s, her early work had immense influence on the fashion of the decade, because it typified the interest in the links between art and fashion. The body was seen as a canvas to be decorated with images. Schiaparelli's clothes are always somewhat surreal and highly dramatic, although not exactly theatrical, for they are still very wearable and well-made. The first impression is one of immensely stylish, tailored elegance. Second to the workmanship and the quality of cloth and cut, is the originality of the design, although it is the latter which has come to characterize her work as it is described in books or shown in photographs. Schiaparelli was always particularly admired by the Americans – in fact it was a buyer from a New York store, when ordering forty of that first black and white bowed sweater, who launched Schiaparelli on her career. Her style was eclectic: she sought inspiration in the shapes of African burnouses, Eastern harem outfits, medieval costume and circus fancy dress, and for colours she looked as far away as the hot reds and pinks of South American folkloric traditions and to the purples and blacks of her original city, Rome.

Beach life became fashionable in the 1910s and 1920s. Chanel is reputed to have made the suntan respectable. This scene from Illustrations, *a French magazine, in 1927, gives a good suggestion of shapes and colours in 1920s textiles.*

'Picture dresses' from Jeanne Lanvin. Femina, May 1922.

Right *Lanvin again: she loved rich plaids and ornate printed designs.*

Something of an anomaly during the 1920s was the work of Jeanne Lanvin, who departed from the predominant *garçonne* style by producing much more feminine and frilled dresses. Famous among these are her 'picture' dresses in soft taffetas, and her exotic evening clothes in rich, Eastern-style velvets and satins. Her daughter, the Princesse de Polignac, one of the leading hostesses of Paris at the time, became her main symbol. Lanvin 'created' a particularly beautiful shade of blue which was supposed to have originated in the colour of medieval stained glass, typical of her sources of inspiration. Her models are mysterious rather than outrageous. In 1923, for instance, she created a 'sports dress' in primrose wool jersey with checks of gold and silver thread running through it; in the mid-1920s she produced some stunning examples of the beaded dance dress which was the rage of the period, and perhaps its best known legacy for collectors today. Her love of bright, jewel-like colours is seen in all her work – even in her use of glittering buttons and embroidery on black. Perhaps because they were so feminine and easy to wear, Lanvin's clothes are equally hard to find in good condition, although her styles were much copied by big stores in London and New York. (Current saleroom prices in New York range from $1,150 to $1,600 for her dresses.)

Where Vionnet, Schiaparelli and Lanvin may be considered the most original and individualistic of the designers to emerge in Paris during the 1920s, other couturiers of note were perhaps more typical, more wearable, and more far-reaching in their effect on modern fashion, particularly in the transformation of high style into the commercial reality of ready-to-wear fashion. In this respect, names such as Louiseboulanger, Augustabernard, Lelong and Cheruit come to mind.

At the time, probably the most outstanding name for the latest fashion look was that of Jean Patou. His first collection in 1914 had been bought in its entirety by a New York store, but the war prevented him from developing his business further. In 1922 he moved to new premises in the rue St Florentin, and began producing a range of highly versatile, young-looking clothes that captured the sporty, dance-crazy girls of Paris for his clientele. Patou was always much loved by Americans, because his casual clothes seemed to suit the shape of the American female so much better than the work of other European couturiers. There is a considerable quantity of Patou clothes in America worth collecting as a result. In 1924 Patou visited the USA and came home with six American model girls, who were to be his mannequins, acknowledging a major source of his revenue. Patou had a way of proposing design ideas which looked more extreme in the hands of other couturiers: in *Paris Fashion*, edited by Ruth Lynam, there is a colour plate from the house of Patou showing long-line sweaters which have all the surreal quality of Schiaparelli designs, but appear somehow more relaxed and wearable. Patou's colours are less strident and demanding, and his evening clothes always offer a romantic relief to the sporty elegance of his day clothes. Patou rivals Chanel at this period as the inventor of 'separates', lounge pyjamas, cardigans over dresses, beach clothes. In his newly opened sports shop he even sold swimsuits, which *Vogue* described as looking 'as if you might be able to swim in them', in jersey and marocain. The output from this highly successful and commercial house is so varied that it is difficult to characterize it in a description of particular dresses: whatever was the fashion for each year of the decade, Patou was in the forefront, designing, with charm and gaiety, youthful interpretations of the look. A

Deauville fashions, 1929. Compare the Patou design on the right with the illustration of the work of Sonia Delauney – Cubist designs were everywhere.

Top left *Louiseboulanger, a designer who enjoyed great but short-lived success in the 1920s, drawn in Harper's Bazaar (1926), with, on the left, another minor name of the time, Jenny, and, centre a gown from Berthe.*

Left *The work of a designer who had an enduring and practical impact on fashion: Jean Patou. Femina, April 1922.*

A simple and characteristic Molyneux evening gown photographed for Femina, *July 1922.*

Right *A somewhat unexpected early Norman Hartnell design, 1924.*

good example from 1929 is a 'little black dress', with the latest uneven hemline, dipping at the back, a blouse top shaped rather like a little bolero, and a sash, draped round the waist, adding a softness to counteract the stark effect of a deep plunge neckline. The whole garment, so carefully constructed, is made of panné velvet, ensuring by the luxury and shining beauty of the fabric alone that the dress would be a pleasure to wear. Patou always combined high fashion with femininity and practicality.

If this last couturier provided the style for the 1920s lady while she relaxed on the beach or in a jazz bar, then Edward Molyneux gave her the uniform for her more emancipated day-time activities of travelling or working. Molyneux was one of the few Englishmen (though officially of mixed Irish and Hungarian descent) to make a name for himself in Paris, and his distinguished military career gave him a romantic cachet that helped him after the war. He had worked in London for one of the few high-level British couturières of the time, Lucile, but developed his own idea of elegance and moved to Paris to realize it. His clothes were instantly successful, because they were endlessly wearable. Couture can supply either originality and uniqueness, or high-quality perfect tailoring, and it was in the second category that Molyneux excelled. His tailor-mades were impossible to describe but always popular. They combined the right blend of mannishness with frivolity which was a speciality of the 1920s. His day dresses have the same combination of tailored austerity and relieving softness, expressed either in the drapery or in the pattern of the fabric. His clothes are, however, difficult to collect because, like those of Mainbocher, later, they

were worn to shreds by their owners.

Molyneux's career serves as a reminder that the world of fashion in London was indeed capable of producing some designers as good as those to be found in Paris, and that at the time a number of talents came through that had a marked influence on the development of ready-to-wear manufacture in Britain. The first of these is Norman Hartnell, who, like Molyneux, served an apprenticeship with Lucile, but by 1923 was working for himself from Bruton Street. The dominance of Paris was still so great that Hartnell decided the only way to establish his reputation was to show his collection in the French capital, which he did with great success. During the 1930s he maintained his high popularity by dressing English socialites and actresses in a uniquely smart, English way – a look that is a mixture of the traditional pastels and pearls of the upper classes with a little hard-edged tailoring. Hartnell is perhaps best remembered for his work, over subsequent decades, as dressmaker for the British royal family, and especially for the stunning 'picture dresses', or crinolines, which he has made for so many State occasions for the Queen. His skill with embroidery is consummate, and his tailored suits and dresses have been adapted by ready-to-wear manufacturers for decades in Britain.

Equally significant as an encouragement to the home-grown industry were the improvements in machinery and work regulations during the 1920s. The garment industry's unions became better organized and more widely recognized. For the first time, magazines began to refer to manufacturers by name in their pages, instead of discussing only models from Paris, bought as originals from smart London stores, or as copies carefully made by that store's own dressmaking department. (America, as we have seen in the preceding chapter, was well ahead of England in this respect, and had good ready-to-wear clothes available for the market at least ten years earlier.) No doubt, this process was speeded up in the 1920s by the simplicity of the

Above & right *Designs from Vogue's pattern book service, for readers, 1927. Clothes made at home or by dressmakers were still the norm for most comfortably-off, as opposed to wealthy, women.*

prevailing fashion: a straight tube is a fairly easy object for a manufacturer to copy, requiring little expertise in the shaping, and presenting few problems as to sizing. The London stores of Dickins & Jones, Marshall & Snelgrove and Debenham & Freebody attracted out-of-town purchasers, only too glad to give up what Alison Adburgham describes as 'the tyranny of private dressmakers and their interminable fittings'. Madge Garland, in *Fashion*, comments:

> Hitherto styles had been created exclusively for the rich and leisured and filtered gradually down the social and economic scale; now the ordinary woman began to be considered, and the two years previously required for a Paris fashion to become universally seen and worn in London gradually shrank to one, and is now merely a matter of weeks. . . .

At this time, the retail industry in New York was developing much faster than that in the United Kingdom. All the big stores ran departments which imported French model gowns, and often made up their own copies using house dressmakers. Paris still dominated the international fashion field, and few designers could match the stature of the Parisians described above. One man who began his career in the 1920s, and was to become America's first great 'home-grown' couturier, was Norman Norell. A young man from the Midwest, he came to New York and was dazzled by the excitement and beauty of the imported beaded clothes – possibly the Lanvin models previously mentioned which were so exotic and beautifully made. P. Lee Levin writes in her history *The Wheels of Fashion*: 'The freewheeling days of the 1920s, the women with their skimpy black dresses, short hair, fake jewelry, the gaiety and the jazz were to insinuate themselves in Norell's work for his entire career and probably to account for a vein of drama that has always been a part of his collections, either in their presentation or in the designs themselves.' Norell's early work in the 1920s included designing costumes for the lovely 'high yaller' girls at the Harlem Cotton Club, where Duke Ellington enthralled the high society white audience; creating clothes for such glittering stars as Gloria Swanson; and designing for the richer clients who came to Hattie Carnegie, the haute couture house where he worked for a while before branching out independently. Miss Levin says, 'Norell spent the 1920s leaping from the Astoria, Long Island studio of Paramount Pictures, to the Brooks Costume Company, to the Seventh Avenue manufacturer Charles Armour until he arrived at Carnegie's, his circuitous route being somewhat comparable to reaching the Plaza's Persian Room by way of Roseland.'

Such mixtures and contrasts seem to be the stuff of the 1920s. It is fascinating to view the clothing of the period, so minimal in cut, so elaborate in fabric and colour, and wonder at the contrasts inherent in the styles. The favourite fabrics were elaborate in the extreme: chiffon slips heavily beaded and embroidered; varieties of crêpe de chine, marocain and georgette; printed silks, light wools like the famous 'kasha' made by Rodier from the silky, soft wool found on the backs of the Himalayan sheep. The colours were magical, ranging from soft eau-de-nil greens and light blues to peachy pinks and spring yellows. Texture was as important as colour, with satin shine or fur trimming completing the seductive impression.

A pyjama suit for 'informal dinner' designed by Worth and imported into the USA by Hattie Carnegie: photograph by Steichen, 1928.

The clothing industry of New York moved at this time from the Lower East side to Seventh Avenue, Manhattan, where it still retains its nerve centre. To this area, all the beautiful lines from Paris and all the exotic fabrics and furs found their way and were rapidly interpreted into lines that every woman could afford. The Charles William Stores catalogue described the influences of American fashion at the time in words of Shakespearean grandeur:

As all roads lead to Rome, so all fashion inspiration reaches New York eventually. Paris sends wonderful creations in frocks and blouses and lingerie, a thousand and one ideas that bear the stamp of that artistic race and exhale the perfume of rare beauty. London contributes fashions in that garment that American women love best of all – the tailored suit – and also sends smart hats to match, and from Berlin come wonderful coat styles. The Philippines offer embroideries, veritable cobwebs of fine underwear; and Japan, that wonderful country of little people and great accomplishments, sends rich fabrics, sumptuous embroideries, kimonos that ravish the eye for color and design, and a hundred silken treasures of the East. . . .

Slightly outside the normal channels of couture, but supplying America with the exotic from afar, exactly as described here, was Mariano Fortuny, who by the 1920s had established shops selling his unique clothes in Paris and New York. The market in Fortunys is at present verging on the hysterical: prices are reaching astronomic levels. A sale held in New York in May 1980 produced a buying price of $2,600 for a Fortuny cloak, and $1,100 for a beautiful black silk pleated dress with the label intact. At these prices, Fortuny's work is probably beyond the means of most new collectors, but his story is worth quoting as an example of the artist-craftsman who was not in the mainstream of fashion in his time, but who has become a rare collectable since. Perhaps there are other craftsmen, not necessarily of Fortuny's stature, working today who could be collected for the same enjoyment of fabric and skill. Collecting fashion need not always mean going for the recognized but can include the individually delightful.

In 1909, Fortuny, a young Spaniard who had settled in Venice, patented a new system for making a dress. He described his idea as 'a type of garment for women . . . basically in the form of a central neck opening, with two side openings for the arms and along the full length of the side seams which are laced together with slanting eyelet holes, which can be adjusted under the sleeves.' A dry, technical explanation for one of the most beautiful garments ever conceived for twentieth-century women – the 'Delphos' dress. Essentially classical in style, Fortuny's dress has something distinctly modern about it. The Delphos dresses were made in the most exquisite silks and pleated by a method which still confuses the experts. The large, batwing-shaped pieces of fabric, laced as described, and moulding over the shoulders and body, fell in a way that flattered almost any figure within. The 'modern' aspect of Fortuny's design is the way in which the skirt fans out, Hollywood-style, in a dramatic circle round the feet. Such a design could only exist after the invention of photography or the film still. It recaptures the perfection of a Greek statue, but was made in an age that already knew how to create an atmosphere of illusion on the stage and on the screen. It is not a coincidence that Fortuny enjoyed designing for the theatre, although some of his designs were so elaborate that they were considered too expensive to use.

For wearing over the Delphos dress (a style that he continued to produce with slight variation until his death in 1949), Fortuny created the most magnificent wraps, cloaks and three-quarter-length coats, some in rich brocades, others in deep-pile velvet of a sumptuous quality unseen elsewhere in twentieth-century fashion. It is still a mystery how Fortuny applied the metallic oxides that give rich gold or silver lustre designs to his velvets. They have the atmosphere of aged medieval tapestries. The colour of the velvet is of such a luminous, deep quality, and the applied designs are so carefully added, in processes which may have involved six or seven stages of application, possibly by stencil or by hand painting, that the fabric appears ageless in its design. Fortuny's palette adds to this air of timelessness; the colours are soft oyster pinks, sea greens, blues like the inside of a shell or the bottom of a pool. With his artistry, Fortuny combined a talent for marketing; he controlled the network of boutiques that sold his work personally, his garments being available only through his Palazzo d'Orfei in Venice and his boutiques in Milan, New York, Paris, Berlin, London and Zurich. He was seldom featured in the fashion magazines of the 1920s, but anyone with any pretension to taste who was making a trip round Europe bought one of his dresses, which were sold twined round like a skein of wool, so soft and finely pleated was the silk, and swaddled into a distinctive small cream box.

Fortuny was copied by lesser talents such as Maria Monaci Gallenga and Madame Babani, who also sold their goods in Paris, Italy and New York in the 1920s and 1930s. The quality of the fabric and design is usually a way to distinguish the work, but a cautionary story from Phyllis Magidson of the Museum of the City of New York illustrates how even the expert eye can be misled. Miss Magidson, who works in costume conservation, was once submitted a Fortuny, bearing the typical silk 'rat-tail' cord running along the sleeve joinings, with the pretty glass beads, from the Murano glass factory in

Two pieces of fabric created by Mariano Fortuny: the pleating process he created is still a secret, as are the exact methods of using oxides on brocades and velvets to give them an antique patina of colour. (c 1911).

Venice, which he used as decoration. The dress did not bear a label, and the beads looked somehow atypical, which led Miss Magidson to doubt the provenance of the dress. However, some time later a second Fortuny appeared, this time with a label, and decorated with exactly the same beads. It seems that for a while, in one year only, a different type of bead was used, and both garments were therefore authentic. Miss Magidson went on to comment that the rules about the 'signature' or 'handwriting' of couturiers can often be misread for similar reasons – a couturier may lose the services of an expert dressmaker, take on someone new with a different technique of finishing, and throw the collector off the scent for a while.

New collectors may never have the chance to worry themselves over the identity of a Fortuny, but at least the predicament described above acts as some comfort for the inexperienced entering the maze of the collecting world. There are no rules, and the main criterion for collecting must still always remain the individual response to the beauty or style of a garment. Collecting is meaningless without it.

Apricot silk Delphos dress photographed in 1971 by Cecil Beaton.

Mrs Jack Scudamore, fashionably dressed by Jean Patou in white crêpe and satin, trimmed with white fox, in 1929, when hemlines fell dramatically.

Above, left *Exactly the image that James Laver would have selected to show his theory that clothes follow the architectural and design forms of the time. (1928).*

Above, right *Zig-zag designs and sporty styling: Worth advertisement, 1927.*

The 1920s ended with a uniform that appeared so successful that the manufacturers of Seventh Avenue, New York, and Bond Street and Oxford Street, London, were happily settled in their mould. Knee-length dresses, cloche hats, wrap-around fur coats of three-quarter length, separates for day wear, with dress and cardigan ensembles predominating – the generally sporty, casual look seemed perfect for the time and mood. Then, suddenly, on the eve of the Depression and the Wall Street crash, Paris turned. In 1929, Patou (of all the French couturiers a man most able to manipulate the forces of the press and general publicity to his own advantage) launched a new, long look. *Women's Wear Daily*, the American rag-trade journal which still has complete authority when it comes to forecasting trends and passing judgement on styles, recorded the event: 'In August 1929, on the eve of the Wall Street crash, Patou's collection showed day-time clothes at mid-calf and even to the floor, when Americans were still wearing them at knee length. . . . The long dress caught the American garment industry both retail and wholesale unawares and caused tremendous losses.'

The change of style at the end of the decade was one of those inexplicable volte-faces which are open to wide interpretation. Why was 'activity' replaced by a ladylike 'romanticism'? It could be said that the style of the 1920s was truly revolutionary, and that a period of reaction was bound to set in. A more political view would see the 1920s as a period of escapism before the harsh economic realities of between-war Europe began to be felt. This final act of regal defiance from Paris proved to be the end of the city's dominance of international fashion. For a while, women in America and Britain tried to find the money to buy the models of the new long Paris styles. But when the manufacturers of New York and London returned to Paris after the Depression in the mid-1930s it was not to buy models, but to buy 'toiles' (muslin versions of the finished garment) which they would carefully unpick and use as guidelines to produce fashionable and acceptable ready-to-wear fashion, at a much reduced price. They wanted the cut, but not necessarily the quality. Independent ready-to-wear manufacturing dates from the 1920s, and becomes more significant in the history of fashion from the close of the decade onwards. For the novice collector, the scope widens, in terms of price, availability and choice, from now on.

THE THIRTIES

After the dramatic rejection of curves and flounces in the 1920s, it is a surprise to the eye to look at 1930s styles. The hemline had never receded much above the knee, but now it dropped to mid-shin, while the whole shape of a garment seemed to droop. It must be said that many 1930s dresses look dowdy, because colours could be muddy and patterns frumpish. But, at its best, it is the decade of fashion which had the greatest charm and the subtlest innovation. The period sees a gradual move towards a philosophy of clothes-making that we can call modern by our own standards – we require ease of wear, and suitability of the clothes to the activity, before seeing them as decoration. In comparison, the styles of the 1920s appear artificial and forced.

From the point of view of the collector, the 1930s have a great deal to offer because the fashion manufacturing industry developed very significantly. New synthetic fabrics came into use, as did new ways of cutting for mass production, and in general, on both sides of the Atlantic, the fashion industry took on a new professional-merchandising bias (which is discussed more fully below).

One aspect of fashion in the modern world remained unchanged. That was the complete dominance of Paris as the arbiter and originator of all things good in the field. The emphasis was still very much on the names of the great couturiers, and the works that they produced, because the ready-to-wear industry, in its infancy at this time, slavishly copied the styles, colours and finishing details of its superior French counterparts. So, for the collector, a survey of what was happening in French couture gives a clear idea of the look and the line that will be found in surviving model or ready-to-wear garments of the period. Socially, too, the world remained small: smart women in Rio de Janeiro, New York, London, Berlin and Paris wore almost identical clothes, carried the same accessories, and floated from place to place on the international circuit of acceptable society. For the collector, this represents a tremendous bonus. Fans, hats, shoes and scarves frequently turn up even in the most remote corners of the globe, the property of some distant maiden aunt who had travelled extensively – and who had often, perhaps, made her purchases in the Place Vendôme. Particularly in the field of accessories, the most beautiful objects can turn up in mint condition in a suburban attic or country mansion.

The most dramatic change in fashion from the 1920s to the 1930s was in

Fussy 1930s lines: a complete contrast to the boyish elegance of the preceding pages. Berlin, 1934. The gauntlet gloves were fashionable everywhere.

MODEL 58
Ready-to-Wear Dress in printed Sungleam crape. Finished with hand-embroidered organdie.
4 guineas
Sizes : small, medium and large.

Asymmetrical lines are characteristic of 1930s clothes: look for unusual buttons, fur trims, and exaggerated cuffs or shoulder lines.

Above, right *Simple ready-to-wear dress from the London store, Liberty, always valued for its distinctive fabric designs. This dress has all the hallmarks of the 1930s 'droopy' look: low neckline, elongated skirt, falling soft cuffs, and a shady-brimmed hat to match.*

the shape of the day dress. The *garçonne* look, with no waist, abbreviated hemline and deliberate denial of all womanly curves, gave way to a longer, more figure-hugging shape that defined the waist, accentuated the shoulders and added all kinds of detail at the neck and wrists (sometimes to excess) to produce a more mature image of womanhood. The typical dress of the early 1930s had a many-gored skirt, a waist marked by a sash or self-fabric belt, a draped neckline, or possibly a turned-back collar in contrasting piqué, and long, tight sleeves that added to the elongated, elegant outline. Cross-over closing on the bodice, often asymmetrically positioned with a 'novelty' button closure, or a white gilet tucked inside an accentuated vee-neck, were other variations on the same theme.

This new modest femininity was a great change from the boyish stridency

Below *All interest at the back: black satin with flying panels.*

Below, centre *Schiaparelli designs with the new high shoulder, and the focus on novelty buttons and unusual hats, 1938. Note the Cupid clips on the suit on the far right.*

The famous Schiaparelli sheath dress with fabric, featuring surreal tears, designed by Salvador Dali, 1937.

An original design drawing by Schiaparelli, showing her innovative use of buttons and other trimmings. (1937).

of the 1920s, but was very much in key with the financial mood of the time. The New Deal from President Roosevelt in 1933 and the slow revival from the Depression of the 1920s meant that American buyers returned to Paris to buy merchandise for their New York stores. Soon Paris models and, to a greater extent, toiles, were being shipped across the Atlantic once more, this time in softly sensible colours such as greys, muted beiges, and rose pink (a great favourite). A notable introduction in the fabrics of the period was cotton, largely due to the impact of Chanel with her new beach and sportswear range. The shortage of servants meant that clothing needed to be easier to maintain and cheaper to replace. But, while day and beach clothes became more practical and easy to wear, evening clothes gradually became even more romantic and delicate. The archetypal image of the 1930s hostess sees her in a backless chiffon creation, with a silk rose tucked into the nape of her neck, and a long string of artificial pearls decorating a smoothly tailored bodice. Her skirt falls seductively flat across the stomach and drifts into bias-cut folds around her knees.

To cover the bare backs left by these flimsy dresses, a whole new range of evening wraps became the rage. Hip-length jackets and capes in monkey fur, thick, Chinese-patterned brocade, and satin-lined velvet are often found, together with even fussier and more fragile 'wraps' in boa feathers, ruched chiffon and spangled organdie. Schiaparelli was perhaps the most famous and original couturier for 'after-six' ensembles. She collaborated with French textile manufacturers to produce some outstandingly unusual evening clothes, such as her 'cellophane cape' and her glittery glass fibre fabric 'rodophane'. Her evening accessories, such as fans, necklets and box-shaped bags made of perspex, set a new value on plastics. Now many women who could afford to wear diamonds chose to wear artificial glitter and transparent synthetics.

These new materials often provide the collector with a clue to the date of a dress. In my chapter on Buttons, a complete survey of the substances used in the 1930s acts as a useful reference point for identifying the date of a dress. For example, another innovation from Schiaparelli was the use of 'novelty' buttons, very much influenced by the art of the Surrealists (Dali actually designed some fabrics for her). The buttons would take the form of the theme for a particular collection: for the 1937 Autumn 'Circus' collection, buttons were made in the shape of little jumping horses, and clowns' faces. On another famous occasion, Schiaparelli made a wonderful tailored suit that had enormous hand-mirrors running up the front closure. Her wit and originality sparked off a tremendous enthusiasm for lifelike copies of everyday objects, so that many dresses of the period are adorned with 'realistics' – buttons in the shape of lemons, posies of flowers, smiling faces and even minute lamb chops. It is an interesting reflection on the period that plastics, which we now associate with rather cheap mass-production, provided a source of inspiration when they first entered the market and enabled manufacturers to produce some amusing distinctive items.

Another special feature of evening fashion for the 1930s was the vogue for beaded clothes. This had been extremely popular in the 1920s, too, but in the 1930s new manufacturing advances enabled dresses to be produced at a

A Chanel evening dress photographed by Cecil Beaton, 1935. Even the hairstyle in silhouette copies Chanel's own preference for neatness with a bow.

Right Functional fashions by Chanel: a skirt with braces, 1936.

Centre right Vionnet at work on a model, in the round – the art of the couturier that ready-to-wear can never achieve.

Far right A Vionnet ball gown worn by Mary Taylor, photographed by Cecil Beaton for Vogue in 1934.

cheaper, ready-to-wear level with the same decoration. In England, one of the first ready-to-wear companies to specialize in beaded work was Marley Gowns, established in 1933 by Julian Lee, one of the foremost champions of the British garment industry. He employed twelve beaders to produce his line of inexpensive beaded 'dance dresses' in the mid 1930s.

Schiaparelli's greatest rival as the most influential couturier of the period was undoubtedly Chanel. By the early 1930s she was a well established figure in Paris, working from her salon at 31 rue Cambon. She produced a range of clothes that were youthful, sporty and very easy to wear. In 1931 she was invited to England to help Ferguson in the promotion of a new range of cottons as fashion fabrics. In the same way that Schiaparelli was helping to make synthetics available, Chanel gave her blessing to this most simple and natural of fabrics. Evening dresses in piqué, cotton lace, spotted muslin, organdie, lawn and net were featured in her 1931 collection, and continued to be popular throughout the decade. By 1938–9, on the eve of the Second World War, these ultra-feminine evening dresses had become veritable crinolines, reminiscent of the Winterhalter paintings of the Empress Eugénie in the 1860s.

Madame Vionnet was a third designer whose work was perhaps less copiable than that of her contemporaries. She was a supreme artist with fabric, being best remembered for her draped afternoon dresses of heavy silk crêpe. They flowed and fell round a woman's body, producing a seductive yet very easy to wear garment. The other unique feature of her dresses was

Ready-to-wear styling improved enormously during the 1930s: cheap day outfits from D. H. Evans, London, 1937.

that they could be adapted to fit any physical shape, although in theory they were ideally suited to the rather large-framed, small-bosomed figure that enjoyed such approval at this time. The bodice top is cross-cut, falling softly away from the neck. A unique triangular seam moulds the bodice into the waistline, and the skirt is caught at the side, on the hip, with a single fastening. The dresses were worn with a contrasting coloured belt. Very few of these dresses have survived, because they were worn and loved until they fell apart. However, her beautiful suits with gored or bias-cut skirts and dramatic collars or high-set shoulders are also very typical of the period. She made some handsome wrap-around coats with side fastenings, often decorated with rolls of fur, or large wooden buttons down the front. Everything she made was produced with the greatest craftmanship, and many of her methods were kept secret. Her style was most influential, but her craft remained essentially her own.

The shock of the Wall Street crash continued to have its effect on couturiers throughout the decade. While it is true that Paris retained its dominance in taste and invention, this was the time when most of the great fashion houses established ready-to-wear boutiques, and model gowns sold to New York and London were eagerly copied to be sold in cheaper lines for the masses. Schiaparelli's and Chanel's links with the fabric industry are indicative of a trend towards providing value for money, and exploring ways of making high fashion more cheaply. The collector may be lucky enough to find some examples of 1930s clothing with manufacturers' labels sewn inside the garment for the first time.

It must be admitted that these early efforts to make off-the-peg clothing were not entirely successful. At first, dresses were made up in three sizes only, the ubiquitous 'small', 'medium' and 'large'. All the big stores had sizeable alteration departments to adapt the dresses to the figure of the individual. Off the peg they might be, but the customers still required these dresses to fit them exactly. A good indication of the period of a dress would be where industrial machining is modified by handwork – particularly in the set of the shoulders, or with the enlarging or diminishing of a shoulder-pad.

Below *a simple summer frock from Debenham & Freebody, London, 1939.*

Bottom *The high-shouldered look much favoured by Hollywood star, Joan Crawford.*

Centre *1930s accessories are great fun to collect and a wide variety of objects are still available: a page from Liberty's catalogue, 1935.*

'Pyjamas de Bateau', the mannish casual uniform of the 1930s.

A useful page of designs from Harper's Bazaar, *spotlighting the new silhouettes for 1938.*

LEATHER BELT

LARGE SIZED SCARF FOR BATHING BAG

This last feature, so typical of the period, has been claimed at different times as the particular invention of both Schiaparelli and Rochas. It certainly helped ready-to-wear manufacturers enormously, because it allowed for the armhole to be of a fairly generous standard cut. The 'shaping' came from the high set of the pad on the shoulder. There are certain perfections in dress which couture can achieve, and which ready-to-wear cannot follow: a well-tailored, scrupulously cut armhole is one of them.

The high-shouldered silhouette was accentuated by the smallness of the waist and the length of the skirt. It was an outline made famous by the Hollywood stars of the period, notably Marlene Dietrich and Joan Crawford. (Both Schiaparelli and Chanel designed for many films, made in the USA and the UK, and were heavily copied by Hollywood costume designers, such as Adrian and Howard Greer.) Couturiers' clothes in films had the unfortunate tendency to date rather quickly, so there developed in the 1930s a highly influential, separate machinery for costume designing, where the essence of current fashion was extrapolated and turned into a more enduring image of Hollywood glamour. For this reason old films are not as reliable a source of information or inspiration for the collector as magazines of the period. To get the 'feel' of the time there is nothing so helpful as riffling through old copies of *Vogue* or *Harper's Bazaar*, paying particular attention to the small advertisement sections, where ready-to-wear clothes are most accurately described and sketched.

In one respect Hollywood was responsible for creating fashion rather than following it. As the decade proceeded, evening wear, which had always remained highly fantastical, became increasingly bizarre and varied. As has

Molyneux. A tight little
jacket and a deep-pleated shirt

Alix. A plaid blouse under
a mulberry suit, and over
all an off-white coat

1K? 38
Also at Alix, a great coat
of rainbow plaid with all
the fulness swept to the front

Paquin's dark brown
antelope sports coat
lined with plaid.

Left *'Indisputable evidence that Paris is plaid mad' . . . Designs by,* **left to right,** *Molyneux, Alix, later Mme Grès, and Paquin. Harper's Bazaar 1938. All these give an excellent representation of late 1930s length, line and colouring, to help you identify similar finds, even in ready-to-wear.*

IT'S WONDERFUL WHAT A
LIBERTY SCARF CAN DO
FOR YOU
TUCKED INSIDE YOUR TWEED
COAT, AND WITH GLOVES
AND HAND-BAG TO MATCH~

IT VERY NEARLY
GIVES YOU
CONFIDENCE
AT THE MOMENT OF
ARRIVAL.

More ready-to-wear details emulating the new Paris chic: Liberty advertisement, 1935.

been mentioned, by 1939 the crinoline came back into vogue. Along the way, costume epic films, such as Alexander Korda's *The Private Life of Henry VIII*, or Von Sternberg's vehicles for Marlene Dietrich, created sudden waves in fashion, with slashed velvet sleeves or cossack fur hats as examples of their influence. The high fashion magazines helped this trend to gain significance, for whereas a decade earlier they might have confined their celebrity portraits to the ranks of the European aristocracy or the Latin American *nouveaux riches*, they now photographed Hollywood stars such as Jean Harlow, Marlene Dietrich, Mary Astor or Joan Crawford on location, setting up ideals of glamour and chic which were at the same time even more artificial and remote than the blue-blooded variety, yet somehow more able to be copied by the dreamy metropolitan secretary.

The mid-decade saw a great increase in sportswear and outdoor clothing as areas for fashion rather than apologetically utilitarian garments. Chanel had shown that casual wear did not have to be devoid of chic or femininity, and Patou justifiably claims that his house was the first to put 'separates' and co-ordinated sportswear into high fashion profile. Bathing suits became briefer, and had a plunging back similar to that seen in evening wear. Matching wraps in bold-patterned cotton or synthetic fabrics became popular. Schiaparelli made an amusing design in 1932 from a 'newspaper' print, with raffia accessories. A 'Tyrolean' fashion, a rather ominous foreshadowing of Hitler's rise to power through Bavaria, produced divided shorts, embroidered braces and tilted, narrow-brimmed hats. In 1935, adopting the idea that clothing should be practical and cheap, Mainbocher (one of the few American designers to make a considerable name for himself in the 1930s) produced mid-thigh-length shorts and below-the-knee bloomers for the beach in checked gingham and linen crash.

As the decade progressed, the twin themes of glamour and practicality produced an increasingly hard-edged, sophisticated day-time look. The dress and jacket or suit became the ultimate in elegance, and examples are often seen that are so dashing and impeccably co-ordinated that they could easily be worn today: they have a timeless elegance. English tweeds, checks, tartans and textured fabrics enjoyed a boom. The style, brilliantly executed by Chanel, Mainbocher, Rochas, Molyneux and others, employed a mixture of fabrics – a dark colour for the jacket, a paler, toning one for the skirt, with an equally harmonious pale silk or satin blouse. The ensemble would be topped by a small, ludicrously perched hat, always worn well to the side or forward over the brow. Colours became more intense towards the end of the decade, with Schiaparelli's incredible 'shocking pink', and a proliferation of plum, purple, red, and black and white checks. The year 1939 saw a strange innovation in the form of 'Louisa May Alcott' day dresses – the original shirtwaisters – which had white collars and cuffs, tightly cinched midriffs and full skirts. Hats became even more extravagant, ending the decade as a complete circle of straw, like a Mexican sombrero. Turbans, toques, pill-boxes: the hats of the 1930s are such an extraordinary

Below, right *The epitome of late 1930s elegance: a Maggy Rouff design, with hat from Reboux. The metal clasp handbag, elbow-length, knotted gloves and overtly chunky jewellery are also typical of the period. (1939).*

A good example of the Austrian influence in fashion towards the end of the decade: A Viennese suit shown in London, complete with Tyrolean hat.

Hand-knitted clothing became popular during the 1930s: Vogue produced a series of knitting books at the time. Designs from Vogue's 8th Book of Knitting, 1932. The scoop neck helps to date clothing from this period.

mixture of folly and invention that a collector could concentrate on this ten-year span alone and produce a most satisfying portrait of feminine coquetry.

A most significant development took place in the area of knitted clothing. Unfortunately these garments are more difficult to acquire now; jumpers and cardigans seem to survive less often than day or evening clothes, perhaps because they are more easily worn out or deteriorate more rapidly in storage. The 1930s were a time of tremendous development in knitwear, not simply for day wear but for that emerging new category of clothing, early evening or cocktail wear. Schiaparelli had revolutionized the dowdy image of knitting with her splendid *trompe l'oeil* jumper, first produced in 1928. From then on knitwear became increasingly important, and was seen in the form of smart evening jumpers, racy, bright-patterned sports sweaters, and extremely brief but beautiful bathing suits (including the first knitted two-pieces to be seen). One of the smartest fashions of the mid-1930s was a small, strapless, knitted top, striped or in a plain, dark colour, matched with shorts in white, black or navy blue. By the end of the decade, knitwear had become very fashionable. Owing to the prevailing taste for the Austrian *dirndl* look, white cardigans with flowers, bobbles and other forms of peasant embroidery added a European ethnic flavour.

Even stranger in those final years was the sudden tightening of the waistline. Waist corsets, or 'waspies', made an appearance, and one of Patou's 1939 models sported a twenty-inch circumference. Tiny bodices without straps were combined with stiffly starched petticoats. It is intriguing to note that this waisted silhouette is exactly what Dior 'discovered' after the Second World War for the famous New Look. But, on considering the whole range of novel ideas at the time, this forecasting is more an accident than a trend, for fashion generally became absurdly chaotic. Oriental extravagances, harem trousers, Russian coats, Greek draperies, all these ethnic styles were copied – or exaggerated – at the end of the decade. Tourism had enjoyed a great boom throughout the 1920s and 1930s, so perhaps the menacing nationalism that foreshadowed the war produced a sudden rush of interest, in fashion at least, in the benefits of that kind of international exchange.

THE FORTIES

Severe fashions reflect the sombre mood of the period: Berlin fashion, 1940.

On first sight the 1940s, or at least the war years, might appear to be the least inspired and varied of decades in the fashion history of this century. But for the historian and the collector, these years produced important changes. The apparently limiting factors of rationing imposed by wartime shortages, and changes in the life style of women caught up in the war effort, demanded an entirely new approach to clothing, and, of necessity, a new industry emerged.

The six years of war, 1939–45, were followed by Dior's 'New Look', which transformed the fashion world and proceeded to dominate it until the end of the 1950s. For the collector, the war years offer the exciting prospect of gathering samples of documentary and social significance, as well as the pleasure of finding engaging items of clothing. No one can claim that the 'Utility' garments were enchanting or stylish in the manner of the 1920s or 1930s but, by the same token, a collector now entering the field stands an excellent chance of finding interesting examples which will increase in financial and nostalgic value as time goes by.

The crucial event in fashion was the total loss to the rest of the world of the creative and guiding force which had been provided until that time by Paris couture. Most of the Paris houses had closed their doors in 1940, when the German army occupied France. Many couturiers left, some moving to Free France, others to America or England. A few carried on their business in Paris, not because they were willing to collaborate with the occupying forces but, on the contrary, to protect the industry for the future, and to thwart the German intention to shift the whole couture operation to Berlin and Vienna. The Chambre Syndicale de la Couture Parisienne, an organization led by Lucien Lelong, was specifically created to protect the industry. Jane Dorner relates in her history of the period:

> Lelong managed to persuade the Germans that such a move would kill the industry dead. Paris had been regarded as the centre for chic ever since the sixteenth century, when France's supremacy in silk and lace making was undisputed, and from that time onwards a system of complementary industries essential to the fashion trade had been built up. To separate Paris and fashion would have been like removing the heart from its fine web of interacting veins and arteries. Besides this, it would have been fatal to remove the designers from the milieu of elegance from which they drew their inspiration. By repeated discussion

(fourteen conferences in four years) Lelong managed to keep open ninety-two houses (though only the top twelve had privileges) and 112,000 skilled workers were saved from compulsory labour in German war industries. Paris retained its traditional position as the centre of the fashion trade, while Germany failed to produce a single designer of note.

Among the designers who continued to work at this time, the most distinctive were Grès, who made (and still makes) timeless day dresses and the most exquisite classically draped evening gowns, and Balenciaga, who remained aloof from the mainstream of Paris fashion while creating an elegance that was to become as influential as that of Dior by the end of the decade. Others were Paquin, Jaques Fath, Marcel Rochas and Piquet; Chanel shut down at the start of the war, not to reopen until fifteen years later, in 1954.

Developments in women's fashions during the lean years reflected what was happening in the world: the feminine opulence of the previous decade gave way to a more severe, masculine look. The square shoulders which Schiaparelli and Rochas had introduced in the late 1930s, which gave an effect of provocative, hard-edged elegance, now combined with a fitted waistline and straight skirt (often enlivened with a pleat or two at mid-front and back). This became the new shape for the tailleur, the two-piece suit which more than any other outfit expressed the style of the time. The same outline prevailed in dresses of the period – simple shirtwaisters with a few buttons down the front, small, turned-back revers, a slim belt to define the waistline, and a sparely cut skirt, lightly pleated or gathered. The hem, reaching a few inches below the knee, now made the lavishly trimmed tea gowns of the 1930s, all bias-cut and floating to mid-calf length, appear outmoded indeed.

Some notable designers, having left Paris, began to make a considerable impact in fashion in other cities. Opening a boutique in New York, Schiaparelli introduced to Americans a new ideal in glamour and chic. The American Mainbocher, who had embarked on a successful career in the

Above *Schiaparelli moved to New York during the war years. This sketch of her on tour in America shows her revolutionary sackbacked coat, a shape that reappeared after the war in the work of Balenciaga and Dior.*

Left *Schiaparelli's little black wool suit from the Spring Collections of 1940 (the last before the German invasion), with the square-shouldered look which remained popular throughout the decade. The gold chain instead of buttons is a typical innovative touch. (Jean Morel photograph).*

Sketches from Harper's Bazaar, September 1942, full of money- and energy-saving ideas, give an excellent view of the period's styles.

French fashion centre, crossed the Atlantic back to his native country, where he was to remain permanently after the war, and demonstrated that the acceptance of economic stringencies need not prevent a woman from looking well turned out.

In London, Molyneux, Creed and Angèle Delanghe provided noble support for the government in its exercise of the economy measures that were necessarily imposed on the fashion industry. The British couturiers Norman Hartnell and Hardy Amies joined Molyneux and Creed in designing 'Utility' clothing, stamped with the official 'CC41' sign to show that it conformed to the government regulations limiting the amount of fabric used in a garment by restricting skirt length and discouraging such excesses as elaborate turned-back cuffs, decorative pockets and costly trimmings, even limiting the number of buttons. Manufacturers in America were soon forced to work under similar restrictions laid out in the Limitations Order L–85.

The sixty-six coupons a year allotted to each adult in the United Kingdom at the start of clothes rationing during the war had dropped to thirty-six by the end of hostilities. A Utility tweed suit was rated at eighteen coupons, a coat at fourteen, a woollen dress at eleven, blouses, cardigans and jumpers at seven each. Even a couple of handkerchiefs accounted for two coupons. As children also had to be provided for out of the adult allowance, the war years in England produced a style of dressing that was serviceable, hard-wearing and at times ingenious. Women cut down their own coats to make skirts or children's romper suits, they unravelled knitted jumpers, reworking the wool many times, and found cheerful uses for such unlisted categories of material as curtain fabric, ribbons and blanketing in sporty jackets and eccentric dresses.

Such limited buying power naturally meant that Utility clothes had to be made out of the highest quality of cloth allowed in the circumstances, so

Far left *A classic wartime 'tailleur' by Peter Russell (1945). Many designers felt that the Utility restrictions helped in creating suits that relied on their cut rather than trimmings for elegance.*

Left *A smart yet simple suit (1941) designed by Molyneux: a little propaganda on the wall emphasises the need for home knitting and sewing as an economic necessity.*

Below *Models at an exhibition of 'Make Do & Mend' ideas in 1942. The lady's suit is cut down from a man's old dinner suit (even her hat is made from a topper!), while the jacket and skirt on the right are converted from a waistcoat, with home-knitted sleeves, and a pair of plus-fours.*

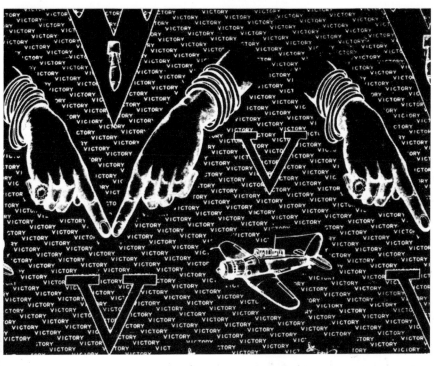

Centre left *A wartime print: this 'Victory' cotton, probably made for headscarves, even had the morse code signal for Victory worked into the selvedges.*

CC41: *this label indicated a garment or article was manufactured to conform to Utility regulations, so look out for it as a guide to dating clothes.*

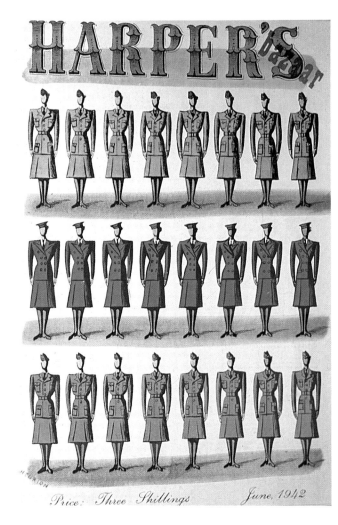

*Pyjamas for women were
more popular than
nightdresses – perhaps more
suitable for a quick remove to
the air raid shelter. With
wings on the pocket, these air
force blue pyjamas are a nice
example of how patriotic
themes were used at this time.*

*'World War II' would make
an excellent theme around
which to form a collection –
including examples of 'Make
Do & Mend', military and
civilian uniforms, and Utility
fashion.*

that they could withstand the hardest possible wear. Both in Britain and in
America, garments of the period were generally made from natural fibre –
cotton and linen for summer, wool for winter. The cotton prints of the
1940s demonstrate a gallant spirit, with their vigorous, splashy, abstract
designs in boldly contrasting colours. Some typical examples also include
patriotic motifs of flags, anchors or other militaristic emblems; colour
combinations of red, white and blue were followed in popularity by black
and white, with polka dots or checks. In Britain, Paul Nash and Graham
Sutherland were among the well known artists who collaborated with the
Cotton Board under a government subsidy to provide overseas trade
(notably with Latin America), and set a taste for cheerful, dramatic textile
design.

Rayon crêpe, a successful substitute for silk when such imported luxury
fabrics were very difficult to find, frequently occurs in evening clothes of the
period, and manufacturers made a virtue of necessity in producing thick
rayon stockings in bright colours such as lilac, rose and apple green. After
the ban on silk stockings in 1941, women even went so far as to draw black
lines in eyebrow pencil up the backs of their legs to simulate the seams in the
forbidden hose. Ankle socks became the day-time fashion, worn with
brogues.

Determined to exploit the financial security of the American market by
exporting British clothes, several English designers banded together to form

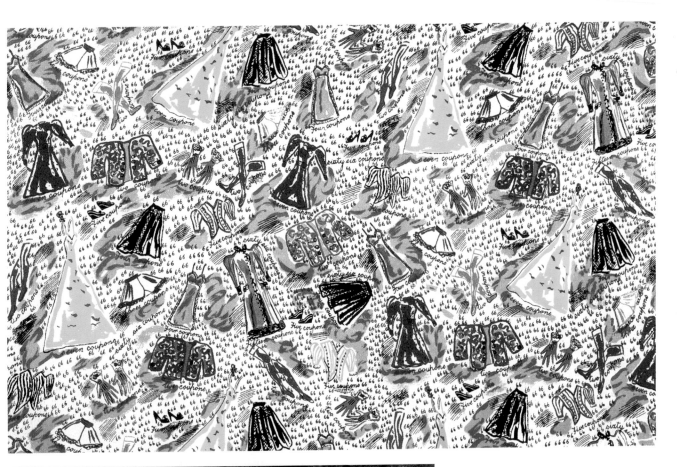

Fabric echoing British Utility and Patriotic themes: a rayon crêpe dress fabric showing the number of coupons required for each article of clothing shown in the print, set against a background of 66, the total allowed for a year's purchases.

An elegant way of turning the stocking shortage to advantage: designs by Rahvis create couture ankle socks with tweed turnovers matching the tweed of the suits.

American influences in fashion become apparent in ready-to-wear during the 1940s: a latter-day 'Prairie' style (1941) sold on coupons in London.

Centre *The drive for export during the war years kept the British fashion industry going – all these models went to New York in 1940. Note the abundance of buttons and the width of the lapels, in contrast to designs for home wear.*

the Incorporated Society of London Fashion Designers. Of the output produced by the British fashion industry, fifteen per cent was excluded from the stringent Utility regulations in order that much needed trade links could be kept open through export. 'Buy British' shops soon opened in New York, and for once the urgent necessity of war-time regulations had a favourable effect on the organization and dynamism of the home industry. Faced with reduced facilities and a continuing shortage of staff, the trade responded by evolving a new professionalism, with improvements in mass-production, the development of time-saving equipment, and a new spirit of co-operative effort. The experience of producing, in quantity, varied styles of uniform consolidated improvements in cut, sizing, fitting and finish that were to persist after the end of the war.

According to several London dealers, fashions of the early 1940s are still not very widely collected, possibly because the styles remain easily recognizable, and many women of the present generation continue to associate the straight-skirted look with some of their mothers' dowdier clothes. However, the field is rich in possibilities: the fabrics have considerable charm, and the supply is plentiful in second-hand dress shops, junk shops and markets. This holds as true for the American collector as for the English. Because the clothes of the war years were in general so toughly made there are good prospects of building up a substantial and well preserved selection from the period. There is an interesting development in the importation by many dealers of American 1940s dresses for sale in the English second-hand market, not simply from outlets in New York, but from other centres such as Chicago, Detroit and the west coast.

American clothes have an added freshness in style, since ready-to-wear designers turned to cheap and cheerful sources of inspiration. 'Mexican' peasant blouses, polka-dot 'Pioneer' dresses, boldly checked 'Country-and-Western' skirts, and of course the crucial introduction of tough denim working trousers originally manufactured by the Californian firm of Levi-

Strauss & Co. from the 1890s onwards, all added vitality to young people's clothes.

California grew as a significant centre for a thriving new sportswear industry. One of the main reasons for its enormous increase in output was the popularity of Hollywood, which reached its peak in 1946. The desire to emulate the actresses portrayed with such glamour on the screen was not confined to the imitation of the elegant, romantic evening clothes, or even the sharply tailored outfits favoured by Joan Crawford and made for her by the Hollywood designer Adrian (considerably influenced by Schiaparelli). Gossip magazines made a highly profitable business of 'revealing' the lives of the stars off the screen. They photographed Bette Davis, Katharine Hepburn, Lana Turner and other famous actresses of the day relaxing at the pool-side, on the golf course or in the paddock. The emphasis on sports made possible by the favourable climate meant that Californian designers were adept with youthful, active styles, which exerted a nationwide influence on ready-to-wear and, in turn, on fashion in general. Schiaparelli said in New York, 'It is amazing what America does with reasonably priced clothes, especially sports clothes. So much taste.'

It may well be that sheer distance from Europe encouraged Californian styles to seek their own inspiration; New Yorkers always had Paris to turn to. Even before the outbreak of the Second World War, California was so well established as a centre for sportswear that eighty-five per cent of the output was sent to the large eastern stores, and many manufacturers were happy to give exclusive lines to shops in the west because they bought in such large quantities.

Robert Riley, until recently head of the Fashion Institute of New York, suggests that a most interesting line of fashion from this era came from the Hollywood designer Irene, who produced a ready-to-wear range for the Los Angeles store of Bullock's Wilshire. Any items with this label would be collector's pieces. Adrian, too, produced a ready-to-wear line (apart from

"of san francisco"
...city of sophisticates
and superlatives
... of longest bridges and
suddenest hills, and fairest flowers
and smartest women.

Logo for Lilli Ann of San Francisco, a label worth looking for, as the maker of some handsome little suits.

Top *A dress created for Loretta Young by Irene, one of the most successful Hollywood designers of the 1940s.*

Top left *Hollywood stars were promoted for their style off-screen as well as on: Mr & Mrs Ronald Reagan (Jane Wyman) on their honeymoon at Palm Springs, sporting the best of American labels in swimwear during the 1940s: Mabs of Hollywood sharktex suits.*

71

his very successful film work in the late 1930s). In 1942, he went into a small line of couture clothes, which are even rarer.

Most famous of the Californian manufacturers are Cole of California and the Catalina Knitting Mills, headed by Edgar Stewart. For the Mexican-inspired clothes so popular in the west, the name of Louella Ballerino is worth looking for. She liked to use Mexican or Indian motifs in her cottons, and was one of the first American designers to use hand-blocked designs, which give a fabric an 'ethnic' quality. It is very interesting to compare her style with similar developments in the decades that followed – particularly the crumpled peasant look so popular in Paris and London in the past few years. To prove that even the most bizarre of fashion habits always has a forerunner, consider the following description (taken from *Fashion Fundamentals*, a history written in the mid-1940s by Bernice Chambers) concerning another well known Los Angeles designer of that time:

> Agnes Barrett created a sensational broomstick skirt made by wrapping a wet cotton skirt around a broomstick and tying it securely with string while it dries. This procedure produces an uneven crinkled effect. Such skirts were tremendously popular before wartime restrictions limited the use of cotton cloth. The skirt was sold to customers on the broomstick so it could be washed and 'recrinkled'.

Much more enduring and classic casual clothes were made in California at this time by White Stag, Koret of California, and Pendleton (the Pendleton Woolen Mills had been established in the state since the 1930s, though the firm began by making bright Indian blankets in Oregon in 1909). These labels can be found fairly easily in second-hand clothing stores, and good examples of their output would be worth preserving in a ready-to-wear or sports collection.

In England, too, the war years were marked by the development of leisure wear other than outfits specifically intended for such active sports as tennis or golf. Women's new duties provided the impetus: the 'siren suit' became

Wartime work had an enduring affect on women's clothing. Land girls watch a squadron of fighters returning. Dungarees remained part of female wardrobes ever after.

Bouquets from the Army

standard wear for land girls, factory workers, even for Winston Churchill himself. Headscarves, which had hardly existed as a fashion accessory before, came in at first for severely practical reasons, and gradually became acceptable headgear for casual occasions. As hats were exempt from the rationing system, many a plain Utility outfit was enlivened by a concoction of flowers and ribbons set on a small bonnet, worn well forward or fixed close to the temple with a hatpin. Straw boaters, snoods and net bags for chignons were further economical and stylish accessories of the period. Knitted or crocheted gloves completed the modest wardrobes of the resourceful women. Fashion illustrations from the war years soon dispel the idea that stringency was dull or unfeminine; the overall effect is one of restrained gaiety.

However, at the end of the war, the mood of carefulness was instantly dispelled by one of the most dramatic changes of direction that has occurred in fashion in this century. The New Look was primarily the creation of one man, Christian Dior. After working for some time in the house of Lucien Lelong, Dior attracted the confidence and business resources of the French textile magnate Marcel Boussac. He boldly suggested to Boussac that they collaborate on the launching of a new fashion house, thinking that the idea would sound so preposterous that Boussac would fade away and he would thus have removed the temptation to leave Lelong, who had cared for him for so long. But Boussac, aware of Dior's talent, offered to back him with double his asking stake. By 1945, Dior had gone independent and was established at 30 rue Montaigne; he gathered around him a brilliant team of technical and marketing experts and stunned the Western world with his first major collection in Spring 1947.

Dior developed a look that was in complete contrast to the style of the war years. Skirts became as full as crinolines, sweeping almost to ankle level (eleven inches from the ground) from a nipped-in waist, for which Dior devised a special 'waspie' corset that was sometimes built into the garment.

Designs from the Paris Shows in 1944, the first after the Liberation, show the extravagant outlines popular in France, so different from the severely elegant London line. **Left** *an ensemble from Robert Piguet, and* **below** *from Maggy Rouff.*

A famous design from Christian Dior's collection in February 1947: 'Bar'. A new nipped-in waist, a new length, a general air of luxury – the New Look.

Centre *A selection of frivolous hats from America.*

73

Above *A Dior coat, 1947, superbly tailored.*

Right *The 'waspie' that made the heavy, generously cut dresses sit as they should.*

Jackets were figure-hugging, with décolleté necklines, long, narrow sleeves and a mass of fine decoration – pleating, tucks, feathery lace trims for evening – or matching draped stoles. 'Bar', the most famous outfit from that first major Dior collection, consisted of a tight shantung silk jacket over a widely pleated black skirt. Bettina, the mannequin who wore it, was one of the first of the French couture models to win international social stardom.

There were, of course, commercial advantages in Dior's style. With financial backing from one of France's leading textile manufacturers, the New Look was destined to provide the fabric industry with a necessary boost, now that the war was over. In addition, there is no doubt that women were yearning to the lavish romantic styles that the economic restrictions and practical considerations of the war had denied them. In 1946, *Vogue* featured a photograph by Norman Parkinson of a woman in a flowing white ball gown with a caption that described her as ' . . . wistful with the frustrations of youth, or the longing for a charm and an elegance abandoned without question during the wartime years, now hard to recover in a Utility world'. There was scope for a revival of femininity, and Dior seized the opportunity.

Not surprisingly, there were fierce reactions to the sudden outburst of frivolity and luxury. Sir Stafford Cripps, the President of the British Board of Trade, indignantly denounced the New Look: 'It seems to be utterly stupid and irresponsible that time, labour, materials and money should be wasted upon these imbecilities.'

American women, who had suffered the same deprivation from the L–85 wartime restrictions as their British counterparts under the Utility scheme, had adopted ballooning sleeves and full skirts to the new mid-calf length almost immediately the war ended in 1945, but government restrictions still prevented manufacturers from making copies of the Paris fashions. However, in 1947 Neiman-Marcus invited Dior to Dallas, Texas, where he received the first 'Oscar' awarded to a non-American for services to fashion. By the following year, Dior had opened a boutique in New York to produce a separate line of his creations for the American market. (The Dior boutique in London followed in 1954, and operated on the same lines.)

Dior's style was received as excitedly in America as it had been in Europe. Local reactions to the New Look were extreme. A group formed in Texas as the 'A Little Below the Knee Club' stood out against the new length, and magazines contained a flurry of protest letters, as well as cartoons caricaturing the French innovation. Nevertheless, the New Look opened up an important increase in trade between France and America, notably in the business of buying model dresses from which to make 'line-for-line' copies, and selling them for very high prices in the city stores.

Two pioneers in this business were the New York firms Macy's and Ohrbach's. Both used a labelling system whereby they sold Dior copies as 'Monsieur X' dresses; Jacques Fath copies were labelled 'Monsieur Y', and Givenchy's 'Monsieur Z'. The clothes were faithful copies of originals bought in the Paris showrooms, and one of the attractions of fashion shows at Macy's was the appearance of two mannequins together on the catwalk, one wearing an outfit from Paris and the other a virtually indistinguishable Macy's copy.

Dior was eventually forced to prevent the pirating of his lines when Alexander's store began to use his name openly in selling their copies in the 1960s. The couturier needs his exclusiveness to maintain the value of his designs, and Dior, who exerted so dominant and far-reaching an influence for the fifteen years immediately after the war, was particularly vulnerable. Alexander's returned to the use of a pseudonym on the label, although like Macy's and Ohrbach's they were making replicas of Paris models. As a documentary piece in the history of fashion, a 'line-for-line' Paris copy would be well worth buying for a collection centred on New York.

Good examples of the New Look have a durability that makes them irresistible to the collector. Apart from the waist corset, dresses were distinguished by the first use of a firm nylon fabric ironed into shape and inserted as a stiffener in the lining of the bodice. In 1947 *Harper's Bazaar* ran a page of detailed sketches showing how each panel of a full New Look skirt was individually lined, with an extra ruffle at the waist to make pleats or gathers jut out sharply over the hips. Padding was built up gently over the shoulders to give jackets a wide-necked, curving but tailored line, emphasizing the slimness of the waist. Enormous bows were frequently added to the front of dresses, or fitted to resemble a bustle at the back. The almost Edwardian feel of the ensemble was accented by elbow-length black gloves. In his most important collections, Dior paid particular attention to hats, whether they were small and head-hugging, with a long, swooping feather set at an angle, or enormous and wide brimmed, with a small, low crown. The hats complemented each outfit with a harmony and ingenuity rarely equalled in couture after the 1950s.

It should not be thought that Dior was the only creator of fashion in the late 1940s. In retrospect, it appears that the improvement brought about in manufacturing skills by the stringencies of the war had its counterpart in the fruitful output of a whole generation of couturiers, Dior and his competitors, who were superbly skilled and diverse in their talents. They were all highly influential in the development of ready-to-wear fashion, and their work might form the basis of important collections concentrating either on model couture clothes, or, more cheaply, and possibly more interestingly from the historical and documentary viewpoint, on good copies of the period's Paris lines.

Dior's greatest rival, the Spanish designer Cristobal Balenciaga, could hardly have provided a sharper contrast with him in presentation. While Dior loved, or at least valued, the commercial ballyhoo surrounding his work, and was always ready to open a boutique or sell the franchise for a range of scarves or perfume, Balenciaga always remained aloof from the bustle of Paris and even showed his collections a month later than the rest of the couturiers, forcing foreign buyers to stay on in Paris, or to return there, for he was too important to miss.

His designs were less dramatically varied than those of Dior, who moved from long, full skirts to the slim sacs of the early 1950s. But a Balenciaga model has certain telling features. The clothes are often made in plain, black fabric, or dramatic, splashy prints. Balenciaga favoured extremely elegant, formal lines, and was renowned for the expertise of his workrooms in the setting of shoulders and the almost sculptured sit of a turned-back collar. Balenciaga's work is so distinctive that he is one of the first couturiers to become identifiable to beginners in fashion history or collecting from photographs in glossy magazines.

Equally distinctive, though possibly appealing to a different type of wearer, was the work of the young Jacques Fath. He exerted a strong influence on American fashion, as his copies under the 'Monsieur Y' label show, and took back to Paris many refreshing innovations from his twice-yearly trips across the Atlantic. He would take with him a designer, some 'toiles' and a workroom première, as André Ostier wrote in *Paris Fashion*:

> In a few weeks, not even a month, he would put on a collection of dresses, coats, and tailored suits, for Joseph Halpert, one of his important buyers. He would start with twenty models, and add up to forty for the ready-to-wear manufacturers. He was criticised a lot at the time for selling himself outside his house. His example was taken up and other couturiers were soon delighted to be approached by other American off-the-peg manufacturers.

Fath's clothes have an air of being designed for a light-hearted, amused and amusing woman, not necessarily as wealthy as the classic Dior or Balenciaga customer. He was a great favourite with models and actresses, and enjoyed cheaper, zanier fabrics, with bright, young colours – blues, greens, pale yellows and pinks – at a time when beiges and muted tones were considered elegant, and black and white the ultimate in good taste. His own monochrome designs were dramatized by the prettiest pointed collars standing up beside a kiss-curl on the cheek, or set off by an outsize flower or bow at the neck. Fath possibly had sufficient flair to rank along with Schiaparelli as one of the greatest originals of Paris, but he died of leukaemia in 1954, at the age of forty-two. His wittiest and silliest invention, which hardly does justice to the appeal of his other creations, was the 'hobble' skirt of 1948. In this style, he out-Diored Dior with a skirt so long and tight that it was almost impossible to walk in. But the shape made a wonderful silhouette, immediately beloved of fashion photographers, for Fath was well aware of the couturier's need to maintain keen public interest.

Another name of considerable power in American ready-to-wear was

that of Pierre Balmain, who was, like Fath, one of the new generation of designers to emerge after the war. He was originally an architectural student, but turned to fashion as a career and trained, significantly, with Molyneux, whose talent for beautifully tailored suits may have coincided with Balmain's own preference for structured, classical clothes. He then moved to the house of Lelong, where he worked for a while with Dior, but left to establish his own house in 1945, doubtless encouraged by the success of his former colleague. In 1947 he made his first trip to America, where he arranged to supply exclusive designs for the Magnin stores in California. Like Dior, he also made an arrangement with Neiman-Marcus in Texas. Balmain was one of the first designers to cater for the shape and style of the American figure, employing several American mannequins to show his collection in Paris. By the end of the 1940s he had opened a ready-to-wear boutique in New York, and was selling his designs to wealthy customers in Latin America and to the new European stars of the cinema – notably Brigitte Bardot, Sophia Loren and Melina Mercouri.

British couturiers, too, made a fine contribution to the improvements in the standard and variety of ready-to-wear clothes. Hardy Amies, who had helped to create interesting designs for the Utility label during the war years, also exported his clothes to the USA, and worked closely with big retailers such as Marshall Field. Charles Creed, who had started his fashion career in the New York retail business, spent the war years in London, moved for a while to Bergdorf Goodman and subsequently designed for A. Beller, a famous 1940s label. Eventually he rejoined his father's couture establishment in Paris and in doing so came into contact with Patou – a house which, like Balmain's, produced a sporty style of clothing well suited to the American market. Creed then spent many years taking over small collections of Paris fashion to America, and greatly influenced the taste and

A classic travelling coat by Pierre Balmain (1949).

*Two British designers to look for: **Right** a yellow wool evening suit from Charles Creed and **left** a smart dress from Hardy Amies.*

style of manufacturing in New York. During this period, he created many ready-to-wear clothes with his own label for the firm of Philip Mangone.

Balmain, Patou and Creed illustrate the cross-fertilization of ideas and talent that took place in the 1940s between Paris, London and New York. The Paris designers still set the pace for new ideas, and lent their expertise to a ready-to-wear industry which was improving dramatically in quality and variety. New names established by the end of the decade were to become very familiar in the 1950s. In London, the firms of Polly Peck, Horrocks, Linzi, London Town and Susan Small figured frequently in the pages of *Vogue* and *Harper's Bazaar*. Fourteen new companies formed the Model House Group in 1947 in order to promote their own interests jointly and to attract overseas buyers to their combined shows; and the firm of Marks & Spencer began to make a name with well-cut and -finished dresses for the modest spender, retailing at about £5.00.

The great influx of Jewish refugees during the war years added further to the pool of talent that had been steadily building up the New York ready-to-wear industry on Seventh Avenue. But it was perhaps in the 1940s that a truly American style of ready-to-wear, no longer merely imitating Paris, came into being. Norman Norell and Clare McCardell figured as two outstanding examples of national talent at this time.

Norell lived in his native state of Indiana until the age of nineteen, then moved to New York to study at the Parson School of Design and the Pratt Institute in Brooklyn. His background may have kept him in touch with the combination of practicality and glamour that is essential in clothes for the American woman. He had executed a great many designs for the cinema, and worked for the noted ready-to-wear company of Hattie Carnegie (a label that is well worth collecting) by the 1940s, when he linked up with the Seventh Avenue manufacturer Attilio Traina to produce clothes under the name of Traina-Norell, aptly described as 'the Tiffany's of the dress industry'. Phyllis Lee Levin pictured the clothes in *The Wheels of Fashion*:

> It [Traina-Norell] became famous for jersey chemises, 2,000-dollar slithering sheaths sewn with 50,000 paillettes, for the sable-bordered organdie, mink-hemmed chiffon, sweater-topped dirndls, evening shirt-waists. The firm was synonymous with masterful craftsmanship, revolutionary silhouettes, and astronomical prices.

A collector in New York, Stan Weaver, who specializes in Norell's work, spent half an hour describing in loving detail how exquisitely made Norell's clothes always were. One example, typical of his famous beaded designs, was decorated with trailing flowers that wound their way around the skirt. The beading had been applied to the finished garment, so that the movement was unbroken across the seaming. Norell is a designer's designer, justly deserving his eminence in American fashion history.

In a totally different way, Claire McCardell originated many ideas that helped the modern woman to find clothes that truly suited her active, liberated life. As originator of the modern taste for separates, she is most famous for her 'pop-over' style, a wrap-around cotton pinafore dress with wide sleeves, which was soon adopted in a variety of other fabrics – denims, checks, ginghams and corduroys. In fact, her practical, sporty look seems so familiar that it hardly looks dated. She also added originality and taste to the famous all-American shirtwaister. Many of her designs came out under the label of Townley Frocks Inc. in New York; collectors may well find something quite distinctively McCardell bearing this other name.

The list of well made American ready-to-wear labels from the 1940s is impressive: Ceil Chapman, working for Samuel Chapman Inc., produced an identifiably American version of the Dior New Look, with bone-bodiced evening dresses, hooped skirts and flounces – the classic *ingénue* ball dress. She was also responsible for a young-looking range of suits and day dresses for the same firm. Nettie Rosenstein made evening dresses of a more sophisticated appeal, specializing in 'little black dresses', simple in line and cleverly made to flatter older figures of less than perfect proportions. Pauline Trigère was actually a French dressmaker, daughter of a Parisian tailor, who arrived in New York in 1937 and produced some fine examples of sophisticated dresses and cocktail outfits in subtle 'French colours' – greys, soft blues and mauves. A particular innovation was her use of fur as a lining for capes and coats, which were often designed to be reversible. Vera Maxwell's name gained in popularity during the war with her clever use of the war-time L–85 regulations. She made a stylistic advantage out of economy with some interesting collarless, cuffless, beltless coats, finished with welt seaming and fabric-covered buttons. Her styles were much copied by other Seventh Avenue manufacturers.

It is interesting to note the extent to which women dominated the American fashion scene at this time, but many companies were run by male designers who maintained a steady output of finely tailored suits, coats and

An evening gown designed by Pauline Trigère for de Pinna of New York.

Often considered the leading American couturier, Norman Norell worked in both couture and ready-to-wear; his couture clothes are already very highly priced at auction sales, particularly the beaded evening dresses. **Far left** *a dress designed for Traina-Norell, in red silk taffeta.*

An outfit from the 1940s by Claire McCardell, whose novel ideas for casual clothing made her the most distinctively American of modern designers.

dresses in quality fabrics: Herbert Sondheim, Larry Aldrich, Maurice Rentner and Philip Mangone. A most interesting collection might be based on the work of these excellent ready-to-wear manufacturers, possibly on the lines suggested in a statement by the Seventh Avenue professional Stanley Marcus: 'A style is any particular and individual article made differently from another article. Fashion is a process of change in the development of styles. . . .'

We could extend this to say that couture is concerned with the development of fashion, capturing the new mood, the new aesthetic, as it seems to the eye of an intuitive, creative couturier-designer. Styling is the manufacturer's translation of fashion into something wearable, and suited to the lives of women in the working, democratic world. The 1940s saw both forces dramatically in action, from the exigencies of war-time economies to the inspired revolution of Dior's New Look and the subsequent adaptation of his line by many talented manufacturers.

A nice assessment of levels of spending power in 1948: the 'wage earner' dresses at Jaeger, the salaried woman at Dorville, and the lady with capital at Digby Morton.

A stunning golden-yellow Adrian Original in rayon crêpe. The padded shoulders help to date the dress – 1944. Even in America with wartime economy fabrics were limited as was the yardage allowed for each garment.

THE FIFTIES

The 1950s offer tremendous prospects for the collector. It is true that, as the decade is nearer to us, it is more difficult to see the long-lasting significance of some designers' work; and clothes which may appear to us to be significant now may have to be reassessed at a later date. But the two great characteristics of the 1950s were the growth of the ready-to-wear industry and the dramatic change in source of influence for fashion. It could be said that, with the New Look, Dior had made the last definitive statement from Paris. After this, other inspirations for new fashions came into being, the most important of which was the growing influence of younger people's street fashion – with London boutiques as the centre of a thriving new business. In America, the films of Hollywood produced a whole new set of fantasy heroes and heroines with whom the young could identify: Marlon Brando, James Dean, Marilyn Monroe, Jane Russell (and in Europe, Brigitte Bardot and Jean-Paul Belmondo). All these gave impetus to a new style of wearing casual clothes, the same outfits for all occasions, marking a younger set's style which was totally different from, and much more relaxed than, that of their parents.

An 'A' line Dior suit, 1955.

The remarkable changes in fashion from the beginning of the 1950s to the end suggest that a social revolution was working its way through all levels of society in the developed world. At no other time have clothes so clearly illustrated such dramatic changes in values in so short a period. Magazines and films at the beginning of the decade create the impression of a reasonably stable world, recovering steadily from the ravages of the Second World War. Dior's New Look, with its generous yardage in the skirt, its nipped-in waist and tailored, tight-fitting bodice or jacket, had about it an air of formality and dignity. In his subsequent collections, Dior continued to produce 'looks' which gave an elegant femininity to the wearer. In 1951 came the 'Princess' line, with beautifully cut, long seams running down a waistless dress which flared out gracefully to end at mid-shin level. In 1954 came the 'H' line (coincidentally reflecting in its name the current preoccupation with the Bomb), and in 1955 the 'A' and 'Y' lines. The 'A' line consisted of a dress or a jacket and skirt in a pronounced flaring line, often emphasized by double rows of buttons down the front, or with flat pleats breaking out where the horizontal stroke of a capital letter 'A' would be. Gradually the line became narrower at the hem, and more shapeless in the body, so that in 1956 and 1957 the shape was a simple chemise with long

The new soft-shoulder look,
Dior, mid-1950s.

or short sleeves and a slightly puckered, full back. One of Dior's first examples in 1957, in soft wool, had a small, stand-up, rolled collar, tiny sleeves, a curved back, and a tapering hem that reached a few inches below the knee. It appeared to be quite simple, but was in fact very difficult to cut and make well, and therefore was also difficult to make flattering to the immensely varied physiques of European and American women. For once, the ready-to-wear industry was defeated by it, and the gulf that divides excellent couture from the world of off-the-peg clothing showed up dramatically. It perhaps signifies the last time that manufacturers in New York and London unthinkingly took the line from Paris and tried to adapt it. The sac, as it was called, clearly did not work, and from that moment on Paris lost its unquestioned superiority as the exclusive source of all style innovations. Norman Norell describes what was wrong with the sac or chemise line:

Many manufacturers thought all they had to do was run up two seams, put a bow on the behind, and they had it. Actually, the chemise is a very difficult dress to make properly.

The chemise is not a tube, which was what you saw on the streets. It is supposed to be soft and clinging. Instead they made them for the summer out of stiff cottons. You saw those sights on the street that made everybody sick.

Women didn't realise how they were supposed to look. They wore them too long. Also, they used an uplift bra, so that instead of falling against the body, the dress was pushed away.

Many manufacturers who based their entire collections on the sac in 1958 suffered serious losses, or even went out of business. For once, Paris had defeated its imitators, and produced a shape that only expert cutting and beautiful fabric could create with justice.

Balenciaga made some fine examples of the new loose look, but his clothes are extremely difficult to find, even from this late date, on the collectors' market. He made for a highly individual, very rich and elegant set and refused to come to any compromise, as did some of the younger designers in Paris, with ready-to-wear manufacturers. His clothes were in any event very difficult to copy, being based on elaborate structures and immaculate, painstaking tailoring. He had a way of setting collars so that they stood up and curved outwards in a sculptured shape. The set of his sleeves was finely seamed, generous and high. He liked plain colours, favouring black, and used beautiful laces and striking patterns for his dresses and evening wear. Born in Spain in 1895, he began his working life as a tailor in San Sebastian, not arriving in Paris until 1937, at the age of forty-two. He had by that time perfected the art of tailoring, and the elegant, secluded ladies of Spanish high society left their mark on the kind of couture he produced in his salon in the avenue George V. His designs were always well ahead of their time. He introduced soft leather boots for women, and redefined the wool day suit, with a new, soft-curving back that was a revolution in dress in comparison with the tailleur and Dior's 'New Look' – both of which were very structured and could be difficult to wear, though they were glamorous and feminine. Balenciaga's suits were altogether more modern, and deceptively simple. When Sir Cecil Beaton came to look for a 'little black suit' by Balenciaga to include in his big exhibition of modern fashion at the Victoria and Albert Museum, London, in 1971, he had the greatest difficulty in finding one in good condition – all their owners had worn them out.

A designer who inherited Balenciaga's mantle was Hubert de Givenchy, who trained with Lelong, Piguet and Jacques Fath, before spending two

Left *Barbara Goalen, a British model who epitomised the adult, sophisticated style of the 1950s – here wearing a sumptuous ball gown in black velvet and pleated tulle designed by Jacques Fath, 1951.*

Left *Rival to Dior as the king of couture, a design by Balenciaga sketched in* Harper's Bazaar. *The white satin sheath dress is finished with a huge chestnut taffeta bow. (1950).*

Below *An American comic view of the 'sac' or 'chemise' dress – and how not to wear in, 1957.*

TIFFANY

Audrey Hepburn sporting the classic elegant 'sheath' dress typical of the late 1950s/early 1960s. Givenchy was her favourite designer. Breakfast at Tiffanys (1961).

Right *A grand Balmain design, 'Bizance' in ivory satin, embroidered and appliquéd in yellow, 1954.*

A very narrow full-length evening dress from Balmain. Harper's Bazaar 1950.

years as a designer with Schiaparelli. In 1952 Givenchy opened his own salon. His work in the 1950s is readily called to mind by the clothes he made for Audrey Hepburn to wear in her various films – little, neat, tailored wool dresses, 'A' line coats with channel seaming, small, high-standing collars, and double rows of buttons. He liked to use clear, soft colours – pinks, yellows, beiges and blues. His look was readily copiable, and he produced many clothes under licences in the USA. His youthful, *ingénue* style of couture suited the American market very well. Other designers of note at this time are Pierre Balmain and Lanvin-Castillo.

Pierre Balmain worked for five years at Molyneux, then at Lelong at the same time as Christian Dior, when the two men became good friends. Dior obviously had a great influence on Balmain, and perhaps overshadowed the recognition he might otherwise have received. Balmain's elegant, simple clothes made him a great favourite with the world's monarchs and aristocrats, and with American buyers in particular, who adapted his styling for the mass junior market. His distinguished working life came to an end on 29 June 1982.

Antonio Castillo studied architecture in Spain before going to America, where he opened a *haute couture* department in 1945 for the Elizabeth Arden salons in New York: this led rapidly to his acceptance as one of the leading American designers of the period. In 1950 the Princesse de Polignac, Jeanne Lanvin's daughter, invited him to join the house, after her mother's death in 1946, and the house continued under his direction as Lanvin-Castillo.

Shannon Rodgers, one of America's leading manufacturers and a man possessing the largest private collection in the country, has described how, in the 1950s, American stores and ready-to-wear manufacturers would go to Paris (or to Italy) to look for suitable models to buy and copy for their coat, suit or dress ranges. He recalls that Bergdorf Goodman was very active at this time in acquiring Parisian models, producing a Petite Couture range for younger buyers at high but less than couture prices. Shannon Rodgers and his partner, Jerry Silverman, would go to Paris and find smaller, lesser-known couturiers, whose prices were more modest, but whose line and taste for the new, looser-fitting styles was original and copiable. From about the mid-1950s onwards, this became a great trade for American manufacturers, and indirectly caused the birth of the French 'Prêt-à-Porter' exhibition. It had soon become apparent to the couturiers that there was more money to be made from producing their own 'boutique' lines, and selling them internationally, than in relying on the sale of models, toiles, or patterns, where there was a once-only sale with no spin-off profit. (Incidentally, Shannon Rodgers considers couture to be no longer a serious business, but merely a front for products such as perfumes, stockings, scarves, and so on. Only Givenchy evoked from him a respectful murmur of approval.)

Shannon Rodgers' collection covers a vast range of periods and styles. Of the modern, twentieth-century material, he obviously collected less, having the time, the money and the contacts to buy exquisite museum pieces from earlier eras. But he has the expert's eye for enjoyable and beautiful modern objects worth preserving: among the names he mentioned are those of Norman Norell for his beaded dresses, Hattie Carnegie, Pauline Trigère and Claire McCardell, of the American designers, and earlier European names such as Lanvin, Poiret, Piguet and Lucile. He advises young collectors to go outside big cities wherever possible, and to try for the 'period' ready-to-wear pieces, such as Catalina Sportswear, Lilyann suits, Cole of California – landmarks in ready-to-wear – where the collector finds couture prices prohibitive. He agreed that the value of a well documented, off-the-peg collection would be significant in years to come. (Shannon Rodgers' outstanding collection is soon to be given to Kent State University, as he regrets the lack of any collection west of the Alleghenies and would like to adjust the balance.)

There is no doubt that Shannon Rodgers regrets the falling-off in standards of modern clothing, even at the couture level. He demonstrated this with a telling anecdote about Hardy Amies, who came to dine with him a few years ago. A friend, Ruth McCarthy, was wearing a beautiful, bottle-green dress which Shannon had persuaded her to put on from his collection. She looked wonderful, and Hardy Amies could not resist asking where the dress had come from. 'It's one of yours!', Shannon exclaimed delightedly, 'a stunning fifties evening gown!' Hardy Amies had to confess that he did not recognize it, and furthermore commented, 'I couldn't do it today; we never made anything that good, did we?'

The 1950s brought the end of the kind of expensive, time-consuming workmanship demanded for such elegance. Nowadays, style is much more evident in a casual chic, a blend of fabrics, colours and textures and the use of expensive materials such as leather, suede and silks – natural substances that are difficult to come by and therefore exclusive. These materials do not require the elaborate 'reworking', or detail of seaming or embroidery that marks the difference between couture, or high-class ready-to-wear from before the 1950s, and the best work that comes afterwards.

The enduringly popular Chanel suit, 1959: a suit of this kind could fetch as much as £3,000 at auction – such as the sale of Chanel's own collection at Christie's, London, in 1978.

Right *Teenage fashions from America (1952) – a new influence in the 1950s.*

Only one designer in Paris understood intuitively all that was about to happen in ready-to-wear and couture, and reopened her doors in 1954 with the express purpose of capitalizing at the fashion crossroads. This was Gabrielle Chanel. In Spring 1954 she re-launched herself with a collection that was unchanged in spirit and line from her clothing of the 1930s, before the war. Soft, jacketed suits were made in pastel colours, with thick braiding round the edge of the jacket, teamed with a colour-toning silk blouse, tied softly at the neck with a floppy bow. The suits would be weighted inside the lower front edge of the jacket, so that they hung open in a straight, uncluttered line. The famous two-toned, sling-back shoes with black toe appeared, and the endless rows of gilt chains, costume jewellery and pearls. Slowly Chanel's apparently classical style of dressing gained in popularity, and she was widely copied by ready-to-wear manufacturers, the most important being the firm of Geoffrey Wallis in London, and Saks Fifth Avenue, New York. She also made an enormous amount of money from her subsidiary products, such as costume jewellery and perfume. (This was reputed to bear the name 'Number 5' because she was superstitious, the number being her favourite, and also, more suitably, so that Americans in Paris would not be embarrassed to buy a bottle when all they had to do was hold up five fingers and say 'Chanel'!) Her style was enduringly popular in the USA, where its understated, casual elegance suited the less formal ideal of chic which is typical of the best dressed American woman.

A circus design print skirt, 1950.

The contrast between America and England during the 1950s is an interesting one, and shows the diverging social picture of the time. Youth and teenage fashions had been growing in importance ever since the end of the war, and the influence of Hollywood and the popular music of Rock 'n' Roll was producing a whole range of ready-to-wear fashion which had hardly been defined as such in Europe, although, by the end of the decade, Britain caught up with a vengeance. The 1950s was the first decade in which teenagers had the money to distinguish themselves as a consumer group. Most big stores sold specific teenage or 'Young Miss' fashions; the boys invented their own styles, with help from rock and film stars, taking leather jackets from bike riders (like the Hell's Angel which Brando depicted in *The Wild One*), jeans from the country, and checked shirts from the workers. A quite distinctive phenomenon in England, well worth the interest of collecting, was the 'Edwardian' or 'Teddy boy' style of the early 1950s. The movement began in London's East End in 1952, with extraordinary drape jackets reaching to the knee, 'drainpipe' trousers, thick, crêpe-soled shoes and bootlace ties. Their girls wore tight skirts, tight sweaters, big earrings, and the infamous female version of the 'winkle-picker' pointed shoes, which came from Italy from about 1957 onwards. In *Fashion in the Forties and Fifties* Jane Dorner describes an equally bizarre American fashion among the young men known as 'Dudes', who marked themselves off from the 'greasers' by wearing white buckskin shoes. Jackets were fastened with five buttons and the trousers, which were pleated at the waistband, had turn-ups. The outfit was enlivened by gaudy or jazzy accessories, such as polka-dot hats, wampum belts – made of coloured shells – or Indian beaded bags.

Girls reacted to this male display with a bewildering variety of outfits, each verging on pastiche or fancy dress. There was a 'Country-and-Western' look, with huge, circular or tiered skirts, ankle socks, bouffant 'paper nylon' petticoats (often starched at home with sugar or glycerine and water mixes). A simpler, more 'correct' style of dress, found on the American campus, was the circular felt skirt, often decorated with nursery motifs such as poodle dogs, balloons, clowns and the like, worn with a white blouse and wool cardigans. A third group identified themselves with the busty Hollywood goddesses such as Jayne Mansfield and Jane Russell, and wore tight-fitting jumpers and pencil-slim skirts with stiletto-heeled shoes. It became very popular to wear black cardigans the wrong way round, with the buttons down the back – this more original sweater style was boosted by the new French influence in the cinema, particularly the style of Brigitte Bardot.

The new fashions in glamour were further popularized both by newly developed synthetic fabrics and by innovations in existing materials. The 1950s was the decade for mohair – Balenciaga used it, as did Lanvin-Castillo, and it became ubiquitous in a range of 'sloppy joe' sweaters, cinched at the waist with wide, soft, leather belts. Terylene, invented in England but developed in America, led in 1958 to Dacron, a revolutionary fabric which lent itself well to trouser-making and 'permanent pleating' for skirts. Circular skirts of knife-pleats became very popular in mid-decade. Other new fabrics, such as Orlon and Banlon, super-soft synthetic jersey materials, suited the new teenage fashions very well. Tight-fitting stretch 'torero' pants became a hot favourite. The American Enka Co. of North Carolina produced a rayon crêpe that that could be dyed as fabric rather than at the yarn stage, so that designs could be made more seasonally. Kirby Block and Co. made a puckered nylon in 1949 that lasted well throughout the 1950s in popularity; it dried in fifteen minutes, and was ideal for girls' blouses. Ease and practicality were new, and in great demand. Fabrex made Chinzano, a silk and Orlon mix that was crush-resistant, and Monsanto's Acrilan, launched in 1954, gave washable pleats for the first time.

The bright new synthetics found a wonderfully imaginative designer to express their possibilities in Ken Scott, an American who had settled in Italy. Working from Milan, initially as a fabric designer, he created a stunning range of bright, flowery prints which were adopted all over the world by manufacturers for dresses, scarves and many kinds of household and fashion accessories. He is best remembered for his designs for the launching of Banlon.

Even more significant was the work of Emilio Pucci, who also worked with knit jersey, and in 1954 produced a range of bright, swirling, patterned dresses and two-pieces (tunics over floppy trousers) which were so soft that they could be folded up and carried in a handbag. In an age when the life style of every model and jet-setter was grabbing copy in all the major newspapers, these clothes were swiftly successful. Pucci's slightly Art Nouveau, slightly 'psychedelic' prints, in vivid and clashing colours of shocking pink, leaf green, purples and mauves, emphasized with outlines of black, were easily identifiable, and were a high-status purchase at the time. (Pucci now combines the best elements of the fashion market by producing elaborately embroidered, custom-made dresses, at the rate of about eighteen a year, alongside a range of 'Pucci Accessories' including bags, belts, and a bigger range of ready-to-wear dresses. He also designs products for other companies, such as porcelain for Rosenthal, pens for Parker, and uniforms for Qantas. His latest venture is to enter the 'designer jean' market with his own range of denims and casuals.)

Pucci was one of the four boutique owners who collaborated in a venture

A typical Horrockses outfit:
permanently pleated cotton
sunsuit (1955): permanent
pleating was new and very
popular.

Above left *Italian print
playsuit designed by the master
of sportswear for the rich,
Emilio Pucci, 1957.*

Left *Clothes specially designed
for Rock n' Roll enthusiasts by
Teddy Tinling, 1957.*

Right Designs for sportswear by Teddy Tinling in the new synthetic, Celanese 'Tricel', 1956.

Italian fashions emerged with tremendous force during the 1950s: a design by Capucci, in a new fabric, Toninelli's 'silk foam', photographed by Tenca for Harper's Bazaar in 1957.

Right Boussac's French cotton, imported to the UK by Berkertex, 1957.

in 1951 to launch Italian fashion on to the American market. The impetus came from G. B. Giorgini, an agent and exporter who had long desired a bigger interest from America in Italian designers, whom he considered the most original and talented in Europe at the time – certain to be worthy rivals to the Parisian couturiers. In Spring 1951 Giorgini invited representatives from B. Altman, Bergdorf Goodman of New York, I. Magnin of California, and Morgan of Montreal to see a collection of Italian couturiers. Those participating were soon to become famous names in both couture and ready-to-wear designing internationally: Simonetta, Fabiani, Fontana, Antonelli, Schubert and Carosa, all from Rome; Marucelli, Veneziani,

Noberasco and Wanna of Milan; and, besides Pucci, influential boutique owners ('boutique' in the sense that Mary Quant was a boutique owner – a highly influential source of fashion): Baroness Gallotti, Avolio, and Berto-li. The show was a total success, and large orders were placed by all the Americans. For the following year's show, and for several succeeding years, the event had to be moved to a large locale – the Palazzo Pitti in Florence. By 1959, Simonetta and Fabiani had decided to withdraw from the group activities, and signed an exclusive contract with John Fairchild to present their collections in Paris. But the remainder stayed faithful to the idea of a concerted Italian presentation, and gradually this has evolved into the present-day pattern: high fashion – couture – is centred on Rome, while the more influential and big business operation, the ready-to-wear show, has in recent years taken place annually in Milan, having moved there from Florence.

The Italians brought a new flair to women's clothes, with unusually smart, dramatic couture (particularly from Mila Schon and Valentino), and in characteristically gay and pretty sportswear and separates from the ready-to-wear people. In the 1950s their attentions were turned first to casuals with new stretch fabrics used for tight-fitting but flattering pants, witty new cuts such as fringed ponchos with matching trousers, three-quarter-length 'toreador' pants, and off-the-shoulder knitted tops. With the affluence of Europe, winter holidays came back into fashion, and the Italians produced some bright new ski-wear in vivid colours instead of the traditional black or grey; new synthetic fabrics such as nylon could be ruched, elasticated and zipped with ease, and also dyed to a new intensity of bright blue, canary yellow or hot pink.

On the subject of sportswear, mention should be made of the work of Teddy Tinling, an English designer who specialized in couture work for particular sports such as tennis. He revolutionized the dress of women players, beginning with 'Gorgeous Gussy' Moran, who came to the 1949 Wimbledon in a fitted dress with frilled lace pants to match. He has subsequently dressed nearly every international tennis star, and innovations have passed on into ready-to-wear manufacture of not only tennis clothes but casual dress in general. In reverse, Tinling also brought couture lines into sport – he designed an 'A' line, pleated-skirt tennis dress in 1954. Other areas of his work include general casual wear (skirts, blouses and pretty cotton summer dresses), golfing outfits and swimwear.

Teddy Tinling did much to boost the image of British designing abroad. Britain had gained some ground as an exporter of fashion because of the inevitable problems faced by Paris during the war years. Now London couturiers continued this expansion. The eight founder members of the Incorporated Society of London Fashion Designers were Norman Hartnell, Edward Molyneux (who had moved over from Paris), Angèle Delanghe, Digby Morton, Worth of London, Victor Stiebel, Bianca Mosca and Peter Russell. Hartnell is chiefly remembered as the designer of Queen Elizabeth's clothes (he had designed her wedding dress in 1947). He also worked for the firm of Berkertex, who made elaborate but inexpensive dressy clothes in the 1950s.

'The vase look' by Polly Peck,
London 1958.

Top *White barathea suit
designed by Digby Morton,
the London couturier.
Photographed for* Harper's
Bazaar *by Richard Dormer.*

In Britain at this time society was still stratified, although this disappeared by the end of the decade. Girls still wanted to look like ladies, and demonstrated their class by the quality of the clothes they wore. The débutante set was in full swing. A collection of 1950s evening wear could provide endless enjoyment with bouffant skirts, boned bodices, flaring medieval collars, tight sleeves, flashing fabrics with gold or silver Oriental brocades and plangent flowers in greens, purples and yellows. Cotton became popular as an evening fabric; the firm of Horrocks produced some full-skirted, brightly printed styles at this time. Other labels worth noting for a collection of party clothes would be Polly Peck (who specialized in well made copies of French clothes), Linzi, London Town, Susan Small, Dorville and Jaeger. (These last two made some beautiful day suits at the same time.)

Mass-produced clothes became a significant feature of British clothing during the 1950s, the most important company being that of Marks & Spencer, who made good-quality clothes with a hint of 'class'. Their designers would buy Paris models, and work out styles that had a touch of high fashion in some detail of collar, sleeve length or the use of pleats, but the clothes were manufactured in such quantity that the prices were sweepingly low. 1950s examples of Marks & Spencer clothing are remarkable for the quality of the fabric and the high fashion of their styling, and therefore could make part of any self-respecting period collection. The couturier Michael began working as a consultant designer for the company at this time. 'Runs' were limited, so that the market would not be flooded with a particular design. The problem of ubiquity therefore does not yet apply to the label.

Three Irish designers came to the fore and were very influential in the American market. First was Sybil Connolly, who 'rediscovered' Irish fabrics such as linen, thick crochet and beautiful tweeds; the second was John Cavanagh, who made very stylish evening clothes; and the third was Digby Morton, who had trained at Lachasse and specialized in well tailored Irish tweed suits.

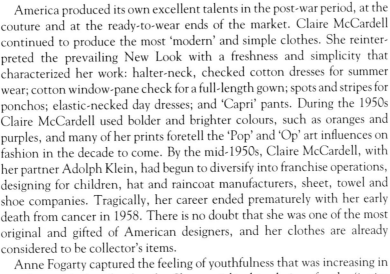

America produced its own excellent talents in the post-war period, at the couture and at the ready-to-wear ends of the market. Claire McCardell continued to produce the most 'modern' and simple clothes. She reinterpreted the prevailing New Look with a freshness and simplicity that characterized her work: halter-neck, checked cotton dresses for summer wear; cotton window-pane check for a full-length gown; spots and stripes for ponchos; elastic-necked day dresses; and 'Capri' pants. During the 1950s Claire McCardell used bolder and brighter colours, such as oranges and purples, and many of her prints foretell the 'Pop' and 'Op' art influences on fashion in the decade to come. By the mid-1950s, Claire McCardell, with her partner Adolph Klein, had begun to diversify into franchise operations, designing for children, hat and raincoat manufacturers, sheet, towel and shoe companies. Tragically, her career ended prematurely with her early death from cancer in 1958. There is no doubt that she was one of the most original and gifted of American designers, and her clothes are already considered to be collector's items.

Anne Fogarty captured the feeling of youthfulness that was increasing in significance during the decade. She specialized in designs for the 'junior miss' market, under the label Margot, Inc. Anne Fogarty took the American classic, the shirtwaist, and made it feminine and fashionable. Her 1950s version had very full skirts and fitted bodices. A similar look can be found in designs made by Anne Klein, and in those of Nettie Rosenstein, who was one of the first designers to work with knitted wool jersey. Other names to look for are those of David Crystal, Clare Potter (who liked to use unusual motifs for her printed fabrics, such as African or American primitive sources, and made some witty sports clothes including bathing-suits and ski outfits), Mollie Parnis, Greta Plattery and Carolyn Schnurer.

Some ready-to-wear manufacturers became well known by their label, while the designer behind it may have remained unknown, or while the company may have employed different designers at different times. Labels worth collecting from the 1950s would include Larry Aldrich, who made some classic suits adapted from French couture models, Davidow & Sons, Anthony Blotta, L'Aiglon, and Sloat and Co.

A designer whose work influenced many Europeans was Bonnie Cashin, who recognized the increasing interest in natural fabrics and softer lines, and produced sports clothes in a very chic combination of tweed, knitted wool, leather and suede. Pauline Trigère, who had started her business in 1942, continued throughout the 1950s to make a wide range of coats, dresses and suits in a slightly more sophisticated style than the prevalent 'young miss' look. Norman Norell also continued to produce beautifully made, high-fashion, ready-to-wear clothes throughout the decade under the label Traina-Norell.

A designer who resolutely refused to manufacture on a wholesale basis was Mainbocher. He had returned to America from Paris after the war, and remained highly successful as a couturier until he retired in 1971. His most famous client was the Duchess of Windsor, for whom he designed the trousseau for her marriage to Edward VIII in 1937. He also dressed some of the most important style-setters of New York society – among them Princess

Centre left *Horrockses produced an infinite range of pretty cotton dresses, like this evening dress, 1957. Boleros and bust-draping are typical of the time.*

Centre *Leisure clothes, 1954. Raglan sleeves, cinched waists and straw accessories strike the note of the period.*

Classic Bonnie Cashin, 1960: good wool and leather combined.

Beautifully sculptured evening dresses by Charles James, photographed by Cecil Beaton.

Paley, Mrs John C. Wilson, Gloria Vanderbilt Cooper and Daisy Fellows – and it was through the photographs of these elegant women in newspapers and magazines that Mainbocher's understated, elegant style remained in the public eye. Among collectors his work is not valued as highly as that of, say, Charles James, who was always diametrically opposed to Mainbocher – the first interested in cut, the second in drape and fabric. But he made innovations, as Dale McConathy listed in his tribute to him in *American Fashion*: 'the short evening dress; the famous beaded evening sweaters; bare-armed blouses for suits; the costume-dyed furs; novel uses for batiste, voile, organdie, piqué, linen, embroidered muslin; the waistcinch; man-tailored dinner suits. . .'.

Mainbocher once said, speaking of the difference between himself and his great rival, Charles James, 'Mr James is madly in love with cut. Anyone who eliminates as much cut as possible *would* seem familiar to him.' James's style was completely the opposite of his contemporary: he saw clothes as a form of sculpture, and gave them an ageless quality which comes not from their wearability but from their abstraction of style. The Victoria and Albert Museum in London exhibited in 'Fashion 1900–1939', in 1975, a satin quilted jacket, made in 1931 with exaggerated puffed curves rising from the top of the bodice and extending over the shoulder head and down the arm – more 'space age' than anything Cardin or Courrèges produced in the 1960s. Charles James has become a cult figure among collectors and fashion students or designers; his original career as a milliner in Chicago perhaps had some influence on his highly structured designing, which spanned sojourns in Paris, New York and London, from the 1930s to the 1960s. His garments are expensive to collect. A range he produced for the ready-to-wear firm of Samuel Winston in the early 1950s was sold in New York in 1980: a typical pink taffeta mid-shin-length evening dress, with a cut-away collar, elaborate empire-line seaming and puffed, full-length sleeves, sold for $140 – not even a couture dress. Another in paisley silk with bell sleeves sold in a lot with a second design with ruched dolman sleeves, and merely catalogued as 'in the style of Charles James', reached the figure of $180 – some indication of his value in the field. All the Charles James clothes I have seen, particularly the evening wear, appear rather severe and hard to wear, in spite of the sumptuous beading or embroidery. They have such a 'created' atmosphere that a woman would always look as if she had been 'dressed' by Charles James; but many of his admirers would disagree. When he himself staged a showing of his 1930s designs in the early 1950s, they were as praised and coveted in terms of style as ever before.

However, Mainbocher's and James's clients were soon to see their position as arbiters of taste evaporate in face of a completely new mood in fashion. The revolution had its origins in the opening of a small shop in the King's Road, London, in 1955. This was Bazaar, run by an ex-art school student, Mary Quant, and her business partner, later husband, Alexander Plunket Greene. The whole atmosphere of the boutique gave a confident impetus to the market of young people's clothing. Mary Quant's dresses were not made to last, and were often unlined, but they had a delightful, iconoclastic humour and great charm. They were simple and unconven-

tional, in strange colours – bright lime greens, pinks and browns or blacks, in unusual combinations – and simple fabrics. The decade had started with women wearing their hair swept up, their bodies poured into tight-fitting, tailored New Look suits or waspie-waisted dresses reaching to mid-shin. The chemise and the sac had prepared the way, and now the image was to appear as young and classless as possible. Débutantes with grandeur were un-fashionable; being an art student, wearing a minimal dress, or jeans and jumper, was more acceptable. For the first time, a teenage girl lost all aspiration to grow up and look like her mother. The ideal woman had lost about ten years in one decade. A collection of 1950s dresses or sportswear that encompassed these changes would make an unusual social record, and, luckily for the new collector, the material is readily to hand. Salerooms rarely deal in clothing beyond the 1940s, so prices are reasonable. However, as the 1950s are brought back in nostalgic revivals (there have been at least two within the past five years), good examples of the movements described may in time become more difficult to acquire.

Roger Burton runs a company in London under the name of Contemporary Wardrobe. It is based on his personal collection of 1950s and 1960s clothes, which he started as early as 1970 while running a second-hand shop in the Midlands. At first he collected clothes for his own interest, then gradually found a market for them in London, and finally moved there to set up his own enterprise which specializes in dressing films and plays of the period. One of the larger tasks was the costuming of *Quadrophenia* with The Who. Over the years he has become immensely knowledgeable on the period, and advises new collectors to start by reading contemporary magazines, and to study the films which depict the period, to develop a sense of style. His collection comprises men's and women's wear, and some accessories, such as the wide, wildly patterned ties and the stiletto-heeled shoes which were so prevalent.

Among the most interesting items in Roger Burton's collection are a drape suit with inverted pleats concealing vertical slit pockets, designed by band-leader Xavier Cugat, and a magnificent tie adorned with a curvaceous Hawaiian dancing girl, also designed by Cugat. Encouragingly, Roger Burton noted that he had paid £15 for the tie as a rare piece ten years ago, whereas he felt that with the stimulated interest in the collecting field, which has brought more goods out of attics and old stores on to the market, similar items might now sell for about £2 to £3.

It is interesting to note that Roger Burton finds the standard of period costuming in British films to be far inferior to those of Italy or Germany. This adds to the collector's difficulties. At any auction there will be costume buyers for films, with budgets ranging from an average of £7,000 up to as high as £90,000, looking for 1950s clothes, for example, and bidding over the top for a lot of 1920s hats perhaps because they are bright green, are decorated with feathers, or are just 'period' in a nostalgic way. It simply adds further pitfalls for the serious collector. But Roger Burton's collecting experience acts as an incentive for the beginner: the enjoyment he derives from the bouffant-skirted dresses, the block-printed fabrics, the rock 'n' roll ties and the white patent shoes is an example of the rewards that the hobby

A Charles James ballgown as featured in a Modesse advertisement in the 1950s. Fashion magazines are as valuable for data as old fashion books or the clothes themselves.

Right *Charles James at work dressing a model (1948). Even his ready-to-wear clothes fetch high prices at auction.*

can offer. His Contemporary Wardrobe is situated in a magnificently solid warehouse tucked in behind Southwark Cathedral on the Thames. It is by a wholesale food market which dates from the last century, with wrought ironwork above the Israeli fruit boxes. His enterprise is a study in retaining the best flavours of the past. As he, like many other collectors, confirmed, once he was established in his chosen field he received offers of goods and information from all quarters. A search in a closing-down hat shop would lead to an address of an old factory, where boxes of 1950s clothes would be lying untouched. Friends visiting America would bring back 'specials' like the Cugat suit. Now he has a team of helpers scouring the countryside, and with his connections in the north of England still finds useful hoards in attics and closing warehouses.

Riffling through a rack of 1950s styles produces a mixture of reminiscences, quite unique in recent history. There are the fluffy débutante dresses, the ornate dark brocades that so many of our mothers used to wear, the printed, flocked nylon that may have been some teenager's first party dress entirely of her own choosing; the consciously French-style prints, with lettering or poodle dogs, halter necks in black, and full skirts in primary colours. The clothes are gay, confident, vulgar and egalitarian, with none of the aggressive anti-feminism in shape or cut which distinguishes the styles of the 1960s. And in the menswear the peacock finally returns. This decade after the war sees, in its clothes, the very essence of the current social and political climate; and if, in viewing a collection like Roger Burton's, the individual can sense the personality of the time in his or her own imagination, then the purpose of collecting is achieved to perfection.

THE SIXTIES

This chapter in the survey of dress styles and innovations from the beginning of the century is significantly different from the rest in composition: the decade of the 1960s belongs primarily to the rise of a whole generation of designers working first and foremost for the ready-to-wear market. Individuals of genius, such as Mary Quant, Barbara Hulanicki, Galanos and Gernreich, transformed the social values of fashion. Parisian couturiers, such as Yves Saint Laurent, Cardin, Courrèges and Ungaro, responded to the new attitudes, but the radicalism started in the streets – firstly in London, but soon spreading to other countries. And it was Italian, rather than French, designing that ended the decade by capturing the inspirational role in both ready-to-wear and couture clothes. For the

A 'working girl's' version of the Paris 'A' line dress, available from Debenham & Freebody, London for 10 guineas in 1958. A good basis for a collection might be of ready-to-wear revealing such clear Parisian influences.

Left Mary Quant in her own 'schoolgirl' look boutique clothes, 1967. Her early Ginger Group clothes are well worth collecting.

collector, the period is rich in possibilities, ranging from cheap and accidental discoveries of early Mary Quant clothes in jumble sales to a more deliberate investment in garments which are sure to become collector's items of the future, such as Jean Muir's matt jerseys, or Galanos' embroidered woollens.

Two important events presaged the change of direction that typified 1960s fashion. First was the death of Christian Dior in 1958. His house was handed over to his assistant, Yves Saint Laurent, who launched, in a stunning first collection, the 'Trapeze' line – a wide-skirted, flaring shape that hinted at the freedom about to overtake all fashion silhouettes. His second collection for the house of Dior was much less successful, and soon after this Saint Laurent left his master's salon, opening up independently a few years later, in 1962, significantly with American backing. The second event, of even greater immediate importance, was the opening in London of Mary Quant's new boutique, Bazaar, in the King's Road, Chelsea. Much has been made of the amateurish origins of Mary Quant's operation, her art-school background and the fact that she bought fabrics across the counter at Harrods in the early days, so ignorant was she of the workings of the wholesale manufacturing business. But she and her husband partner, Alexander Plunket Greene, were obviously rapid learners. Furthermore, they were listeners, and that was how fashion changed irrevocably with the boutique boom.

Following in the wake of Bazaar's success, hundreds of other little shops opened up in London and, more gradually, in other big cities in Britain. For the first time, dresses were sold to young people by young people, often with rock 'n' roll accompaniment. The boutique owners, and through them the makers of these cheap fashions, were able to take note on a day-to-day basis of the reactions of their customers, and to see which styles were popular, and which were less successful. Young girls became accustomed to spending a minimum amount of money nearly every week on a whole outfit for a weekend – and also to merely browsing and trying clothes on in a relaxed way without feeling the need to purchase. It was all a far cry from the atmosphere of the big stores where their mothers shopped, stopping on the top floor for a cream cake and coffee and to watch a fashion parade of near-Parisian interpretations in ladylike colours and 'grown-up' tailored shapes, the way fashion was in the 1950s.

Early Quant clothes put paid to all that. Sleeveless dresses, neat little pinafores, unusual combinations of 'sludge' colours, greys, purples, gingery browns and, most important of all, the disappearance of the waist in favour of a simple shift garment: all these elements produced a style of dressing that the new, affluent youth of the 1960s – the growing-up, post-war generation – could relate to and use as a means of divorcing themselves from their parents' values. Essentially, the style of the 1960s was anti-establishment. In the 1950s, women had enjoyed the formal glamour created by Dior after the war, for they remembered hardship. The girls of the 1960s did not share that special appreciation of luxury. They wanted throwaway, gay clothes that made the wearer feel entitled to be irresponsible. This trend culminated in the 'mini' of the mid-decade, and went to impossible extremes with

the 'hot pants' that Mary Quant designed in 1969. Neither of these styles caught on in America to the extent that they did in Britain – even the dramatic mini took a year to become established. (When I went to live in California in 1966, in spite of flower power and the 'hippy' revolution, my short skirts caused disapproval at work and open mouths in the streets.)

Mary Quant quickly established herself. By 1961 a second Bazaar had opened. Soon Mary Quant had found a solidly professional manufacturing organization, Steinberg's, run by Leon Rapkin, who helped her to launch the 'Ginger Group' range. Mary Quant toured America in 1965, with immense success, and J. C. Penney took a whole range of her designs which proved outstandingly popular. By 1966 her success was seen to be so dramatic that she was awarded an OBE for her services to British export.

Other designers soon caught the mood from Mary Quant's achievement in creating a 'look' which expressed the wearer's independence and personality. Two of the most wearable designers were Sally Tuffin and Marion Foale; a collector's item without a doubt would be one of their pretty cotton lace mini dresses which combined wit with femininity. Many of the early 1960s ready-to-wear clothes were made in clearly 'unsuitable' fabrics: satin for trousers, velvet for day dresses; in 1966 Mary Quant used a fashionable 'Op Art' look for a black and white striped suit that closely resembled mattress-ticking. Even the plainest mini was enlivened by equally unpractical tights: by the mid-1960s, in the coldest weather, girls would go to work in a skirt barely covering their bottoms, with lacy or dotted tights below. Mary Quant also experimented with footwear, using the new synthetics, such as Corfam, and plastic to make short boots in primary colours. Silver shoes and lurex-threaded clothes were no longer found permissible only after six.

Elasticated fabrics, previously used only for sportswear, crept into fashion

Centre The new silver look for the 1960s: designs by Gerald McCann and John Craig, both successful names in London at the time.

Left Mary Quant's Ginger Group designs, 1969, mini, but little-girl-modest too.

Twiggy epitomised the new youthful look, here wearing Mary Quant clothes, 1966.

America was never swayed to
the same extent by the
phenomenon of 'Swinging
London': culotte suit by
Norman Norell, 1961 (with
Norell in the background).

Right 'Op Art' Orlon knitted
dress and contrasting
stockings. 'Penguin' boots
were made in moulded plastic.

clothes. Mary Quant's 'Ginger Group' made some particularly appealing
dresses in stretch terry towelling, in candy-sharp colours – lime green, pink
and yellow. A longer-lasting innovation was the combination of a mini
dress with trousers, and authentic trouser suits (launched simultaneously by
ready-to-wear manufacturers in London and by Courrèges, the French
couturier, in 1964) came to be a permanent feature of women's wardrobes.
Poiret had devised trouser suits in the 1910s, and Chanel had sold some
wide-legged, sporty outfits in the 1930s, and their practicality made them
popular in the Second World War; but a mannish trouser suit, worn
cheekily for the same functions as men wore theirs, in boardrooms and
offices, was a totally new departure of the 1960s. English manufacturers
extended the joke by making them up in charcoal-grey pinstripe and
herringbone tweed, besides a more alluring black velvet or corduroy.

Innovations in fabric were also the province of John Bates, who rivalled

Hardy Amies offers a jacket to
wear with either trousers or a
skirt, using consciously
masculine tweed, topped with
mannish hats (1964).

Vinyl 'Glue it Yourself' dress designed by Betsey Johnson for Paraphernalia. The see-through mini was sold for $15 together with a $5 pack of giant foil scallops, wiggly strips or stars for the owner to create her own outfit. Ephemera like this is a real collector's treasure, and often hard to find.

Left *A daring design by Ossie Clarke and Alice Pollock of Quorum, King's Road, London, now very collectable. The fabric print was by Celia Birtwell. 1968.*

Mary Quant in his daring designs. One, created in 1965, won the Dress of the Year Award: a scoop-necked, flower-printed linen slip with a blue nylon mesh midriff.) A very lucky collector might come across a 1960s paper mini dress, printed in 'pop art' colourings and demonstrating the ultimate limits to which fabric fashion experimentation would go. Paper throwaway knickers were also introduced at this time, and lasted rather longer as a commercial venture than did the gimmick of the dress. Paper dresses, by their very nature, are rare and a great find.) Foale and Tuffin made dresses with cut-outs under the arms; so did Mary Quant. Exposure of the body and the use of zany fabrics are signatures of the 1960s. John Bates is also to be remembered for his influential designs for Diana Rigg in the television series *The Avengers*: he popularized the 'Op Art' look coming from the Parisian couturiers (itself a dramatic response to ready-to-wear revolutionary energy). Another designer who made the most collectable designs in fabrics printed exclusively for him by his wife, Celia Birtwell, was Ossie Clark of Quorum, another King's Road boutique.

All these names were picked up by the American wholesaling organization Puritan, for its younger division, Paraphernalia. In 1965 it began a promotion known as the Youthquake, taking the best of young British talents to America, and launching the London 'look' for the first time. Americans were outraged by the mini and the trouser suit, the 'Op Art' prints and the cut-out holes, with PVC fabric, lace and synthetic shoes or boots completing the picture. One American designer who worked for Paraphernalia in these days, and who was one of the first to respond to the new styling, was Betsey Johnson. At the age of twenty-two she was designing whole collections under this label. However, she soon broke away from the restrictions of mass marketing to open a boutique on 53rd Street, producing slinky, simple tee-shirt-style dresses, vinyl outfits and minimal

Jean Shrimpton, the most photographed model of the 1960s, wearing a John Bates design, 1967.

shapes reminiscent of petticoats or nightgowns. From 1970 to 1975 she designed clothes under the Alley Cat label, and then freelanced for a number of companies, including Butterick Patterns. Currently, her boutique 'Betsey Bunki and Nini' operates on Madison Avenue.

American acceptance of the 1960s boutique styles took some time to come. Interestingly, when I commented on the conservative nature of New York working girls' dress even in the 1980s, I was reminded reprovingly by Robert Riley that the reason for this was that American women are more liberated than their English counterparts. The office is not seen as a place to demonstrate personality. The difference lies in a theme running through America's fashion history more pronouncedly than through Europe's: the 'democratization' of dress. The New York woman buys an office suit for the same reasons as her male colleague: for quality, durability and anonymity in a smart way. The 1960s trouser suits were definitely cheekier than that.

Whatever the philosophy, the business was thriving. In Britain, the boutique trend was soon adopted by the large stores, before they lost too big a slice of the market. Their fears were real: *Vogue* reported that by 1967 fifteen-to-nineteen-year-olds were buying about half the female clothing sold in the country. Boutiques within stores soon became popular. Two of the most enduring of these have been Way In at Harrods, which often purchased special lines from manufacturers to be sold under its own label, and Miss Selfridge at Selfridges. Ready-to-wear manufacturers also introduced younger ranges with separate labels to sell in the new departments and smaller shops, two of the prettiest being Dollyrockers, produced by Sambo, and Miss Polly, by Polly Peck. Other noteworthy labels of this period are John Marks, Mono, Rhona Roy, Harvey Gould, Emcar, Elgee, and Janice Wainwright at Simon Massey. (John Bates also worked for a time at Jean Varon in the second half of the decade, producing some fine evening dresses.) A rainwear company that produced some of Mary Quant's designs, and contributed substantially to a change in High Street fashions, was the firm of Alligator, which manufactured some of the most attractive PVC designs of the decade.

One designer of the 1960s remained outside the wholesaling business, preferring always to sell her fashion in her own boutique. This was Barbara Hulanicki, who started by running a mail-order fashion operation in 1964. The most surprising aspect of her clothes was their price. Even Mary Quant's Ginger Group dresses were still outside the reach of many buyers, but Biba clothes, on the contrary, were ludicrously cheap and very pretty. Barbara Hulanicki designed her own fabrics with patterns in a characteristic blend of Art Nouveau and Art Deco, with some English country florals added in. Her cut remained essentially the same throughout her period of fame: high, tight shoulders, often crowned with gathers, or padded; straight, tight-fitting sleeves, subdued colours, and a gradual movement towards a nostalgic, 1930s romantic look. Biba expanded from a small mail-order business in Abingdon Road to a shop in Kensington Church Street in 1963, then moved to the High Street itself, and finally in 1973 went into the former premises of Derry & Toms. Here, the 1960s trend towards adopting a 'look' burgeoned into a total environment, with wall-

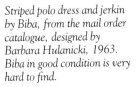

Striped polo dress and jerkin by Biba, from the mail order catalogue, designed by Barbara Hulanicki, 1963. Biba in good condition is very hard to find.

paper, fabric, furniture and other accessories co-ordinated into a complete 'Biba' scheme. But by the end of the decade, the impetus of the boutique movement had been lost, and the vast Biba empire came crashing down in 1975. Barbara Hulanicki went to Brazil to make expensive, exclusive designs for the new rich, returning to London only in the early 1980s.

While England was producing these revolutionary talents, the Parisian couturiers regrouped to defend their established position. A change in mood had become apparent under the reign of Dior and Balenciaga in the 1950s: Chanel, Patou, Lanvin-Castillo and Griffe had been concerned with a softer, less structured style of dress. Yves Saint Laurent had made the first statement for the decade in late 1958 with his 'Trapeze' line, and went on to express the trend towards clothing that reflected the wearer's personality rather than her status. As the decade proceeded, Yves Saint Laurent launched a number of 'looks', each season's show providing collector's pieces for those lucky enough to find one and able to afford the price. As modern couture is not yet widely collected, it is an open guess where prices will go.

Some of the most noteworthy examples of Saint Laurent's originality are in the 'Pop Art' style of the 1966 collection, typified by dresses that have faces or torsos in pink profile running down a black dress – not dissimilar to

Dior still supreme, 1961.

Far left *Pinstripe trouser suits were very popular – Twiggy and her partner, Justin de Villeneuve, symbolised youthful classless success in the 1960s.*

Above *Mary Quant's Ginger
Group dress, 1967. Brilliant
clashing colours were part of
the youthful, cheeky
atmosphere created by
boutique fashions.*

Centre *King's Road boutique
fashion: silver-pink lurex
hipster dress by Susan Locke;
and the 1960s version of 'a
little black dress' by Sybil
Zelker.*

the surreal embroideries done for Schiaparelli in the 1930s. (One superb
example, a beautiful jacket with a woman's golden hair flowing down one
side, in gold thread and beads designed for her by Jean Cocteau, now
belongs to the Philadelphia Museum of Art.) In 1965 Saint Laurent
produced a range of Mondrian-inspired sleeveless dresses, with large checks
divided into segments by black bands. These were soon copied by London
designers – some of John Bates's *Avenger* clothes bear a similarity to Saint
Laurent's concept. Towards the end of the 1960s, Saint Laurent sensed the
breaking-up of the 'look' philosophy which was the essence of the decade's
fashion. His clothes became more romantic and individualistic, and, more
than any other couturier, he encouraged the interest in 'ethnic' clothes,
with 'safari' suits, 'Hollywood' collections, fringed Indian beaded outfits,
Moorish robes, and a continuing delight in fantastic evening clothes.

Saint Laurent started his boutique business, Rive Gauche, in 1966 –
another step towards the style of the present day. Saint Laurent not only
introduced the 'Trapeze', he adjusted our view to blazers over dresses, and
the use of print with print. His contribution to general principles of style has
been considerable. There has been a growing tendency over the past two
decades for women to wear clothes according to their personal taste, rather
than to follow the dictates of fashion from Paris, London or New York, from
season to season. In fact now there are no 'seasons' in the old sense of the
word, but there is instead a gradual evolving of styles. Saint Laurent's Rive
Gauche clothes are classic but varied. They include accessories, knitwear,
men's clothes – everything. Day clothes are practical, and evening clothes

Far left *The pinstripe trouser suit* à la carte *from Saint Laurent, 1967.*

Cardin, 1967, a combination of classic tailoring and 'space age' design. This apricot wool coat zipped up from top to bottom.

Yves Saint Laurent's Rive Gauche line, 1971, bringing back the knee-length hem.

very glamorous. He makes the most flattering trouser suits, and has the most refined use of satins, silver and feathers in modern couture: a trend that started with his 'see-through' clothes, including a 1968 model in black chiffon with ostrich feathers round the hips, and nothing else but a gold serpent waist bracelet, to emphasize the nakedness of the breasts. Somehow the effect was to make the wearer appear elegantly revealed rather than ostentatiously nude.

The combination of day-time chic and night-time romance seems to be the theme for most 1960s couturiers, including the group who identified themselves with the glories of the 'space-age': Cardin, Courrèges and Ungaro. Cardin, also like Saint Laurent, has pursued a varied career through his ready-to-wear operation, his licensing, and his contracts to design such disparate objects as theatres, aeroplanes, hotels, china, glass and linens. Interestingly, his training reveals the main aspects of his own taste: first with Schiaparelli, and subsequently with Dior. From the first of these masters Cardin learnt how to be original and daring, and to question standard forms; from the second he learnt how to be a magnificent tailor. He too followed the 'Trapeze' line in his 1967 collection, but added the most impeccable scalloped edgings, channel seam details, and magnificent collars. Like Schiaparelli, Cardin explored the possibilities of new fabrics, liking the 'scientific' feel of vinyl and plastics. He created some dramatic variations of unisex designs, using ribbed stockings and tabards – again, way ahead of the 1980s interest in track suits, ribbed knits in layers, and athletically proportioned clothes. Cardin's cut-out dresses of the mid-1960s were in sympathy with the styles of London ready-to-wear, but had a more futuristic feeling. His clothes can vary from items which are elegantly easy

Paco Rabanne's metallic dresses excited great press interest in the 1960s, and are now highly prized by collectors – and hard to find.

to wear to those which require three months' mental training in order to adopt the right 'modern' attitude.

This slight schizophrenia in the couturiers of the 1960s was wittily described by Jean Muir, one of Britain's leading couturiers, who emerged during this time (she is discussed more fully in the next chapter). She noted in a succinct lecture on 1960s fashion, given at the Victoria and Albert Museum in London, how Courrèges 'invented the moon girl'. '"I am a child of the moon" was the message – and then he showed broderie anglaise crinolines!' White and silver were the colours that typified his look in 1964 (he had opened his salon only a few years before, in 1961). He was the first couturier to take notice of the mini, and invented white, mid-shin-high boots to accompany his versions of the style. He also dignified the trouser suit, with pale-coloured gaberdines, beautifully cut and seamed, modelled by towering black mannequins – a favourite show stopper. Courrèges had trained with Balenciaga, and indeed was from the Spanish Basque country, like his teacher. He inherited or adopted Balenciaga's ruthlessness with clients, and this shows in his clothes, which are uncompromising state-

Emanuel Ungaro's ready-to-wear range, Parallèle, showing a typical bold and 'arty' print, 1967.

Courrèges exploring the possibility of extra-terrestrial travel.

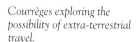

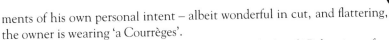

ments of his own personal intent – albeit wonderful in cut, and flattering, the owner is wearing 'a Courrèges'.

The same is true of Emanuel Ungaro, who worked with Balenciaga after his friend Courrèges had departed. In 1964 he joined Courrèges himself for a brief period, before setting up his own salon in 1965. Ungaro collaborates with a fabric designer, Sonja Knapp, and between them they have established a look which is uniquely theirs – highly distinctive, but also influential internationally. Sonja Knapp produces fabrics in the most varied and subtle colour-ways, and Ungaro designs conjunctions of clothes which explore the possibilities of pattern on pattern, shape on pattern, and form on colour. Of course, Ungaro participated in the general revolutionary fervour of the 1960s to define the modern woman, and had her running about in breastplates, stockinged, all-in-one, striped cat suits and the like: but essentially his most collectable items are the couture and boutique clothes produced under the name 'Paralèlle' in Italy, which combined careful structure (learnt from Balenciaga) with fascinating colours.

Lastly, a brief mention should be made of the even more moon-like offerings of Paco Rabanne, who excited 'jet-set' ladies with his extraordinary confections in perspex and metal, plastic and acrylic. Chain-mail minis, cubes of brilliant colour linked together on white crêpe, stole the couture scene in 1966. They will become collector's pieces and already fetch high prices in sales, but they are novelties at the extreme edge of fashion history, and will not be found easily.

While Parisian couture suffered convulsions, and younger designers tried to find ways of expressing the new mood of youthful mockery, British couturiers continued to cater for the often forgotten market: the establishment itself. As Jean Muir pointed out in her summary of the situation, Norman Hartnell, Hardy Amies, Creed and John Cavanagh designed for the rich and aristocratic, and were scarcely innovators. However, they too felt the need to change direction. Cavanagh turned over more or less entirely to a boutique operation; Hardy Amies turned to designing for wholesale menswear and licensing; while Michael (one of the younger designers of the London group) continued to make a substantial business out of designing for Marks & Spencer on the side.

The couturiers were also energetic promoters of British fashion abroad: The Incorporated Society of London Fashion Designers launched a special

Hardy Amies expanded into ready-to-wear and several other licensing operations. This 1965 suit typifies his classic tailoring, with soft stand-away collar and bracelet-length sleeves.

collection in Paris in 1960, which enticed a number of American buyers to London, and resulted in increased orders. In 1964 a group of couturiers and accessory manufacturers of very high quality such as Edward Rayne, the shoe manufacturer, went to America on tour and sold their wares. This activity was mirrored by the London Model House Group representing the bigger wholesale manufacturers, who capitalized on the 'swinging London' image by promoting British fashions in America and Europe. Elizabeth Ewing details the Group's activities, and concludes with the words of one of its promoters, Moss Murray: 'It was too successful. It quadrupled exports and in some cases increased them tenfold. But some firms began to feel they were doing so well that they did not need the joint activities – and costs – of the Group and also that benefits were rubbing off too much on non-members'.

However, a further group, the Associated Fashion Designers of London, established themselves in 1964 to take advantage of London's reputation as the centre of fashion at the time. This group comprised mostly younger designers excluded by the two previous organizations. Their activities were stylish and confident in the extreme: spectacular fashion parades, jumpy music, and ready-to-wear fashion that responded magnificently to the ideas promulgated by the King's Road boutiques and the avant-garde designers of Paris. Any of their labels would be worth noting and collecting in the fullness of time.

American designers of the 1960s were not slow to respond to the new upsurge of activity seen in Europe. The pace of change was slower, however, perhaps because of the sheer volume of the market, and the size of the country. Trends take a little time to become accepted fashion, however much fuss is made by the press. And, as in Europe, it was difficult for the public to accept the often appalling standards of workmanship in British fashion. Visitors to London from Italy or California would stand amazed in a King's Road boutique, suffering a mixture of grabbing excitement because the clothes were so youthful and gay, and downright indignation because buttons fell off in the changing-room. American ready-to-wear has always maintained consistently higher standards of workmanship, and even the so-called 'boutiques' always had an air of solid industry behind them, which was exactly what the London equivalents lacked, and were pleased to lack. The London boutiques wanted to do away with the atmosphere of 'big business backing'.

One of the Californian designers who captured the zest of European fashion without any loss of quality was Rudi Gernreich, who will principally be remembered for his topless bathing-suit, but in actuality designed some fabulous sports clothes too. He caught on to the Parisian idea of 'Op Art' and Mondrian-inspired blocks of colour to produce some simple but very stylish tops, skirts, and beach co-ordinates. He designed a new, soft bra for Warners, the lingerie company, which has had an influential effect on the way women view their bodies: the 'uplift' of the 1950s seemed artificial and dated.

Most other collectable names from the 1960s in America tend to be those working at the quality end of the market. One of these is Gus Tassell (another designer working in California). He uses soft fabrics to make

Psychedelic print jumpsuit and tunic in silk crêpe by Rudi Gernreich, the Californian designer, 1967.

dresses that are simple and unadorned, with a characteristic, close-fitting cut at the neck and sleeves. His clothes are sometimes criticized for being too 'ladylike'; but his success lies with his buyers, not with the fashion pundits, and he proves all that has been said above about the differences between American and European tastes and needs. He works on a small scale, with about fifty employees, and produces between forty and fifty pieces in each season. The small scale of his operation reflects his perfectionism.

A different style of talent lies in Donald Brooks, known principally for his theatre and film designs (such as his stunning outfits for Carol Channing's 1966 television spectacular), but he also runs a ready-to-wear operation which introduces new elements into American fashion. In 1966 too he launched a number of evening dresses with dipping hemlines, and some midi-length day dresses, a season before Paris launched them. Brooks designs his own fabrics, a trend seen to be prevalent among this crop of fashion makers.

James Galanos is another west-coast designer whose workmanship is supreme – his use of bias cuts in woollen fabrics and the thoroughness of his construction techniques put him into the couturier class. Some critics find his clothes verging on the vulgar – his colours are vibrant and his embroidery lavish – but they have imagination and originality.

In another corner of the market is found the name of Anne Klein, who in the mid-1950s started a ready-to-wear label called Junior Sophisticates, a range of clothes for the younger petite woman. She made these clothes in very small sizes, and was influential in getting other manufacturers to increase the range of sizing in their collections. Anne Klein died in 1975, but the company continued, with the designing shared by Donna Karan and Louis Dell'olio working under licence for a number of manufacturers producing leather clothes, textiles, accessories and separates.

Another firm which produced high-quality clothes at fairly high prices for ready-to-wear was Tiffeau & Busch. (He came from men's tailoring in France, she from an American dress manufacturing background, as daughter of Max Pruzan.) Together they established a highly successful, classic, ready-to-wear label. No doubt the influence and name of Max Pruzan, who had been making American fashion for over fifty years, enabled the couple to gain attention from journalists and manufacturers, but their own taste and talent enabled the firm to survive. A somewhat larger organization, but one that is equally elegant in output, is Burke-Amey, which specializes in suits and co-ordinated day clothes that are smart without being imitative of Parisian lines. Both these firms supply stores all across America.

In more specialized areas, the names of Stavropolous and Jean Louis should be mentioned, the first for some classically draped evening gowns, sold in major cities throughout America, the second for his glamorous and luxurious evening wear designed for the stars of Hollywood and a few other selected stores outside California.

For more practical, mass-market day wear, the 1960s story would be incomplete without mention of the revolutionary output of the knitted fabric companies: revolutionary in technique if more classic in style.

French ready-to-wear at its best: Karl Lagerfeld's designs for Chloë, 1976.

Centre *Ankle-length overcoats briefly made their appearance in the late 1960s.*

Double-knit jerseys became immensely popular at this time, and formed a staple of any practical American wardrobe as a result. Butte-Knit (part of Jonathan Logan) and Garland Knitwear are two of the biggest companies in this field. Kimberley, who started in 1946, continued to dominate the market with mixtures of wool and Orlon or Dacron, and produced many interesting designs in the 1950s and 1960s. Geist & Geist also favour wool knits or mixtures, and from their origins in the 1920s as sweater makers they have expanded to offer a complete range of garments in knitted fabric, often with high-fashion styling rather than practicality as their main attraction. In the 1960s they produced mini skirts and sleeveless black sweaters, absolutely in line with London street fashions.

Ready-to-wear manufacturers in France also added their creations to the rising tide of variety and individuality which marked the close of the decade. Among the names worth collecting are Daniel Hechter, who produced some sharply tailored trenchcoats, with a totally French answer to the classic English Burberry; Sonia Rykiel, who started a revolution in knitwear which was to last through the 1970s, and Emmanuelle Khanh, who produced a range of soft, droopy-collared clothes which captured the imagination of the youthfully fashionable towards the close of the decade. She created one very flattering innovation – a petal-layered collar. All Emmanuelle Khanh's styles had a curving line, in either the hem, the collar, or the neckline, which produced a much gentler style of dressing in comparison with the tailored, stiffer styles of the current couturiers, such as

Courrèges or Cardin. Lastly, but even more significantly, Karl Lagerfeld, who designs under the label Chloe, and Kenzo Takada, under the name Jap, both came into prominence. Lagerfeld's high-quality, ready-to-wear clothes are adventurous but easy to wear, a talent in designing which has led him to work under licences for a number of other companies, including Fendi Furs, leather and shoe manufacturers, and textile companies. Kenzo Takada became even more influential during the 1970s, but in the late 1960s he was prominent in the movement towards 'ethnic' clothes, with his batwing-sleeved jackets, Eastern-style tunic dresses, and his return to natural fabrics with the use of cotton and knitted wool.

The hippy look which signalled the breakdown of centralised fashion authority.

The late 1960s saw the influences in popular culture moving away from London once again to America, with the rise of the 'hippy' movement, and the internationalizing of some of the stars who made London 'swinging'. The Beatles went to India, and a drug-induced 'psychedelic' element came into fashion, bringing swirly printed fabrics, full-length floating dresses, and peasant outfits with origins in any corner of the Third World. The 'unisex' tendencies in ready-to-wear fashions, the satin pants and the frilly men's shirts, became even more ambivalent in style as the developed world's youth of both sexes grew their hair uniformly long, and 'poverty' became increasingly a fashion statement. Buying second-hand clothes to wear became sensible and chic. Fashion rules broke down in a chaos of styles and mixed matches – minis with long coats, tight-fitting trousers with frilly Mexican blouses, and the ubiquitous Levi denims. By the end of the decade the midi had established itself, but skirts of all lengths could still be seen. Fashion dictates had truly disappeared, making the task of the collector increasingly difficult. What could possibly stand as archetypal for the look of the late 1960s?

The following chapter will try to identify the designers and the 'looks' from the last ten years which may prove to have been significant contributions to the history of fashion.

THE SEVENTIES

During the last ten or eleven years, fashion has settled down into a new scale of values. A few general trends can be clearly seen, and a few outstanding names can be suggested as possible 'collectable' names or labels in years to come. In general, the movement of the past decade has been towards a new simplicity, almost an austerity in style of dress, reflecting not only the economic difficulties facing the Western developed countries, but an awareness of the low quality of life for people in other parts of the world. It is often said that the ecology movement has had a strong effect on fashion, so that women nowadays would seldom care to be seen dressed from head to foot in real animal pelts, as the mood turns towards protection and preservation of all things natural. This is undoubtedly an overstatement, for there are still many women who would wear a good-quality fur coat, there being no really elegant substitute in harshly cold weather. Besides, styles have reached such a degree of simplification and modesty that the mink-lined raincoat (a theme running through twentieth-century outerwear since those driving coats of the 1910s) would be considered both chic and practical.

Practicality is very much a characteristic of recent fashion history. Paradoxically, the trend came out of the burst of 'ethnic' and 'hippy' clothing which caught the fancy of so many younger people in the late 1960s. The whole world was plundered for easy-to-make, easy-to-wear examples of peasant clothing. Wrap-round Indian skirts, tie-dyed tee-shirts, patchwork leather jackets and hand-embroidered Afghan dresses were highly popular. Some studio examples of hand-made clothing, including hand-knitted or locally woven fabrics, would be well worth conserving. A fascinating collection could be made of do-it-yourself clothing books from the 1960s onwards. Even if this fashion developed mostly with the young, it left its mark on the more established world of wealthier women. And this market was no doubt influenced by the long succession of interviews with film stars such as Jane Fonda, who succumbed to the mid-1970s trend towards army-surplus clothing, and wore battledress and boots. At the other end of the scale, Diana Vreeland, ex-editor of American *Vogue*, and since 1972 Special Consultant to the Costume Institute at the Metropolitan Museum of Art in New York, is given to wearing three black cashmere sweaters rotated with three black Givenchy skirts as her working outfit in winter, according to *Cheap Chic*, a typical fashion Bible first published in

Clothes by Ralph Lauren, current hero of the American fashion scene.

1975 (although in reality, at the Museum she wears tunic pantsuits on account of the cold!). *Cheap Chic* outlines ways to be fashionable on very little money, and sums up the attitude of the time very well. The idea is to use expensive 'basics' such as classic leather shoes and boots and Levi jeans and couture-quality blazers or jackets. These are teamed or alleviated with eccentric items such as hand-embroidered Guatemalan or Mexican blouses, with second-hand splendours from the 1920s, 1930s or 1940s, or with some simple effective, everyday ready-to-wear items, such as men's shirts, plain tee-shirts, or standard garments like the British Shetland sweater, with the Burberry raincoat, or, in America, flannel shirts from the mail-order firm L. L. Bean.

This so-called 'simplicity' has another explanation. The 1970s were the decade when women's liberation really took hold as a force in America and Europe. Couture had lost its authority, and ready-to-wear manufacturers were producing a range of styles from flagrantly teenage or hippy to sedate, middle-aged classic. No single fashion authority existed any longer. After a short burst of eccentricity and frivolity in the early 1970s, with full-length dresses vying on the streets with jeans, the modern woman settled for a more limited view of fashion, as something expressing her individuality, but largely functional. Inevitably, classics made a comeback. Also, the burst of energy in synthetics which had been such a feature of the 1950s and 1960s was replaced by a revival of interest in worthwhile, real materials, such as

A theatrical design by Yves Saint Laurent, one of the few French couturiers who has survived the ready-to-wear revolution and still launches new ideas, 1977.

wool and cotton. Underlying this interest was perhaps the awareness that all things natural are not to be taken for granted.

It is significant that the outstanding names of the 1970s are those people who work most exactly in this area of fashion. Without doubt, the leading taste-maker of the era was still Yves Saint Laurent, who managed to reflect the current mood but translated it into ready-to-wear clothes which were the epitome of relaxed elegance. Any Rive Gauche (let alone couture) piece would be worth saving for posterity. So, too, would any garment made by the British designer Jean Muir. She began her career working at Liberty's, where perhaps her sensitivity to fine fabrics was enhanced. She became a designer, suitably for the firm of Jaeger (still to this day making a high-quality range of tweedy classics which epitomize British traditional dressing) and in the mid-1950s began her own career as a manufacturer with the firm of Jane & Jane. This label marked a range of 'young' clothes, with the emphasis on good cut, youthful styling, and a look that suited petite women. In 1966 Jean Muir began her own wholesale operation, which now employs about a hundred people and is based in Bruton Street, in Mayfair, London. She has strong views on what the 1960s did for fashion design, few of which are complimentary (see previous chapter). In summary, in an interview in the *Observer* in 1980, Miss Muir said: 'The sixties made everything seem instant and easy: you put a sign on your door, got your name in the paper and that was that. Few people were given any chance to develop or learn. And it's still like that. I have girls who come to me after three or four years' training who have not been taught how to make a production pattern!'

Even more significantly, she points out that the 1960s marked the end of the era when women would turn a dress inside out in order to decide whether or not it was worth buying. Any garment produced by Jean Muir herself would survive such a test without doubt. Her speciality is matt jersey, which she styles into the simplest but most flattering dresses, often mounted with soft gathers or pleats into a yoke. She works equally well in suede, leather and silk. Her styles over the years since 1966 have changed gradually from one season to the next, so that they always appear to be of the moment; yet, paradoxically, buyers of her garments find that they can wear a Jean Muir dress for many years without feeling dated. (It is interesting that, like Diana Vreeland, she wears a very limited wardrobe herself, preferring simple navy-blue jerseys and skirts. And yet she tries on all her toiles personally, and adjusts the fit for a perfect size 10 on herself. When completed, her models can be equally successful from size 10 to size 16.)

Only two other British designers come near to Jean Muir in eminence or in individuality of 'look'. The first of these is Zandra Rhodes, who began her career, like Mary Quant, at the Royal College of Art in London. Zandra Rhodes specializes in the most imaginative, not to say surreal inventions for glamorous evening clothes, and exports all over the world. She began her working life by printing her own textile designs, and continues to place great emphasis on the originality of her fabrics. Some of her ideas were revolutionary, such as her practice of shredding the hems of chiffon dresses to create a floating, fairy-like effect. Permanently pleated silks and chiffons

are used to make wild, stand-away collars, or flutes of dresses reminiscent, in their exaggerated forms, of Fortuny. Zandra Rhodes has recently had immense success in translating 'punk rock' fashions into high-style collector's pieces, with torn holes and safety-pin decorations. Her clothes are always original, if not shocking, but are somehow so individual that they hardly date. Like Jean Muir, she believes that the main ingredient for her success has been a constant search for technical perfection and professionalism in her production work. Anyone can be a designer, but few people have the application to be a producer.

Bill Gibb is the third designer from the 1970s whose output was also of a consistently high standard, verging on couture. He produced some fine knitwear, reflecting the interest in soft, thinner fabrics, layered upon themselves, which originated with the Italian school of designers, notably the Missoni family, who started in the mid-1960s when Italian fashion experienced an international revival. He also made some beautifully elaborate outfits in printed wool, often using Liberty fabrics: in 1970 he followed the interest in ethnic styling with some mixed patterns, pleated, beaded and fringed separates. In mid-decade, he created stunning leather clothes using the softest of skins for coats and jackets with wide collars and peplums. Through most of the 1970s he ran a small wholesaling house, but was forced into liquidation. A brief period of financial support followed, but it is doubtful whether Bill Gibb enjoys the restrictions and deadlines implicit in such an arrangement. His name will always be one to watch for collector's pieces, however, whatever form his designing will take.

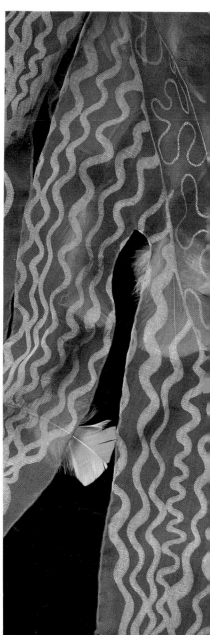

Right *Zandra Rhodes is a modern English collectable – her 1977 version of punk fashions, originated by Vivienne Westwood, is an expensive comment on the look of the time.*

Below & centre *Zandra Rhodes' fabrics are as fascinating as her designs, and enviable possessions.*

A beautiful use of a contemporary pattern: English designer Bill Gibb – another modern collectable (1977).

117

Sonia Rykiel: French
ready-to-wear of the utmost
chic.

Bill Gibb's problems serve to exemplify the pressures on designers today. The cost of fabrics and making – even the mere cost of running a small studio operation – force designers into mass production; often, as Jean Muir has said, they lack the professionalism and the acumen to withstand the difficulties involved. Fashion is now big business, and the 'boutique' operation of the 1960s is difficult to follow. At the same time, women themselves are imposing new demands on their clothes suppliers, and this may well be the reason for a general return to more classical, well made, hard-wearing clothes, which has been a trend for the past five to eight years. A young Japanese designer working in Paris, Kenzo Takada, experienced all these difficulties from the first. He came to success through his designing under the label Jap for his own boutique, and in 1971 caused enormous excitement with his wide, gathered skirts and big-shouldered tops – all shapes somewhat reminiscent of his Japanese background (and readily pirated by slicker ready-to-wear manufacturers). But Takada has stayed the course and continues to provide a vigorous and fresh designing inspiration to modern fashion. His knitwear is simultaneously original and amusing, with a worn and comfortable atmosphere which seems to typify much of 1970s fashion. A rival in this area is Sonia Rykiel, who transformed the 1960s idea of knitwear from the dull twinset-and-pearls, cricket-sweater and golf-cardigan rut which it had become. Her knitwear was at first figure-hugging, with tighter than usual armholes and sophisticated combinations of colours. Sonia Rykiel reintroduced knitted two-pieces, which had been out of fashion for several decades. New knitting techniques enabled her skirts to be clinging, shape-holding, and quite the reverse of dowdy. Her more recent lines have also adopted the looser look, and she remains a forceful personality in French designing, and a name worth acquiring.

No history of 1970s fashion could possibly look at the advance in knitted fashion without considering the tremendous impact of Italian fashion internationally over the past twenty years, from the key American launching in 1951. The influence of such names as Missoni, Albini and Armani is to the 1970s like that of Dior, Balenciaga and Chanel in the 1950s. Taj and Rosita Missoni started what has now become a family business with sportswear in the mid-1950s. By the 1970s they were producing a range of exquisitely mixed and matched patterns in wool, tweeds, soft fabrics in subtle colours, for a select band of 160 international customers. Their myriad jersey knits in patchwork colours are breathtakingly beautiful, with zig-zags in purples, pinks and blues – checks, stripes and all manner of patterns which seem readily identifiable as 'Missoni'. A new study of Italian fashion, *The Who's Who of Italian Fashion* by Adriana Mulassano and Alfa Castaldi, describes their sources: 'a pile of fabrics from Guatemala, an old Hermès scarf from the 20s lying on the floor, fabulous Afghani silks under a chair, a shred of "gobelin" [tapestry] in an open suitcase. . .'.

It is significant that Italian fashion is still in the hands of a number of old families and aristocrats, who have, as in pre-war France, always been involved in its promotion and marketing. As early as 1956, nine aristocratic ladies, rather like the *mannequins de ville* (those socialites and beauties of Paris who were asked to wear couture clothes at important public and private gatherings, so that they would be seen by the right people) travelled to America with cases full of Italian styles, which they wore to their social functions in New York. Everyone began asking where the clothes had come from, and Italian fashion was suddenly on the map. The tradition continues in the work of Valentino, who was employed for a while at Jean Dessès and then for five years at Guy Laroche in Paris. In 1962 he launched himself at

Centre *Soft, interesting knitwear from the Italian firm of Missoni, with a return to natural, luxurious fabrics and fibres.*

Valentino 1968: he has always been popular with the international jet set and his clothes have often been copied by Seventh Avenue and the British 'rag trade'.

the Palazzo Pitti showings, and received business worth eight million lire from the first collection. Then all the present-day international set began to buy from him. His most famous outfit was the lace-topped wedding dress which Jacqueline Kennedy wore for her marriage to Aristotle Onassis. Consuelo Crespi, Merle Oberon, Cristina Ford and Gloria Guinness all became his patrons. From 1969 Valentino began to produce a ready-to-wear line, and handles franchises for bathing suits, leather goods, linens, sportswear and accessories of all kinds. (Even collecting his franchised goods might be a proposition for the not-so-wealthy.)

The ready-to-wear specialists are treated with as much respect as the couturiers in Italy, and none has had more success than Walter Albini. He began his career by designing for Krizia, but gradually linked himself with a secondary group of manufacturers – Basile, Sportfox, Callaghan and Escargot – who launched a breakaway fashion fair in Milan. His most attractive designs under his own label, which he launched in 1970, have been variations on the military theme, or ways of using men's clothes, such as tailored shirts, in sets of separates for women. Albini uses 1930s and 1940s styles as his source of inspiration for suits and 'little' dresses.

In that same year, 1970, Giorgio Armani went independent, after eight years spent with a large industrial group for which he designed both men's and women's clothing. At first he worked on contracts, running a design studio, but in 1975 Armani launched his own range, which has been outstandingly successful. One of his most influential ideas has been the combination of tweed on tweed, sometimes as many as three different patterns being used for a skirt, a blazer and a waistcoat. Armani has now rejoined big industry in the form of the Gruppo Finanziario Tessile, and has been busily launching boutiques around the world in Milan, Brussels, New York, Toronto, Paris, London, Zurich and Montreal, besides others in Italy.

Mariuccia Mandelli is behind the Krizia label. She exhibits at the annual Milan Ready-to-Wear Fair, and is a producer of the softest and prettiest separates and dresses. Her career began in the mid-1950s when she launched herself as a designer. In 1964 she held her first show at the Palazzo Pitti, and was granted the journalists' Press Award for fashion; in winning this prize she was preceded only by Emilio Pucci, a fact which demonstrates the impact made by so new a designer. Walter Albini joined her as designer for a while, and in 1967 Miss Mandelli began her work in knits with Kriziamaglia. Now she too is opening boutiques in Europe and America.

Even newer on the scene, and possibly even more promising, is designer Gianni Versace, who started in fashion at the close of the 1970s, and has been hailed as a new Saint Laurent. He offers his clothes through two boutiques in Milan and Paris, besides working for franchise arrangements with other companies (Complice; Genny, owned by Arnaldo and Donatella Girombelli; and a knitwear firm, Callaghan). The industry and talent in Italy are impressive and distinctive. Italian fashion has never quite lost the characteristic glamour and Latin high style which sometimes makes it hard to wear – it is too demanding and too dramatic for some tastes. But the new generation of designers is adjusting to the world's market forces and adding an admirable energy and inventiveness to international fashion.

Elegant 1980s fashion from Gianni Versace.

Far left *An Autumn/Winter 1982/83 design from Giorgio Armani, a comparatively new name in Italian fashion.*

Left *A striking Krizia design – high class Italian ready-to-wear.*

Calvin Klein, considered the most important of contemporary American designers, specialising in softly tailored, classic separates, like this blouse and skirt in silk crêpe de chine.

'Sleeping bag' coats by Norma Kamali.

For further ideas and advice about possible modern 'collectables', I spoke to Philippe Garner of Sotheby's who is also the author of *Contemporary Decorative Arts*, a survey of new designs in every field from 1940 to the present day. Mr Garner collects clothes which evoke the spirit of a particular time, and like many specialists in the field, looks upon articles of clothing very much as works of art, as fluid sculptures. For a purely documentary view of a particular era of fashion, he suggested that designs by Vivienne Westwood, the Londoner who did much to create the 'punk' fashion of the late 1970s and early 1980s, would be items worth preserving. A similar proposition, though more recondite, would be the work of Antony Price, a King's Road designer who created many startling designs for rock stars, male and female, from the 1960s onwards, and is still well in the forefront of custom-made clothes today. From Paris, an equally distinctive and daring designer is Claude Montana who makes quite extraordinary leather coats and ensembles, some of which are decorated with flashes of colour, gold dragons, militaristic epaulettes and angular shoulders or collars in a mixture of Berlin Nazi and Hollywood glamour – a description which is in no way derogatory, for the final effect is feminine and stylish to a degree.

Two American designers favoured by Mr Garner are Calvin Klein and

Norma Kamali. Calvin Klein is almost single-handedly responsible for the return to classic, deceptively simple clothes – silk trousers, shirts and softly cut tailored jackets – which are very much the current tone in fashion. Norma Kamali runs a much smaller operation, OMO (On My Own), a New York boutique where she introduces a new idea every few weeks or so, and which is constantly referred to as a source of new mainstream ideas by the American fashion trade. Her clothes are now becoming available in American department stores; Gimbels in particular feature her designs. Mr Garner believes that Japanese designers, from Kenzo Takada onwards, are a major source of new inspiration in fashion – perhaps because their tradition-al clothes are cut on very different lines from Western shapes, and this inheritance enables the younger generation to approach Western clothes with a wit and originality which our own designers may not share. Boutiques in New York and London often stock some interesting and inexpensive items, frequently in unusual prints, which will gain in importance and value as the years go by.

As I have tried to keep a balance in this book between what is desirable and what is feasible, I also asked Philippe Garner for his suggestions about current ready-to-wear manufacturers whose styles perhaps sum up a current feeling and are well within the reach of the modest collector. His clear choice in this area would be the work of the Italian-based but international firm of Fiorucci, which started in 1967 with a boutique in Milan. Fiorucci not only makes some simple and dramatic separates for young people – starting with labelled jeans that made Levi-Strauss anxious, and going on to knee-length trousers, kimono-shaped tops, denim and patterned co-ordinated outfits – but also runs its operation with a most distinctive control over its advertising, packaging, and shop-designing. The head of the company, Elio Fiorucci, was a mere twenty-two years of age when his fashion business turned into an international enterprise, and he now has shops in New York, Boston, Beverly Hills, London, Zurich, Rio, Tokyo and Hong Kong. The whole atmosphere of the Fiorucci enterprise is one where clothing and presentation are worked out to the smallest detail, creating a unique and striking image. To give an example, Philippe Garner produced from his own desk drawer (a surreptitious gesture I have enjoyed so many times in dealing with born collectors) a small plastic bag, brightly patterned in red, with flecks of yellow, blue and white. This contained a smaller clear vinyl zipped purse, trimmed with yellow, white and blue binding, revealing inside an even more minuscule red, yellow, white bikini. For under £15 the entire package sums up the sharpness of style and the amusing eye of Fiorucci's chief designer, Ettore Sottsass, imposed throughout the concept.

A final word, which many fashion collectors and dealers have always emphasized in giving their advice for this book. While an inexpensive example such as Fiorucci's swimwear will summarize a feeling to perfection, there will be times when collectors will have to aim high in their acquiring in order to maintain standards of quality and excellence. Susan Mayor, of Christie's South Kensington, confirmed that the great variety in pricing at sales is often due to the range of quality in the clothes and accessories up for auction. Dresses which are not particularly distinctive in terms of cut or

Centre *Punk 'Bondage' suits – fashions from the street are worth keeping if they are distinctive and unusual.*

Philippe Garner of Sotheby's choice of a modern collectable: Claude Montana, 1979.

essential historical value will often sell remarkably well because they are in immaculate condition and very attractive. This is even more reason, therefore, to concentrate on articles which both have a real documentary value and are in excellent condition (and likely to remain so owing to the collector's own care in storing). Serious collecting will eventually involve the occasional bold decision calling for considerable outlay of capital, so it is as well for the collector to read copiously and to visit sales time and time again without necessarily purchasing anything, in order to get an 'eye' and to become more knowledgeable about the field. It is impossible to give rules and regulations – to say that satin feels this way, grosgrain like that, and that a couture hem sits so. Half the purpose of collecting is to develop that knowledge for oneself; the purpose of this book is to help to give the novice collector further enthusiasm for the task.

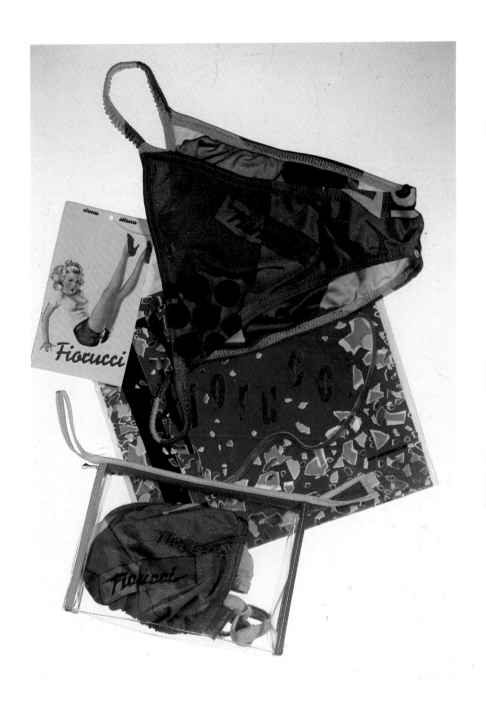

A Fiorucci 'package' showing
the cleverness of the firm's
merchandising style.

CHILDREN'S CLOTHES

Eternal teatime – this delightful couple were photographed in the 1920s.

Children's clothes are not very widely collected, perhaps because they are less subject to the vagaries of fashion than women's clothes, and are therefore less glamorous and interesting at first glance. But a great deal can be learnt about the nature of social changes in this century from a study of the altering shapes and increasing practicality of children's wear. Introductions of new fabrics have often been spurred on by the necessity to provide cheap, durable, hard-wearing outfits for active youngsters: movements towards liberation for women, later so often inculcated in schools by the Miss Jean Brodies of the world, had found first expression in young girls' dresses in the Edwardian eara, while Mamma was still imprisoned in stays. Attitudes towards liberty and progressive education for children affected

young costume more directly than was permissible in adult wear. All these changes could be exemplified in a useful documentary collection. For those more interested in nostalgia, the exquisitely hand-worked layettes and christening clothes of the 1910s and 1920s still retain their charm.

The collector has a rich field of documentary evidence for the look of early-twentieth-century clothes in the illustrated books and magazines of the period: smug little girls in ringlets and smocks, comic infants in sailor suits, and solemn male babies in full-length lace dresses show us the styles of the day. For England, the presence of the Royal Family has always exercised a near-magical influence on style: photographs of the young Princes Edward and George in sailor suits typified the idea of small children at the time. Little boys also sported small versions of the Norfolk jacket, or the aristocratic 'Eton suit', which had a dark jacket with wide lapels and a short, rounded front. Both of these were worn with knickerbockers and thick, knee-high socks. The round-edged shirt-collar that accompanied the outfit must have been Sunday-best wear at its most extreme form of discomfort – it was high and starched, and had a wide black bow at the neck opening.

The Royal Family have always set a style for children's fashions in names and clothes: the Queen Mother with Prince Charles in 1948.

Top right *Two somewhat desperate looking schoolboys in their 'Eton' suits, 1902.*

Top left *Cheerful family photographs reveal a great deal about children's clothes: a naval jacket, complete with brass buttons, worn with leggings. 1920s.*

Above, left *A 'Kate Greenaway' print dress c1900; almost a replica of adult styling.*

Princess Elizabeth, not quite a year old, photographed in 1927: the traditional look has always been popular with the Royal Family.

Top centre Ada Wayter with her 8 brothers and sisters whom she rescued from a fire at their home in Battersea in 1913. Even a modest family laboured over whites for small children.

Centre The gym slip – a first move towards freedom, well in advance of grown women's fashions for the 1900s.

Right Nursery scene at Bognor, Sussex. The elaborate lace and tucks in these clothes must have provided hours of work for the servants.

If formal wear seemed determined to restrict exuberant spirits, then sportswear offered some hint of liberation to come. Rugger and football clothes for boys consisted of knee-length white shorts, open-necked shirts and knee-high socks. Aristocratic boys sported striped blazers and boaters for summer wear. (A mark of difference between the classes was the amount of variety in suitable attire for hot and cold weather.) For girls, the breakthrough to liberty through sportswear was even more pronounced than for boys: the 1910s saw the general introduction of the gym slip – which derived its name from its primary use as an article of clothing worn by more privileged girls in private education. These movements were contemporaneous in England and America. Miss Buss, headmistress of the North London Collegiate School, is credited in England with the introduction of a gym outfit for her girls at the close of the nineteenth century. In 1890 the school magazine recorded a sports day when 'each girl wore a light coloured skirt reaching only to her knees, a white blouse loosely belted at the waist, a cap either blue striped (arts) or red striped (science)'. The true 'gym slip' as it is thought of today probably originated at Dartford College for Physical Training in America, under the direction of a Madame Bergman Osterberg, around 1885, but variations on the theme were appearing in some English public schools too in the final twenty years of the last century. A similar outfit appeared at Wellesley College in about 1880: bloomers, like those introduced for bicycle riding by Mrs Amelia Bloomer, were teamed with a pleated, loose-fitting tunic, sashed at the waist, and worn over a white blouse.

By 1897 gymnastics were being taught in most good girls' schools on both sides of the Atlantic. The link between an interest in physical fitness and women's liberation is an interesting one: it appeared to be a prime motive behind the boyish styles of the 1920s, and was lost in the reactionary 1950s, when women appeared romantically hampered by the billowy skirts of the New Look, and when irregularities of the figure were cured by firm corseting. Only in the 1970s and 1980s has a renewed interest in health and fitness brought back a style of fashion that combines practicality with the absolute necessity to keep the figure youthful and in trim. (In passing, it is

Bottom *A magnificent seaside bonnet – in artificial city sand, Fulham 1910.*

Below *Even at play, hats and pinafores were de rigueur: Regent's Park, 1908.*

worth noting that many of the film stars of the 1930s, and many of the designer clothes for that period, reveal a slackness and plumpness which would not be well received today: Mae West's stomach and Madeleine Vionnet's all-disguising bias-cut dresses attest to the prevailing shape.)

While school clothes for girls and boys showed some signs of adapting to the needs of the growing energetic child, infant clothing in this respect at the beginning of the century lagged far behind. But for the collector, such wardrobes offer a wealth of interest in rich hand-work, exquisite laces and good-quality objects. Fine baby clothes, then as now, are always hoarded by doting mothers. No one who has seen Ibsen's *Brand* can forget the harrowing scene in which the forlorn wife is made to give up the baby clothes she has lovingly stored away after her child's death. There is something universal and timeless about the desire to preserve these symbols of a short-lived phase of infancy. Layettes for babies in the Edwardian era are just as splendid as those for a bride's trousseau. Little boys wore white frilly dresses decorated with lace until well beyond infancy, up to the age of four or five, and often wore their hair long, in ringlets, until that age as well. Little girls endured lace bonnets, frilly collars and lace-trimmed pinafores worn

Charles Dana Gibson's view of Everyday People, *New York, 1904.*

Centre *Small boys wore their caps everywhere: Regent's Park, 1912.*

over dark-coloured dresses. And, in spite of the trend towards freer-fitting clothes in schools, formal attire for Sundays and holidays still consisted of a stiffly starched white cotton, lawn or cotton piqué dress, decorated with fine embroidery and with a contrasting sash, and a bonnet in straw with ribbon trim to match the sash. Even fairly modestly incomed families strove to maintain this standard of dress in surroundings that made such use of white an epic struggle.

Only one outfit in the first decade suggests the freedom that was soon to come for children – and more directly the trend towards clothes which are no longer copies of grown-up styles, but designed specifically for children's own lives. The innovation came from an unusual source in America – a comic strip called 'Buster Brown' which appeared in 1908. The eponymous hero wore a sensible, tweedy wool suit with knee-length pants and a double-breasted, belted jacket with a round collar; and a jaunty straw hat. (Hats were essential for children, as for adults – even the poorest always walked the streets in some kind of headgear, even if it was a rough old cap.) A second introduction from America was the dungarees which became practical and popular day wear for smaller children from the close of the First World War: they were no doubt inspired by the tough farm overalls manufactured by Levi-Strauss & Co., and have continued to be the most popular outfit for toddlers ever since. (It is interesting to note that just as trousers for adult women have taken some time to become acceptable, the same is true for little girls: even in the 1950s most mothers dressed a small daughter in a frock, whereas nowadays trousers or dungarees are not merely informal home wear, but are also made in smarter fabrics, such as velour or jersey, with matching sweaters, for going out on more formal occasions.)

The First World War did much to liberate children, as mothers had less time for the labour involved in maintaining the older style of children's wear. The gym tunic gained in popularity, also because it fitted with the levelling, democratizing movements after the war. Economy had its part to

A well-wrapped-up family and equestrian friend at the Croome Hunt in 1922. Note the buttoned leggings which took ages to do up and undo.

Top left *Ready for the holidays – 'Buster Brown' style suits at Waterloo Station, 1925.*

Left *'Dainty and Pretty' smocks complete with sun bonnets: Harrods 1919.*

play in this change: children's clothes became shorter, so that, in the 1920s and 1930s, little girls' dresses barely reached their knees. The smock-shaped dress or top gained in appeal, in knitted versions with matching knickers for babies, and in knee-length styles for girls. Smocking itself became immensely popular, and the collector may find some fine hand-made examples from the inter-war years. Underwear for children became as simplified as outerwear, the principal innovation being the 'liberty bodice', a fleecy-lined cotton knitted vest with tapes sewn down the length, instead of the boned garment of earlier years. Liberty bodices continued to be worn until well into the 1950s: some had loops so that knickers could be attached for a snug, draught-free childhood. A principal reason for the demise of the liberty bodice must lie in the general rising of house temperatures with the installation of central heating systems, which in Britain at least did not become widely available until the late 1950s.

The so-called 'Liberty' bodice for ages 6–9, 1909.

Cut-out dolls like these were used by several manufacturers of children's clothes including Horrockses, to advertise their wares. The fabrics in the bottom row are equally useful as a reference for ladies' clothes of the late 1920s/early 1930s.

Handsmocked dresses for Liberty, made in silk, crêpe de chine and velveteen, in the 1930s. Note the waistless styles for the younger children, in contrast to the elaborate clothing for children in the Edwardian era.

402. Overall, in linen with hand-appliqued figures. Sizes: 1 to 6 years. 10/6

405. Frock, in velveteen, hand-smocked. Collar and cuffs of georgette, 27 to 33 ins. long. £2.16.6 to £3.2.6

Princess Elizabeth and Princess Margaret Rose in the Garden at Royal Lodge, Windsor.

Bottom Designs by Jeanne Lanvin for children. Gazette du Bon Ton 1914.

Shirley Temple, the cult image of childhood in the 1930s: polka dot dresses like this one were widely copied.

The 1930s saw a general increase in sporting activities for adults, men and women: this too was reflected in simpler, more active clothing for children. Girls could wear shorts, or sun-suits cut like dungarees, and sun-dresses became popular. Just as Chanel made the suntan fashionable for women, so children too were allowed to run about in minimal clothing on the beach or in the fields. As children began to have purpose-made clothes, they also acquired models for elegance: in England the Royal Family provided this, with the famous 'Margaret Rose' frock of 1932 which was quickly adapted by manufacturers and carefully imitated by home dressmakers. (The Kennedy children in the 1960s wore clothes reminiscent of classic European children's wear; particularly the velvet-collared coats of young John Kennedy.) Child film stars also influenced American children's clothes, most spectacularly the style worn by Shirley Temple and Jane Withers, rivals at different Hollywood studios: polka dots and floppy collars, white shoes and knee socks.

There have always been designer-made clothes for the children of the wealthy; Jeanne Lanvin's were her entrée into clothes-making. 'Lanvin blue' was originally created for her daughter, who became the Princesse de

Hand-knitted dresses and suits like these may not have the bandbox appeal of earlier, elaborate styles, but at least they allowed ease of movement. (1921).

Polignac. Her mother-and-daughter outfits feature charmingly in many of the illustrations from the *Gazette du bon ton* and *Jardin des dames* in the 1930s. Dior and Cardin have produced children's ranges, so in more recent times have Betsey Johnson in the USA and Jean Muir in Britain (though she no longer does so). The majority of well made children's clothes before the war in Britain came from large stores such as Harrods or Marshall & Snelgrove, or were still made by the local dressmaker for special occasions.

The Second World War increased the trend towards simplicity: children's coats, trousers and dresses were made from cut-down curtains or old adult garments. A page from *Harper's Bazaar* in 1945 gives ideas for simple pinafores for five-to-eight-year-olds, with illustrations, and suggests: 'Sacrifice a linen tea-cloth, and hunt up some narrow bits of lace to edge the ruffles of this fresh-as-a-daisy party-pretty pinafore like Alice wore when she went to Wonderland. . . . Put your own, or your husband's khaki uniform to good new use by converting it into a different sort of battle-dress, the perfect pinafore for a tom-boy; match it with a khaki jersey.' A vogue for home knitting burgeoned into a complete outfitting of children in rather shapeless, not particularly flattering pullovers, knitted shorts and knickers. But the effect of war-time restrictions was to pare down the garments thought necessary in a child's wardrobe, and the shapelessness of hand-knitted garments was in the 1950s replaced by better-seamed, factory-produced, synthetic stretch fabrics. American fashions had a significant effect on taste in England, because of the importation of second-hand bundles of clothing to help out with refugees or evacuated casualties of the war. Iris Brooke, in *English Children's Costume*, comments:

> It was all part of the 'Costume' of war years to find small boys in loudly checked or plaid three-quarter-length coats with belts, brightly coloured knitted caps and the strangest ankle boots with toe caps and low lacing. . . . long trousers and knee breeches with elastic at the knee, and snowsuits hitherto unknown in England were everywhere to be seen worn by girls and boys indiscriminately. So thick and cosy were these useful garments that conventional children's clothes in England practically disappeared in favour of the much prized 'Yank' possessions.

By the end of the war, and into the early 1950s, children's clothes had acquired a new individuality, it is true, with many styles reflecting the recognition of the separate identity of children, and the peculiar needs of their everyday attire. But where close imitation of adult styles was replaced by childish fashions, a new 'cuteness' came in – perhaps influenced by the idealized portrayal of childhood seen in American films and television series. Homespun fabrics, denims and checks came in, but so did appliqué motifs – clowns, poodle dogs, lambs and kittens, rather similar to the teenage fashions prevalent at the time. Mickey Mouse reached a new zenith of fame, along with Minnie Mouse and the rest of the Disney characters, their popularity since their creation in the 1920s boosted yet further by the opening of Disneyland in California in 1955. The same year marked the launching of the Davy Crockett films, starring Fess Parker, by Disney studios, and this too led to a wild enthusiasm for moccasins and fringed leather outfits for children. All aspects of American culture flooded Europe

134

Pinafore, rompers, gingham hat: practical American children's clothes from Saks Fifth Avenue, 1940. American parcels to the UK during the war had a great influence on the development of children's styles in Britain.

Centre *A Mothercare all-in-one suit, based on the original 'Babygro' design launched in America in 1962.*

The kind of classic look that Britain still exports all over the world: from Debenham & Freebody, velvet-collared overcoats, 1938.

with new trends; this was only reversed with the arrival of the Beatles and the 'swinging London' boutique era of the 1960s.

Over the past fifteen years a marked difference has emerged between the styling of European children's clothes and those of America. As with other manufactured goods, such as shoes and handbags, the American industry has maintained its lead in terms of quality and durability. The famous 'Health-Tex' range of children's clothing is unmatched in the UK, yet in other respects Europe has taken the lead in responding to the changing tastes of young people and producing gay young clothes, often in unconventional colours, which have taken much longer to become acceptable in America. Children under ten, boys and girls, can wear brown, purple or sludge green, from the ubiquitous 'Babygro' stage right through to teenage jumpers and jeans. (The 'Babygro', a one-piece stretch suit for babies, was invented by Walter Artzt in New York and launched in 1962.) American children are still outfitted in plaids and poplins from label manufacturers, whose ranges are sold within big stores, whereas in Europe the cheaper chains have taken over – notably Mothercare, established in 1961, and Marks & Spencer, who started a separate children's section in 1975. (A collector's tribute to this successful enterprise, in the form of a widespread and thoughtful cross-section of their output, would reveal much about the

It's good to grow up in 'Viyella'

Here is the perfect cloth for children —
attractive, plus-proof,
and made to be washed.
'Viyella' stays beautifully soft and fresh-looking
for years; and people say
"The more you wash 'Viyella' the better it is."

Viyella
IF IT SHRINKS WE REPLACE

1940s models from Viyella.

Right *Lace christening robes at a double ceremony, 1925.*

changes in British society over the past thirty years.) Other chief names in the field are Viyella, Chilprufe and Ladybird; along with Health-Tex, an American name of importance in the field is Carters.

Children's clothes today have a completely different character from those of seventy years ago: childhood is now recognized as a phase of life with its own requirements in dress, not a time when children should be made to conform to adult patterns of dress in miniature. It is perhaps regrettable that with practicality comes dullness, and with mass manufacture a singular lack of interesting designs (although French, Italian and Scandinavian examples can be found that disprove this observation). No one now has the time to hand-embroider a christening robe. If the baby is christened at all it is a matter of note rather than a norm.

Noreen Marshall of the Bethnal Green Museum of Childhood suggested that a collection of children's clothes within a family might be a good starting-point for the collector. Such a theme could provide an excellent basis for documentary evidence: the dates of the lives of family members, the places where clothing was purchased, the number of children who wore the garments as hand-me-downs, the price when purchased (or the value of the material that went into the making) – all these points are part of collecting and make a piece of research worth handing on to posterity. Children's clothing may have changed less dramatically than women's dress, yet the alterations reflect significant shifts in public attitude, and echo the upheavals of the century. Collecting children's clothes can provide a cheap and absorbing hobby. The prices are still very reasonable, with the exception of christening garments hand-embroidered or decorated with fine lace. Four nineteenth-century Ayrshire-work christening robes fetched £55 at a sale in London, at Phillips, on 28 August 1980, while an Edwardian child's costume in ivory worsted, complete with maker's label and a rich piped trim, went for the princely sum of £80. In America, prices are more modest: a collection of baby clothes including six white dresses trimmed with lace and embroidery sold for $50, and a similar lot for $65. At least these prices indicate that there is scope for the new collector to start cheaply, and acquire good pieces for a reasonable outlay.

FANS

There is no doubt that for collectors of fans the early twentieth century must represent the end of the long and distinguished life of their favourite object. No fan produced in the twentieth century reached the heights of beauty, workmanship and sheer romance found, for instance, in the historical painted fans of the eighteenth century. However, modern fans offer other compensations, and romance of an ephemeral, nostalgic kind. We are so nearly in touch with the women who carried them, and indeed can often find out details of personal or family history which make the object itself doubly precious. In my researches among collectors, what has impressed me most besides the knowledge and perseverance displayed in acquiring fine pieces is the sheer enjoyment of the objects themselves, and it is this quality of delight which makes collecting fashion objects uniquely worthwhile. Fans in particular were treasured possessions for special occasions – weddings, great balls, cocktail parties, days of celebration and moments of feminine excitement and anticipation. To open a box lined with white satin, and see a set of initials curled along the stick of a fan, is to make a leap of imagination into elegant Edwardian society, and to be in touch, if only for a moment, with a situation of intense interest in another being's life.

The most romantic and dramatic of twentieth-century fans are undoubtedly the evening fans of the Edwardian era. There are three main types, none of which is beyond the pocket of even a modestly set-up

Beautiful ostrich feather fan showing how subtle the dyeing process could be to match chiffon silk dresses in the Edwardian era.

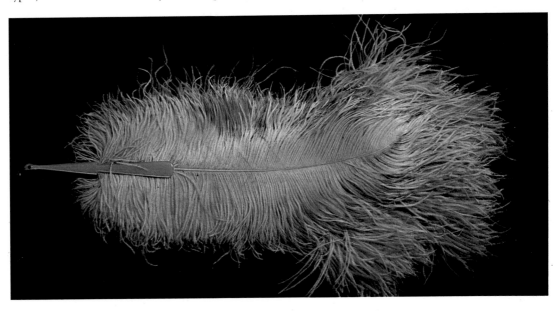

collector: feather, lace, and spangled gauze. The first of these are the glorious ostrich-feather fans, immaculately curled and lying back against solid sticks of tortoiseshell, whose mottled markings complement so well the subtle variations of colour in the feathers. Some of these fans are enormous half-circles, as much as thirty inches in depth from handle to tip. The female ostrich feathers in brown, or brown with a white tip, were often used in their natural state, and curled over each other with a special set of curling tongs. The male ostrich has white feathers, which were left in that colour for formal weddings or gala balls; but both types could also be dyed in a myriad of soft hues – blues, purples, pinks, deep turquoises and greens – to match exactly the shade of a silk or brocade dress. Tortoiseshell was the best choice for the sticks, because it is strong, light, and slightly pliant. Blond tortoiseshell, being softer in colour, like amber, and also much more expensive, was the first choice for those able to afford it. Other fans were made with sticks of ivory or wood.

An equally elegant evening fan would be made of lace, sometimes supplied by the customer from old hoards and remodelled. An advertisement in the *Connoisseur* in 1905 offers to supply 'replicas of old designs from customers' own lace'. Sometimes the lace would be applied to a base of net, to give it strength, or would form only part of the overall design: black lace mounted on white net, for example. By late Edwardian days, bolder colour combinations, such as gold net over purple silk, are found. Often the lace would be decorated with spangles for added richness. The sticks of a lace fan are most often of perforated ivory, but sometimes plain-cut mother-of-pearl may be found. In cheaper work, only the brins – the lower part of the sticks below the leaf – are of pearly shell, or ivory; the upper parts are of a cheaper material, such as bone or wood. Sometimes tortoiseshell is imitated in horn, or a cheaper material known as 'imitation amber' was used. Alternatively a wood or horn handle would be decorated with silver filigree work, often in the spiralling form of initials, inlaid with marcasite or gemstones.

The third type of Edwardian evening fan, which is especially appealing, and not so very expensive for a new collector, is the gauze-and-spangle variety. These are particularly ornate and fragile, and a good example is a delightful treasure. The sequins used on Edwardian fans were stamped from thin sheets of foil, and immaculately stitched on by hand, so that the back of the fan is as perfectly ornamented as the front. In a good-quality fan, small metal discs were inset into the guard and sticks to echo the design on the leaf. The motifs themselves are intensely satisfying to the eye: the half-circle of the fan is echoed in a series of swags or wreaths, with floral-inspired shapes running down each stick towards the centre of the fan.

Gauze is often combined with very delicate painting, echoing the colour of the material; for instance, a soft, pink gauze might be decorated with rosebuds of a slightly darker hue, and mounted, double-sided, on to carved and pink-tinted mother-of-pearl sticks. Black gauze fans might be decorated with spangles of brilliant purple, or a similar shade, to make a subtle combination. These were probably mourning fans, though as Nancy Armstrong comments, in *The Book of Fans*, they were no doubt intended for a very Merry Widow. One of the pleasures of fan collecting is to become

aware of how so small an object can be found in such a variety of designs and colours, each giving a clear indication of the personality of the user, and perhaps the occasion for which it was first required. The first of the two examples just given could have served for a seventeen-year-old's first romantic ball, while the second would have been used by an experienced woman of the world.

A curious novelty in the Edwardian evening fan was Walter Thornhill's patent dressing-case fan, which had a small compartment set into the uppermost guard on the stick, containing a tiny powder box, a puff, a mirror, a glove hook, a comb, scissors, hairpins, needle-and-thread and sometimes other essential items of repair for a dressed-up occasion. Other oddities of the era are blank fans, with spaces for autographs, often mounted on fragrant cedarwood. Other blank fans, made in silk or paper, may have been supplied so that ladies could paint them with their own designs, perhaps to co-ordinate with a favourite brocade or print dress.

Fans for all manner of occasions were the work of a few master craftsmen. The foremost name from the Edwardian era is that of Monsieur Duvelleroy, who had a shop in Paris and another in London. Other centres for fans were Vienna and Berlin. As in the case of many fashion accessories at this time, there was a marked uniformity of taste all over the fashionable world, since the international set encompassed all nationalities, and knew no frontiers. A lady wintered in France or Germany, perhaps; she drifted through the spas of Europe and the country houses of England, and whether she were an

Fans made of net decorated with crystals were very popular in Edwardian days, as were 'picture fans', like this fine example with gilded and pierced mother-of-pearl sticks, and painted chicken skin decorated with a fête champêtre scene.

Top left *Exquisite Edwardian fan of dyed, blue ostrich feathers with dark tortoiseshell sticks, 1900–10.*

Bottom left *Black Chantilly lace piece for a fan made by Gluys-Brougheel, c 1900.*

Austrian countess or an Italian actress, the chances are that she would be carrying a Duvelleroy fan, or one made of Brussels lace or ostrich feathers, which she used wherever she happened to be. This explains why Parisian objects turn up in house sales in Scotland, and why English shawls, hats or fans may be found in all corners of Europe.

By the end of the Edwardian era, the splendours of evening fans were on the decline. The dress styles of the 1920s were so skimpy and slight that a huge half-circle of ostrich feathers looked quite out of keeping. Evening fans were still made, but usually as a decorative fashion accessory, without much real regard to their function. Feathers were used, but for an abbreviated evening fan that consisted of a single, wide stick, with a handful of feathers in a simple, long shape. Sometimes five feathers were set in a slightly larger-than-quarter-circle, still dyed in beautiful hues to match the silk or chiffon of a dress. Smaller silk or lace fans of this period are found with a hinge in the stick, so that the leaf could be folded over the sticks, and the

Centre *A circular paper fan, Paris, 1930s; a most popular oriental style that often figures in early fashion plate illustrations – the colouring and design are typically Art Deco.*

whole tucked into a small beaded evening bag. The sticks at this time might have been made from synthetics, or bone carved in imitation of ivory. In general, the grand evening fan was disappearing from use.

In compensation, the first two decades of this century saw the continuation of a delightful late-Victorian habit, which was the use of the fan for promotional or advertising ventures. These are still in plentiful supply, and can be found in junk shops or flea markets all over Europe and in America too, whence some of the prettiest examples come. Big stores or restaurants would have small fans made of paper printed with their name and decorated with some lively Art Nouveau or, later, Art Deco scene and lettering, and these would be offered as gifts or souvenirs. Some were produced to take advantage of a dramatic or newsworthy event – Blériot crossing the Channel, for instance, or a royal wedding. A typical example was produced as late as 1937 by the brandy company Amer Picon, inscribed with the words, '*La Marque Centenaire 1837–1937*', and showing a pretty Art Deco

Advertising or give-away Art Deco paper fans, very popular in the 1920s and 1930s, and very collectable.

Designs for fans for Paquin by George Barbier and Paul Iribe. Costumes Parisiens *1912.*

scene taken from a sketch by George Scott in 1936. The later 1930s examples are distinguishable by their unusual shape: they rise to a point at the centre, so that when the fan is folded it produces a zig-zag edge, which is often accentuated by a gold line or other decorative border running along the outer edge of the leaf.

Two fan experts, Mr Martin Willcocks and Mrs Everna Zabell, are currently working on a catalogue of the various types of advertising fan, and have so far unearthed over 150 types. The range of styles is endless: scent manufacturers, for example, would have them made with scented wood sticks, or would give away a fan together with a small bottle of scent in a decorative box. Some other examples are of value for the documentary evidence they offer of times gone by: Nancy Armstrong, in *The Book of Fans*, describes one that shows Piccadilly Circus with the Piccadilly Hotel occupying the entire site of what became the big store Swan & Edgar (itself now closed). Such fans are often sold in lots, because they are fragile and deteriorate rapidly. But for one that is torn or frayed the collector can acquire three others in good condition, each one of which will appreciate in value and add up to a worthwhile investment, in terms of both pleasure and finance.

An alternative field for a new collector which offers even greater scope for a low investment is that of modern Oriental fans. The term is used generally here to cover all forms of local, traditional fan making in the Far East, not specifically the work of Japan or China, which in centuries gone by reached great heights of beauty and refinement. In past centuries, all over the East, fans were made from cotton, silk or velvet, and decorated with elaborate designs of spangles, embroidery or gold and silver wiring, but now these are hard to find, and only simpler, mass-produced examples are to be obtained. But the new collector can find some charming examples of everyday fans, still in use locally, and made from simple, easily available materials such as grasses, palm leaves, hide or paper. Many fans have symbolic or religious significance, such as those used in temples in India and Burma. Indian fans tend to be of rigid shapes, made from palm or reeds, densely woven. These fans have integral handles, often woven into the leaf of the fan with fine craftsmanship. They can often be acquired by the traveller for the equivalent of pence or cents, and, considering the beauty of their design and the authenticity of their making, they constitute a fascinating investment in disappearing culture.

Other good examples well worth acquiring are the Indonesian buffalo-hide fans, which are found either in rigid shapes or in the *brisé* style – the name given to fans that have several sections or sticks instead of a leaf, threaded together to form the half-circle with a ribbon or string running through each one. The buffalo-hide is slightly transparent, and has a mottled, creamy appearance. The sections or sticks are pierced with the most elaborate traditional designs, and then covered with gold leaf. Indonesia also produces the loveliest fans with batik fabric leaves, mounted on to wooden or ivory sticks. In India, Indonesia, Malaya and Ceylon, *brisé* fans are also made out of sandalwood. The most ornately decorated of these have finely carved handles and are known as 'processional fans'. Simpler

A magnificent feather fan
carried with a Molyneux dress
in the 1920s.

versions can be found where the sticks are delicately pierced; the delicate perfume of the wood and the fretwork-like piercings give these fans great charm.

The last and most beautiful type of Eastern fan, which is now a little more difficult to acquire, is the Indian ivory fan: outstanding examples were made in the nineteenth century or earlier where the material is carved to such perfection that it really appears to be a rigid form of lace. There was also a large industry making sticks and guards of ivory, for shipment to fan makers in Europe, where the lace or satin would be applied to them. Sometimes auction sales sell lots including such sets of sticks; without doubt, these too will in the future be of some value.

Few traditional paper fans emerge from Japan nowadays, but the traveller can acquire some very attractive modern advertising fans there, in both folding and rigid styles, with pretty bamboo handles. The quality of design is still as pleasing as ever, although coming nowhere near the standards of the classical fans made two hundred years ago and exported all over Europe. Another type of advertising or souvenir fan is made from white plastic, in imitation of the old ivory designs; though once again the designs are cruder in execution, these little *brisé* fans have interest and should be preserved. It will not always be the case that an attempt is made to emulate the beautiful objects of past traditions and place them in a modern context. The souvenir fan is a humble object but is nevertheless a link with a finer past.

The collector may be dubious about the ease with which such curiosities can be acquired, but it is interesting to see how long-established collectors have the knack of falling upon treasures. Fan collectors in both England and America have the great advantage of a well established collector's organization, the Fan Circle, which regularly publishes a newsletter with articles of

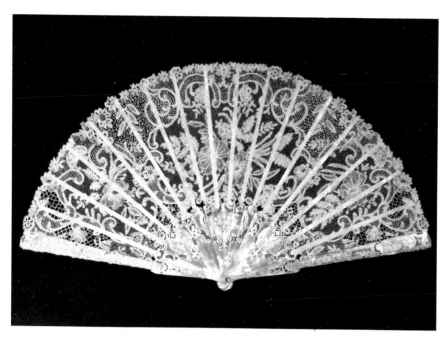

An Edwardian fan with carved, pierced and gilded sticks covered with Honiton lace.

such thoroughness and erudition that the reader is left in no doubt about the standards and aspirations of the Circle's members. As in other specialist areas, the books written on fans come down to a handful of valuable titles (all listed in the Bibliography). However, the information available on modern fans is patchy, because keen fan collectors tend to prefer earlier periods. There are individuals on both sides of the Atlantic with impressive collections of, say, advertising fans, or Oriental fans, but the new collector has to proceed by trial and error with only outlines of information as a guide.

A last word about the acquisition of modern fans. It has already been mentioned that advertising fans in particular can be purchased in a variety of places, from flea markets to auction rooms; and Oriental fans can be bought on travels. But the collector will find that, once he or she is established within the field, other collectors may be interested in buying, selling or exchanging various types of fan, thus affording another venue for acquisitions. Earlier Edwardian evening fans of the kinds described here are most commonly purchased through the sale room; the prices vary tremendously. Good authorities all agree that luck plays a great part in successful bidding. Prices fluctuate in an enticing fashion, allowing the beginner the realization that it is certainly possible to obtain favourite styles without inordinate expense. However, it does seem that once bitten by an enthusiasm such as fan collecting, personal sacrifices are often made by the devoted without any reaction beyond a self-satisfied smile.

BUTTONS

Although purists in the button-collecting field might be disparaging about twentieth-century buttons (in fact several specialist books on this subject end with the Victorian era), modern buttons offer tremendous scope for the collector, and have great charm besides considerable originality. It is easy to see why there is a great divide between the nineteenth and twentieth centuries for the collector, because most earlier buttons were either hand-made or produced at such a high standard of workmanship (such as the cut-steel buttons of the English Midlands) that, by comparison, twentieth-century efforts look crude. But, on the other hand, modern buttons are much more varied, and reflect social history in a more direct way. They have humour, and a brightness of colour and design that was not acceptable before.

Top right French glass cameo button decorated with flowers. The fine lacy look helps to place them. c 1900.

Right, clockwise *Cut silver button with enamel painted flower: Edwardian emaux peints. Art Nouveau painted porcelain dress button. Solid-cut abalone button, probably for an overcoat or cape, 1920s. Cloth-covered buttons with painted leaves and ribbon embroidery – possibly made to match a specific fabric. c 1910.*

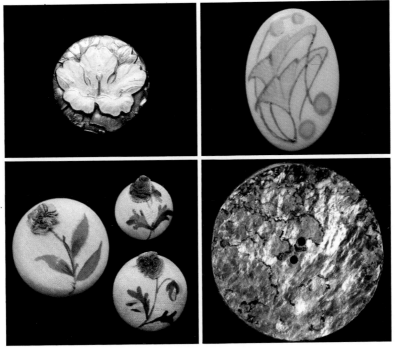

Below *Painted enamel buttons, Edwardian in motif.*

At the turn of the century, buttons were still being made in the patterns that were popular with the Victorians. Edwardian dress called for an extensive use of buttons, all the way down the front of tight-fitting jackets and bodices, and also on outdoor wear. There were two main types of button in the first decade: cut metal with coloured enamel decoration, and cloth or crochet ones, often home-made to match a particular outfit.

Looking at the metal ones first, we find that these employed all the various styles of enamelling that can also be found on jewellery of the period. In *champlevé*, the metal is carved or stamped to make hollows in the surface, and these are then filled with enamel. For instance, a trellis effect might be carved into the metal, and pools of blue or pink might form the flowerheads of the design. *Cloisonné* buttons are found, where thin wire is soldered on to a plain base, and the divisions thus formed are filled with different coloured enamels and fired. *Émaux peints* are further examples where various colours of enamels are laid one on top of the other and painted to look like oriental enamel work. *Plique à jour* is a fourth style, somewhat similar to *cloisonné* in that wire is used to make *cloisons*, or wells, for the enamel, but there is no base plate, so that the final effect is like stained glass.

These Edwardian metal buttons are mostly found with floral motifs, or with swags, wreaths and semi-classical forms, rather baroque in flavour. Not surprisingly, these match the favourite fabrics of the period, when sprigs of flowers, classical wreaths, spots, stripes and lace decoration on sleeves and necklines were popular. The influence of Art Nouveau is often to be seen in Edwardian buttons. The movement gained a great hold in Europe, and was best translated in England through the work of Voysey, Butterfield and Napper in fabrics and William Morris in furnishings and wallpaper. It led to button designs with a flowing, naturalistic feeling rather different from the classical designs of the 1880s and 1890s, which were more formal and Roman in inspiration.

The second type of Edwardian button is a little more difficult to find, because it is made of fabric or crochet work to match a specific dress, and many have either disintegrated with bad storage or discoloured with age. Pretty examples can be found, however, where satin fabric is stretched and stitched over a wooden or metal base, and then hand-painted with a motif to match the rest of the outfit. Sometimes, little seed pearls are hand-stitched on to a small leaf or floral design to represent buds or stamens. Barbola work is also commonly found: little mounds of narrow ribbon are twisted round to represent a flower rosette, again decorated with seed pearls. Crochet buttons are beautifully made, the delicacy and minuteness of the stitches giving a pleasing, textured effect. Mother-of-pearl, abalone and other shell buttons were also popular, especially because they looked very attractive with lace, a high-fashion fabric at the time. Sometimes these buttons will have plain, polished faces and a rim of silver or metal in a filigree design.

The 1910s and 1920s were a period of decline for buttons, because clothing became more draped and sashed, and button closures went out of fashion. Only in sportswear and outdoor wear did they remain useful, and it is possible to find some fairly plain, utilitarian buttons made of wood or gilt.

Of course, military buttons also in gilt were produced in large quantity during the war period, and form a separate possibility for a collector. A particular trade in 'woodbacks' – a wooden-based button with a thin metal veneer – grew up at this time. These were exported to the USA in great numbers.

During the 1920s and 1930s, button manufacturers began to experiment with synthetic materials, partly owing to the rising costs of natural materials, such as shell, and metals, such as silver and brass. Casein was one of the first of these; it was discovered in 1903, but did not enter serious production until after the First World War. The firm of Internationale Galalith Gesellschaft in Hamburg produced significant quantities of casein buttons, both from the sheet (stamping out round buttons from a large flat area) and by making round bobble shapes from rod casein. These buttons give the first indication of changes in machining and mass-production techniques, which really came into their own in the 1930s. A second synthetic which enjoyed ever greater popularity was celluloid. It was invented as early as 1869 by John W. Hyatt of New Jersey, and at first was welcomed as a substitute for ivory, having a thick, creamy colour. Early celluloid buttons sometimes have a metal trim or paste diamonds set into the top, copying the styles that had been used in the Victorian era for true ivory. Some are carved in imitation of eighteenth-century rococo designs, while another type has a hollowed-out, turned dome, with a metal plate at the back and a shank cut through the celluloid. However, the major drawback with celluloid buttons was that they were highly inflammable, and eventually they were banned in both Europe and the USA.

A third type of synthetic which made a pretty button was artificial resin, or plexiglass; tiny pieces of metal are often set into the liquid mixture to produce a square or round button with a glittery transparency. This substance is often described in books or on original shop stock lists as 'aeroplane glass', because it was used in the early days of aviation to make shatterproof windows. Its transparency also lent itself to another design variation, where a pattern would be stamped on to the reverse side of the button, to show through from the base as one looked at the button head.

A similar technique is found in glass button making, where a pattern is stamped or etched into the back of the button, and the top polished smooth. Sometimes glass would be moulded or pressed into a slight convex shape, and the underside painted with flowers or leaves, giving a shiny, distant effect to the design. The problem with glass buttons, if they are not carefully made, is that the thread used to attach them to the garment rubs and frays on the edges of the shank holes. For this reason, the collector will be lucky to find a complete set that has not lost its shine, or had too much of the painted decoration chipped or washed away.

A large number of 1930s glass buttons were made in Bohemia or Czechoslovakia, and from there they were exported all over Europe and to the USA. It is interesting to see that many Parisian couturiers would place special orders with firms as far away as this, in order to enjoy their expertise and workmanship. (Madge Garland, then a leading fashion journalist, once scooped the press by revealing the source in Bohemia for some of Chanel's

Top: *A large celluloid coat button, typical of 1920s designs, and* **below** *celluloid dress button, late 1920s.*

Experiments in the 1920s and 1930s produced buttons made in a wide variety of materials, such as this button made of plexiglass, or artificial resin.

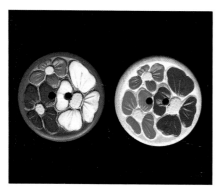

Top *Plexiglass or 'aeroplane' glass buttons – the smaller design has a cut base to create the flower pattern, and* **bottom** *Austrian painted wooden buttons, c 1935.*

Far right & above *Czechoslovakian glass buttons were a major industry, and supplied many Paris designers in the 1930s.*

famous 'junk' jewellery.) Czechoslovakia also manufactured some pretty wooden buttons to fasten the tweeds, checks and big wrap-round coats of the 1930s. They are often as much as two or three inches in diameter, but would be worn only one or two at a time.

Schiaparelli delighted in buttons, and had them specially created for her model clothes. She used buttons of every type but the normal small round ones; a particularly beautiful lovat green suit for her March 1938 collection had four huge, square buttons set on the front. She made buttons in the shapes of fruit, flowers and animals – and even used mirrors. Her originality sparked off a whole style of button-making in the 1930s, the results being known as 'realistics'. Bunches of fruit, little baskets of flowers, bowls of cherries, pieces of furniture, faces, plates of food, breads, musical instruments – almost anything that could be depicted was turned into a button for novelty's sake in the 1930s. Children benefited enormously – characters like Mickey Mouse and Betty Boop were miniaturized in plastic. One of the best known of the American designers of realistics was Marion Weeber, who worked for B. Blumenthal and Company in the USA, and who produced a series of sets called 'The Vegetable and its Blossom' and some nut and shell shapes called 'The Nutcracker Suite'. As might be expected, this craze for realistics also gained in popularity during the Second World War, with 'Patriotics' – cards of buttons in suitable designs, such as flags, stars, eagles, anchors, chevrons, V for Victory, and so on. (The cards, if you can find them intact, have a value of their own – they often bore inscriptions or colours to encourage the war effort.) By the 1940s, the materials used for

these cheap buttons were endless in their variety: plastic, glass, china, metal, celluloid, leather, wood, pressed sawdust, straw, cloth and cork are commonly found. The plastics dating from this time are just as legion, being produced from waste materials and substances like skimmed milk, cornstalks, coffee beans, nutshells and so on. At first button cards would specify the plastic, but this soon stopped and collectors now tend to lump all plastics together. It can be quite difficult to see the difference between some plastics, especially if they are coloured, or have altered with age: polystyrene buttons tend to go yellow.

After the war, wooden buttons came back into popularity for a while, mainly due to the scarcity of other substances. Turned, carved, inlaid, veneered or painted wood buttons from the late 1940s are well worth collecting. Some of the best known names in the field are the firm of Rademacher, who manufactured wooden buttons for a Berlin distributor called Adolf Gans; and Alfred Schweitzer, another Berlin wholesaler who supplied buttons all over Europe. Schweitzer also specialized in types made from rare or unusual woods, such as thuja tree roots, macassa wood and ebony. Gans is known to have used coconut shell that he acquired from a chocolate factory in Berlin. The Irish too specialized in wood: a William Griffiths of Dublin displayed bog-oak buttons as early as 1851 at the Great Exhibition, and his styles continue in manufacture to this day. They are particularly suitable for the hand-knitted garments of Aran and elsewhere in Ireland.

A final category of button which the collector can consider is the 'studio' button. This style became popular in the 1930s, but the ardent pursuer can find many beautiful examples up to the present day, and could build a very satisfactory collection on this topic alone. Studio buttons are what they suggest: the output of an individual craftsman in small numbers. Many were made in the Art Deco period of the 1930s in London, New York and Paris, in metal and enamel work, and also in ceramics with a glaze. Carved wooden buttons are also found in this category, and are very popular with craft studios today.

It is virtually impossible to describe the infinite variety of button manufacture in the twentieth century – this survey at least reveals the enormous variety of materials, and the different styles that can be found, from glittery evening buttons to rustic wood for chunky cardigans and cheap plastics for a child's organdie party dress. In the 1950s, however, buttons began to be manufactured along simpler, mass-production lines, and this variety declined. The improvements in machinery have enabled button manufacturers to produce the same design of button in a host of carefully measured sizes, and a range of colours. The wide use of the zip fastener has seriously reduced the importance of the button as a fashion accessory. Buttons are now required for utilitarian, mass-produced ready-to-wear, such as school cardigans or men's suits and shirts, and little else.

The field for the collector still offers immense potential, and prices are not at all overbearing. It is possible to find even good-quality 1930s buttons in junk boxes and sales all over England the the USA. Some of the prettiest examples are found at the flea market in Paris, so long the centre of fashion and its allied trades, for old stocks in warehouses are still coming to light. The problem for the collector is that it is difficult to be precise about dating buttons, except through experience in handling them, because the styles and materials overlapped each other. Even the backs of buttons, which in earlier periods can provide a reasonable guide, are not always reliable – for instance, loop shanks with a small round plate, attached to the back of a glass button, were used throughout the nineteenth and twentieth centuries. Some styles were adopted for shorter periods, however, among them the practice of cutting into a metal back-plate and lifting up a small arched or

Centre *Buttons still intact on their original cards are sometimes worth more than those sold loose; but beware, some dealers re-stitch buttons on to old cards, so check the threads before paying out a significant sum.*

Hardy Amies used plastic buttons, carved in imitation of men's leather Burberry buttons for this herringbone tweed suit, 1948.

triangular piece as a shank. This usually indicates a cheaper button, made after the Second World War – cheap, and unsatisfactory too, because the thread would undoubtedly fray against such a crudely created shank. The collector should, however, learn the different styles of loops and shanks since they act as a further means of identification and help to build up a 'feel' for the subject (Primrose Peacock's little handbook on buttons, listed in the Bibliography, can be recommended for this).

Methods of displaying a button collection vary enormously. The simplest way is to mount the buttons on cards with a ribbon or a stitch in wool thread, and encase each card or sheet in a plastic case. The pages can then be clipped into a large, loose-leaf folder. The only disadvantage of this system is that the button heads may rub against the cover and lose some gilt or enamel. A splendid way to house a small collection is to use one of those Victorian specimen boxes, which have a lot of small compartments. Ornate variations can be found with glass lids, and some are in the form of a cabinet, with drawers. It would not be at all difficult to design or build a small specimen case of this type oneself. It is important to remember that, if you acquire buttons mounted on the original card, this too has a value: a complete set should preferably not be divided from its original card, which adds to its historical and documentary worth.

The aspiring button collector is luckier than those starting out in other areas of fashion. The basic material is in fair supply, and a number of specialist shops and books already exist to help – although the collector will soon find buttons which are not described in the books as such, but are definitely from a particular period. In compensation, button collection does not require a special skill, such as those needed for mending lace or repairing fans, and calls for considerably less financial outlay. The most expensive buttons in the whole span would probably be early Edwardian silver or enamel, and a set of six of these might fetch as much as £50 or so at a sale. But small sets of delightful Art Deco buttons from the 1930s can be bought from reputable dealers for a few pounds; and there is little doubt that, as the button declines further in use and quality, a beautiful collection from the early twentieth century will increase significantly in value over the next few decades.

COSTUME JEWELLERY

Twentieth-century jewellery is one of the most accessible and adventurous areas for the collector, particularly if he or she concentrates on costume jewellery and semi-precious substances only. I have excluded precious stones from this survey because the prices are already so high that a novice collector would be unrealistic to think of embarking on an attempt to collect them: fine styles such as Art Nouveau, or good-quality pieces of Art Deco, can change hands for several hundreds of pounds, and involve problems of expert identification and insurance which are outside the field of collecting fashion as discussed in this book.

This chapter looks at the main types of costume and semi-precious jewellery to be found in Europe and America and suggests various themes for a collection. None of the types of jewellery discussed would call for an expenditure in excess of £100, and on many occasions a pretty example can be acquired for only a few pounds. Unlike other areas of collecting fashion, jewellery can be stored in a limited amount of space, and once cleaned up in the ways suggested in this chapter, will provide a source of pleasure that does not deteriorate with the passing of time.

Certain types of jewellery reflect the style of dress fashions in a particular era, which gives some help to the collector in deciding how to date a piece. In the first decade of the century, Art Nouveau styles reached the height of popularity, obviously because the sinuous, twisting forms of the brooches and ear pendants suited the ultra-feminine styles of dress, the laces and bows and satins of the time. Although the finest Art Nouveau pieces set with precious stones, for example the work of the Frenchman René Lalique, can cost hundreds at auction, the shapes were imitated in cheaper metals and mass-produced so that very attractive samples can be found inexpensively. Art Nouveau styles span the period from 1890 to 1910. In England the style was taken up as a development from the Arts and Crafts Movement, a reaction against increasing mechanization and a desire to return to hand-crafted principles in design. This produced a range of studio jewellery which is expensive, but which had its influence on the designs of the mass manufacturers. A collection that illustrated the shapes and subjects of these

The epitome of Art Nouveau: an advertisement for La Maison Moderne, *a Parisian treasure house for jewellery and objects for the home.*

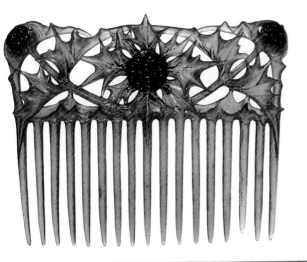

Left *Pretty tortoiseshell hair comb, designed by Frenchman, Lucien Gaillard, and demonstrating how natural forms were stylised into Art Nouveau shapes.*

Romantic Art Nouveau jewellery set with semi-precious stones, designed by Sybil Dunlop.

A hair comb made by Georg Jensen of Copenhagen.

French and American 1920s powder compacts with enamel lids – the user had to grate the face powder before applying it.

153

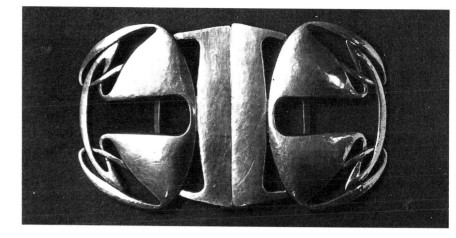

A 1930s Liberty silver buckle.

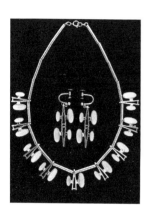

Another Scandinavian design, necklace and earrings in enamel on silver, 1950.

movements would have some narrative structure, besides providing the collector with a fine sense of the differences inherent in pieces made in various countries. French Art Nouveau is very different from English, while some of the most distinctive examples I have seen emanate from Barcelona, in Spain. Art Nouveau was such a popular design trend in Spain, large quantities of artefacts – jewellery, glass, china – were brought into the country for sale to wealthy Spaniards. Tourists to the country should keep an eye open for cheap acquisitions. Old costume jewellery was made in such quantity that the collector can enjoy a wide range of choice in building up a worthwhile collection, and has the scope to develop a fine sense of discrimination.

Some of the cheaper examples of Art Nouveau do not incorporate gemstones, but are made in enamel, an ancient technique much favoured by the new designers, and especially René Lalique. There are various techniques for enamelling, which the collector can easily identify. (These are also mentioned in my chapter on Buttons, where much the same design developments as for costume jewellery can be seen. A comparative collection of buttons and jewellery would be well worth the effort to assemble.) The first of these techniques is *cloisonné*, in which thin strips of metal are soldered on to a base and the different colours of the enamels poured into the separate compartments so formed. *Champlevé*, by contrast, is created by carving out areas on the surface of the metal (frequently silver or cheaper metal alloys) and filling in these 'pits' with enamelled colour. Enamel colours are alternatively painted on to the surface of the piece, often at successively lower temperatures, so that a layered range of colours can be built up without the colours running into each other. Enamelling in any of these techniques was used widely for the manufacture of brooches and belt buckles; the high-necked blouses and tight-waisted, full-length skirts of the time called for adornment at the midriff, neck and ears.

The Victorian delight in colourless gemstones persisted into the Edwardian era. Soft, creamy colours, combined with piled-up coiffures and big picture hats, produced a style of dressing which was as romantic as it was impractical. The jewellery of the era has a peculiar period charm, not as heavy and ornate as Victorian pieces, and smaller in scale. Bar pins, droplet earrings, and frankly sentimental designs such as hearts, little flowers, stars and floral sprays were the most typical motifs of the time, alongside the more abstract versions of natural forms typifying Art Nouveau – the stylized fern and curving leaf shapes – and copies of medieval pieces which were popular with the Arts and Crafts design designers. Celtic motifs appear frequently in Art Nouveau brooches or buckles, twisting tendrils twining round a central semi-precious stone such as an agate or moonstone. Belt buckles like this were made for Liberty's, the Regent Street store which was the home of the Art Nouveau and Arts and Crafts design; cheaper versions of designs following the principles of the Arts and Crafts ideal were marketed here under the name of 'Cymric', first appearing in 1899. The original pieces in this range were made by Archibald Knox, and it was he who inspired the so-called 'Celtic revival' which took place in the Edwardian era, and the influences of which can be seen widely even in imitations of Liberty pieces. Vivienne Becker's excellent survey, *Victorian and 20th Century Jewellery*, observes:

> Marked Liberty jewels have that extra attraction, partly because the designs were very good, and partly because of the close association of the name with Art Nouveau. Murrle, Bennett & Company holds the fascination of the strong, German modernistic style . . . and Charles Horner pieces, interesting because he was the original totally-commercial manufacturer, are easier to appreciate, and make a very good starting point in many cases.

The moonstone was one of the favourite stones of the Edwardian jewellers, its watery, milky colour being uniquely suited to mounting in silver, and its subtlety allowing for the intricate tracery and twining shapes for the foils which the jewellers wished to create. Moonstones cannot be imitated successfully: opaque glass, quartz or chalcedony are substituted at times, but never with the same effect. At the turn of the century, rings set with a single round moonstone were very popular and can still be found.

Opals were as commonly sold, perhaps because mining in Australia released a fair supply on to the market in the Edwardian era, and prices were low. The principal types are black opal – not discovered until 1905 in the vast Lightning Ridge Black Opal field in New South Wales, and so helpful for the dating of a piece as Victorian or Edwardian; white opal, the name explaining itself; water opal, which is paler in background colour, with flashes of yellow, green or red, and fire opal, which has less flashing quality, but a more pronounced flame or orange tint than the other types. Lillian Baker's fine guide *Old Costume Jewellery* provides the following comment on its identification: 'Often effectively imitated by glass or Bakelite. . . . When the stone (in its setting, if necessary) is immersed in a clear container of carbon tetrachloride, the outline of the stone and its facets are barely visible. Imitations of glass or plastic show quite distinct outlines when subjected to the same test.' (Miss Baker's book is highly recommended for the collector, as it is the only comprehensive book specializing in this field.) Also, very usefully, Miss Baker recommends that as opals are so easily chipped, and actually contain water, they should be stored separately from other jewellery, in a cool place, and bathed several times a year in a glycerin and water bath to prevent them from drying out. For the same reason, opals should not come into contact with strong liquids as they may pick up a stain.

Another gemstone popular in the 1900s was the garnet: the deep blood-red stone was especially favoured in the rose-cut forms made by Bohemian jewellers. These are usually set with closed backs for rings or brooches. Sometimes small pieces of cardboard were inserted in the back of

Good-quality costume pearls, the most popular jewellery of the 1950s.

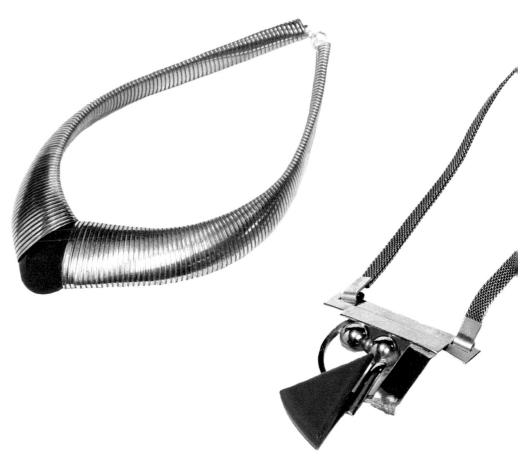

Typical Art Deco jewellery in chrome and plastic.

Far right *Synthetics were used to wonderful effect when they first appeared: a plastic and chrome necklace from the 1920s.*

A good example of the vogue for 'Egyptian' jewellery in the 1920s: a scarab pendant, made in glass by Gabriel Argy-Rousseau.

the setting to create an impression of a bigger stone, and with immersion in water this can of course disintegrate and the stone may fall out – so care must be taken to wash only the surface of Bohemian garnet jewellery with a brush and a little soapy water, and then to dry the piece quickly with a soft cloth.

Interest in less familiar and ostentatious stones was helped by the discovery in 1922 of Tutankhamun's tomb in Egypt. The extraordinary beauty of the head-dresses and collars, combining dully shining metals with brilliantly deep coloured substances such as lapis lazuli, turquoise and cornelian, opened up new possibilities to modern designers. The blues especially could be imitated in enamel work, and some fine pieces were made in the 1920s using the *plique à jour* technique, which is similar to *cloisonné* except that there is no base plate, and the finished effect resembles a stained-glass window, with colours in separate compartments linked by a metal structure. The collector can identify this 'Egyptian' jewellery by the distinctive motifs – lilies, scarabs, and small birds, with geometric linking metal chains or foils. Significantly, some of the best pieces were made in France or Germany. I have also seen several fine pieces in collector's shops in Spain. All manner of pieces were made, from collars to earrings, belt buckles, and small charms for bracelets – a popular style for this last being the 'Moses basket', a small casket with a hinged lid and a metal baby inside. Scarab rings were made in abundance, and, of course, tiny mummy cases, also hinged to reveal the body inside. There are still sufficient examples of this style available for the collector to begin by specializing in it.

The first two decades of the century were also a time for experimentation with much cheaper materials for costume jewellery. As with buttons, celluloid was one of the first of these cheaper substances to be used. Celluloid items are still to be found in enormous quantity. An Englishman is

156

credited with the first actual plastic, a cellulose nitrate, as early as 1855. In the following decade, he set up an enterprise, the Parkesine Company, to produce a large number of jewellery pieces and hair-combs in imitation of a wide variety of substances including horn, tortoiseshell, ivory, amber and malachite. His firm was taken over by Daniel Spill, who added to this list by creating a very attractive synthetic version of coral for jewellery. In America, a Belgian immigrant devised in 1909 another well known synthetic, Bakelite, which became widely used for jewellery and button-making. A number of other synthetics followed over the next twenty years, some of them based on casein – a resinous substance discovered in Germany and produced in England from 1919 – with such derivative names as 'Erinoid', 'Keronyx' and 'Lactoid'. In America, jewellery was made from 'Gemstone Marblette', 'Opalon' and 'Prystal'.

In the 1920s and 1930s, plastics came to be seen also as a substance in their own right, not only as an imitation of another material. Designers in Paris helped to bring about this change in values. Schiaparelli, with her fascination for new fabrics, such as cellophane or man-made fibres, also created some splendid Art Deco pieces in the mid-1930s. Evening purses in clear plastic, collars in imitation of African tribal decoration (much favoured at the time in French café society) and the jazzy effect of plastic with glittering paste stones seemed to reflect the new bright chic which had little to do with inherited emeralds or diamond tiaras. Chanel also made it

1920s and 1930s necklaces, also in paste, chrome and plastic – on a Lorenzl statuette of the same time.

A set of belt, bracelet and clip in 'Crystal Bakelite' from Asprey's, worn with a typical 1930s dress (1937).

acceptable to wear frankly fake costume jewellery – bright swags of multi-coloured beads sometimes exploited their very synthetic nature by matching the colours with the fabric of the dress. Much of Chanel's costume jewellery, or 'Illusion Jewellery' as it was first called, was made by Comte Etienne de Beaumont. The brightly coloured stones Chanel popularized were made of glass by the traditional glass-workers of Czechoslovakia. This style developed to the point that women liked to wear real jewellery as casually as they did fake – there seemed little difference in effect between the two. In *The Indecisive Decade* Madge Garland describes a classical 1930s beauty, dressed by Chanel in the new manner: 'Alicia Nikitina, the great ballerina then dancing in Auric's *Les Biches*, wore Marie Laurencin's poetic chiffons on the stage at night, but by day was dressed by Chanel in a sober navy-blue suit which was a mere background to a constellation of immense diamond and ruby bracelets, clips and rings.' Similar designs were made in inexpensive, semi-precious stones by Mauboussin, using aquamarines, turquoises or topazes. He made some pretty strands of beads with tasselled ends which were instantly popular. Platinum now came into favour as a suitable foil for these less brilliant stones, where previously its dull shine was thought suitable only for button manufacture. Cartier of Paris found a way to make platinum into very fine wire, which set off the character of these large, cheaper stones – a totally new style of decoration in comparison with the ornate silver or gold settings and small clustered gemstones of previous decades.

While semi-precious stones were being used in this original way, the new plastics also led to a completely new range of ideas in the 1920s and 1930s for decorative accessories. Copies of other materials still proliferated – the tortoiseshell, amber and bone as mentioned earlier – and the use of plastics enabled designers to create fanciful designs too difficult to attempt in rarer substances. If a mistake was made, there was no great loss in scrapping the idea and starting again. So plastic brooches can be found imitating carved ivory, in the shapes of bunches of flowers, animal or human heads; or combined with other materials such as base metals or wood, to make fantastical copies of boats, bowls of fruit, lidded boxes, animals, and scores of other designs. As the Art Deco movement got under way, the synthetics designers began to create more abstract objects, with stripes of colours set into the typical Art Deco 'three-dimensional' forms – the sunray shapes, or

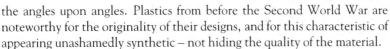

1930s plastic clasps and buckles: still widely available, and worth collecting before they disappear.

Top *Novelty animal shapes became popular in the 1950s – gold plastic winged horses, English.*

the angles upon angles. Plastics from before the Second World War are noteworthy for the originality of their designs, and for this characteristic of appearing unashamedly synthetic – not hiding the quality of the material.

A few simple tests can help the collector to establish the identity of these early plastics. Because there were so many different types, it is inaccurate to describe a piece simply as 'plastic' without some attempt to define its substance further. (I am indebted to Lillian Baker's book for this and other technical pieces of advice passed on in this chapter.) Bakelite, for instance, will not react in any way if touched with a drop of ether. A simple burning test will distinguish between a piece made from a resin, and a piece made from a synthetic plastic: a hot needle will melt resin, making a small hole, whereas the synthetic plastics char and burn slightly. The hot needle test also provides a useful clue to substance by smell: celluloid produces characteristic camphor fumes, whereas casein smells like burnt milk. Even simpler is the friction test: synthetic plastics are more inclined to become electrified; casein pieces are not. It is quite useful to know whether a piece is casein or another resin, as opposed to bakelite, because the former respond well to cleaning with baking soda, if there is grease and discolouring dirt on the surface. Celluloid is best cleaned with a creamy car wax.

Synthetics were frequently combined with glass or with crystal quartz to make some stunning evening clips or hat-brooches for evening caps. The cutting of glass, to give it a faceted surface and a brilliant shine, first came into vogue in the middle of the nineteenth century. 'Paste' jewellery remained popular from that time right up until the 1950s. In the modern era we associate it most perhaps with the 1930s and 1940s – possibly because it worked very well in black and white film, and played a major part in the glamorizing of such Hollywood stars as Marlene Dietrich and Jean Harlow, in their shimmery satins, black felt hats and rich furs. The illusion of the cinema enhanced the brightness of the glassy shine, and made it acceptable elegance for lesser mortals off the screen too. The collector might do well to concentrate on paste as a theme for a costume jewellery collection, beginning with the pretty floral sprays of the Edwardian era, the pendants and long necklaces of the 1920s, and the interesting combinations of plastics and glass in the 1930s. According to Irina Laski, who runs a shop in London specializing in Art Nouveau and Art Deco pieces, good-quality paste on silver can still be found, especially in Paris, and well designed pieces will sell for over £100. In the 1940s, glass 'stones' were gradually increased in size, so that they look even jazzier, not to say vulgar at times. Novelty pieces in the shapes of animals, umbrellas, musicians' heads and so on date from this time.

In a curious reversal, real jewellery was often designed to look fake: these parachutist earrings are made in gold, set with sapphires, diamonds and rubies. (1940s.)

"Meteor"...

starburst finds of
baguette rhinestones
showering from golden
Trifanium.
Necklace $20.00,
Cuff Bracelet $12.50,
Earrings $7.50,
Plus tax.

In the foreground of Fashion

Jewels by
TRIFARI

French necklace, mid-1920s, in paste, jade and silver.

Right *An advertisement for rhinestone jewellery by Trifari, with the necklace, earrings and hat all based on similar forms. American Vogue 1949.*

Far right *Balenciaga always favoured black – even in his accessory designs, like this jet collar, a popular substance in the 1950s (and expensive to collect today).*

Glass can be successfully distinguished from real gemstones because it lacks the refractive qualities of facet-cut gems, and frequently has tiny air bubbles in its interior which can be seen with the naked eye. Most gemstones when viewed through a magnifying glass have a double line of refraction, whereas glass has only one. Diamond is single-refracting, but obviously distinguishable because it is so much harder, and will cut glass.

Other substances used in costume jewellery for their brilliance and lack of colour are rhinestones, crystal, cut steel and marcasite. Rhinestones are a type of quartz, and originate, as one might expect, from around the Rhine in Germany. Crystal is another type of quartz, much used for some prettily faceted beads to make the long necklaces favoured in the 1920s and 1930s. It is harder than glass, and does not scratch or chip so easily. Whereas glass always feels warm to the touch, crystal beads have a cool, heavy feel. Confusingly, there is an imitation crystal made of glass and reflecting its origin in a slightly cheaper price: most coloured 'crystal beads' are more likely to be this glass type than true crystal quartz. Miss Baker also offers this interesting test for the difference between the two: ' . . . because most colored quartz crystal is dichroic (that is, the color of the stone varies depending upon the direction from which you view it) while glass crystal is not, you can frequently differentiate between the two by rotating the stone slowly and observing the color closely.'

Cheaper and less aesthetically pleasing pieces of work contain marcasite – especially the pendant earrings of the 1920s, and later, the clip-on evening earrings of the 1940s. Marcasite is made from iron pyrites, not from the mineral marcasite. The shine comes from the facet and polish of the surface, which will reflect any light that falls on it. Most twentieth-century examples will have the marcasites glued into place rather than set by hand individually. Cut steel is commonly found in later periods of the nineteenth century, when die-stamping came in: the early pieces somewhat resemble marcasite in effect, and the faceted surfaces can be very finely made. But later pieces look mass-produced. The collector may often find either type of

metal work surrounding an imitation cameo, or enamel-painted ceramic centrepiece.

An interesting sideline to glasswork was the black glass produced towards the end of the nineteenth century, when mourning jewellery was so popular. 'French jet', as it was called, was made in designs imitating the true and magnificent Whitby jet of the 1870s. Whitby, a small seaside town in the north of England, specialized in this work, which was exported widely to the United States and Europe. It fetches very high prices in the antique jewellery market, whereas 'French jet' is comparatively cheap. Lockets, bracelets and pendants, possibly set with paste in the form of an initial, or with little pearls, were popular made of jet and imitated in glass. Predictably, these forms experienced a resurgence at the times of both World Wars, and the cheaper types can still be acquired easily. Many American examples incorporate patriotic motifs, such as eagles or flags. The Whitby examples are distinguished by their fineness and elaborate nature of the cutting: some pieces look almost like a shiny black ivory, with fruit, flower, petal and animal shapes made in the most delicate of designs. The difference between the two can be seen in the quality of the faceting, and a simple test is that glass will scratch jet, while jet being softer will not leave a mark on glass. Good quality pieces already fetch hundreds of pounds or dollars and are probably beyond the reach of the modern collector, but black glass 'jet' is most attractive and well worth seeking out. The black beads are often strung with clear paste or crystal, and the combination of colouring and the unusual shapes of the glass lead to some fascinating pieces.

True jet was also used by the finer designers, who worked with gemstones to create some new, modernistic designs, in contrast to the Art Nouveau and naturalistic trends of the earlier part of the century. Modernist jewellery is distinguished by its abstract motifs, clarity of shape and brilliance of execution. Among leading modernist jewellers are Georges Fouquet, who gave up working in Art Nouveau styles in favour of the new look; his son, Jean Fouquet, Jean Després, Gerard Sandoz, and Raymond Templier. A

Left Typical 1950s naturalistic designs for costume jewellery – flower clusters, leaves and fruits were often used.

Above & centre Superb Art Deco cigarette cases designed by Raymond Templier, 1930s.

Brigitte Helm, a film star of the 1920s, wearing a stunning set of Templier jewels.

study of the work of these artists can help the collector to develop a sensitivity to its quality, and a useful talent for picking out good copies, for their own products are probably well outside the financial range of the new collector. Strangely, Art Deco jewellery is rarer and more prized than Art Nouveau, according to dealers. England and France are both good sources of objects, though the latter tends to be more expensive as a supply centre. Many German collectors come to London to buy pieces which may originally have emanated from their own country, because prices are lower. A warning for Art Nouveau enthusiasts: there is a substantial trade in reproductions, which the inexperienced can easily mistake for the genuine article. It is essential to look at as many good examples in museum collections as possible, to train the eye.

In New York, Tiffany, Cartier, and Van Cleef & Arpels can provide a source of inspiration. A collector would do well to find examples of jewellers' work in contemporary magazines, in photographs or old catalogues, and use them as links in a collection made up of cheaper copies. Such visual comparisons add immeasurably to the historical value of the enterprise. Once the collector starts looking, it is surprising how many sources can be found: old biographies, newspapers, fashion magazines, postcards from art gallery exhibitions of contemporary portraiture or books on design theory for any of the periods mentioned in this chapter. The joy of collecting old costume jewellery lies in its abundance, its comparative cheapness, and the variety of the designs to be found.

An advertisement for Van Cleef & Arpels, Gazette du Bon Ton, *March 1920.*

Great names in jewellery in the 1930s: designs by Van Cleef & Arpels and Cartier illustrated in Vogue 1930.

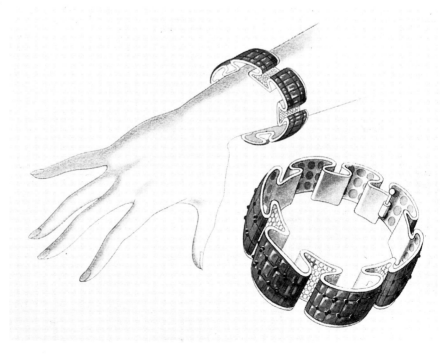

HATS

Hats are fairly difficult items to collect, chiefly because good-quality examples are hard to find. Unless it is immaculately preserved in a box, a hat will usually end up squashed out of shape or torn. The trimmings often fade because of bright sunlight in a way that even the gayest and lightest summer clothes resist. And up until the Second World War at least, a woman would often take apart an old hat to re-use the trimming on a new model.

In spite of these disadvantages, however, there are times when the collector is offered the possibility of a dress and hat together, and this enhances the value and interest of each. Alternatively, a hat may be so perfectly a reflection of its era, or of its original owner, that the collector cannot resist buying it. One of my favourite fashion arbiters has long been Mrs William 'Babe' Paley; her picture in *Vogue* or *Harper's Bazaar* or *Women's Wear Daily* always caught my eye because her taste in clothes was an enviable mixture of the elegant with the dramatic. Subsequently, I saw the massive Monet exhibition at the Hayward Gallery in London, and without hesitation picked on a wonderfully insouciant picture of a woman, dressed in black with a jaunty hat and lace veil, as my favourite of all the portraits in the gallery. And who owned it? The picture – not the hat! – was the property of 'Mrs. W. B. P.' – Babe Paley's taste at work again.

In London in 1980, Mrs Doris Langley Moore, the finest fashion collector in the country, sold her hat collection through Christie's South Kensington; this résumé of hat history will be in part a record of that sale, as a tribute to Mrs Langley Moore's great work as a collector (her dress collection forms the basis of the Museum of Costume at Bath). Although the figures will become meaningless with time, prices have been included because some interesting vagaries of the saleroom can be explored in this way.

At the turn of the century, hat fashions looked back to the Victorian era, besides introducing some intriguingly daring new styles. It was still quite common for a woman to wear a lace cap – particularly a married woman or a widow receiving visitors at home. 'Boudoir' caps remained popular right up until the 1920s; these small lace confections were prettily decorated with ribbons and small clusters of artificial silk or velvet flower sprays. The quality of the workmanship found in these indoor caps can push the prices fairly high; the following trio from Mrs Langley Moore's sale fetched £65: 'A boudoir cap of cream lace trimmed with pale pink satin ribbon – c 1920; a

An advertisement for
'Delightful hats at John
Barker, Kensington' from
The Lady, October 1908.

Above A 'Charming Toque'
covered in rose petals:
Harrods 1919.

A Suzanne Talbot hat design
in natural coloured straw with
a very large puff of feathers,
1922.

boudoir cap of cream lace trimmed with silk flowers, pale blue thread and silk ribbon – c 1921; and another similar, trimmed with pale pink ribbon and thread – c 1925'.

For outdoor wear in the first decade, hats replaced bonnets. At first the brims curved outwards, and by the end of the decade the hat size was tremendous, reaching out well to the level of the shoulder edge or beyond, and lavishly decorated with flowers, feathers, or even entire birds. Cecil Beaton gave a vivid description of his Aunt Jessie and her hats in *The Glass of Fashion* (1954):

> Then there were the hat boxes – great square containers that held six hats apiece. In those days, mesh moulds were pinned on the sides, top and bottom of a box so that the crown of a hat could be placed over the mould and fixed into place by a long hatpin piercing the mesh. In such manner, six hats could travel in a box without being crushed. And such headgear! Vast discs covered with funereal plumes of black ostrich feathers or white ospreys; hats for the evening and hats for the afternoon; hats for her garden parties. . . .

Hats for all occasions were made in every material, from straw, lace, chiffon and raffia to panné velvet. Colour was immensely varied too – navy, black, white, cream, or any bright colour to match a particular dress. Also in this first decade, beside the wide-brimmed shapes, the toque appeared. This was a small, forehead-hugging shape rising high on the crown, rather like a traditional Turkish hat, also made in a variety of materials, from felt to straw. The Langley Moore sale included a typical model from about 1914; in black raffia, it was trimmed with black and white plumes at the side, and a black net veil, edged with black beads, was draped to fall down over the ear and shoulder.

In 1907 came the heyday of the tall, nearly straight feather, curling at the tip, worn at the front of the hat; for obvious problems of practicality this was a short-lived style. In the following decade, the idea was translated into some simpler but very dramatic evening styles, with a single feather held in place by a jewelled headband. Hats in the 1910–20 period were varied and obligatory; no outfit was complete without one. Some of the shapes were so top-heavy that to the modern eye they look quite disproportionate; they sat well down on the brow and had broad, deep crowns and fairly wide, hard brims – though not as wide as in the Edwardian era. Trimmings remained as elaborate as ever, with many kinds of feathers, lace veils, ribbons and satin.

By the end of the decade, the prevailing hat shape was closer to the head, and had less of a brim – what there was would be turned back close to the crown shape of the hat, and the whole pulled down even further on the head, nearly to eyebrow level. Mrs Langley Moore's collection included a beautiful late-decade example of a toque, in beige georgette, decorated all round the brim with large shaded brown velvet flowers, and intended to be worn fairly well down on the head. In exquisite condition, it fetched £38 at auction. Two other hats, both dated c 1924, went for quite different prices: one of navy blue felt, trimmed with shaded blue feathers and marked '*Court Milliner, C. Errington, 6 Lower Grosvenor Place S.W.*, sold for £35, and an unlabelled pink velour hat with black velvet brim, trimmed with plaited

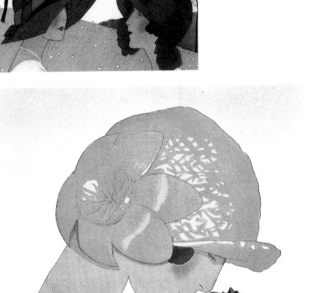

Left 'Sad Winter gives way to Spring', hats by 1920s Parisian milliner Marthe Collot; gradually deep brims disappeared in favour of the close-fitting cloche, like the petalled hat by the same designer. Gazette du Bon Ton 1924.

ribbon, went for a mere £12, although it was a delightful example of its type. The existence of documentary evidence to show provenance adds measurably to the value of any collected article: as suggested in my chapter on Conservation, the collector should always make a note of the date of the purchase and the circumstances (vendor, price, any details of previous ownership discussed at the time, where bought, and so on). Such information is soon forgotten or lost unless a consistent effort is made to record it at the time. This was certainly a major reason for the difference in price between two hats quite similar in aesthetic appeal.

In the 1920s, a new style emerged from the Eastern splendours of Poiret and Paris. This was the head-hugging turban, often made in shining satins or rich brocades, and decorated with paste jewels or feathers. Fancy dress, or theme hats, were also very popular: tam o'shanters, Spanish torero hats, varieties of 'helmets' with cut-out or appliqué decoration in felt; 'vagabond' hats like those of some pantomime character, with tall crowns and brims worn well down over the face (one of this type in printed red plush, trimmed with red, ribbed, silk ribbon and made by Derry & Toms, Kensington, c 1927, sold for £30 in Mrs Langley Moore's auction); 'Bowlers' in felt or straw, for summer or winter, Juliet-style skull-caps – the innovation and

A pretty array of 1920s hats, showing the most popular shapes of the time. Femina, May 1922. Hats in good condition from this date are difficult to find, but often not very expensive.

Left A striking evening hat illustrated in Gazette du Bon Ton, 1912.

Typical hat shapes – and the appropriate necklines for each: Berlin, 1917.

Right *A cloche hat from Victor Jay, 1928.*

Three designs by well-known French names – left to right – Jane Blanchot, Camille Roger and Lucienne Lange. Jardin des Modes, August 1932.

Right *Acute angles, lace, bows and veils were characteristic of hat designs towards the end of the 1930s: Legroux Soeurs, Agnes and Mme Suzy, 1939.*

variety of hats in the 1920s is without end. For the collector, it is difficult to provide information on hat shapes which is sufficiently exact to allow precise dating. As with some shoes, certain hat shapes remain popular for several decades, or alternatively, like the 'bowler' shape, reappear at odd intervals. Therefore, any outside information, such as a label in a hat box, or a photograph of the owner wearing such a hat, or an advertisement for a similar model from a magazine, will add to the documentary value of the hat, and eventually to a greater financial prospect on its sale. But as an alternative reason for some high prices at auction, there were hats that were timeless in their prettiness, and sold perhaps for stage or film use – or even, one suspects, for wearing by the new owner.

Hats in the 1930s reached a new level of impracticality: at least the cloches of the 1920s could be jammed well down and would stay in place during a hectic life of dancing, sports, cocktails and fast car outings, which is how the socialites of the decade would have history remember them. The fussy femininity of 1930s clothes called for more subdued headgear to complement the dress: hats were gradually pushed up off the face, and worn at any angle, however absurdly tilted. Berets, pill-boxes, small militaristic shapes were all popular. It is very likely that the influence of Hollywood made a great impression on hat shapes at the time: the curious angles and snappy brims of 1930s hats looked very good for some quizzical profiles, or over luminous eyes in close-up. Towards the end of the decade, a variety of

picture hat with a wide, curving brim and a very shallow crown, often secured with a hatpin, became the fashion. Two such examples from Mrs Langley Moore's sale were some of the most seductive hats I have ever seen: 'A summer dinner hat of black net applied overall with shaded pink roses – c 1932; and a hat of brown felt embroidered overall with shaded brown sequins by *Amy, New York*, c 1932' (together, they fetched £32).

A black straw hat with a crown of black ribbed silk, trimmed with satin ribbon and two jet buckles, was teamed with another low-crowned felt hat, trimmed with red, black and white ribbon (sale price £45); the first came from one of the best French milliners, Caroline Reboux. Reboux, a leading milliner whose styles accompanied couture clothes, is also credited with the invention of the cloche. Madge Garland makes an interesting comment on the hat styles of the 1920s and 1930s in her book *The Indecisive Decade*:

> The indecision of milliners resulted in a spate of alarmingly bad millinery, for no one seemed to know whether a hat should tilt backwards, forwards or sideways. It did, however, often team with the costume it accompanied and hats of matching fabric were as much a feature as matching gloves. Diana Wynyard, newly a star in London, set off for Hollywood wearing a pointed cap of the same crinkled black silk which made her Scap dress; Victor Stiebel showed a sailor hat and gloves of floral silk with a dark suit; Marcel Rochas a navy dress accompanied by a jacket and gloves of blue and white striped linen. This was the style which the London firm of Matita made very much their own, and their striped woollen suits with matching or plain skirts, together with striped gauntlet gloves, turban or cravat became their definite hallmark at a time when few wholesalers had acquired a personal idiom.

Incidentally, Schiaparelli made some mad hats in her heyday, the most famous being the 'leg of lamb' hat worn by Mrs Daisy Fellowes. 'Scap's' hats are so individualistic and surrealistic that they fall outside the mainstream of hat history and in any event are very seldom found for sale. Significantly in the 1930s Schiaparelli made a deal with an English manufacturer, Lincoln Bennett, to supply hat designs for the mass market, but her ideas became so diluted that there is little of her character in the hats bearing her name for this label.

French hats continued to have the greatest cachet until the end of the Second World War. The house of the Legroux Sisters was one of the most popular, and widely known, for Madame Germaine Legroux made regular trips to the USA from 1930 onwards to carry the best of French millinery to

During the war years hats became very frivolous particularly in France. This example of sensational bad taste was photographed in 1941.

New York. In the 1930s their address was in the heart of the couture area: 4 rue Cambon. A Legroux hat ('A hat of tan straw trimmed with checked silk ribbon by Legroux Soeurs, 4 rue Cambon, Paris') was included in a lot of three from Mrs Langley Moore's collection which was sold for the miserly sum of £25. Divided by three this can hardly have been more in real terms than the original price paid for the hat at the time of its first purchase, around 1937. The business began with Germaine and her sister Héloïse in 1913, just before the outbreak of the First World War, in Roubaix, near the Belgian border. It was continued in the family tradition when a niece, Maino, joined the company in the mid-1940s.

Other Parisian milliners from the 1930s and 1940s whose names may be encountered are Paulette, who designed many hats for the couture house of Robert Piguet, and executed many theatre designs in collaboration with Berard; Albouy, who made hats in pretty colours to match special dresses and used unusual materials during the war years, when many couturiers and milliners gave an inspired lead in economizing; and Madame Jane Blanchot, who eventually became President of the prestigious Chambre Syndicale de la Mode Parisienne – the couturier's official organization.

Towards the end of the 1930s, with the onset of war, hats – and particularly French millinery – perforce lost their influence over international fashion. War-time restrictions reduced hat-making to an industry for uniforms, and women 'made do' during the war years with confections made of a fragment of net, a bunch of fabric flowers carefully procured on coupons, and a great deal of inventiveness with home-made efforts. Knitted hats were popular, and also 'snoods', or nets which encased the longer hair then in

fashion. Schiaparelli had launched ridiculously small hats in the mid-1930s, and this trend, combined with the need for economy, led to some bizarre concoctions with snoods at the back, tiny hats on top, or a hat with a wimple or veil wound round the neck. It was as if a hat was hinted at, rather than actively worn. Turbans were the exception; they maintained their appeal from the 1920s continuously through the next two decades.

R. Turner Wilcox details, in her encyclopedic study of hats in history, how the Audubon Society of America was successful in preventing the use of feathers from rare birds for millinery in America as early as 1905, while the whole of Europe paraded about festooned with ostrich feathers or egret's wings: 'In 1941 in New York, a new agreement was reached between the National Audubon Society and the Feathers Industries of America, Inc., whereby the use of wild bird plumage for millinery and decorative purposes ceased. At the end of a six-year period, any remaining stocks of paradise, egret, golden or bald eagles were to be turned over to the State Department and the agreement was to be countrywide.' This at least helps the collector to recognize a European as opposed to an American creation, and is a reminder that in some respects America was more conscious of depradations on wild life than Europe at this time.

In England during the war years, a fashion started for the use of headscarves, sometimes tied turban-style as a protection while working, but also used as a fashion accessory, and tied Babushka-like beneath the chin. In retrospect the disappearance of the hat as a necessary accessory for the fashionable lady was a start towards a levelling of society, a process much accelerated after the war. Hats, like other accessories, cannot be matters of economy without showing their lack of quality. A headscarf is another matter. Little round evening caps, Juliet caps, berets, pill-boxes, these were all the styles of the war years, and easily achieved by mass-production or home ingenuity.

Perhaps that was why, after the war, with the birth of Dior's New Look, there was a violent reaction against war-time averaging out. The New Look dresses were accompanied by hats of the utmost glamour, starting with Balenciaga's dramatic, wide-brimmed black hats, owing much of their panache to the Spanish traditional shapes. Dior and Fath showed some delightful head-hugging hats, beautifully ornamented with elaborate embroidery or trimming – feathers, pompons, sequins – for evening wear.

Hats designed by leading American milliner, Lilly Daché: turbans like these were very popular. American Vogue 1940.

Some important milliners of the late 1940s and early 1950s were Lilly Daché in New York, and Aage Thaarup and Simone Mirman in London. Mirman made hats for the Christian Dior salon in London; Aage Thaarup, Danish in origin, worked for a while in Paris, led a peripatetic life through the last throes of the Empire in India, and settled in London to become milliner-in-chief to the London couturiers Victor Stiebel, Norman Hartnell and Peter Russell. During the 1930s he made hats for a variety of socialites and film stars including Marlene Dietrich and Gloria Swanson; in the 1940s and 1950s he received a royal recognition and made some wonderful hats for Queen Elizabeth, now the Queen Mother, and the Princesses Elizabeth and Margaret. Perhaps his most interesting hat historically is the tricorne which he designed in 1950 for Queen Elizabeth's Trooping of the Colour ceremony – a feminine version of a military style which has become famous all over the world. After the Second World War, Thaarup visited the USA, and designed hats for stores in New York and across America. He was a man of immense charm and creativity, who in his own words made designing sound effortless and instinctive – which it probably is for those with the talent for it: 'I might buy flowers from France but I never bought ideas. If I may be excused from boasting, I have never felt any dearth of ideas. As for forecasting fashion, one simply 'feels' what is going to happen. Shoulders are going to do this . . . it is inevitable.'

In one of the surprises of Mrs Langley Moore's sale, several lots of Thaarup hats sold comparatively cheaply: a description serves to show the prettiness of his creations (the entire lot was sold for £75): 'A red felt toque trimmed with black ostrich feathers and black velvet ribbon by Aage Thaarup – c 1942; a hat of blue felt trimmed with black feathers by Aage Thaarup – c 1943; and a hat of rust red velvet and underbrim ruched, trimmed with a rust red velvet wired bow by Aage Thaarup – c 1943'.

Left *A charming hat designed by Aage Thaarup. In black velvet with a black and red bow – 'the red to match the lips', and* **below** *Aage Thaarup at work on a rough of the hat above (1940).*

The return of luxurious glamour: John French photograph, 1950.

Right *Hat designed by Peter Shepherd, London: toques and pillboxes came back into fashion to balance the width of the New Look dresses and coats. Photographed by Richard Dormer for* Harper's Bazaar.

The flat, wide-brimmed 'coolie' hat was very popular in the 1950s, balancing the new fullness of skirts.

Right *Flower hats were very popular in the 1960s: Lilies by Paulett, Daisies by Graham Smith, London 1965.*

One of the innovations of the 1950s accompanying the wide-skirted New Look dresses was the flattering coolie hat shape, often trimmed with feathers, made in straw, or sometimes created out of pleated fabric (several such designs by Simone Mirman were included in Mrs Langley Moore's collection). It is worth noting which of recent shapes this famous collector purchased, as it provides a guide for the beginner, who may find similar shapes widely copied by cheaper manufacturers, and worth preserving as typical examples of the age. Pill-boxes and toques continued to be popular throughout the 1950s – this was a shape of hat much favoured by Mrs Jacqueline Kennedy, and suited the little white or pale dresses in the Courrèges and Cardin mould which she preferred. Turbans have continued in vogue until the present day, even in a time when hats are increasingly rare. Turbans seem to reflect the style of the wearer, and are less 'hatty' than other shapes. Besides, their usefulness as a cover-up make them invaluable

The ultimate hat for the grand occasion: a creation by Claude Saint Cyr for Empress Farah Dibah of Iran, jewels by Mauboussin, 1963.

in an age when few women can afford or expect to go to a hairdresser with the regularity that was usual, and stylish, in the 1950s.

Garden hats were also represented in the Langley Moore collection, and these, like turbans, remain a fashion accessory, even with younger girls who would otherwise never wear a hat. Biba in the mid-1960s specialized in a range of floppy-brimmed, pull-on hats, and with Biba's demise came the end of the hat as a fashion accessory. Their use with the mini-skirt seemed at the time a strange anachronism, a last-minute nostalgia for more impractical feminine accoutrements. It is significant that Mrs Langley Moore's collection at sale came to a conclusion with turbans from the late 1960s, and one ranch hat, stamped Rockmont, Denver, c 1975. Hats for particular purposes have remained in fashion in the past three decades, beginning with the raffia and straw beach hat craze of the 1950s, and continuing with 1960s PVC rain-hats, helmets, 'baby bonnets' and winter fur 'cossack'-style pull-ons. The 1970s revived the countrified appeal of the large straw hat, to complement the peasant-style, full-length dresses of the young, but these were as much carried as worn. Nowadays, hats are worn for ceremonial occasions, by Heads of State or their wives, at the most formal and conventional levels of society for weddings and such occasions, but, in general, only the utilitarian list mentioned above survives. Perhaps for this reason, the market in second-hand hats is fairly active; the current breakdown of fashion rules, and the prevalence of 'fancy dress' or fantasy clothes for evening wear means that pretty, well-made hats from earlier decades are admired for their dramatic femininity. There are many individual milliners such as David Shilling in London who are creating very stylish designs for women who have always adored hats and will continue to wear them. A representative collection of hats over the past fifty years documents the changes in women's status more evocatively than any other article of female clothing.

Left *A striking evening hat illustrated in* Gazette du Bon Ton, *1912.*

*Three hats by David Shilling,
the well-known London
hatter.*

HANDBAGS

Handbags, like hats, can be problematical collector's items. They suffer badly at the hands of their owners, and seldom reach old age in very good condition, except perhaps for the beaded evening purses of the 1910s and 1920s. In antique shops these fetch extraordinarily high prices, quite beyond the intrinsic worth of the object – they are usually too small and fragile and can never be viewed solely as a handsome antique. They always retain a functional air. For an energetic and enterprising collector, however, it is still perfectly possible to find characterful and unusual handbags in the cheapest places – flea markets, jumble sales, and as lots at auctions. The great advantage in collecting handbags is that so far it is not much done, and prices for other than the delicate and rare items are, therefore, low. But a pitfall for the inexperienced is that there is very little detailed information about handbags available in book form; starting a collection of handbags means building up your own references, poring through old magazines for styles and types to act as a guide, and learning about the materials as you proceed through stalls and trunks in the search.

The following notes are a brief guideline to some possibilities, for which I am indebted to John Jesse and Irina Laski, who run an antique shop dealing mostly with Art Nouveau and Art Deco pieces, in Kensington, and who staged the first handbag exhibition (outside more composite collections in museums) in 1981.

It is interesting to note in fashion plates of the Edwardian era that handbags were nowhere near as popular as they are today. A well dressed woman would just as easily accessorize her outfit with a muff, a parasol, gloves, or a fur wrap. This reflects a woman's social situation; a lady would have little need for cash in hand, as supplies would be purchased by housekeepers or maids, and she would move about in private transport. Little purses in suede or leather are sometimes seen, and the 'Dorothy bag', a pouched bag of fabric on a drawstring, was also popular. Handwork is found in *petit-point* or Berlin-work embroidery for evening purses, and sometimes chain mail was used. Styles of jewellery are emulated in the handles, which helps to date them (although as John Jesse points out, dating handbags is a hazardous affair, as the same shapes and styles continued over many decades). Fine examples of Edwardian bags have curled leafy designs in silver for the clasp, and sometimes have the mark of a well known manufacturer inside the closure. Small bags or 'pocket books' set with

A typical little beaded purse, carried with an outfit from Madame Beddoes, London 1910.

175

Right *Dramatically lined Art
Deco bag, showing how even
an accessory can be a work of
art.*

*Early twentieth-century
French beaded reticule.*

Centre *A beautifully
embroidered, beaded evening
bag, and* **below** *a woven
check bag, echoing the interest
in cubist geometrics. Both
were made by Maria
Strauss-Likarz, a member of
the* Wiener Werkstätte, *the
Austrian association of
artist-craftsmen, 1920.*

semi-precious stones and with some mark as to provenance can cost a great deal of money; an example marked 'Dew', which I viewed before a sale at Sotheby's, New York, fetched about $100. Tiffany bags may be even more expensive. According to Julie Collier of Christie's East, New York, Victorian and Edwardian bags sometimes go for lower prices than those from the late 1910s and early 1920s, especially those which were imported from France to America at that time.

The 1920s styles in bags reflect the contemporary taste for glitter and lightness; small chain-mail bags with long chain handles are found; sometimes bags were made with a hook to attach the bag to the waistband of a dress. Mansfield and Cunnington in *Handbook of English Costume 1900–1950*, describe 'safety underskirt bags' with a belt and chain to attach them to the wearer's waist that are sometimes encountered. Prices for good examples of 1920s evening bags can be very high. John Jesse's sale included some in the area of £150–£200. Quite often this price reflects some other valuable feature of the bag, so that it becomes a collectable item for other antique specialists: a particularly splendid example was a Chinese bag made of blue silk, with ornate embroidery, and a clasp made with a *netsuke* – a decorative toggle worn on the end of the sash in traditional Japanese costume.

The 1920s and 1930s bags can best be identified by a close comparison with other more easily dated objects, such as jewellery, or shoes. The period produced some unusual examples in rich brocades – small clutch purses to match a dress or coat, for instance – and some eye-catching designs in the Art Deco style, with sun-rays or fan-shapes being common. Early experi-

A representative collection of Art Deco handbags and shoes – note the waisted heel of the 1920s.

Below *Beaded bag of the Edwardian era: these are popular and very expensive if in good condition, often because they are sold, like fans, in general antique shops besides those specialising in fashion.*

ments with plastics are interesting to acquire: celluloid for the frame, enamel set in silver-coloured metal for the clasp. Diamanté clasps were much admired, and it is possible to find evening bags set with real gemstones such as diamonds or emeralds, which will obviously sell for several hundred pounds.

Evening bags with brocade or embroidery, and tassels at the bottom corners, are also typical of the 1920s. Besides the variety of substances used for the handles and clasps, the collector will find a diverse use of animal skins, which was not the case in later decades. Antelope, suede, kid, elephant-hide, ostrich-skin, sharkskin and crocodile were often employed, and are still worth preserving. John Jesse's sale included a brown crocodile *minaudière* with a silver-gilt clasp in a 'Chinese' design, made by Finnigans (a name to note) and valued at £120.

The 1930s saw a move away from the extravagance of the 1920s styles. A page from a 1931 copy of *Vogue* chastises a woman for over-accessorizing a plain black evening dress:

She is enchanted and buys long glittering earrings, a diadem of brilliants for her hair, and giant court shoe-buckles, from under which peep coquettish wisps of tulle. To all this splendour she adds a massive coral beaded bag, which swings from a long chain. One does not need to see to know that in due time she will produce from that bag a long chiffon handkerchief of the tie-and-dye variety and a very long cigarette holder. Alone and unaided, she has ruined a good dress.

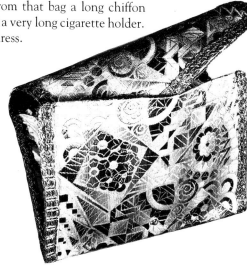

Further evidence of innovation in the new synthetics: a plastic cosmetic set for the handbag, 1930s.

Immaculate Art Deco bag, 1930.

Below, centre *Clear plastic novelty bag carried at Ascot, 1949 (though the lady and the bag are American).*

The cruise age: a striking 1930s bag design.

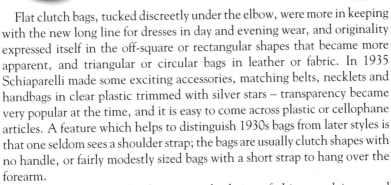

Flat clutch bags, tucked discreetly under the elbow, were more in keeping with the new long line for dresses in day and evening wear, and originality expressed itself in the off-square or rectangular shapes that became more apparent, and triangular or circular bags in leather or fabric. In 1935 Schiaparelli made some exciting accessories, matching belts, necklets and handbags in clear plastic trimmed with silver stars – transparency became very popular at the time, and it is easy to come across plastic or cellophane articles. A feature which helps to distinguish 1930s bags from later styles is that one seldom sees a shoulder strap; the bags are usually clutch shapes with no handle, or fairly modestly sized bags with a short strap to hang over the forearm.

In the 1940s, shoulder bags came back into fashion, and increased generously in proportion, reflecting the more practical and businesslike atmosphere for women at work for the first time because of the war. Box-shaped bags, often with two handles side by side, one for each half, were an innovation, and allowed more objects to be carried conveniently than ever before. To comply with restrictions on the use of leather for accessories, alternative materials such as cotton fabrics, raffia, straw and plastic were introduced for bags, engendering designs which are quite awe-inspiring in their ugliness. Beach bags with an all-in-one looped section for the handle date from this period too; in general handbags with a purpose-made rather than purely decorative air are typical of the period.

The 1950s offer the handbag collector hours of amusement for very little outlay. Obviously there is a great variety of types still in existence, and these are sometimes to be found in very good condition. If 1940s bags looked large and practical, 1950s bags became exaggeratedly proportioned and impractically silly. A twelve-inch deep model in clear vinyl mounted over bright-coloured fabric was designed which looked splendid against a wide-skirted summer dress, but it either tipped its contents into the street or lost objects beyond recovery in its depths. Large clasp catches came back into fashion, in the form of knobs of perspex or gilt set on the edge of envelope-shaped clutch bags. Wrist-length handles once more returned, besides some girlish designs in boxy shapes, with clasps like those on jewel-boxes for their lids.

Below *Mini-suitcases and other box shapes were very popular in the 1950s: this design by Susan Handbags, London 1953.*

1950s bags grew to enormous and awkward proportions: the bucket bag, 1954.

Right *1950s clear plastic handbag, with perspex handle, often found in flea markets and jumble sales, and still worth preserving.*

A stylish hat-box handbag, 1950, and **below** *a plastic and perspex design, 1950.*

Above, right *A series of objects designed by London specialist Clive Shilton – the kind of 'studio' work that will be much admired in decades to come.*

Pearlized plastic and imitation patent leather in black or white, gold spangled perspex and shimmery iridescent synthetics were typical of the period. John Jesse exhibited an unusually beautiful bag from the 1950s, with a silvered metal handle, a trapezoid boxed frame, and pale pink butterflies glowing in the plastic side panels. This was valued at just under £100.

When boutique clothes caught on towards the end of the decade, classic handbags temporarily went out of fashion as a reaction against the posed and elegantly arranged look of the early 1950s. It was no longer possible to buy a high fashion dress in a boutique and find suitable accessories in other shops – the gap in styling was too wide, between the new and the orthodox. Fashion

180

photographers seldom accessorized their pictures in the way their counter-parts ten years previously had done. The new woman was definitely unencumbered. As if in comment on previous styles, Biba produced a range of tiny purses on long, thin, leather straps, which could hardly conceal more than a lipstick, and the bus-fare home. In more practical circles, the European style of quilted leather with a long gilt chain (originally designed by Chanel) was adopted. And by the end of the decade, all rules about matching accessories were firmly destroyed. The taste for 'ethnic' clothing made voluminous Afghan 'camel bags' worn over a trench coat, or even with a full-length summer dress, seem quite in keeping. Peasant-

More examples of Clive Shilton's work revealing the superb craftsmanship that makes such items always collectable.

Left *A 'Mod' shopping bag in cream and blue leather from the 1960s.*

Typical 'pop art' handbag, 1966; a hand-made design, from Woman *magazine.*

embroidered holdalls, ex-army dispatch bags and fur-covered sacks suddenly turned handbags into nomadic equipment.

As one might expect, the 1960s brought a return to more classic shapes. Buckled shoulder bags, or double-handled bags with an extra outside pocket, went with the fashionable military look.

It is always difficult to see collectable trends in styles nearer to the present day; a certain distance and perspective is necessary before one can judge what would be considered noteworthy in fifty years' time. One possibility from the 1970s and 1980s would be to look at the growth of designer-labelled accessories. As in jeans, the addition of a couture name somehow gives a cachet to a utilitarian object. Gucci, Pucci, Hermès, Cardin, Yves Saint Laurent, are names that suggest themselves in this respect. The sophistication of advertising nowadays could well be reflected through a collection of accessories including handbags, or even carrier-bags, although these count more as ephemera than fashion. Some leading cosmetic houses have produced most carefully designed small pouches containing samples of their products: Estée Lauder, Lancôme and Revlon are worth a look, particularly for their special presentations at Christmas time. These little creations have some of the charm that the earlier advertising fans offered, and although they appear trivial today they could look much more interesting years from now, when the majority have been lost or discarded. The most important rule when collecting fashion is to develop a discriminating taste and the courage to buy things which are personally appealing. There are many independent designers producing custom-made or small-run goods, both in shoes and in bags, whose work will look particularly distinctive in the near future, let alone in distant time. One such craftsman is Clive Shilton, who worked first as a designer for the British shoe company Saxone, but now has a small shop in London's Covent Garden. He produces all kinds of accessories, besides shoes and boots, and his exquisite satin or velvet purses, with fluted edges and stitched or jewelled covers, are reminiscent of the Art Deco clutch purses of the 1930s.

Studio work of this high standard can be found in many major cities. A further possibility for a collector outside main centres such as New York or London would be to make up a selection of the best of locally made craft work. In America this is probably more feasible than in Europe, because the interest in individual creativity has developed apace in the past few decades. Hand-tooled leather offers tremendous scope for a modest collector, wherever based. Studio buttons, bags, belts and, individually, scarves would make a handsome regional selection, especially if the collector paid attention to the documenting of the purchases: the price, date, maker, and circumstances of the acquisition. The great advantage of such accessories is that they are easy to store, less costly to acquire, and often as evocative of a time and style as a complete outfit might be.

SHOES

Shoes are a decidedly odd subject for the collector. Aesthetically speaking, there is something a little unpleasant about handling or hoarding large quantities of other people's discarded footwear. However, there are many ways of approaching the subject – not least being that of the industry which in England has helped the creation, at Northampton, of the world's largest shoe museum. Here the curator, Miss June Swann, presides over more than 7,000 pairs of shoes. She has diligently collected from all kinds of sources, including closing-down factories, the sales of rich, hoarding old ladies, and the more bizarre acquisitions of foot fetishists – a hazard in her profession. (Most are kept in store, with a mere ten per cent of the museum's holdings on display, owing to lack of space and money.) In such a setting, the value of collecting shoes soon becomes apparent.

Any self-respecting fashion collector will inevitably acquire shoes as an accessory to other main lines of endeavour; sometimes shoes are bought with a dress – especially dyed-to-match evening slippers, or babies' shoes with a christening robe. Earlier examples from this century have a beauty of their own, being made just like a dress – inside out and then turned – but the turn-shoe industry died out with the coming of the Second World War. Most shoes from then on were made with moulded uppers, and there is less variety of materials: none of the velvets, moiré silks or brocades of earlier times were used.

As with clothing, most of the improvements in mass manufacture of shoes came from America. The first machine for 'closing' a shoe, that is, attaching the upper to the sole, was made in America as early as the 1850s. Machines to do the lasting of the upper, moulding the shoe to the foot shape, followed in the 1880s. In general terms, however, the USA is more conservative than Britain or the continent of Europe in its foot fashions. It is noteworthy that Europeans and Americans spend more money on their accessories than the British: modern English shoes are not made to last, and are often more extreme fashion items. American women prefer shoes which can be worn with various clothes for a longer period of time – and which will

Left 'La France', a high fronted, laced evening shoe.
Below Brocade and satin evening shoe – 'La Soiree'.
Bottom Mule slipper in brocade or velvet. Evening shoes and slippers from Rayne, London 1912.

keep. It certainly seems, as one views the footwear of even the brief span of the twentieth century, that standards in comfort and fit have deteriorated, in spite of the invention of many practical synthetics and of machines to speed production. That perhaps is the key to the problem: in order to fit well, shoes cannot be made on a conveyor belt. Standardization of sizes and shapes cannot be imposed on a part of the body where there is such a variety of width, length and height of arch.

Women's and men's shoes from the early decades of this century are works of art, and most complicated in their conception. In the 1900s, the lady's laced boot was very popular, with a smallish, thin heel, which was pedestal-shaped, or straight-sided. The shoes of this time always appear very much narrower than ours today, and it seems to be a fact that people's feet have increased in dimensions over the years. While the methods were not as severe as Eastern foot-binding, practices certainly existed to prevent a child's feet from growing. The narrow boots of this period were often scalloped along the buttoning edge, and the collector may like to acquire the decorated buttonhooks and tiny boot-buttons which were essential for the neat, tight fit of the shoes. Kid or cloth was used for the upper part of the boot.

The shoes of this era follow the same shape as the boot: the ever-present single-strap bar shoe with an approximate two-inch heel was a favourite style, alternating with a high-fronted dress shoe, often decorated with a tab folding over the gusset (where the shoe laces up at the front). High vamps in general were common in the Edwardian years, often decorated with a paste buckle, or with a free-standing front concealing the lacing. Toe shapes

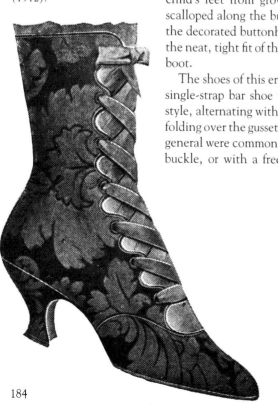

always give a clue to the date of origin, although Miss Swann of the Northampton Museum emphasizes that there are few hard and fast rules, and that it is often possible to find a shoe of a certain shape that predates the era of its popularity by as much as twenty years. Just as often, an 'out-of-date' shape will continue to be found for many years after its introduction. As many of the shoes from the early part of the century were made to measure, it is understandable that women stuck to a toe shape or heel height that suited them in spite of changes in current fashion.

England was also dominated by American imports in the ready-made market, and the quality of these goods is often very inferior. The First World War brought a revival of the British shoe and boot industry, and its products were able to maintain their hold on the domestic market for a time. A major influence on the shoe and boot styles of the late Edwardian era and the 1910s was the increase, for both men and women, in motoring and sporting pastimes: fur-lined motoring boots and overshoes were devised to cope with the difficulties of early motoring, just as dress fashions reflected the new necessities. Men at this time wore boots or 'Oxford'-style shoes, and spats were still very popular. Rubber began to replace leather in machine-made shoes quite pronouncedly at this time; latex had first been discovered in 1790 in South America, but the first real landmark for shoe manufacture was the development of a liquid rubber which could be spread over cloth, such as canvas, to make a waterproof shoe or cover. Rubber soles and heels began to be used in the 1910s and 1920s. But it was not until after the Second World War that rubber soles were 'vulcanized' on to uppers – as in tennis shoes, for instance. Nowadays, most shoes have stuck-on rubber soles

Above '*Balmoral' button boot, and **below, centre** *crocodile leather shoe: men's styles, 1905.*

Luxurious glacé kid front-lacing boots, made by Bally of Switzerland c 1914.

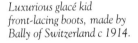

and heels, and the complicated and technically skilled business of stitching a leather sole to an upper is a thing of the past except in rare hand-made items.

One of the most interesting shoemakers of the 1920s was Yantourny, Curator of the Cluny Museum in France, and a craftsman-shoemaker; a rarity in a field where designers do not figure prominently by name. His shoes commanded the astronomic sum of about £1,000 from the customer: Yantourny worked as an eccentric shoe magician, using rare Byzantine fabrics and the finest soft leathers and suedes. His shoes are well beyond the dreams of a private collector, but his name is worth remembering when visiting museums, for his creations are extraordinary and deserve close observation.

Designers of the couture world in the 1910s and 1920s made a considerable impact on shoe fashion. Not the least of these was Paul Poiret, who showed mid-shin laced boots in brilliant colours with various of his creations. Colour is a significant feature of the shoes of this period, as well as such exotic materials as snakeskin, lizard-skin, bronzed kid and all varieties of suedes and special-finish leathers, often with applied decoration. The popularity of the dance, especially the tango, led to a partiality for light-weight pumps, bar shoes, and the new 'tango shoes', which had cross-over laces worked up the leg. Men's shoes were equally bold, the famous 'co-respondent' or 'spectator' shoe, a brogue in two tones, being one of the most popular styles. With both men's and women's shoes of the 1920s, there is a definite feel for streamlined, elegant shapes, slightly elongated, egg-shaped toes, and a beautiful line to the decorative details on the sides or toes.

Above *Red Genoese velvet shoes embroidered in gold, with diamanté buckles, designed by master shoe-maker Yantourny of Paris c 1920.*

Unusual skins were a feature of 1930s footwear: black python court shoes by Randalls c 1930.

Above, right *Lace-up boots in patent leather and black cloth with waisted, Louis XV heel, from Harrods 1919.*

The famous 'co-respondent' or 'spectator' style in Russian calf and white buckskin, made by Manfield's, 1935.

Left Hollywood style, 1934: spats were still worn, and the lady in satin underwear is wearing very pointed shoes.

In the 1930s, American styles in footwear began to prevail over the European, notably French designs of the previous decade: this was doubtless helped by a slump in European industries, and by the increasing influence of Hollywood as a source of fashion generally. The shoes of the 1930s were heavier, more ornate than those of the previous decade: heels were higher, a platform sole made its appearance, and ankle straps came in. The shoes were varied, and often verged on the vulgar. During the 1940s this trend increased, with the most exaggerated platform soles, ankle-breaking high heels, sometimes reaching five inches or more, and heavier, darker materials coming into vogue: black or brown suede, black patent leather, and silver or gold kid. The highest wedges became flights of architectural fancy: some have cut-outs in the heel itself, or a highly ornate curving shape. Sometimes the wedge is made in sculptured layers, rather like a pile of tyres in their inspiration. At the same time, open toes and slingbacks made their appearance.

During the war years rationing applied to shoe material as much as to the cut of clothes: substitutes for leather had to be introduced for non-military shoes (leather being reserved for army boots), so that many women's fashions at this time were made in plaited straw, canvas, or gaberdine. Cork in place of leather was a summer substitute for sandals. War-time shoes are heavy and not very feminine or pleasing in shape.

Men's shoes by contrast acquired a new informality from the 1940s onwards: the moccasin came into fashion in the mid-decade, and dress shoes were lower cut, replacing the ankle-boots favoured earlier.

French shoe, late 1930s: the platform sole became widespread.

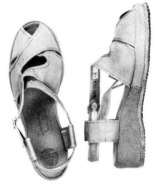

A good example of Utility footwear – Dunlop 'Liftees' in denim from the late 1940s.

As shoes were precious and used up five coupons, only sturdy, well-made styles were acceptable.

Left A clog sandal with raised sole, 1936: such styles increased in popularity in the 1940s. Unusual fabrics, like the grey tweed illustrated, were typical.

Far right The difficulties of coping with chic: pencil skirt, straight seams and ankle-breaking four-inch 'stiletto' heels, 1953.

Right American fashions – red and gold dinner shoes, 1940. **Below** A startling design in black and silver by Ferragamo of Florence, 1947.

Right A pair of evening shoes in ivory silk and gold thread brocade, designed by Schiaparelli, with a narrow toe and low heel, 1950.

A Charles Jourdan design, 1950s.

The greatest change in silhouette came for women with the New Look launched by Dior in 1947, after the end of the war. Skirts suddenly became longer and fuller, and war-time restrictions on materials were at an end, so that shoes could once more be delicate, well made, and all leather. The chief identifying feature of late 1940s and early 1950s shoes is the slimming-down of the heel: at first the height of the shoe was at a modest two to three inches, but during the 1950s heels were pushed higher and higher. England lagged behind Europe in the adoption of the true 'stiletto'; the first examples to be seen in the country arrived in 1953. The most noted shoe designer of this period was the Italian Salvatore Ferragamo, who had emigrated to America from his home in Naples, set up a shop in Santa Barbara, California, and had been responsible for some imaginative costume-shoe designs for early films, particularly the epics of Cecil B. De Mille and D. W. Griffith. On his return to Italy, Ferragamo established himself in Florence, and by the early 1940s was already famous for the inventiveness of his designs which combated the difficulties of war-time economies. But his international fame arrived in 1947 with the 'invisible shoe' – a top part made of nylon so that it hardly showed against the skin, and a black suede heel several inches high. Toes to shoes became exaggeratedly long: the winkle-pickers of the 1950s were the most stylized of the tendency towards pointed rather than round-toed shoes. Many of these styles were imported from Italy to northern Europe and America.

In the USA the growth of the teenage market in the 1950s led to some more youthful shapes in shoes: low black pumps, often cut so that the toes nearly showed, were popular: likewise pumps resembling ballet shoes, which went well with the full-skirted, 'country', shirtwaist styles which were so widespread at the time. The colour of shoes in the 1950s was generally more conservative than in earlier decades: mechanization produces its own rationalizations too. As the youth market increased, so did the size of the average person's shoe wardrobe: different shoes for sports, beachwear, city and country became feasible even on a modest income.

Just as shoe styles seemed to have stabilized, another revolution took place: this was largely born from the impact of boutique clothing fashions emanating from London, principally from Mary Quant's boutique, Bazaar, in the King's Road, which opened in 1955. It is significant that both Mary Quant and her subsequent rival, Barbara Hulanicki of Biba boutique, both sold not only dresses but all accessories too: the style was for a complete 'look', and this involved buying exactly the right shoes and handbag to match the outfit. Shoes had not been so consciously matched with dresses in this way for some time: the ladylike court shoes of the 1950s could be worn with several outfits, interchangeably. Suddenly, white shoes, plastic shoes, black and white 'Op Art' shoes, and above all knee-high boots (for both men and women) provided an exciting new focus for inventive dressing. The quality of these shoes, however, left much to be desired, though American manufacturers did not drop their standards to the levels found in some cheaper British products. Shoe styles varied tremendously between America and England in the late 1950s and early 1960s. The habit of buying good quality and keeping it was never abandoned in the USA, even if 'dolly' dresses caused a sensation and swept the market for a while. One of the most distinctive features of 1960s shoes, for both men and women, is the chisel toe, balanced by a low heel, often squared at the base to echo the toe line. Colour and shine came back into fashion, with patent, aniline leathers dyed in wild colours such as purple and scarlet, and glittering evening shoes. Lace and lurex were further alternatives.

Men's side-laced winkle picker and ladies' Swiss lace, stiletto-heeled shoe, 1965.

Left *Winkle-pickers, low black pumps, 'Op Art' plastic boots and Dr Scholl's ubiquitous clogs – a fair range of 1960s footwear styles, showing the great variety worn at the time.*

Silver boots, designed by Courrèges, 1966.

Paris once more asserted itself as a source of inspiration for shoe designs: one of the most widely copied boots of the early 1960s was the white, bowed, mid-shin boot created by Courrèges. Roger Vivier was responsible for many of the shoe designs taken up by Parisian couturiers, although his influence did not much extend to the ready-made industry. French and Italian women's shoes gradually gained in distinction as the most finely made and best designed – a trend which continues to this day, as leather becomes more expensive, and substitutes more commonly used by the mass-market industry in other countries. A confusing feature of better-made examples from the 1960s is the bewildering variety of toe shapes, from the almond point of 1960 to the chisel toe of the mid-decade, and a more obviously square toe for a more sporty style at the same period.

More recent shoe fashions have been as inconsistent as ever: the mid-1970s provided every known style as fashions became increasingly varied, and called for different shoe styles to match. Knee-high boots under full-length peasant skirts, sneakers with jeans, open sandals with socks in the depths of winter – it seemed as if shoe rules were disregarded even more than dress regulations. In general, the trend seemed to be moving towards a more practical, utilitarian view of footwear – young people often went to the lengths of having shoes hand-made once again. Hand-made boots in imitations of rock-star styles are a phenomenon of the 1970s, and would make a splendid documentary collection of the taste of the time: silver or gold, with appliqué stars, stripes and snakeskin cut-outs, these boots are fantasies of costumery. More recently, a reversal took place: a grotesque artificiality emerged in shoe fashions. Platforms reappeared, followed by high, thin heels and pointed toes: at a time when women's role in society gained significant liberty and new possibilities, shoe shapes seemed to regress. For men, the brief flare of dandyism in the 1960s and early 1970s has receded, and the majority of men's styles remain true to the moccasin, the lace-up, and the boot in its various practical manifestations from cowboy to rough hiking styles. According to Miss Swann, shoe shapes often reflect the style of government: when a Socialist administration is in power, shoes tend towards thicker heels and square toes. A Conservative government produces a change towards more elegant shoe shapes. A shoe collection could easily summarize, in a few carefully chosen examples, a whole complexity of social changes from decade to decade of this century – and at prices never embarrassing to a modest purse.

Most recent trends in fashion point to a return to more classic styles in dress and accessories: in shoes, low-heeled pumps – a remodelling of 1950s styles – seem to be popular, and clutch handbags have made a return after the dominance of capacious shoulder bags over the last ten years. The Amer-

A Yuki dress worn with some unusually-heeled shoes, 1970s.

Bottom Classic 1960s 'Op Art' outfit, including see-through boots. These would be very difficult to find second-hand.

A selection of children's shoes: styles have barely changed for the past forty years.

ican 'college' style of co-ordinated separates, re-styled with much sophistication by Calvin Klein, Bill Blass, and Halston, seems more appropriate than the excesses of originality prevalent in the mid-1970s. It is always difficult to guess which current styles will remain significant in a decade or so; but, apart from the well known designers whose work has already been described in each chapter, my own preference for modern collectables, in clothing and in accessories, would be to search out the work of small atelier and boutique owners who are producing hand-crafted work of great beauty. Hand-painted or elaborately embroidered silks or velvets, well cut custom-made shoes, fine-stitched leather bags, should be mixed with dashing examples of the best in mass-marketed ready-to-wear – where flair and colour are combined in prints which provide a stylish commentary on modern taste. Cartoon-inspired designs on cheap fabrics; exotically patterned machine-knits; together with a world-wide trade in village-made ethnic clothing (like the gold-threaded ensembles from India or the yoke-embroidered dresses from Mexico) now offer a varied choice for the constantly changing, energetic marketplace of fashion. Above all, the collector must keep a firm hold on standards of quality and taste, and acquire only the best examples of any area that holds appeal. A collection will be not only a record of an age, but an expression of your own personality. That individuality gives any collection its particular value.

Suede extremes by the British shoe company Elliot – a mass production company with a consistently high design reputation. 1960s boots, silver, gold and multi-coloured shoes were always identified with their name, like the hot pants and 'wedgies' shown here.

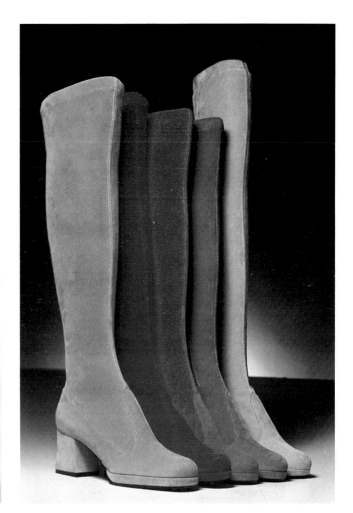

After the thicker heels of the 1960s and early 1970s, thin-heeled boots made a reappearance, in keeping with more varied fantasy fashions at the close of the 1970s.

Very 1980s designs by Clive Shilton.

GLOVES

Right *Suede and leather gloves, in neutral colours, were an essential accessory from the 1900s to the 1920s. These were offered for sale at Harrods in 1919.*

Bottom right *Wartime cheap and cheerful knitted gauntlets: 1941, from Harvey Nichols.*

Below, centre *Leather and knitted gloves, 1930s, by Jaeger.*

Good-quality gloves are fun to collect. They often sell quite cheaply at auction. A pretty pair by Worth, 1923.

Accessories can so often summarize the look or 'signature' of a particular fashion period, in a way which makes them a particularly appealing focus of interest for the collector. Gloves, like fans, have often been the possession of a proud owner: a woman with fine hands is likely to look after her gloves well, just as a woman with small feet are more likely to keep beautiful shoes than those ashamed of their boats. The small selection of gloves presented on these pages summarize many important points of reference for the fashion historian.

Edwardian accessories reflect the high standard of craftsmanship available to those (the few) who could afford to dress well; leathers, fine kidskin, satin, velvet were the favoured materials, like the buckskin, fringed example illustrated. Gloves were often made for a particular dress or suit, with matching buttons or other trimmings. Less prosperous women would buy ready-made gloves in plain colours, like gloves in various skins available from the large department stores. While women would seldom carry a handbag, gloves were obligatory.

Gloves that matched an outfit were still considered appropriate throughout the 1920s and 1930s; couture fashions, such as the outfit by Worth, were modelled with specially made accessories, and stores such as Liberty's advertised co-ordinated articles in 1935. The 1930s were the last years when fashionable ladies could expect such detailed craftsmanship; hand-embroidered gloves, with bugle beads and gold thread, look almost out of date for the period. Already, mass-market production for the growing middle-class market was improving so that stores could offer a supply of gloves, in many styles, knitted wools, stitched leather, all made to suit various purposes, but not necessarily intended for use with one outfit exclusively.

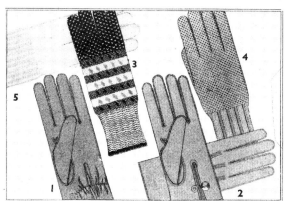

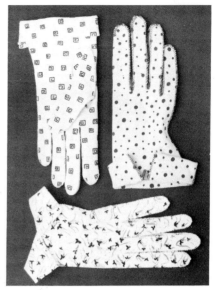

During the war years, many women had to make do with home-made gloves, as leather and tough materials were reserved for official use. Precious coupons would be saved to buy gloves for a special occasion, so it is not surprising that ideals of elegance should involve long, long gloves up to the top of the arm, not to say shoulder – a wish satisfied by some of the post-war designs from Paris. Intriguingly, co-ordinated gloves, that sign of luxury, were very much favoured by the new doyennes of fashion, the Hollywood designers and their stars, who perhaps liked wearing gloves so much because they were useful in close-up.

1950s fashions in gloves were obviously a reaction to the limitations of the war years, by their sheer impracticality, taking ages to peel on or off, satisfying a desire to enjoy leisure anew, and not be ruled by necessity. I suspect too that after the war, for working women who had a chance to better themselves as a part of the new economic prosperity, long gloves were a symbol of upper-class elegance (or hid a multitude of sins – for those who had no servants to wash the dishes any more). Many 1950s fashions were frankly vulgar – accessories in general seem to go oversize in the second half of the decade, and over-trimming became common, in both senses of the word.

American teenage fashions, which created a market well ahead of anything similar in the UK, produced some pretty, fresh styles in complete contrast to the older, elegant look, and soon gained widespread popularity. For a while the two looks existed uneasily side by side, but by the 1960s fashion no longer dictated to young people what they wore, and gloves went out of vogue – as other accessories did too. Of course gloves were worn, of necessity, but co-ordination was viewed as a bourgeois preoccupation. It is noteworthy that some of the most popular gloves in the 1970s were simple forms, such as handknit mittens, or traditional styles like the multi-coloured Inca designs from Peru, or the Fair Isle patterns from Scotland, which satisfied the current feeling for function, but provided decorative pleasure as well.

As with other accessories, the collector today should look to the work of studio designers for some stunning examples of modern glove craft. Some examples veer towards the surreal, but they do illustrate that where a clothing object is still needed, there will always be a designer inspired to re-interpret the shape according to his own aesthetic.

Far left *Sexual overtones hardly need discussing: long, peelable gloves, worn by Ava Gardner. The Killers, 1946.*

Centre *The return to the long glove after the war: designs by Rahvis, 1951.*
Right *Spick and span short gloves; very much part of the youthful American style, 1955.*

Left *Long gloves have always been the symbol of elegance: design by Arpen c 1938.*

A last look at post-war elegance, 1960.

Compare this gauntlet glove with the Liberty catalogue design; although suggesting an older date the flowers are unmistakably Art Deco in concept and date from c 1925–1935. Made by Alexandrine of Paris.

A beautiful cream buckskin glove, custom-made, and fastened with a tab and press stud, 1910.

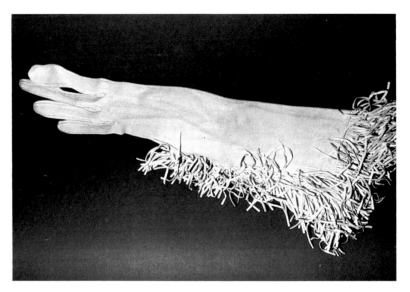

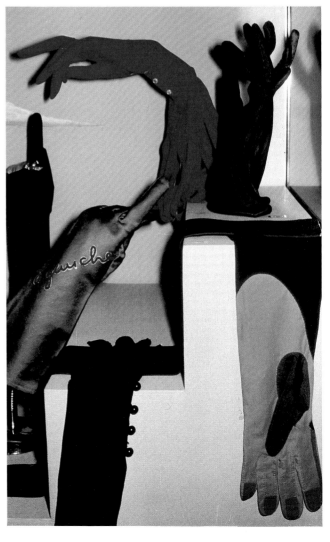

Designs for 1930s accessories shown in a catalogue from Liberty's, c 1935. Note the pretty gauntlet shape of the gloves matching the handbag in an Art Deco design.

Right Contemporary gloves showing that young designers still enjoy experimenting with traditional forms. Any collection has room for individualistic objects such as these.

LINGERIE

The trend in women's underwear during this century may seem to go from restriction to liberation, but in fact the change in style and shape from the Gibson Girl of the 1900s to today's active working woman has not followed an undeviating course. It is probably better to view the female form as a canvas, with endless possibilities to portray an altered silhouette and varying centres of interest.

The corsets of 1900 were stiffened with whalebone, straight-fronted below the bosom and extended well below the waist in order to produce the 'S' bend shape. Some of these corsets claimed to reduce the size of woman's waist by as much as two inches 'without causing the slightest discomfort or inconvenience' according to an advertisement for 'Ye Daintie Corsette', from Mesdames Perkins and Tinsley, London, 1910. The relief of sinking into the lavishly trimmed night clothes illustrated must have been intense. At every level, great workmanship went into the lingerie for both trous-seaux and less formal wear, as can be seen from the depth of trimming shown on ready-made examples here.

When dresses became briefer, in the 1920s, underwear took on a new purpose: to conceal the figure without altering the outline. Suspenders (introduced in the 1880s) and stockings offered new sources of attraction, as they emerged, half-visible, for the first time. Retailers of fashion gradually

Above A 'Swanbill' corset 'for well-developed figures' designed to create the characteristic Edwardian shape, c 1900. **Below** Edwardian camisole trimmed with Valenciennes lace and ribbon.

Far left A 1920s beauty, demonstrating the new charms of suspenders.

A tummy-trimming corset for the new soft-draped clothes, 1934.

I dreamed I led the
Easter Parade in my
maidenform
Chansonette

Pre-lude—
A touch of pure genius

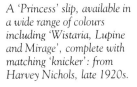

*A 'Princess' slip, available in
a wide range of colours
including 'Wistaria, Lupine
and Mirage', complete with
matching 'knicker': from
Harvey Nichols, late 1920s.*

Far right *One of the most
successful advertising
campaigns ever: the new uplift
bra for the 'Sweater Girl'
look, 1957.*

*Wartime economy in
underwear: home-made
ruched bra and pants.*

became more skilled at satisfying the demand for finery and delicacy, while keeping costs low, as mail-order advertisements for lingerie in the 1920s show. But the two opposing forces of high fashion and manufacturing practicalities are just as apparent in underwear manufacture as in outer clothing, and have worked on each other, a two-way exchange, throughout the century. It is interesting to note that underwear was available, right up to the 1950s, in a vast array of colours; unlike today, when our choices are in general limited to white, black, coffee or peach. The slips and cami-sets of the late 1920s and 1930s were made in as many as a dozen shades, to contrast or combine with the transparent fabrics of the prevailing dress styles.

As described in the chapter on 1930s fashion, ordinary women were fascinated by film stars' wardrobes, just as they had been by the elaborate 'toilettes' of Edwardian actresses. The monochrome cinematic glamour of satin pyjamas, white fur and lace are typical of the period. The charm of 1930s underwear is its femininity, and its lack of artificiality; women's figures were left more or less undistorted by underpinnings, in contrast to what happened before – and after. A probable cause of change was the invention of synthetics, the use of elastic and rubber corsetry, which began during the 1920s but came into its own with the wartime developments in the industry. Women who had grown accustomed to home-made cami-knickers and hand-ruched underpinnings during the war, must have revelled in the transforming effect of uplift bras and 'waspie' waist corsets that became the style in the 1950s. The photography and advertising of the period emphasize the fantasy element in women's view of their figures.

But fashion never follows one ideal for very long; an inevitable reaction to the tailored, grown-up 'New Look' of the early 1950s had reduced the female ideal age by about ten years at the end of the decade. 'Baby doll' fashions in lingerie and nightwear suggested this new mood which was soon to change all fashion. The centre of interest in the figure shifted to the thighs and midriff; John Bates' cut-out mini-dresses of the mid-1960s called for minimal underpinnings – bikini knickers, throwaway paper panties, and bras that offered no uplift at all. Fashion magazines suggested that girls who could not hold a pencil under their breasts could follow fashion dictates, and emerge bra-less; an opinion feminists were soon to condemn. Good authorities confirm that no-one ever actually burnt a bra, but the inaccurate symbol persists. 1970s fashions in underwear have pursued a trend towards

The Underliners

*Even today, the Edwardian
boudoir look still sells in large
quantities: Janet Reger design,
1982.*
Far left *Natural-shaped white
tulle bra designed by
Emmanuelle Khan for Erys,
1968.*

physical freedom; body stockings, minimal bra and pantie sets, knee-socks,
all combine with the layered, multi-purpose clothes of the period, although
the vogue for jeans in the 1970s virtually crucified stocking and tights
manufacturers.

It is interesting to note that nowadays women still need to choose
between two extremes. They have the active, functional body clothes, such
as leotards and tights, which are incorporated into costume, with skirts,
trousers and leg warmers, but they also require (to judge from the booming
business of such designers as Janet Reger, in England, and such outlets as
Victoria Falls, in New York) the romantic, lacey, sensuous underclothes
in which Edwardian ladies reclined. Changes in fashion have often been
described as the swing of a pendulum – but the history of underclothes
suggests some more fundamental ambivalence.

*Mary Quant underwear in
revolutionary 'Op Art' style,
1966.*

Three examples of highly ornate and original ladies' knitted lisle stockings from the 1900s. These were imported to America from Germany.

Elaborately painted silk stockings and hand-painted shoes for Coronation year in England, 1911.

Right *Hollywood glamour to the tips of her toes: novelty stockings with diamanté hearts from the 1920s.*

Centre *The delights of nylons, after wartime scarcities: Charnos, 1950.*

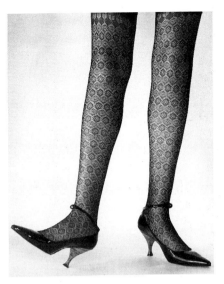

Far left *A good example of 1950s vulgarity: each stocking has 25 rhinestones down the seam, 1952.*

Left *Mary Quant 'Bazaar' designs for stockings in the early 1960s. Tights didn't become commonplace until the late 1960s.*

STOCKINGS

In the course of researching this book, we discovered a host of pictures of unusual and decorative stockings. This gave us reason to believe that a splendid collection, infinitely easy to store, could be made of stockings and tights from the last eighty years.

Bouffant petticoats and rose-decorated hose: 1950s romanticism photographed for Harper's Bazaar by Richard Dormer.

MENSWEAR

The most obvious feature of menswear in the twentieth century is its relentless sobriety. Volumes have been written, and will no doubt continue to be written, on why women's clothes change so frequently, while in modern times men's clothes have changed so little, and remained so sedate and colourless. Theories abound, but James Laver, in *Style in Costume* (1959), links architectural forms with dress shapes, an idea which is visually convincing: he pictures captains of industry gathering for a formal business meeting, in the days when they were the new power in the land. Their sleek black top hats exactly resembled the stove-pipe chimneys of the burgeoning industrial centres. Plainness in men's clothes reflects a social truth: men have no need to dandify, because women are still, in spite of the suffragettes, more or less in their pockets. Society works to man-made laws.

Mansfield and Cunnington, the great experts on fashion history (in *Handbook of English Costume in the Twentieth Century*), quote the editor of the *Tailor and Cutter*, who stated that the lounge jacket has remained unaltered in its construction since its origin some hundred years ago. The illustrations on these pages show just how little the styles have altered – even the revolutionary 'drape' jacket from America, in the 1940s, was merely a widening of the shoulder line. One only has to look at the sketches of Norfolk jackets, identical even when they are twenty years apart, to see that in casual clothing, too, development has been remarkably slow.

Perhaps one of the most liberating changes for men was the death of the

Unchanging styles: the Norfolk suit, 1905 and, **above right** *in 1920 seen together with smart riding gear.*

Lower centre *The Varsity look for young men, 1917: note the knickerbockers.*

Right *The epitome of male elegance this century: six-button suit, spats, cane, Trilby-style hat, Paris 1922.*

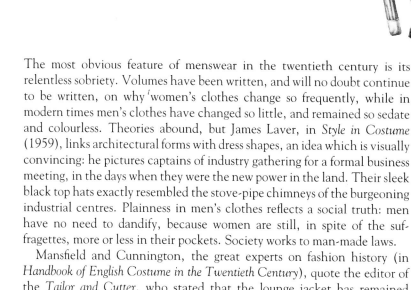

separate shirt collar. It was described by Cecil Gee, one of the leading menswear manufacturers in England, who started his business in the late 1920s: 'In those days,' he said in a long profile in the *Sunday Times* in 1969, 'the ordinary working man just wore a muffler; a young fellow didn't know how to put a collar on his shirt. So I started to market the shirt with collar attached, all sewn in one. I used to sell it with a diagram showing how to tie a tie. But to put it on over your head was difficult – it used to ruffle my hair, and I didn't like that. So I cut it down the middle, added a few buttons, and that was the birth of the coat-shirt!'

It is plain to see that the epitome of male fashion, well into the 1940s, continued to be the well-heeled countrified English gentleman. Hollywood stars, who knew as little about grouse moors and worsteds as they did about stage acting, were made to pose in fantasy gentleman's clothing, in order to conform to current standards of male elegance.

The most important single factor to change menswear was the effect of wartime restrictions and shortages, between 1939 and 1945. For example, turn-ups disappeared: the material was simply not available. A little book published by Moss Bros, the famous London firm of men's outfitters, at the end of the war describes two common disasters which befell men's wardrobes at that time: one was to be hit for six by a well-directed bomb, the other was to be chewed to shreds by moths while the owner was away at the front. The booklet continues, 'All over the country strong men are weeping at the final dissolution of some cherished garment they think is irreplaceable. . . . We of Moss Bros face the fact that it will take years to build up once more the vast and varied stock we offered you before the war, but . . . in addition to such stocks as we can gather there is always our hire service'. From then on, the tendency was for men to hire formal evening clothes, rather than have dinner suits made to measure. The cost was often prohibitive, and besides, the gradual democratization of society made such pretensions to class outmoded.

American merchandise became very popular – Mr Gee remembers the names he imported, which the collector could do well to note: 'We'd make the suits in England – straight cut with big drapes – and import the ties and shirts and socks. I was selling Manhattan shirts, Arrow shirts, Adam hats, Mallory hats, Stetson hats, the glove shoe. The shirts had big, long pointed collars – the Spearpoint, that name became a symbol.'

Top *Robert Taylor offering something different – a more rugged, American relaxed style. No shirt! 1937, and the alternative: Errol Flynn looking terribly British in checks, 1936.*

Above, left *Men's fashions, 1926: the trouser legs are wider, and turn-ups predominate.*

Centre *John Gilbert giving a good impression of an English aristocrat in Hollywood, 1928.*

Below *The image that changed young men's ideas of attraction: James Dean in* Rebel Without a Cause *(1955), and* **right** *Marlon Brando, equally threatening in leather for* The Wild One *(1954).*

Above, right *Robert Taylor and Robert Stack wearing good examples of the sports clothes American manufacturers produce better than anyone else (1950s).*

Hollywoodiana, always worth collecting: a Fred Astaire shirt c 1963.

While innovations in shirts and jackets may have been acceptable, other changes were less rapid. For example, the zip was first used in menswear in 1935, in place of buttons in trouser flies, but in 1973 Mansfield and Cunnington were still able to write, 'Its popularity in these regions took some time to establish and it has not yet completely conquered the older method'. This is no longer true – and certainly, developments in the last twenty years have moved a great deal faster than in the early part of the century. Lightweight fabrics and two-piece, as opposed to three-piece, suits made their appearance after the Second World War, but it was not until the late 1950s that synthetic materials made any significant impact on styling, and then only in leisure wear. It is still not considered smart or acceptable to use a knitted fabric for a suit, although Cardin did his best to suggest alternative styling for suits in the 1960s. Among the most successful of modern-day designers is Tom Gilbey, who has at least managed to break away from the numbing conformity of the lounge suit, introducing mixed and matching tweeds with exceptional originality and taste.

Prudence Glynn, in *In Fashion*, sees the occasional emergence of Italianate, sharp styling in the suit, such as the excessively tight-fitting, flared-trousered versions sported in England in the 1970s, as 'a reaction of men in a welfare state' – where women could find other sources of support and men, by asserting themselves in a peacock fashion, might regain their dominant

One of the best modern menswear designers: clothes by Tom Gilbey.

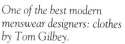

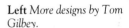

Darling of the jet set – a suit made by Tommy Nutter worn by Ringo Star in 1975 – even this modest advance in styling, mixing checks, never caught on.

Far left *The Italianate style popularised in Britain by Cecil Gee. 1960s.*

Left *More designs by Tom Gilbey.*

role. It is noticeable that in the 1980s men wear exactly what they feel comfortable in, so that one will see a woman dressed up to the nines in a little black dress, accompanied by a man in lumber jacket and jeans. What this says about women's independence, or men's view of their social position, is once again open to theory. Men seem to be moving towards a less hidebound style of clothing – women's ambivalence is a sign of the times.

Menswear in good condition is very hard to find – in earlier decades, before the war, men would probably hand on their clothing to the gardener, chauffeur or odd-job man. Nowadays, when hand-made suits cost a fortune, it is interesting to note how many men wear suits originally made for their fathers or even their grandfathers. This reflects not only on the excellent quality of the cloth, but also on how the styles remain essentially unchanged and can be worn from decade to decade. In this way many suits just do not survive and even the better examples of 'Teddy Boy' clothing from the 1950s, or 'mods and rockers' gear a decade later, are scarce. Paramilitary or unisex clothing might be an interesting starting point for a novice collector; perhaps combined with printed ephemera from the period. On a more aristocratic level, there is plenty of scope for collecting within fabric areas, such as woollens or worsteds. However, men's suits in their entirety are space-consuming, and likely to succumb to the moth: collectors may find they share the plight of the customer in the Moss Bros booklet whose 'dear collection might have passed well enough in Gruyère, but not in Piccadilly'.

Present-day casual wear from Gianni Versace, Italy.

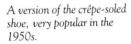

A version of the crêpe-soled shoe, very popular in the 1950s.

Above, centre *The Teddy Boy, in drape jacket and 'drainpipe' trousers, 1954.*

Left *In the 1940s, lapels grew wider, and the jacket looser-cut: Tailor & Cutter, May 1941.*

Prestige label clothes: suits from Cerruti, 1982.

LACE

Lace filet work dress from The White House, New Bond Street, 1920, advertised as 'special for the tropics'.

In collecting lace it is impossible to remain within the confines of this century if one wishes to enjoy the subject to the full. Hand-made lace has rarely been made in any quantity since the 1920s, and most people consider lace based on machine-made net to be inferior to the hand-made article, so the twentieth century does not seem to have a lot to offer the collector.

Lace is still a collectable commodity, however, because it is reasonably available and moderately priced. As one goes back in time, the quality of design and workmanship improves dramatically. The aspiring collector must learn about antique lace because this represents the ideal which later laces tried to achieve, and often imitated – some machine-made lace is very hard to distinguish from hand-made Mechlin or Valenciennes.

The terminology of lace-making is complicated, and the collector must have at least a nodding acquaintance with it in order to understand the intricacies of identification. The mesh or net in lace, the filmy backing across which lacy figures are dotted or joined, is known variously as the 'reseau', 'mesh', 'net', 'ground' or 'fond'; I shall call it the reseau. Similarly, the rows of thread which join the motifs are called 'brides', 'bars' or 'bridges'; I shall use 'brides'. 'Needlepoint' lace is made by stitching on a piece of work held in the hand or in a frame; 'bobbin' lace is lace formed on a pillow, using little bobbins for each fine thread, and weaving a pattern by twisting the threads round each other. Some of this is done round pins in the pillow, or against a paper pattern laid under the work in progress.

Right *Lace advertisement for a 'give-away' sheet to help boost sales of machine-made lace: New York, 1924, and* **Far right** *'How Paris Is Using Lace' – lace trimming continued to be very much in fashion in the 1920s. The Lace & Embroidery Review & Dress Essentials, New York 1922.*

In general, needlepoint laces were the earliest types, dating from the 1600s onwards, while bobbin lace made its appearance in the 1700s. Machine-made lace came into being in the late eighteenth century, with the invention of machines that could make the reseau automatically; it then became a much less tiresome task to add hand-made motifs. The difference in quality between a lace made on a machine-made reseau and one made entirely by hand can clearly be seen. A mechanically-made reseau compares poorly with hand-made work, where the motifs slightly distort the shape of the little holes in the net producing a fluid, sparkling quality in the lace.

What follows is little more than a catalogue of the main types of lace that can be found. However, this litany of names and places should give an idea of the rich and varied field that awaits the collector. The earliest form of lace was the embroidered work of the sixteenth century, such as cutwork, where the fabric was literally cut into holes of geometric shapes, and the edges neatened with hand stitching such as buttonholing or oversewing. The same technique is found in broderie anglaise, so popular in the Edwardian era. In filet or Buratto work, a simple geometric reseau was worked over with a filling to give a darned effect. Pieces are still inexpensive and a new collector can probably acquire examples for under £5.00.

The early styles of needlepoint are the noblest of laces. The beautiful Venetian laces are good examples – *gros point*, *rose point* and *point de neige*, which has a glittering frosty effect that well deserves its name. They have

Detail of Bedfordshire Maltese lace, made to compete with the imported variety until just after the beginning of this century.

Left *A dinner dress encrusted in Venetian lace by Doucet, 1903.*

Centre *French needlepoint lace c 1720, shows the elegant motifs and beautiful workmanship in antique lace.*

Duchesse lace leaf design, with flower sprays and scrolls used for a fan; late nineteenth century.

Far left *Early twentieth-century white work for baby's clothes.*

Lace on everything – boudoir cap, corsetry, pillows etc: from The Lace & Embroidery Review, *1922.*

A beautiful dress of Chantilly lace c 1900.

For the house of Worth: Chantilly lace flounces c 1900.

A seventeenth-century English sampler showing several designs in cutwork.

strange encrustations, known as 'cordonnets', which are small, padded curves or crescents laid on top of the floral motifs. The motifs are edged with little 'picots', pointed buds or whiskers, like some half-imagined hairy fern. Another lace-making centre in Italy is Burano. Collectors should be aware of the dangers with some of this work: Burano produced wonderful copies of the old Venetian laces, and also of the later eighteenth-century French laces.

All the French laces are ornate and sophisticated. The finest are *point de France*, Argentan, and Alençon. In Holland, some equally fine needlepoint lace was created in the eighteenth-century, particularly *point de gaz*, a typically romantic lace, with swirls of roses and the prettiest of fillings-in.

Bobbin lace differs substantially from needlepoint in its effect, and the fineness of the work is amazing: bobbin-made lace is generally flatter, filmier and softer in texture. It is quite easy to find pieces where the two techniques are used together – bobbin work for the reseau and needlepoint for the motifs. One of the early bobbin laces much copied in later work was Milanese lace. The design consists of scrolling shapes, large, trellising, fern-like leaves and stylized flowers, such as lilies or tulips. The lace was perfectly suited to deep flounces and is usually found in this form. Equally popular and often imitated was the Maltese lace produced from the seventeenth-century onwards. It was made in cotton or linen, or in a shiny, golden thread, with the combination of a wheatear motif and a Maltese cross worked into the edging of the design. This is a popular lace with which to start a collection.

Brussels needlepoint and Brussels appliqué are two extremely beautiful nineteenth-century laces, often re-used on Edwardian clothing when older, rare laces were highly prized, all lace being very fashionable at the time. Duchesse is a similar Belgian lace, with ornate designs employing clusters of flowers and elaborate leaf-shapes. Another beautiful Flemish lace is Mechlin or Malines lace: it has delicate motifs of flower-heads and arabesques, so generously worked that the reseau can hardly be seen. Late nineteenth-century examples have pretty, sprigged borders, tiny flower-heads and dots above the border design, known as *point d'esprit*.

Valenciennes is a typical example of the French lace which was slavishly copied by lace-making machines. Miles of borders in Valenciennes style were manufactured: the pattern is similar to Mechlin, with scrolling leaf

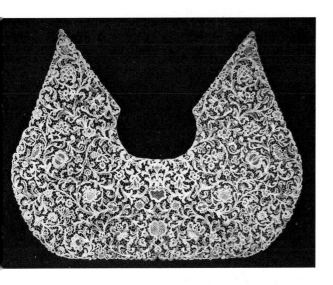

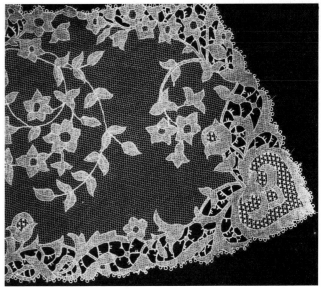

shapes, and flowers with dots or holes between, giving a summery, light atmosphere to the lace. It was much used for trimming underwear and nightdresses, being able to withstand heavy washing. Chantilly conforms to all the notions of glamour that the mention of black lace evokes, with swags of flowers, dots scattered on the reseau, and a light cordonnet running around the motifs.

English laces are considered less perfect than European because they lack a sense of structure and design. However lace from Honiton, in Devon, can be exquisitely made. Even if the motifs lack sophistication, they compensate with naturalistic charm: flowers, such as roses or daisies, plump little birds, or butterflies with patterned wings. The other main lace-making areas in England were Buckinghamshire, Bedfordshire and Northamptonshire, and, of course, Nottingham, the centre for machine-made lace.

Limerick lace, from Ireland, is machine-made: soft, almost velvety, to the touch, and extremely romantic in conception, which explains its popularity for bridal veils and wedding dresses. A rarer type was produced at Carickmacross, with muslin motifs on a machine-made reseau, giving a fine, gauzy effect.

Chemical lace, although it has a fuzziness and lack of distinction when compared with machine-made lace, where the motifs still retain a hand-crafted quality, contains all the elements, in imitation at least, of finer pieces. The collector with limited funds may find this a useful starting point.

The Edwardian age saw the last flowering of lace in fashion, with gowns deep in lace flounces, blouses frothing with frills, and lingerie trimmed with ribbons and yet more lace. As this century has progressed and the working girl washing her own 'smalls', without the aid of maid or laundry, has emerged, the use of lace has inevitably diminished. However, the collector can search happily for lovely Edwardian 'whites', pretty 1930s cami-knickers trimmed with ecru lace, sets of cuffs and collars sold in the 1920s for transforming last year's summer dress, dresses from all decades with inserts and panels of lace. The rock n'roll song of the 1950s, "Chantilly lace and a pretty face . . ." shows how potent the image still is of a pretty girl in sexy black lace (even if the lace is only nylon). While the dedicated collector of fine laces might look askance, I would suggest that a collection based on the use of lace in fashion in this century could be very rewarding.

Carrickmacross lace, late nineteenth-century Irish work. This and other late English laces are still available at modest prices in auction sales.

Left *A Honiton lace collar c 1900.*

Centre *Fine examples of Buckinghamshire bobbin lace, with the naturalistic motifs generally found in English lace.*

HOW TO KEEP YOUR COLLECTION

Conservation

Conservation is one of the thorniest issues for the collector to take up. There are a great many pitfalls, and, as far as textiles are concerned, the science of conservation is still in its infancy, so no hard and fast rules can be given. Betty Kirke, who is responsible for conservation at the Fashion Institute of New York, could only offer the new collector the wariest of policies, illustrating just how difficult it is to decide on the right treatment for any garment or object that is intended for preservation in a collection:

> The whole field is totally up in the air. There are now two different viewpoints at least on nearly everything. Whether to wash, or not to wash an old garment, whether dry cleaning is permissible – the Victoria and Albert Museum dry cleans some pieces, whereas the Metropolitan Museum of New York doesn't do this for anything. The safest thing that can be suggested is a little vacuuming to lift out the dust. Conservation of old clothes is now more experimental than ever before, with each country involved in the business going off in its own different direction, and each one developing its own talents. The best method of conservation, after all, would be to put the clothes in a room full of nitrogen, with no oxygen, and keep them all in the dark! But the decision has to be taken: what are the clothes to be kept for? Attendance at museum exhibitions on fashion has increased steadily over the last decade. In New York, for example, a costume exhibition at the Met seven years ago received 35,000 visitors. Then we staged a special display on 'Sporting Life' which took in 126,000 people. The last big exhibition on 'Romantic & Glamorous Hollywood Design' was seen by 750,000. The interest in costume history is steadily on the increase, and museum conservators have to remember that the clothes will have to be moved about, will have to be seen. And costume or fashion students have to be able to touch clothes in order to understand structure, cut, and all kinds of techniques. So these considerations must be weighed against the ideal environment, and the lifetime of the object will necessarily be shortened by this.

In conclusion, Ms Kirke advised, 'When in doubt, don't do *anything* – beyond asking for expert advice.'

Why is conservation such a difficult issue? The problem is that few people know how long any particular fabric will last. Among fashion collectors dedicated to the idea of preserving our heritage in our costume history, there is a strong disapproval of the increasing amateur interest in collecting. Although I have tried to show throughout this book that there are some fields where articles are rare, and others where pieces are not so few and far between, there are many serious collectors who would frown on any encouragement offered to beginners. Such an attitude is not so much to deny a pleasure, but for fear that the objects, once acquired, would not be treated well. This in the long run would be detrimental to the inheritance which should be preserved and passed on, either through museums or private collections, to future generations. Even on the most modest level, therefore, it is vital that collectors should be fully conscious of the responsibility they take on when hoarding even a few precious objects. In fifty years' time those few pieces might be of inestimable value, in a world where the past is so easily discarded, and our social history so poorly understood.

The philosophy of conservation is in itself something that the collector should understand. For example, conservation is not the same thing as restoration. Karen Finch, who runs the Textile Conservation Centre, Hampton Court Palace, says, 'Restoration aims to make objects look and function according to the intention of their original makers by reproducing worn or missing parts with new materials. Traditional workmanship may or may not be used.' In practical terms, this is what happens to an antique wedding veil which a younger member of the family has mended to use again. A valuable piece of lace which was to be conserved would be treated differently, according to Karen Finch's definition: 'Conservation is concerned with the safe-keeping of objects as examples of their kinds and periods. Conservation treatment must neither add to nor take away from the original but only make it safe for display, storage or future study.' To take the example of the lace veil, this would mean that holes would not necessarily be filled in with new working, but merely supported so that the deterioration would go no further; the piece would then perhaps be carefully cleaned to avoid further damage from rotting with dirt, and stored away following such instructions as are given later in this chapter.

While the issues of conservation and restoration may be hotly debated by museum workers, they are not irrelevant to the modern collector. Everyone entering the field must be aware of the responsibilities that accompany the acquisition of fine old things, and temper their habits with the long-term value of the object clearly kept in mind. For the private collector, the first and most important of these habits must be correct storage and maintenance.

Storage and Maintenance

All experts agree that wearing old clothes is not to be recommended. The reasons are simple. An old dress, for example, contains a certain amount of body perspiration, especially in the underarm area. If the collector starts to wear the dress again, the salts in the textile will be re-activated by contact with body heat, and the deterioration of the textile will be accelerated anew. Even sitting down in a tired old fabric causes an extraordinary amount of additional wear, and a dress that appeared strong and in reasonably good condition may fall apart after very few occasions of re-use.

Cleaning old fabrics is a difficult question. No one can be quite sure how the fibres and the dye in the fabric will respond to either dry cleaning or hand-washing, and these processes are irreversible – which according to the principles of conservation means that the collector is making a change to the state and condition of the object in such a way that it can never be put back as it was before. If cleaning is an absolute necessity, then a small sample of the textile should be tested to see what happens – the colour may run, the fabric may shrink beyond recognition, or go hard and resisting so that the quality of the garment is permanently lost. As Ms Kirke advised, vacuuming is the only method of cleaning that can be safely recommended. For fragile textiles, the object can be mounted between layers of suitable plastic mesh, and the vacuum cleaner used through it, so that the fabric is subjected to the least possible tension. The Textile Conservation Centre at Hampton Court Palace uses for this purpose a nylon monofilament screening, which is cheap and easily obtainable. Brushing the fabric directly must be only very carefully attempted, as it tends to move the dust about rather than remove it completely from the fabric.

Phyllis Magidson of the Museum of the City of New York suggested the use of unscented pharmaceutical talc to lift out grease and oils from the fabric: the talc is shaken on to the textile, left for a short time, and then very lightly brushed out. Spot cleaning to remove grease or other stains is not recommended, because modern solvents may unfix the mordants in a dyed fabric, causing the colours to run. But dry cleaning is probably best left to expert companies, who have a vast range of chemicals for the purpose, and can test the fabric and choose the right substance for it. If, however, the collector feels confident that a dress or other piece will withstand dry cleaning, because the fabric is identifiable and in good strong condition, then a further precaution should always be to remove buttons, hooks and eyes, and any decorative additions that might cause damage to the material in the machine. The recommended method for dry cleaning is to put the prepared object into a big bag made of old nylon curtaining, and sew it up, all round, before the piece is put into the dry-cleaning machine. This subjects it to less direct wear and tear.

There are pieces that can, of course, be washed very successfully: turn-of-the-century blouses would have been boiled in their heyday, and are often still in good enough condition to receive a firm washing process. Laces can respond amazingly well too (one dealer confessed that she still boils lace in a mild detergent, but then her years of experience of handling various pieces have probably enabled her to know which items will survive the process and which will not). Francesca Bianco of Saks Fifth Avenue Bridal Salon suggests sewing small pieces of lace into a muslin bag to give support during a gentle hand-washing process. Larger pieces can be loosely stitched between two layers of fine mesh and laid flat in a large receptacle (the bath is ideal) for a gentle wash. Easing the suds through the object, perhaps using a sponge to help to loosen and lift out the dirt, is sufficient for most old pieces. Whites should not be bleached, as an old fabric may not withstand this treatment after years of storage. A further precaution, which is a little difficult for the collector at home, is the use of neutral water: ideally a water-purifying processor should be used, and the final rinse performed with distilled water. A hand-shower attachment is useful for this process. Failing distilled water, the water used for washing should be boiled first to remove its hardness and other impurities. Karen Finch explains why: 'Pinpoints of iron mould on textiles may have been caused originally by traces of iron in washing water, so it is very wise to give a final rinse in pure distilled water, so that there will be the least traces of impurities to leave marks.'

A further tip before washing a beaded dress was offered by Phyllis Magidson: turn the dress inside out to see if the threads holding the beads have turned brown. If they have, it indicates that the dye in the thread has already oxidized, so that if you wash the piece the threads will simply fall away – and the beading will be lost. Always test a coloured bead to make sure that it does not lose its colour in washing. If the beaded dress also includes sequins you should carefully test these before washing the dress. In the early part of this century sequins were made from a bewildering variety of substances; some, like glycerine or the 'fish-scale' sequins, will dissolve in water.

It should be remembered that any dress with a lining should be treated as two separate garments: the lining should be unstitched and washed separately. Otherwise, it might shrink at a different rate from the dress itself, causing distortion, or the colour might run and spoil the outer fabric.

The drying process needs as careful supervision as the washing: once again, a piece of plastic mesh offers the best prospect, for the garment can be laid out on it with the least possible strain, and the air can circulate freely through the fabric. A conscientious collector will keep various pieces of mesh, labelled clearly, for washing, dry cleaning, and for drying. As the edges of the mesh tend to fray, it is a good idea to bind them with straight tape so that they will not catch on delicate fabrics. The garment, once laid out, should be dried at an even temperature: neither too fast, under direct artificial heat, nor too slowly, which can increase the risk of running dyes or shrinking. Creases can be smoothed out by hand as the drying progresses, which often obviates the need to iron the piece. Professional conservators take the drying process very seriously, constantly watching the garment, adjusting its position, and making sure that no avoidable deterioration is taking place. A useful piece of advice for drying smaller items, such as lace, is to take the measurements of the piece, and pin out the washed fabric accordingly (using glass-topped, stainless steel pins, so that there is no risk of rust marks). During the drying process, the collector can then see if the object is losing shape, and the lace or other material can be gently pulled back into position – very experimentally at first, to ensure that the damage is not irreversible: it is better to have a slightly smaller piece than a ripped one.

When the garment is dry, it is best not to iron it, for this only increases the risk of further damage, setting in stains and ironing in creases. If ironing is necessary and not too risky, then only the coolest setting is to be recommended, and certainly without steam, which merely puts humidity back into the fabric, making it a bad risk to store.

Now that the object is ready to put away, the collector has to decide on the method of storage. It is generally thought best to hang the dress on a dummy, so that the weight of the fabric is evenly distributed, and so that no incorrect creases can form – for these will eventually lead to cracks in the textile. From the point of view of space, this may not be feasible for the private collector. The next best method is to hang the dress on a padded hanger. Tapes, sewn inside the dress at the waist and attached to the hanger, can help to take the weight of a long skirt. Padding the shoulders and sleeves of a dress also prevents creasing and cracking, and helps the dress to remain as close to its best state as possible. If the collector can afford them, cambric storage bags should be sewn to slip over each hanger to keep the pieces dust-free. It is common sense, after all these precautions have been taken, to hang the collection with a little space between each item, so that air can circulate and the objects remain uncreased. (I might add here that auction houses could well afford to take more care of the clothes they sell – it often happens that in a week's viewing before a big sale, the dresses will be so manhandled that an object will be seriously altered by the time the collector makes a purchase. This is unfortunately a risk that has to be taken, but it could be minimized with a little fore-thought.) If cambric is not available, a suitable temporary cover can be made by pinning layers of acid-free tissue paper over each hanger. Never use polythene or plastic bags, for two reasons: they are by nature static, so that they attract dirt rather than repelling it; and they create a greenhouse atmosphere, causing humidity rather than preventing it. Acid-free tissue paper is readily available in the bigger stores. Most ordinary tissue paper is made from wood pulp; wood is acid, and eventually this kind of paper stains the textile folded in it. Even acid-free paper yellows with age, and should be changed as soon as this is apparent. One very important thing to consider when hanging clothes up is the hanger itself; a surprising number of people care enough not to use wire hangers, and then choose unfinished wooden hangers which can seriously damage fabric. Unless the wood is sealed with paint, a wooden hanger will rot fabric where it touches it.

When it is necessary to store clothes lying flat (and some museum conservators are beginning to think that this is preferable to hanging in most cases, imposing less strain on a heavy garment), it is essential to see that each piece is padded out with plenty of tissue paper, inside the sleeves, and especially wherever folds have to be made. Make fat 'sausages' out of tissue, and fold the cloth over this, rather than flat back on to itself. Beaded dresses should always be stored flat. The weight of the beads is simply too great a strain on ageing silk chiffon or net and can cause the fabric to shred at the shoulders. It is also worth considering storing bias-cut dresses such as those from the 1930s, and the bias-skirted dance dresses of the 1950s and 1960s, in the same way. The hems can hang down and distort the cut of the dress. The weight of heavy matt jersey dresses can also pull against the hanger causing the fabric to develop small holes.

Smaller items in a collection also call for some special treatment. Shoes, for example, should be stuffed with tissue paper, or kept on trees – which should not be too taut as an old shoe may have weak stitching. Patent leather shoes are the exception; they should not be wrapped in tissue but kept in a fabric bag. Hats are best kept on stands which fill out and support the crown, or in hat-boxes, well stuffed with acid-free tissue paper. All other small accessories should be stored in individual bags, or wrapped in tissue paper: jewellery in particular will be marked by scratches, and small stones may work loose, if this precaution is not taken. Parasols and fans are better kept folded, because the fabric may be too weak to withstand the pressure of constant stretching when open for display.

The problem about displaying fans is that they were never intended for permanent show in an open position: by their very nature they are flexible, lightweight, and intended to be frequently opened and shut. If they are displayed open, a certain amount of distortion is inevitable, but the risks can be minimized if certain basic rules are followed. The simplest method of display is for the fan to be propped up on a stand. However, a little support must be placed under the leaves (carefully positioned so as not to push into the material). This wedge is necessary to keep the fan exactly horizontal, not tilting forward from the handle to the leaf, which could cause warping. The Fan Circle has devised a small stand for displaying fans, which anyone could copy simply; the chief advantage of the design is that the whole open leaf has a measure of support and suffers the least possible strain.

If a fan is to be displayed lying on a flat surface, for example in a glass-topped case, then the guards must also be propped up, so that they do not fall on to the base surface, but remain in a horizontal position. The clasp of a hand round a fan naturally maintains the spacing of the sticks; left flat, the fan begins to twist. Many collectors display fans in special oval boxes with glass fronts.

Very fine wooden cases sometimes come up for sale at auctions, and the Fan Circle itself can supply names and addresses of people who can build a case to order. Alternatively, there are occasions when fan collections can be purchased in their entirety, say from the estate of a deceased person, in which case they may be obtained in boxes or drawers specially built for the purpose. Mrs Hélène Alexander, one of the leading members of the British Fan Circle, has just such a collection, housed in an immaculate walnut chest of drawers in miniature, no more than eighteen inches in height, with small drawers just deep enough to house about twenty fans, in their boxes, on each level.

One point to think about carefully is that it is now generally considered that any object made of PVC (polyvinyl chloride) will give off a chlorine gas harmful to clothes. Therefore, check that your plastic hangers are not made of this, and make sure that any articles in PVC, such as raincoats, boots, some 1960s clothes and many 1970s shoes, are stored separately.

For every kind of collection some general rules about lighting must apply. Old fabrics respond to light in the same way as water-colours, and fade gradually. The colours in dyestuffs fade fast over a period of time, but eventually reach a point of stability where they will not lose much more colour. Conservationists notice this phenomenon with old pieces of textile that have been 'restored'; threads may have been selected perhaps fifty to a hundred years ago which then matched the textile in question fairly closely. However, during the next span of time, the original textile fades much less obviously, while the restoring threads change colour a great deal, often showing up as a dull clump of crude darning on an otherwise handsomely ageing object. Karen Finch explains the rules about lighting in her book *Caring for Textiles*:

> The international unit of illumination is the lux. In Britain in summer, direct sunlight out of doors could measure as much as 100,000 lux and the measurement on a dull day, inside, would be about 600 lux. From a conservation point of view, the advocated illumination for textiles is no more than 50 lux. Obviously in the open conditions of a house, as opposed to the more controlled ones of a museum, some compromise regarding the exposure of textiles to light must be achieved, but very fragile pieces should always be displayed where light can be excluded whenever it is possible to do so.

Documentation

Throughout this book, a general aim has been suggested to the collector. The acquisition of objects, whether dresses, accessories, jewellery or the ephemera that accompany a fashion collection, is not an end in itself. The point of such activity is firstly to satisfy the desire for acquisition, but this is only truly pleasurable if you take the trouble to become personally well informed about the period covered, the range of materials you are likely to find, and the highest standards of excellence which should be represented in the collection. Your pleasure in the objects acquired unquestionably deepens as you become more knowledgeable. But, in turn, the responsibility of the collector is to create something of value to pass on to others. For this reason, regional collections are of inestimable worth. To collect and find out about the fashion pieces manufactured in a particular area – your home town, for instance – and to document the history of their production, will help to create a collection that a professional would admire.

Significantly, there is now genuine anxiety about the growing interest in modern collecting. In the *Guardian* of 28 January 1981, a group of historians and museum workers complained about the sale of old collections of photographs and postcards without the due realization of their worth. Their letter closed with the words, 'We can only hope that the current passion for collectables, which results in such objects being torn out of their context and locality, will eventually subside. Let us think carefully before sacrificing any fragment of our past for a short-term gain.'

This may seem a stern admonition for collectors interested in pretty old clothes, feathery fans and squashed hats! But any collector will soon be confronted with a dress-box in an attic, accompanied by an old diary; a fan in a case with the shop bill tucked underneath; a hat with old newspaper stuffed inside the brim. All these bits and pieces provide valuable historical evidence which it should be part of the collector's hobby to write up and store. At the very least, the date, price paid, and source of any object acquired should be written down at the time of purchase, because it is otherwise soon forgotten. Either label the item itself, or keep a giant scrapbook of your acquisitions. Avril Hart, who works at the Victoria and Albert Museum in London, believes that the best system is to use a card index, which is more flexible and expandable as a method of storing facts. Who knows what deductions future historians may make from these jottings? It is stimulating to take part in a quest for the past. The world is not so full of beautiful objects that we can afford to be careless about anything that provides a delight to the eye and a charm in its presence – and that, most certainly, is what collecting fashion offers.

COSTUME COLLECTIONS THROUGHOUT THE WORLD

The only way that a novice collector can improve an appreciation and understanding of fashion, in all its aspects, is by looking at as many examples of clothing styles as possible. Fortunately, there are a large number of museums that have recognized fashion as a valuable source of historical information, and the movement internationally is very definitely to build up collections, not merely for view, but for study purposes as well.

In preparing this index of resources, the author and editors wrote to museums with costume holdings, all over the world, asking for details of collections, viewing times, and the exact possibilities for the collector – that is, whether only the garments and accessories exhibited could be seen, or whether close scrutiny of the reserve collection was feasible. As may be imagined, the task was a daunting one; some museums never replied, and although we asked, every time, for further addresses of other holdings, there is always the possibility that some small, splendid and local collection has been overlooked. It would be very much appreciated if any such museum or collection could provide information, for future editions of this book.

The complete list may appear rather weighted towards UK museums and collections; our researchers were conducted very thoroughly, and worldwide, but the balance of the list reflects the tradition in collecting, which has always been well-established in the UK and northern Europe. (However, we are quite sure that there must be – or should be – more than one significant collection in Australia!)

Most of the museums that did respond were obliging and very informative; the entries here also include specific tips and general advice which will help the collector at work. Many curators were caring and conscientious enough to write with alterations and amendments to their entries, and to provide fascinating details of local history, which are a delight to any collector, and certainly serve to show what a rich field of social history fashion collecting can still be. It is worth noting here that the larger national museums, unlike local museums, tend to see fashion as a part of the fine and applied arts rather than as social history.

Throughout this book, I have been at pains to point out that private collecting need not necessarily conflict with the outstandingly valuable work of local museums and galleries. Reading through the list given here, it is very easy to see how much help and support a private, enthusiastic collector can give to the continuing work of the public sector. Many of these collections would simply never have come into existence without the backbone of some individual's donation to add strength to the effort. For example, it is all too sad to see the lack of a Doris Langley Moore at work in Ireland – the National Museum in Dublin has a wonderful tradition of textiles and fashion design to honour, and a collection only in embryo state. So it is hoped that fashion collectors will also look at this list with a view to supporting the work of their local museums, as well as learning from them, to the benfit of their own collecting.

A silk gown designed by Kolomon Moser in 1905. Museen der Stadt, Wien.

EUROPE

AUSTRIA, VIENNA

Modesammlungen des Historichen Museums
Schloss Hetzendorf, 12 Hetzendorfer Strasse 79, 1120 Vienna
Opening hours: Library, Tuesday–Friday, 9.00 am–12.00 am.
Open for professional and research use only.

The costume collection in Schloss Hetzendorf is part of the Historical Museum of Vienna. Principally concerned with items which relate in some way to Vienna, it consists of a library of over 15,000 books and magazines relating to fashion and a collection of costume dating back to the end of the eighteenth century. Unfortunately, the costume collection does not have a permanent exhibition, but items of fashion can be seen on request, by appointment. The twentieth-century holdings include dresses, shoes, hats and other accessories. Of especial interest are the dresses designed by Koloman Moser, one of the founders of the *Wiener Werkstätte*, for his family, and there are also examples of handbags and costume jewellery designed by other members of the group.

There is an excellent catalogue of an exhibition held in 1976/77 – *200 Jahre Mode in Wien* – which is illustrated with pieces from the costume collection.

BELGIUM, BRUSSELS

Costume & Lace Museum
6 rue de la Violette, 1000 Bruxelles (Brussels)
Telephone: (02) 512 77 09
Opening hours:
Weekdays: April–September, 10.00 am–12.00 am, 1.00pm–5.00pm.
October–March, 10.00 am–12.00 am, 1.00 pm–4.00.
Saturdays, Sundays & holidays, 10.00 am–12.00 am.
Closed: 1 January, 1 May, 1 November, 11 November & Christmas Day.
This collection, which centres on Brussels lace, has holdings dating from the seventeenth century to the present day. Although much of the collection dates from before this century, there are some fine examples of twentieth-century craftsmanship, including work by Worth, Doucet, Poiret, and Chanel. As might be expected, much of the lace work is in

wedding dresses; one of the most recent in the collection was made by Valens of Brussels in 1971 for the Princess of Lichtenstein. Exhibitions at the museum change every six months and are usually grouped around a single theme, such as the wedding dress. Many accessories are included in these exhibitions, from buttons and shoes to gloves, belts and jewellery; accompanying these there are exhibits and documentary items which serve to evoke the world in which the fine lace on view was once worn.

DENMARK, COPENHAGEN

Dansk Folkemuseum

Nationalmuseet, III Afdeling, Frederiksholms Kanal 12, 1220 Copenhagen K. Telephone: (02) 85 34 75
Opening hours:
16 June – 15 September, 10.00 am–4.00 pm.
16 September – 15 June, 11.00 am–3.00 pm.
Weekends & holidays, 12.00 am–4.00 pm.
Closed: Mondays, Constitution Day, Whitsunday, 24, 25, & 31 December.
Admission charge.

This is primarily a collection of folk costume, originally set up at the end of the last century and aiming to record social customs from every class of Danish society. The collection was widened by the addition of costumes from the Royal Theatre in Copenhagen, some of which were ordinary everyday clothes. In this century the museum has continued to collect fashion which reflects the increasing influence of foreign styles and the end of the ethnic traditions; that these foreign styles from Paris were not always well suited to the northern climate might be gauged from the local expression, "dress like the French, freeze like the Danes".

FRANCE, LYON

Musée Historique des Tissus

34 rue de la Charité, 69002 Lyon, Telephone: (7) 837 15 05
Opening hours:
Daily, except Monday, 10.00 am–12.00 am, 2.00 pm–5.30 pm.
Closed: Mondays & public holidays.
Admission charge.

This wonderful museum has one of the richest collections of silks and fabrics in the world. Lyon has been the centre of the French silk industry for hundreds of years, and this museum's holdings reflect the beauty and splendour of the fabrics produced in the city, particularly in the eighteenth century. From the twentieth century there are superb examples of fabrics designed by Sonia Delaunay and Raoul Dufy, as well as examples of the work of the world famous Lyonnaise firms of Ducharne, Bianchini Férier and Coudurier-Fructus et Descher.

PARIS

Musée de la Mode et du Costume

Palais Galiera, 10 Avenue Pierre-ler-de-Serbie, 75116 Paris, Telephone: 720 85 23/720 85 46
Opening hours: Daily, except Monday, 10.00 am–5.40 pm.
Admission charge.

This museum contains one of the most important collections of fashion in France. Founded in 1956, the core of the holdings were built up from a collection given to Paris in 1920 by the Société de l'Histoire du Costume; the collection has been added to ever since, and now boasts of 4,000 complete costumes and nearly 30,000 other pieces, covering the fashionable dress of men, women and children from 1735 to the present day.

The twentieth-century section is very strong, built up largely with private donations from people living in Paris and thus providing a very thorough documentation of French fashion, from the influence of the Ballet Russe in the early years of the century, through Dior's New Look to the present-day work of Saint Laurent. The museum has an active exhibitions policy, and there are a number of well-documented catalogues from past exhibitions available. The museum also organizes study group tours to visit the exhibitions.

PARIS

Musée des Arts de la Mode

Pavillon de Marsan, 107–109 rue de Rivoli, 75001 Paris, Telephone: (01) 260 32 14

This museum is due to open at the end of 1984 in the Pavillon de Marsan, part of the Louvre overlooking the Tuileries. Its holdings will be formed from the existing collections of the *Union Central des Arts Décoratifs* and the *Union Français des Arts du Costume*. The former was founded in 1971, and as well as having a large collection of textiles, costumes and accessories, it also has a large library and an extensive photograph and microfiche collection. The latter is an older organisation, having been founded in 1948. It has always been very closely associated with the fashion trade (Pierre Balmain was until his death a Vice President) and as a result its holdings have benefited considerably; it has a huge collection of designer drawings, 6,000 of which come from the house of Schiaparelli, 12,000 from Martial and Armand and 5,000 from Mainbocher. The costume collection numbers some 8,000 complete suits for women, men and children and 32,000 accessories. The library, built up around Madeleine Vionnet's library, contains books on fashion, exhibition catalogues, fashion magazines and a collection of 60,000 photographs, as well as the designer drawings mentioned.

The new museum aims to increase these large holdings and create a facility which can be used fruitfully both by the general public and the professional student; together with this educational role, conservation is seen as of paramount importance. The Musée des Arts de la Mode seems set to take its place among the leading international collections of fashion.

ROMANS

Musée de la Chaussure

2 rue Sainte-Marie, BP 12, 26101 Romans Cedex, Telephone: (75) 02 44 85
Opening hours: January – June & September – December:
Weekdays & Saturday, 9.00 am–11.45 am, 2.00 pm–5.45 pm.
Sundays & holidays, 2.30 pm–6.00 pm.
July – August:
Weekdays & Saturday, 9.00 am–12.00 am, 2.00 pm–6.00 pm.
Sundays & holidays, 2.00 pm– 6.30 pm.
Closed: Tuesday, all the year round; 1 January, 1 May, Christmas Day.
Admission charge.

Devoted to shoes and their manufacture, this museum has examples of boots, shoes and slippers of every shape and kind; Roman sandals, the riding boots of the Empress Eugénie, even an Austrian sado-masochistic boot from 1900! There are two collections of particular interest to the student of twentieth-century fashion, the Unic Collection of casual and sporting shoes (1910–1965), and the Jourdan Collection of more elegant shoes produced by Charles Jourdan between 1954 and 1972. The museum also has a documentation centre, the Institut de Calcéologie, which is open to the public and students alike for the serious study of shoes and the shoe trade. There are several excellent publications devoted to shoes on sale at the museum, a list of which can be obtained from the Association des Amis du Musée de Romans at the above address.

GERMANY, KREFELD

Deutsches Textilmuseum Krefeld
Andreasmarkt 8, 4150 Krefeld 12–Linn, Telephone: (02151) 57 20 46
Opening hours:
April–October, 10.00 am–1.00 pm, 3.00 pm–6.00 pm.
Sundays & holidays, 10.00 am–6.00 pm.
November–March, 10.00 am–1.00 pm, 2.00 pm–5.00 pm.
Closed: Mondays

Founded in 1880, the Textile Museum now holds a collection of over 18,000 items from all over the world. Although only four of these – three dresses by Vionnet and one by Lanvin – can be described strictly speaking as fashion pieces, the collection would be of great interest to anyone interested in the history of textile design. The Museum has a large and active publications programme.

NÜRNBERG

Germanisches Nationalmuseum
Kartäusergasse 1, Postfach 9580, D–8500 Nürnberg 11, Telephone: (0911) 20 39 71
Opening hours: Tuesday–Sunday, 9.00 am–5.00 pm.
Closed: Mondays and most public holidays.

The *Germanisches Nationalmuseum* houses a variety of artefacts which have been collected and displayed to reflect the art and culture of German-speaking countries. Thus the collection contains a large number of fashion items, selected as being typical of what would have been worn in Germany at the time they were made; the foreign items are representative of the kind of foreign clothes and textiles which were worn or used in Germany. The fashion holdings are strongest up to about 1914; after that date there has not been a consistent acquisitions policy and almost all the fashion pieces entering the collection have been bequests. The collection is not on view, and arrangements to see it should be made by contacting the curator in advance.

OFFENBACH

Deutsches Ledermuseum/Deutsches Schuhmuseum

Frankfurter Strasse 86, 605 Offenbach/Main
Telephone: (0611) 81 30 21
Opening hours: Daily, 10.00 am– 5.00 pm.

This museum has a well-known collection of shoes from all over the world, ranging from European high fashion to peasant styles, as well as footwear from many places outside Europe such as Africa, China, the Polar Regions and North America (Indian). The museum also has a very good collection of handbags, tracing the development of the handbag from the Middle Ages to the 1960s. Most of the handbags in the collection are German. The museum has an active buying policy, purchasing shoes regularly from the principal German factories, as well as other European firms in Switzerland, Italy, Spain and France. There are two excellent catalogues available, one dealing with European leatherwork of all kinds, including handbags, and a new catalogue devoted to the shoe collection.

STUTTGART

Württembergisches Landesmuseum
Schillerplatz 6, 7000 Stuttgart 1, Telephone: (0711) 2193–2931
Opening hours: Daily except Monday, 10.00 am–5.00 pm.
Late opening Wednesday until 7.00 pm.

This museum is one of the few in Germany with a costume collection extending through the twentieth century. At present the collection is extensive up to 1934, and the museum is actively building up its holdings to include more recent fashion. While the collection is not exclusively German, it is centred on the dresses and accessories worn by the well-to-do community of Baden Württemberg – a range of fashion from the great 'ateliers' together with good, elegant, mass-produced items.

This magnificent Cheruit gown in white dotted tulle and black Chantilly lace, was worn by a prominent Stuttgart lady, 1905.

IRELAND, DUBLIN

National Museum of Ireland
Kildare Street, Dublin 2, Telephone: Dublin 765521
Opening hours: Tuesday – Saturday, 10.00 am–5.00 pm.
Sunday, 2.00 pm–5.00 pm.
Closed: Mondays.

In spite of the fact that Ireland has produced some of the best fabrics used in fashion – tweed, linen and lace – and, in the twentieth century, has provided some splendid designers, the collection of costume at the National Museum of Ireland is only in an embryo state. The Art & Industrial division hope that the collection will expand and eventually be put on display. They have started to collect information and items designed by the Irish fashion community.. The author and editors of this book can only encourage them in their aims and ask all interested Irish collectors and members of the fashion industry to do the same.

There are some twentieth-century clothes in reserve which may be studied by serious students. Enquiries should be addressed to the Art & Industrial Division at the above address.

ITALY GARDONE RIVIERA

Il Vittoriale

Gardone Riviera (Brescia), Telephone: (0365) 20581/20130
Opening hours:
Tuesday–Sunday, 9.00 am–12.30 pm, 2.30 pm–6.30 pm.
Monday, 2.30 pm–6.30 pm.
Closed: 1 January, 1 May and Christmas Day.

Il Vittoriale was the home of the Italian poet Gabriele D'Annunzio, and the clothes collected there were either worn by D'Annunzio himself, or were chosen by him for one or another of the lovers who shared his exotic life on the banks of Lake Garda. The collection is thus lavish and idiosyncratic, and covers both men's and women's fashion of the highest quality dating from the 1920s and 1930s. The collection was exhibited between July 1981 and January 1982, and the clothes are unfortunately now in storage; only a few military uniforms remain on view. Permission to see items in storage and copies of the well illustrated exhibition catalogue can be obtained by writing to: Fondazione Il Vittoriale, Corso di Porta Nuova 34, Milan; telephone (02) 66 78 49.

Items from the Gabrielle D'Annunzio collection: a grey English bowler hat with grey doeskin gloves and silk bow tie, c 1930–35.

MILAN

Civiche Raccolte d'Arte Applicata

Castello Sforzesco, 20121 Milan, Telephone: (02) 6236 ext. 3954
Opening hours: Weekdays, 8.45 am–12.00 am, 2.30 pm–4.15 pm.
Closed: Mondays, holidays and the whole of August.

The Museum of Applied Arts at the Castello Sforzesco contains what is probably the most comprehensive public collection of twentieth-century fashion in Italy. There are over fifty items from between 1900 and 1960, concentrating particularly on

women's clothes from the 1920s and 1930s and representing the work of both French and Italian designers – Ventura, Salomon, Tizzoni, Chanel, Lanvin, Callot Soeurs, Molyneux, Fortuny and Mötz. There is also a large group of accessories, particularly shoes and hats. There is no catalogue, but a large exhibition in 1980–81 at the Museo Poldi Pezzoli was accompanied by the publication of *1922–1943: Vent'anni di moda italiana*, in which a large part of the collection is reproduced. Due to lack of space, most of it is kept in storage, and you should write in advance to make arrangements to see it.

MILAN

Raccolta delle Stampe Achille Bertarelli

Castello Sforzesco, 20121 Milan, Telephone: (02) 6236
Opening hours:
Monday–Friday, 8.45 am–12.00 am, 2.30 pm–4.15 pm.
Wednesday late opening until 5.00 pm.
Closed: Saturdays, Sundays, holidays and all of August.

The Achille Bertarelli collection contains, among other things, a very large and comprehensive collection of fashion drawings, advertisements, magazines and other publications from the earlier part of this century, concentrating particularly on fashion in Italy. The material can be studied in the normal opening hours of the museum, and permission to photograph individual items is available on request.

GIGNESE

Museo dell'Ombrello

28040 Gignese (Novara)
Opening hours:
October–March: Saturdays, 3.00 pm–5.00 pm.
Sundays & holidays, 10.00 am–12.30 am, 3.00 pm–6.00 pm.
April–September: Every day, 10.00 am–12.30 am, 3.00 pm–6.00 pm.

The Umbrella Museum must be one of the more eccentric fashion museums in Europe. Gignese, on the Lago Maggiore, has been for generations an umbrella-making town, and it was the son of one of the families working in the local trade, Igino Ambrosini, who decided in 1939 to build the museum, which is appropriately shaped like an umbrella. The collection reflects the whole history of umbrellas, from early silk Chinese ceremonial ones to their introduction into Europe as a practical method for keeping dry. Part of the collection is filled with nineteenth- and twentieth-century work in the local artisan tradition, while there are also many examples of modern high fashion work, such as a 1947 Christian Dior New Look umbrella. The museum also houses a collection of photographs and other documentary material.

ROME

Accademia di Costume e di Moda

Via S. Maria dell'Anima 16, 00186 Rome, Telephone: (06) 656 81 69

The opening of this collection is presently scheduled for some time in 1984, and it is worth mentioning here as it represents a very exciting addition to the range of Italian fashion museums. To be housed in the Villa Borghese, the collection will concentrate on the years since the 1950s, and aims to build up a comprehensive group of fashion items representing the work of all the major designers, particularly in Italy but also from abroad. It is hoped that the holdings will be continuously added to by donations from the designers themselves. The collection will be closely associated with the fashion academy, and its educational role will be stressed; a large collection of photographs is planned.

VENICE

Museo Fortuny

Camp San Beneto, 3780 San Marco, Venice, Telephone: (041) 70 09 95
Opening hours:
March–September: Every day, 9.00 am–6.00 pm.
October–February: Monday–Saturday, 9.00 am–1.30 pm.
Closed Sunday.
Admission charge.

After Mariano Fortuny's death in 1949 his widow Henriette, following his wishes, offered the Fortuny home, then called the Palazzo Orfei, to the Spanish Government. Years of indecision ended in the offer being refused; in 1957 the building was given instead to the municipality of Venice, on condition that the artist's studio should be preserved and the rest of the museum be devoted to cultural uses. Today the museum houses a collection of dresses and textiles, all designed by Fortuny, as well as many photographs relating to the Fortuny family. A catalogue of the collection is in preparation.

VIGEVANO

Museo della Calzatura

Corso Cavour 82, Vigevano (Pavia), Telephone: (0381) 701 49
Opening hours: Sundays, 9.30 am–12.30 pm.
Closed: All other days & throughout August.
Admission charge.

Vigevano is one of the main centres of the Italian shoe industry, and has established a wide reputation for the quality of its work. The shoe museum is run by the town council, and is built up around the private collection of the founder, Pietro Bertolini. The range of the collection is very wide, and contains a section devoted to reconstructions of shoes worn by famous historical figures such as Charlemagne and Louis XIV. The holdings of twentieth-century footwear cover all the major Italian designers in all fields – slippers, sandals, formal wear – as well as containing examples from many other countries, some of which are very exotic – Texan cowboy boots with spurs, or lavish Argentinian gaucho boots. The collection is supplemented by examples of shoe-makers' tools and documentary material. Arrangements can be made by writing to see the collection outside normal opening hours.

THE NETHERLANDS, AMSTERDAM

Rijksmuseum

Stadhouderskade 42, 1071 ZD Amsterdam, Telephone: (020) 73 21 21
Opening hours: Monday–Saturday, 10.00 am–5.00 pm.
Sundays, 1.00 pm–5.00 pm.
Admission charge.

The costume collection at the Rijksmuseum concentrates on the eighteenth and nineteenth centuries, and the acquisitions policy for the twentieth century covers European fashion only up to 1945. However the collections from the first half of this century are quite comprehensive, and contain a range of items such as creations by Worth and Paquin, dresses dating from the *Jugendstil* period, bead dresses from the 1920s and 1930s and French *haute couture* work up to 1945 (for example Lanvin and Nina Ricci). This collection has been made up from Dutch sources, so dresses in it represent the sort of thing that would have been worn in The Netherlands before the last war.

Due to lack of space the museum is unable to exhibit this collection, and it is essential that those wishing to see items should write in advance to the curator of costume to arrange a definite appointment.

THE HAGUE

Nederlands Kostuummuseum

Lange Vijverberg 14–15, 2513 AC The Hague, Telephone: 64 28 08
Opening hours: Daily, 10.00 am–5.00 pm.
Late opening Wednesday, 8.00 pm–10.00 pm.
Sundays, 1.00 pm–5.00 pm.
Admission charge.

The Dutch Museum of Costume places its emphasis on fashionable clothes worn in The Netherlands, though not necessarily manufactured in Holland. In building up the collection there are two main themes borne in mind – the history of style, and the cultural, social and economic aspects of fashion. The museum has a fairly representative collection from the mid-eighteenth century to the present day, though in common with nearly every other costume museum, men's and boys' clothes are lacking.

The twentieth-century holdings consist of approximately 200 pieces of women's clothing together with men's suits and overcoats and children's clothes. The dresses are from some of the leading French couturiers, Fath, Chanel, Dior, Givenchy, Molyneux, Cardin, Courrèges and Saint Laurent. In addition to *haute couture* there is also some typical ready-to-wear on show. From 1960–79 examples of Dutch *haute couture* were purchased for the collection – Koos Van den Akker, Ernst Jan Beeuwkes, Leon Bouter, Frans Molenar, Frank Govers, Maarten van Dreven and Cargelli among others.

The museum has an extensive conservation unit and has experimented with new methods of restoration. In addition there is a fine library of books, prints and fashion magazines from c.1750 up to the present day. Among them is a complete edition of the Dutch fashion journal, *De Gracieuse*, Leiden (1865–1936).

UTRECHT

A costume in silk by Dutch designer, Frank Govers (1981).

Centraal Museum

Agnietenstraat 1, Utrecht, Telephone: (030) 31 55 41
Opening hours: Tuesday–Saturday, 10.00 am–5.00 pm.
Sundays & holidays, 2.00 pm–5.00 pm.
Closed: New Year's Day.

The Centraal Museum in Utrecht has been collecting fashion since before 1904, and has recently built modern gallery space in which the holdings are displayed. The collection ranges from eighteenth-century costumes to the mini-skirts of the 1960s and beyond, concentrating mainly on Dutch women's clothes. Only part of the collection is displayed, but the galleries are notable for the thoughtfulness of their layout – fashion pieces are not seen in isolation, but in conjunction with other artefacts dating from the period, such as furniture and paintings. Applications to see items in the reserve collection should be made in writing to the keeper of costumes.

WAALWIJK

Nederlands Museum van Schoenen Leder & Lederwaren

Grotestraat 148, 5141 HC Waalwijk, Telephone: (04160) 32212
Opening hours:
April–October: Weekdays, 10.00 am–12.00 am, 2.00 pm–5.00 pm.
Saturday, 1.00 pm–4.00 pm.
Closed: Sundays and holidays.
Admission charge.

This is the leading museum in Holland dealing with shoes, leather and leather products. Since 1960 the museum has been based in a large Victorian town house, formerly the home of a family in the shoe trade, where the collection is displayed in nine rooms on two floors. Three rooms have been turned into tableaux which re-create the traditional workshop interiors of a cobbler, a clog maker and a tanner. The remaining rooms house a collection of shoes which range from archeological finds to contemporary work. Of particular interest in this century is a range of French, fashionable shoes, and, in complete contrast, a group of very rough and basic shoes made during the Second World War. These exhibits are accompanied by full documentary information.

NORWAY, OSLO

Kunstindustrimuseet

St. Olavs Gate 1, Oslo 1, Telephone: (02) 20 35 78
Opening hours: Daily, 11.00 am–3.00 pm.
15 January–1 May & 15 September–1 December, late opening on Tuesdays and Thursdays, 7.00 pm–9.00 pm
Closed: Mondays.

The Oslo Museum of Applied Art was founded in 1876, and since that date the department of costume and textiles has acquired approximately 10,000 items. During the 1930s the importance of collecting fashion was realized, and events such as a two-week costume cavalcade, or a fashion show displaying pieces from the eighteenth century up to the 1920s, were held. Such events have continued, and the museum has recently opened a new gallery of costume dating from 1750 to the present day. The collection ranges from traditional Norwegian clothes to ceremonial court costume donated by the royal family, and the work of international couturiers such as Worth and Dior in France and Mary Quant in the UK. It is not possible to visit the reserve collection, but items from it are occasionally displayed

in temporary exhibitions.

OSLO

Norsk Folkemuseum

Museumsveien 10, Bygdøy, Oslo 2, Telephone: (01) 55 80 90
Opening hours: The museum is partly closed in December and February. During the rest of the winter season, the hours are as follows:
Monday–Saturday, 11.00 am–4.00 pm.
Sunday, 12.00 am–3.00 pm.
Summer season: Monday–Saturday, 10.00 am–5.00/6.00 pm.
Sunday, 12.00 am–5.00/6.00 pm.

The Norwegian Folk Museum has a collection of twentieth-century clothes. The collection is intended to show how ordinary Norwegian men, women and children, living in the towns and following the general trends of fashion, dressed: it therefore does not have any examples of *haute couture*. Only a small part of the collection has been photographed and research facilities are very limited. However, the museum does have a collection of portrait photographs with people wearing their fashionable best.

This green alpaca dress trimmed with lace, was probably made in Oslo by a local dressmaker. It was bought in 1905 as part of a confirmation outfit.

SPAIN, BARCELONA

Museo Textil y de Indumentaria

Calle de Montcada 12–14, Barcelona 3, Telephone: (03) 319 76 03
Opening hours:
Tuesday–Saturday, 9.00 am–2.00 pm, 4.30 pm–7.00 pm.
Sundays & holidays, 9.00 am–2.00 pm.
Closed: Mondays.

This is the only Spanish museum with a large and comprehensive collection of twentieth-century fashion, containing examples of work by both Spanish and major international designers. The holdings are based around the Rocamora Collection, donated to the museum in 1969 and kept permanently on view. Apart from fine design work from Barcelona houses such as Rodríguez, Pertegaz and Bastida, and Madrid houses such as Berhayer, Zamorano, Villahierro and Camón, there are also examples of the work of Balenciaga, Doucet, Rolande and Paco Rabanne. Beyond this, there is a very large and varied collection which includes men's and children's clothes, servants' uniforms and court dress. Every imaginable accessory is represented, from feather boas, belts and umbrellas to embroidered handkerchiefs. The holdings also include an interesting small group of designer drawings.

TERASSA (BARCELONA)

Museo Provincial Textil
Parque de Vallparadis, Terrassa (Barcelona)
Opening hours:
Tuesday–Saturday, 10.00 am–1.00 pm, 5.00 pm–8.00pm.
Sundays & holidays, 10.00 am–2.00 pm.

This museum has a very wide-ranging collection of textiles and costumes, including a group of tapestries by six modern Catalan artists, a collection of Mexican Indian ceremonial dress, twenty-two antique sewing machines and a small number of twentieth-century fashion items. Although the number of pieces in this last area is tiny – there are only five – they are all of very high quality, representing the work of Balenciaga, Dior, Berheiner and Pedro Rodríguez. The museum also has a library containing research material on textiles and costume.

SWEDEN, STOCKHOLM

Nordiska Museet
Djurgardsvägen 6–16, S–115 21 Stockholm, Telephone: (08) 22 41 20
Opening hours:
June–August: Monday–Friday, 10.00 am–4.00 pm.
Saturday & Sunday, 12.00 am–5.00 pm.
September–May: Tuesday–Friday, 10.00 am–4.00 pm.
Thursday late opening, 4.00 pm–8.00 pm.
Saturday & Sunday, 12.00 am–5.00 pm.

The Textile and Costume Department at the Nordiska Museum has a collection which aims to illustrate the production, character and use of textiles and costume. The holdings embrace both folk costumes and fashion items; there are about 5,000 pieces of men's clothing, 3,000 pieces of children's clothing and 15,000 of women's fashion. The museum also has a large library and an extensive photographic collection.

SWITZERLAND, SCHONENWERG

Bally Shoe Museum
5012 Schonenwerg, Telephone: (064) 40 11 22
Opening hours: By appointment.

Although this museum has been put together by the Bally shoe company, the range of the collection is by no means limited to Bally products; in fact there are many important historical items displayed. The variety of designers represented in the twentieth-century holdings is very wide, and covers all the leading European houses. As well as publishing a guide to the museum, Bally has also sponsored a history of shoemaking which has been translated into English. Applications to visit the museum should be addressed to the museum curator.

THE UNITED KINGDOM, AYLESBURY

Buckinghamshire County Museum
Church Street, Aylesbury, Buckinghamshire HP20 2PQ
Telephone: Aylesbury 82158 and 88849
Opening hours: Weekdays, 10.00 am–5.00 pm.
Saturday, 10.00 am–12.30 am/1.30 pm–5.00 pm.
Closed: Sundays, Good Friday, Christmas Day, Boxing Day, New Year's Day.

This county museum has a small, representative collection of women's fashion covering the period 1900–1980, as well as

earlier material. Many of the garments originally belonged to people living in Buckinghamshire. Men's wear is less well represented, although there are suits from most decades, as well as shirts, ties, shoes, etc. There is a small selection of early twentieth-century babies' and children's clothes. The museum generally has some costume and accessories on display, but this may or may not be twentieth-century material. The museum also has a collection of local lace, of particular interest to the fashion collector as it is mainly worked as trimming for clothes.

As far as study facilities are concerned, storage is such that it is not easy to provide students and researchers with space to work, nor is it always easy to extricate material quickly. At present the collection is only summarily catalogued, but the staff gallantly say they will always do their best to help with any specific enquiry and welcome requests to study the collection. They are willing to provide anything within reason, on appointment. The museum has been building up its holdings of ancillary material such as patterns and magazines and will provide photocopies in response to enquiries. The hope is that one day there will be the staff and display space to do the collection justice.

BATH
Museum of Costume

The Assembly Rooms, Bath, Avon
Telephone: 0225 61111 (Weekdays), 0225 65025 (Weekends)
Opening hours: Daily, except Christmas Day and Boxing Day.

The Costume & Fashion Research Centre
4 Circus, Bath, Avon, Telephone: 0225 61111 ext. 425
Opening hours: Monday–Friday, 10.00 am–1.00 pm, 2.00 pm–5.00 pm.

The nucleus of this famous collection was formed by Doris Langley Moore, OBE, who founded the museum in 1963. A comprehensive collection which ranges from the sixteenth century to the present day, it has excellent holdings of twentieth-century designers and couturiers. Among the designers represented are Alix, Hardy Amies, Balenciaga, Balmain, Callot Soeurs, Chanel, Courrèges, Dior, Doucet, Jacques Fath, Hartnell, Lanvin, Lucile, Molyneux, Paquin, Patou, Poiret, Pucci, Nina Ricci, Schiaparelli, Yves Saint Laurent, Victor

The 'Dress of the Year' 1980 by Calvin Klein.

Stiebel, Vionnet and Worth. In addition to *haute couture* the museum also has a number of ready-to-wear dresses from department stores such as Jolly's of Bath, Debenham & Freebody etc., and firms like Susan Small, Frank Usher and Cresta.

Every year a 'Dress of the Year' is selected for the museum by a leading fashion journalist and is on view for that year. This practice, first started in 1963, has produced a fascinating group of some of the best names in recent fashion design – Mary Quant, Jean Muir, John Bates, Ossie Clark, Bill Gibb, Biba, Jorn Langberg, Missoni, Gina Fratini, Kenzo Takada, Calvin Klein and Karl Lagerfeld. In 1971 a man's suit was included for the first time with the 'Dress of the Year' and the work of Blades of Savile Row, Yves St Laurent, Missoni, Tommy Nutter, Fiorucci and Cerruti have been shown to date. It is also worth adding that accessories – hats, shoes, costume jewellery – are all provided to create the total look of the moment.

The displays in the Assembly Rooms are changed annually and include some charming set pieces. The number of twentieth-century dresses on display at any one time is at present limited to about seventy models, but there are examples of dresses (though not couture models) in the Secondary Collection at the Costume & Fashion Research Centre at 4 Circus which may be handled and examined. The Costume & Fashion Research Centre is open to any interested member of the public at the times given above, but if you have a special interest or plan to come in a group you should write ahead with a note of your plans. Among the resources available at the Centre are *The Sunday Times* fashion photography archives (1957–1972) and an excellent library. The library has a wide range of books and magazines concerned with fashion, including a set of the hard-to-find *Les Modes* (1901–08), the *Tailor and Cutter*, and a more-or-less complete set of *Vogue* from 1930 onwards. It also contains material from the Worth and Paquin archives (which can also be found at the Victoria & Albert Museum).

BARNARD CASTLE

The Bowes Museum

Barnard Castle, Co. Durham, Telephone: 0833 37139
Opening hours: May–September: Daily, 10.00 am–5.30 pm.
Sunday, 2.00 pm–5.30 pm.
March, April, October: Daily, 10.00 am–5.00 pm.
Sunday, 2.00 pm–5.00 pm.
November–February: Daily, 10.00 am–4.00 pm.
Sunday, 2.00 pm–4.00 pm.
Closed: Christmas Day, Boxing Day, New Year's Day.
Admission charge.

The Bowes Museum was founded by John Bowes (son of the 10th Earl of Strathmore) and his French wife, in the second half of the nineteenth century to exhibit a fine collection of paintings and works of art. The museum now has a Gallery of Costume covering the period 1740–1960s with a fair representation of twentieth-century costume including a Hartnell crinoline of the 1950s on loan from H.M. Queen Elizabeth the Queen Mother. The reference collection includes the wardrobe of one Northumberland lady dating from 1920–1960, consisting of nearly thirty couture dresses and suits, with items designed by Worth, Hartnell and Paquin. At the other end of the scale an important acquisition was the stock from a North Yorkshire draper's shop, providing a 'High Street' range of clothes with underwear, women's and children's dresses and suits and a few men's collars and hats.

The acquisitions policy of the museum has an emphasis on twentieth-century clothing worn in the Teesdale area, as well as

the acquisition of further examples of French *haute couture* to add to the good, though small, collection which already exists. The reference collection is open to 'senior students' by appointment on weekdays only.

BEDFORD

The Cecil Higgins Art Gallery

Castle Close, Bedford MK40 3NY, Telephone: 0234 211222
Opening hours: Tuesday–Friday, 12.30 pm–5.00 pm.
Saturday, 11.30 am–5.00 pm.
Sunday, 2.00 pm–5.00 pm.
Closed: Mondays, Good Friday, Christmas Day, Boxing Day.
Admission charge.

This museum has both a costume collection and a fine collection of lace. In common with most small, local museums, most of the clothes in the costume collection belonged to local people and represent the work of dressmakers and large London shops rather than *haute couture*. The twentieth-century holdings represent approximately 25% of the collection and comprise clothes from the turn of the century to the 1960s, including a red leather kimono-style jacket by Bonnie Cashin. The majority of the collection is women's clothes, but there is a small group of men's wear including suits, shirts, underwear, overcoats and cloaks. Babies' and children's clothes and lingerie also feature in the collection.

BELFAST

Ulster Museum

Botanic Gardens, Belfast BT9 5AB, Northern Ireland
Telephone: 0232 668251/5
Opening hours: Monday–Saturday, 10.00 am–5.00 pm.
Sundays, 2.00 pm–5.00 pm.

The Ulster Museum is building up a new costume and textile collection to replace that destroyed by fire in 1976 following the bombing of the house in which it was stored. In this the museum is largely dependent on the co-operation and generosity of local people – and others – who can provide information about surviving specimens of costume, or who are willing to let their private possessions become part of a public collection. The re-creation of the collection has met with reasonable success, but anyone who is interested in helping the museum should contact the Curator at the above address.

As it is obviously easier to collect than earlier dress, the museum has been making virtue of necessity and is actively trying to make the twentieth-century collection as complete and representative as possible. The collection as a whole could best be described as High Street fashion rather than *haute couture*. Already the museum has women's day and evening dresses displaying nearly every stylistic change from 1900. The 1920s and 1960s are particularly well represented. Such designer clothes as there are include Balenciaga, Dior, Fortuny, Grès, Poiret, Pucci, Saint Laurent and Schiaparelli.

The museum collects costume as an applied art and as a weather-vane of the changing taste of the era. One interesting practice carried out by the staff before accepting or rejecting a garment for the collection is to put it on a dummy to decide whether it has the style and proportions which make it typical of its date. This is often surprisingly revealing and can contradict the original impression given by a garment. (This excellent idea could usefully be tried out by the private collector). Any serious student is welcome to study any aspect of the collection. Prior notice is required.

BIRMINGHAM

Birmingham City Museum & Art Gallery
Chamberlain Square, Birmingham B3 3DH
Telephone: 021 235 2834
Opening hours: Monday–Saturday, 10.00 am–5.30 pm.
Sundays, 2.00 pm–5.30 pm.

The strength of the Birmingham costume collection lies in the nineteenth- rather than the twentieth-century holdings. Nevertheless, there are some good examples of fashionable dresses and hats from the period 1900–1960, although most pieces are of ordinary, everyday quality rather than *haute couture*. The majority of the labelled dresses were made in London, although there are a number of Birmingham-made clothes. *Haute couture* as such is represented by three items, a Poiret pink silk and gold brocade evening dress, c 1914, a black crêpe evening coat by Normal Hartnell from the 1940s, and a black and white crêpe day dress with a black straw hat designed by Victor Stiebel. About half the total costume collection of women's dresses and shoes are twentieth century.

Men's twentieth-century costume is chiefly formal wear, including court dress, and there is a limited amount of children's clothes.

The display and storage area for costume is unfortunately limited, and you should enquire well in advance about making an appointment to see items not on display.

BOLTON

Bolton Museum & Art Gallery
Le Mans Crescent, Bolton BL1 1SA, Telephone: Bolton 22311
Opening hours: Monday–Friday, 9.30 am–5.30 pm.
Saturdays, 10.00 am–5.00 pm.
Closed: Wednesdays, Sundays, all Bank Holidays, Good Friday, Christmas Day, Boxing Day.

The collection of twentieth-century clothes in this museum is quite small, but has characteristic examples of dresses reflecting local taste. In general all the material is in store, with the occasional exception of one or two items on display. One interesting part of the collection is the clothes belonging to one Bolton family, with examples covering three decades up to the 1920s, and which present a fascinating glimpse of the evolution of style and taste.

In recent years the collecting policy has had to be ruthless due to pressures of space, and as a result only truly 'local' costume will now be acquired. An appointment should be made in advance to view the collection.

BRADFORD

Bolling Hall Museum
Bowling Hall Road, Bradford, West Yorkshire BD4 7LP
Telephone: Bradford 723057
Opening hours: Daily, except Monday, 10.00 am–5.00 pm.
Bank Holiday Mondays the same.
Closed: Good Friday, Christmas Day, Boxing Day.

Bradford Industrial Museum
Moorside Road, Bradford, Telephone: Bradford 631756
Opening hours: Daily, except Monday, 10.00 am–5.00 pm.
Bank Holiday Mondays the same.
Closed: Good Friday, Christmas Day, Boxing Day.

Cliffe Castle Museum
Spring Gardens Lane, Keighley, Telephone: Keighley 64184

Opening hours:
April–September: Daily, except Monday, 10.00 am–6.00 pm.
Bank Holiday Mondays the same.
October–March: Daily, except Monday, 10.00 am–5.00 pm.
Bank Holiday Mondays the same.
Closed: Good Friday, Christmas Day, Boxing Day.

The costume collection of Bradford Metropolitan Council is housed at Bolling Hall Museum, together with all the relevant documentation. From this collection small displays are maintained at Bradford Industrial Museum and Cliffe Castle. These are changed fairly frequently and do not always contain any twentieth-century material. In addition, small exhibitions are occasionally mounted at Bolling Hall or at Cartwright Hall, Bradford.

The emphasis of the collection is not on high fashion but on what was worn locally, and wherever possible, the museum tries to obtain items made up from cloth manufactured in Bradford. Over half the collection belongs to the twentieth century and the museum has recently increased the number of items from the 1950s, 1960s and 1970s to include a fairly representative selection of ladies' day wear. In addition to a small group of men's clothes, you can find accessories such as fans, parasols, gloves and handbags, as well as babies' robes and some children's clothes.

The reserve collections can normally be made available for study between 9.00 am and 5.00 pm, Monday to Friday. Enquiries should be made to the Keeper of History, Bolling Hall Museum at the address given above.

BRIGHTON

The Fashion Gallery
Royal Pavilion, Art Gallery & Museums, Brighton BN1 1UE
Telephone: Brighton 603005
Opening hours: Tuesday–Saturday, 10.00 am–5.45 pm.
Sundays, 2.00 pm–5.00 pm.
Closed: Good Friday, Christmas Day, Boxing Day and New Year's Day.

The idea of a display of period clothes at Brighton has long been in the air – for over twenty years – and, largely thanks to the tireless efforts of volunteers and the Friends of the Royal Pavilion, Art Gallery and Museums, The Fashion Gallery opened its doors for the first time in 1982. The collection has been built up largely through generous donations and features some beautiful couture clothes.

The Gallery is arranged in two halves – the first, 'Why We Wear Clothes', explores a series of themes such as social and occupational influence on clothes, and a study of the variations in standards of modesty; the second half of the gallery is a chronological survey of fashionable dress from 1830 onwards. Clothes are shown in period settings to demonstrate the vital link between fashion and the fine and decorative arts. The range displayed carries the visitor from elegant court dress of 1916 to a duffel-coated figure of an Aldermaston marcher in 1960.

There is a special display of *haute couture* evening clothes including the work of Balmain, Dior, Jacques Fath, Hartnell, Charles James, Lanvin, Molyneux, Patou, Maggy Rouff and Schiaparelli. Finally, there is a display of recent and contemporary fashion including current work from the Fashion Textile Department of Brighton Polytechnic.

At the time of writing facilities are not yet available for the study of the reserve collections, and enquiries should be directed to the Costume Curator at the above address.

BRISTOL

Blaise Castle House Museum

Henbury, Bristol, Telephone: Bristol 506789
Opening hours: Saturday–Wednesday, 2.00 pm–5.00 pm.
Closed: Good Friday, Christmas Day, Boxing Day and New Year's Day.

Blaise Castle House Museum houses the City of Bristol Museum and Art Gallery costume collection, which dates from the late eighteenth century to the present day. The collection contains 'a mass of costume items collected since 1971 from all dates in the twentieth century'. The aim has been to collect across all social barriers. Examples of *haute couture* include a Jean Patou costume c 1925–30, a Dior 'little black cocktail dress' of the early 1960s, a 1950s outfit from Nina Ricci and a Schiaparelli fur evening top of the 1930s. Away from *haute couture* the museum has collected a range of blue denim clothes of the late 1970s. Since 1979 the museum has picked what it considers to be the most 'typical' dress from those designed for the Bristol Polytechnic Degree course, and it is hoped that this will build into a particularly 'local' collection. Other examples of twentieth-century fashion include several hundred items from 1920–1960, from the stockroom of a draper's shop in St George, a working class area of Bristol. These include a range of 'Utility' shoes and numerous frocks from the 1950s.

The displays at the museum cover a wide range of dresses and accessories, also men's and children's wear. These displays are necessarily limited, but the museum does endeavour to make the reserve collections as available as possible to the serious student and the interested general public.

CARDIFF

Welsh Folk Museum

St Fagan's, Cardiff CF5 6XB, Telephone: 0222 569441
Opening hours: Monday–Saturday, 10.00 am–5.00 pm.
Sunday, 2.30 pm–5.00 pm.
Closed: Good Friday, Christmas Day, Boxing Day, New Year's Day.

The Welsh Folk Museum has an excellent collection of clothes and accessories dating back to the mid-eighteenth century. As far as twentieth-century fashion is concerned, the preponderance of the collection lies in the first two decades of this century. However, the museum has acquired two large and representative collections of 1920–1940, and thus every type of material from pure silk to 'Celanese' is represented. The austerity of the war years can be seen in the alterations carried out on 1930s dresses and in wartime 'Utility' clothing. New materials, such as the early experiments in the production of nylon, can be seen in the full-skirted summer dresses and the bouffant short evening gowns of the 1950s. The 1960s and 1970s are represented by a series of costumes designed and made by students of the Textile Department at the Cardiff & Dyfed College of Art, although the Curator feels that these show 'a greater emphasis on style than that which would be worn by ordinary members of society!' There is a large collection of hats, shoes and other accessories such as gloves, handbags and costume jewellery.

The museum has a small permanent gallery for the display of costume from all periods. However, Edwardian dress is constantly on view, and from time to time there are also examples from the later decades of this century on show. The greater part of the collection is in store and it is advisable to make prior arrangements with the staff if you wish to see specimens from it.

CASTLE HOWARD

Castle Howard Costume Galleries

Castle Howard, York, Telephone: Coneysthorpe 333
Opening hours: Lady Day (25 March)–Hallowe'en, (31 October), daily, 11.30 am–5.00 pm.

The largest private collection of costume in Britain, Castle Howard can present a very comprehensive portrait of twentieth-century fashion. There are day and evening dresses of all periods from 1900 to the 1970s, ranging from Worth to workhouse garments, Dior to jeans. The displays are for the most part in tableau form and a certain amount of twentieth-century material is always included. Although the Galleries are closed to the public during the winter months, the collection can be seen by appointment during that time – there are no actual displays then as the old ones are being dismantled and new ones built. The collection can produce, if required, costumes by Worth, Fortuny, Poiret, Dior, Chanel, Lanvin and many others.

Castle Howard Costume Galleries are also willing, by appointment, to assist private collectors in identification and to advise on the care of costumes and textiles.

CHELMSFORD

Chelmsford & Essex Museum

Oaklands Park, Moulsham Street, Chelmsford CM2 9AQ
Telephone: 0245 353066/260614
Opening hours: Monday–Saturday, 10.00 am–5.00 pm.
Sunday, 2.00 pm–5.00 pm.

About half the women's fashion represented in this collection is pre-1939, but the dresses do come more-or-less up to date and include mini-dresses and hot pants from the 1960s and 1970s. A small number of men's suits, shirts, ties and shoes include án evening suit of the 1920s, a 'demob' overcoat, and a wedding suit of 1962. The collection also includes hats, children's and babies' clothes, lingerie and shoes. Of the shoes most are post-1939 and include pairs of stilettoes, platform shoes and boots. This museum also has an interesting group of military and non-military uniforms. The military uniforms are principally those of the Essex Regiment, while the non-military uniforms include that of the Deputy Lieutenant of Essex c 1912, an air-raid warden's tunic and a 'blackshirt' outfit, which bears the emblem of the 'I' squad, Oswald Moseley's bodyguard.

In common with many local museums, space is at a premium, and there is only one room in the Chelmsford & Essex Museum where post-Second World War clothes can be displayed. This display is changed about once a year. All the museums we have been in touch with have been generous with their offers of help and advice for the serious student and collector, but the Curator here does make a valid point – 'whilst specific enquiries by students and other interested people will normally be answered willingly, people should be discouraged from making vague, general enquiries covering the whole collection.'

A 1962 wedding outfit, when short dresses were popular for formal occasions.

CHESTER

Grosvenor Museum
27 Grosvenor Street, Chester CH1 2DD, Telephone: 0244 21616
Opening hours: Monday–Saturday, 10.00 am–5.00 pm.
Sundays, 2.00 pm–5.30 pm.
Closed: Good Friday, Christmas Eve, and Christmas and Boxing Day.

The Grosvenor Museum's collection of costume dates from the mid-eighteenth century to the present day, but the best-represented period is between 1840–1950. Most of the clothes were worn by members of families living in Chester and the surrounding district – giving a clear picture of fashionable wear in a small provincial city. It is hoped that eventually the Georgian House, adjoining the Grosvenor Museum, will be opened to display period costumes in room settings. The extensive reserve collections can be seen by appointment.

CHRISTCHURCH

The Red House Museum
see WINCHESTER.

COLCHESTER

Colchester & Essex Museum
The Hollytrees Museum, High Street, Colchester, Essex
Telephone: 0206 77475
Opening hours: Daily, 10.00 am–1.00 pm, 2.00 pm–5.00 pm.
The Museum closes at 4.00 pm on Saturdays between October and March.

The costumes belonging to the Colchester and Essex Museum are displayed in a branch museum, The Hollytrees, and cover all aspects of fashion. There are a reasonable number of dresses from the 1900s and, although the collection is rather short of material from the First World War, there is a good series of pieces from the 1920s. The museum is now concentrating on building up the collection from the periods subsequent to 1945. The display area is somewhat limited and the displays are changed about every six months. An appointment should be made in connection with any research, with the Curator, at the Museum Resource Centre, 14 Ryegate Road, Colchester, Essex CO1 1YE.

COVENTRY

The Herbert Art Gallery & Museum
Jordan Well, Coventry CV1 5RW, Telephone: 0203 25555
Opening hours: Monday–Saturday, 10.00 am–6.00 pm.
Sundays, 2.00 pm–5.00 pm.
Closed: New Year's Day, Good Friday, Christmas and Boxing Day.

Only a small fraction of the costume holdings are on display in Coventry. As it is a local museum, a large proportion of the collection is based on clothes which, if not actually made in Coventry, were at least worn in the area, and donated by local people. The twentieth-century holdings concentrate mainly on women's clothes, with good examples for the 1930s through to the 1950s. While very little of this costume is *haute couture*, there are some excellent labelled clothes to be found – Harrods, Liberty, Harvey Nichols, Reville and Worth in London; Rosange, House of Adair and Franchiset Soeurs from Paris. There are also some men's and children's costumes as well as

ancillary study material such as fashion illustrations and paper patterns which can be studied. In addition to fashion items, there is a small number of civil uniforms such as a nurse's uniform c 1910 and wartime ARP uniforms for both men and women. Another piece of wartime interest is an evening dress (1945) with the lining made from black-out material.

DUMFRIES

Dumfries Museum
The Observatory, Dumfries DG2 7SW, Scotland
Telephone: 0387 3374
Opening hours:
April–October only: Monday–Saturday, 10.00 am–1.00 pm, 2.00 pm–5.00 pm.
Sundays, 2.00 pm–5.00 pm.
Closed: Tuesdays.

Dumfries Museum's collection of nineteenth- and twentieth-century costume concentrates on the clothes worn by the people of Dumfries and Galloway, much of which was made locally. Styles are therefore provincial and conservative, with a cautious choice of materials and understated trimmings, many of the clothes being 'Sunday Best'. There is a small amount of men's clothes and costume relating to local trades. There is also an extensive collection of white cotton and linen baby clothes, nightwear and lingerie, much of it hand-sewn including a great deal of Ayrshire whitework embroidery, known locally as 'floorin' (flowering).

The collection is fully documented and most items have details of provenance and local associations. There is display space for clothing and accessories but the displays are changed at least twice yearly. The majority of the collection is held in storage, but is readily available to view by appointment.

DUNFERMLINE

Pittencrieff House Museum
The Glen, Dunfermline, Fife, Telephone: Dunfermline 22935
Opening hours: May–September only: Daily, except Tuesdays, 11.00 am–5.00 pm.

Originally set up by the Carnegie Dunfermline Trust, this costume collection is now administered by Dunfermline District Council. The twentieth-century holdings represent about a quarter of the total collection, comprising dresses and skirts, hats, shoes, lingerie, fans, parasols, purses and a small number of men's suits and uniforms. Unfortunately, due to recent cutbacks the museum is only open from May to September, and specific enquiries and requests to see the collections during the rest of the year should be addressed to the Curator at the Dunfermline Museum, Viewfield, Dunfermline, Fife (Telephone: Dunfermline 21814). There is a little *haute couture* in the collection, principally a Callot Soeurs dress (1902) and some dresses and hats designed by Dior and Worth.

The Curator at Pittencrieff House makes the point that a great deal of costume can be collected locally and very often at very little expense, while pointing out that ' . . . one of the main problems regarding costume is not the actual acquisition of items of a collection, but rather storing it properly so that no further damage is caused to the item in question'.

EDINBURGH

Royal Scottish Museum
Chambers Street, Edinburgh EH1 1JF, Telephone: 031 225 7534

Opening hours: Monday–Saturday, 10.00 am–5.00 pm.
Sundays, 2.00 pm–5.00 pm.
Closed: Christmas Day, Boxing Day, New Year's Day, 2 & 3 January.

The costume collections at the Royal Scottish Museum are extensive and international, and cover the development of fashion from the mid-eighteenth century to today. There is a special gallery for costume where displays are usually thematic rather than chronological and thus may or may not include twentieth-century fashion. The twentieth-century holdings represent a principally middle-class world with few couture pieces. In addition to women's clothes, there are also children's clothes and some men's wear.

As far as enquiries are concerned, requests for information should always be made as specific as possible. This holds true for all museums as in these days of government cutbacks, museum staff are very hard-pressed, though usually very willing to be helpful if they can. Requests to see the reserve collections should be made in writing to the Curator, Costume & European Textiles, at the above address.

EXETER

The Paulise de Bush Collection
Killerton House, Broadclyst, Exeter EX5 3LE
Opening hours:
April–October: Daily, 11.00 am–6.00 pm.

This fascinating collection of costume is administered by the National Trust. It has a large number of twentieth-century holdings, including an important group of Dior dresses. Killerton House provides the background for displaying the collection in some ten or eleven rooms, and the entire exhibition is changed each year. Each room is devoted to a different period, so it is difficult to say how many twentieth-century items might be on view at any one time. However, an indication of the displays in 1980 should serve as a guide to what the visitor might expect to see – a 1930s cocktail party with nine figures, a nursery scene from the 1920s, and a bedroom scene set in 1910 with two Court gowns, a dressmaker and three other figures. There was also a display of early twentieth-century bathing costumes.

Although the collection is stored at Killerton, unfortunately it is not possible for students to study costumes that are not on view.

EXETER

Royal Albert Memorial Museum
Queen Street, Exeter EX4 3RX, Telephone: 0392 56724
Opening hours: Tuesday–Saturday, 10.00 am–5.30 pm.
Closed: Sundays, Mondays, Christmas and Boxing Day.
Admission charge.

The collection of costume at the Royal Albert Memorial Museum has expanded considerably in the past ten years and there are now over three hundred dresses dating from 1900 to the present day. There is a particularly fine group of 1920s beaded dance dresses, and also some Worth models, but few other examples of *haute couture*; many of the 1960s and 1970s clothes come from the High Street chain stores. The accessory collections are extensive: blouses, skirts, shoes, stockings, gloves, handbags, lingerie etc. with perhaps 100 items of children's clothes, and a similar number of men's fashions from the twentieth century. The museum also has examples of twentieth-century lace, mostly Honiton.

Because very little of the storage is accessible, prior arrangements should be made if you require facilities to view the collection.

GLASGOW

Art Gallery & Museum
Kelvingrove, Glasgow G3 8AG, Telephone: 041 334 1134

The Glasgow Museum and Art Gallery Costume Collection is at present inaccessible to the public unless an appointment has previously been made. The entire collection is in temporary store, and as a move is planned it is best to contact the main museum at the address given above for details of where to get in touch with the Curator of Costume & Textiles.

Most of the collection has been acquired locally, and it is basically a 'middle-class' collection reflecting the taste of Glasgow's inhabitants and thus has few examples of *haute couture*. The twentieth-century section of the costume collection is very well represented as far as women's fashions are concerned, including a wide range of dresses from the Edwardian era, which are in superb condition, and beaded dresses from the 1920s, with some splendid examples from a local shop, Murielles of Sauchiehall Street. The 1930s and 1940s are portrayed through a large selection of ladies' suits, dresses and jackets, including wartime 'Utility' clothes. A stunning wedding dress of 1956 is perhaps the best example of this decade in the collection – made in white satin with an overbodice and sleeves in matching white lace, it is superbly tailored. The 1960s and 1970s have not been forgotten and the museum continues to collect from these years as well as from the earlier periods. The 1980s will not be overlooked as contemporary costume is also being acquired.

The collection of men's clothes is small at present, although there is a fair representation from the 1950s, 1960s and 1970s. The collection of children's clothes is also quite limited. However, there is a large selection of costume accessories including hats, gloves, handbags, scarves and costume jewellery from all periods of the twentieth century.

When we first contacted the museum for information about their costume collection, it was hoped that they would be moving into permanent accommodation with display facilities. Alas, due to the economic climate the whole project has been 'mothballed' and it is still not definite if or when this excellent collection will find a proper home. This pattern is reflected all over the United Kingdom, and we can only urge readers to become real 'friends' of their local costume museums and encourage them in every way possible, from raising funds to giving donations of good pieces.

GLENESK

Glenesk Trust Folk Museum
The Retreat, Glenesk, Brechin, Angus, Telephone: Tarfside 254
Opening hours:
June–September: Daily, 2.00 pm–6.00 pm.

As you would expect in a Folk Museum, the costume collection of this small Scottish museum comes exclusively from the working families of the Glenesk district. The collection is based essentially on the nineteenth and twentieth centuries and is primarily women's and children's clothes, although there are a few items of men's wear. There is a range of excellent study material in the form of portrait photographs and local newspaper clippings, but in general there are no study facilities available at the museum.

HALIFAX

Bankfield Museum
Boothtown Road, Halifax, West Yorkshire HX3 6HG
Telephone: Halifax 54823/52334
Opening hours: Monday–Saturday, 10.00 am–5.00 pm.
Sundays, 2.30 pm–5.00 pm.
Closed: New Year's Day, Christmas and Boxing Day.

This local museum has a wide-ranging collection of costume and textiles from all over the world, together with textile machinery relating to the local wool industry. Most of the 'fashion' clothes were made and worn locally and include day dresses, wedding dresses, a representative group of evening dresses, from 1900 to 1970, lingerie and an extensive group of accessories of all kinds. Men's wear is principally confined to Court Dress and military uniform.

There is some excellent study material available – pattern books, dress patterns and fashion publications. The recently opened Costume Gallery has clothes on display in cases and room settings.

HARTLEBURY

County Museum
Hartlebury Castle, nr. Kidderminster, DY11 7XZ
Telephone: Hartlebury 250416
Opening hours: Monday–Friday, 2.00 pm–5.00 pm.
Sundays, 2.00 pm–6.00 pm.
Closed: Saturdays.

Unusually, most of the costume in this collection is not of local provenance. An average of about twelve pieces of twentieth-century fashion are displayed in a year, but there is a large reserve collection of men's, women's and children's clothing and accessories up to c 1950 which can be studied by appointment. The women's clothing covers a wide range from maternity clothes to mourning, and there is a fascinating amount of what might be termed bedroom and dressing table paraphernalia – hat stands and hat pins, buttons and bows, brushes and combs.

There is an excellent library which has costume books, dress patterns, photographs and fashion magazines available for study.

HEREFORD

Hereford City Museums
Churchill Gardens Museum, Aylestone Hill, Hereford
Telephone: (for appointments only): Hereford 268121 ext. 207
Opening hours:
May–September: daily except Monday, 2.00 pm–5.00 pm.
October–April: Tuesday–Saturday, 2.00 pm–5.00 pm.
N.B. The museum opens on Bank Holiday Mondays.
Closed: as above, Good Friday, Christmas & Boxing Day.

The collections in Hereford fall into two main sections, adult fashion and a wide-ranging collection of children's and babies' clothes. Both these collections are stored at the Churchill Gardens Museum, and while there are occasional special exhibitions or fashion shows, in general it is true to say that none of the items is on permanent display. However, the Curator is always pleased to arrange for people to see any particular aspect of the collection in which they might be interested.

The museum is actively building up its holdings of twentieth-century fashion, in particular styles from the 1960s and 1970s and has acquired a good group of Biba and some Ossie Clark. There is some excellent pre-World War I material in good condition, dresses from the 1920s and 1930s, a good group of wartime wear including 'Utility' items, as well as fashions from the 1950s. There is a fairly representative collection of men's wear including 'Carnaby Street' styles, hats and neckwear.

The twentieth-century children's costume is divided into 'children's' and 'baby' wear (although it is tricky to define the dividing line in some instances!). The children's clothes include capes and cloaks, coats, dresses, gloves, hats and caps, mittens, pinafores, school uniforms, shoes and boots, socks and stockings, suits, underwear and night clothes. The babies' costume is categorised into bibs, binders, caps and bonnets, christening gowns, collars, dresses, nightgowns, flannel and cotton petticoats, robes and gowns, shirts, underwear and comes right up-to-date with Baby-gros. This wonderful array of material is stored in date order, and should give a good idea of how rich a hunting ground children's clothes can be.

HOLYWOOD

Ulster Folk & Transport Museum
Cultra Manor, Holywood, Co. Down BT18 OEU, Northern Ireland
Telephone: Holywood 5411
Opening hours:
October–April: Monday–Saturday, 11.00 am–5.00 pm.
Sundays, 2.00 pm–5.00 pm.
May–September: Monday–Saturday, 11.00 am–6.00 pm.
Sundays, 2.00 pm–6.00 pm.
Closed: Christmas Day.
Admission charge; handicapped admitted free.

One of Northern Ireland's two national museums, the purpose of the Ulster Folk & Transport Museum is to preserve and illustrate the way of life – past and present – and the traditions of the people of Northern Ireland. The collection of costume and textiles is mostly of vernacular and middle class clothes and does not extend beyond 1930. All the material is Irish and has been gathered together in the context of economic and social history. There is a very good collection of Irish laces from 1840–1920, but regrettably there is very little on exhibition. Plans for a comprehensive display of costume and textiles had to be shelved as a result of government spending cuts.

Items from the reserve collections can be seen by prior arrangement between 9.00 am and 5.00 pm, Monday to Friday. The museum welcomes enquiries and requests and say that their attitude is one of 'flexibility and helpfulness, if at all possible'.

HULL

City of Kingston upon Hull Museum & Art Galleries
Georgian Houses, 23–24 High Street, Hull
Telephone: 0482 222737
Opening hours: Monday–Saturday, 9.00 am–5.00 pm.
Sundays, 2.30 pm–4.30 pm.
Closed: New Year's Day, Christmas & Boxing Day.

The emphasis of this collection is almost entirely on costume made or purchased in Hull and North Humberside. The twentieth-century holdings are strongest in the period 1900–1918 with good examples of coats and mantles, and a good number of beaded dresses and jackets c 1918–28. The pearl of this collection is the work of Madame Clapham, a Hull dressmaker who first opened her salon in 1897 and continued making clothes 'smart enough for London' until her death in 1952. She numbered among her clients the aristocracy and well-to-do of the surrounding countryside and, most important of all, Queen

Maud of Norway, who ordered gowns from Madame Clapham twice a year. A fascinating booklet, *Madame Clapham, The Celebrated Dressmaker* by Ann Crowther can be obtained from the museum: it outlines her career and is illustrated with examples of her work which are in the museum collections.

IPSWICH

Christchurch Mansion

Christchurch Park, Ipswich, Suffolk, Telephone: 0473 53246
Opening hours: Monday–Saturday, 10.00 am–5.00 pm.
Sundays, 2.30 pm–4.30 pm.
Closed: Good Friday, Christmas Eve & Christmas Day. N.B. The Park closes at dusk in winter.

This collection, based at Christchurch Mansion, a beautiful sixteenth-century house, is at present mainly in store. However, the reserve collections are available to students and researchers on written application to the Curator. The strength of the collection is principally in is nineteenth-century material, but there is a range of twentieth-century fashion from 1900–29 which includes ladies' underwear, shoes and accessories, and 1920s day and evening wear including a good collection of beaded dresses. There are also several items of men's clothing and children's wear.

KEIGHLEY

Cliffe Castle Museum
see BRADFORD.

LEEDS

Abbey House Museum
Abbey Road, Leeds LS5 3EH, Telephone: Leeds 755821
Opening hours:
April–September: Monday–Saturday, 10.00 am–6.00 pm.
Sundays, 2.00 pm–6.00 pm.
October–March: Monday–Saturday, 10.00 am–5.00 pm.
Sundays, 2.00 pm–6.00 pm.
Closed: New Year's Day, Christmas Day and Boxing Day.
Admission charge.

The Abbey House collection of costume covers men's, women's, and children's clothing from the late eighteenth century to the present day. It consists mainly of working class and middle class garments, so as to reflect the general character of the museum, which is principally devoted to imaginative tableaux recreating a view of Leeds life in 'the olden days' – a Victorian parlour, three street scenes, a pub scene, a working class kitchen and period shops – the grocer, chemist and draper.

The museum has an extensive collection of twentieth-century dresses, coats, lingerie, hats, shoes and bags which is not displayed at present. Arrangements can be made to see items if a previous appointment has been made.

LEEDS

Lotherton Hall
Aberford, nr. Leeds, Telephone: Leeds 818259
Opening hours:
May–September: Daily except Monday, 10.30 am–6.15 pm.
Late-night opening Thursdays until 8.30 pm.
October – April: Daily except Monday, 10.30 am until dusk (about 4.00 pm).
Closed: Mondays, except Bank Holiday Mondays, Christmas & Boxing Day.

Lotherton Hall was given to the City of Leeds by the Gascoigne family in 1968 and comprises a beautiful garden, parkland and an important art collection. In 1970 the Leeds costume and fashion collection was added to the museum and since 1973, when dresses by Bill Gibb were purchased for the collection, much emphasis has been placed on the acquisition of contemporary work – not only fashion but also British furniture, ceramics, jewellery and textiles.

The major part of the collection is British, dating from the mid-eighteenth century, and is concerned with 'fashion' rather than the everyday wear of 'the man in the street'. As in many costume collections men's wear is thin on the ground. Of twentieth-century women's fashion, the museum has recently been adding to their holdings of 1920s and 1930s styles and the collection now includes labels such as Bradley, Louis Copé, Russel & Allen as well as some early Hartnell. The glory of the collection is very much the growing number of pieces by contemporary British designers. Work by John Bates, Victor Edelstein, Kaffe Fassett, Bill Gibb, Tom Gilbey, Gail Hoppen, Jean Muir, Zandra Rhodes, Pauline Wynne-Jones and Peter Yovel can all be seen – and the buying continues. The museum has organized some spectacular special exhibitions, in particular on John Bates (which opened the new fashion galleries in 1978) and, more recently, the major touring exhibition of the work of Jean Muir (1980).

There is a little French couture in the collection, with the creations of Callot Soeurs, Grès, Jacques Griffe and Jacques Fath represented.

Although space is limited, the museum is happy to arrange for serious students to see the collections, and will help in as many ways as they can. Recently a special conservation workshop has opened in the Gascoigne Almshouses. It is hoped that the textile department of this new centre may be able to hold 'Open Days' so that people can see work in progress, but you should check first with the Keeper at Lotherton Hall.

A stunning Zandra Rhodes dress from Lotherton Hall.

LEICESTER

Leicestershire Museums, Art Galleries & Record Service

96 New Walk, Leicester LE1 6TD, Telephone: 0533 554100
Opening hours: Daily, except Friday, 10.00 am–5.30 pm.
Sundays, 2.00 pm–5.30 pm.
Closed: Fridays, Good Friday, Christmas & Boxing Day.

The twentieth-century costume collection in Leicester is fairly representative of middle-of-the-road fashion of the period 1900–80, though it contains comparatively few items by major couturiers and designers. There are in the region of 700 complete outfits (men's, women's and children's) and many more accessories. The emphasis is on the period prior to World War II, with Leicestershire manufacturers' goods – hosiery, knitwear and shoes – well represented. In addition to the costume collection itself the museum was given the important collection of corsetry and swimwear formed by Symingtons, a major manufacturer in this field.

The Symington collection is almost entirely of British manufacture. Many of the items dating from before 1920 were made by other firms, but most post-1920 pieces are from Symingtons. The larger part of the collection comprises corsetry, brassières and bust-improvers, but it also includes children's Liberty Bodices, swimwear from 1937 onwards, wartime parachutes, co-ordinated bra-slips and waist slips from the late 1960s, and maternity wear made for Mothercare. The only 'couture' items are some corsets made under licence for Christian Dior (1957–59).

The Costume Museum changes its displays fairly frequently and there is usually at least one room of twentieth-century costume on view. There are also two 1920s period shops, complete with assistants and customers and three shop windows displaying 1920s drapery, shoes and gowns. Appointments should be made well in advance if you wish to see reserve material from either of the two collections.

LIVERPOOL

Merseyside County Museums

William Brown Street, Liverpool L3 8EN
Telephone: 051 207 0001
Opening hours: Monday–Saturday, 10.00 am–5.00 pm.
Sundays, 2.00 pm–5.00 pm.
Closed: New Year's Day, Christmas Eve, Christmas & Boxing Day.

The costume collection, part of the Decorative Arts Department, contains several hundred twentieth-century items, mainly pre-World War II. From 1900–1920 the collection, which is mostly day and evening dresses, reflects both local and national taste, ranging from Worth and other Parisian evening gowns, via many products of the local high class dress shops, to a certain amount of working class clothing. From 1920–40 there are fewer couture items, but a large collection of middle-class, local clothes, including the complete wardrobe of a Merseyside doctor's wife. Post-1940, the holdings are scanty, but an interesting collection of clothes designed and made by Liverpool Polytechnic students vividly portrays avant-garde fashion of the 1960s and 1970s.

There is no permanent display gallery for costume in the main museum building at William Brown Street, where the collection is stored. However, costume items are on display during the summer months (April–September) at Croxteth Hall, West Derby, Liverpool 13. It is possible for students to study the collections by appointment at William Brown Street, though

regrettably both space and staff time is limited.

LONDON

Bethnal Green Museum

Cambridge Heath Road, London E2 9PA
Telephone: 980 2415/3204/4315
Opening hours:
Daily, except Friday (including Bank Holidays), 10.00 am–6.00 pm.
Sundays, 2.30 pm–6.00 pm.
Closed: Fridays, New Year's Day, Christmas Eve, Christmas and Boxing Day.

Bethnal Green Museum is a department of the Victoria & Albert Museum, principally devoted to all aspects of childhood. The Children's Costume Gallery contains examples of children's costume from the mid-eighteenth century to the 1920s. The cases are arranged chronologically so that changes in style and use of textiles can be followed clearly. Adult costumes are also included to give a sense of scale and to enable the visitor to observe the similarities and differences between adult and child fashions. Wherever possible contemporary photographs or paintings have been included in the display to convey a more accurate impression of how the clothes looked when worn.

The displays also include underwear and accessories such as gloves, shoes and hats, and the collection of clothes is further complimented by a display of children's fashion plates. A new addition to the gallery is a range of fancy dress costume dating from the mid-nineteenth century to the early years of the twentieth century.

The museum does not attempt to show a comprehensive survey of baby wear, but the gallery does contain an almost complete baby's layette of 1923. There is also a display of Mary Quant designs for children (1978).

The reserve collection of children's clothes is viewable by appointment only. This contains clothes and shoes and some accessories, ranging from 1900 to the present day. The twentieth-century element of the collection has increased considerably during the past ten years; the collecting policy has now been extended to the acquisition of contemporary children's clothing (partly to avoid a future repetition of the 'gaps' which exist in the museum's 1930–70 holdings).

In addition to the collection of children's clothes, Bethnal Green Museum also has a collection of wedding dresses which spans 200 years from the 1770s to the 1970s. Some are on

A blue child's coat trimmed with fur, with a matching muff (1915).

display in the museum and there are many more in the reserve collection. The twentieth-century wedding dresses represent the work of some of the best British designers and fashion houses – Liberty (1905), Aida Woolf (1924), Reville & Rossiter (1922), Norman Hartnell (1932 and 1957), Victor Stiebel (1932 and 1963), Worth (1961), John Cavanagh (sketches and samples for the Duchess of Kent's wedding dress, 1961) and Gina Fratini (1970). The dresses show a wide variety of styles, techniques and materials. Also on display is a collection of bridal accessories such as fans, shoes, lace and head-dresses. The museum is also gradually acquiring outfits worn by bridesmaids and pages.

LONDON

The Museum of London

London Wall, London EC2Y 5HN, Telephone: 600 3699
Opening hours: Tuesday–Saturday, 10.00 am–6.00 pm.
Sundays, 2.00 pm–6.00 pm.
Closed: Mondays, New Year's Day, Christmas & Boxing Day.

The holdings of the Department of Costume & Textiles at the Museum of London are extremely large, and probably more varied than any other collection of English costume in the United Kingdom. The main groupings into which the collections fall are everyday and fashionable dress, ceremonial clothing and uniforms, accessories, Royal clothing, theatre costume, textiles and dolls.

The collection of everyday and fashionable dress is particularly rich for the period before 1800. However, there is an excellent range up to and including the present day. It includes many dresses from the major London shops and a number of examples from London couture houses – Hardy Amies, Hartnell, Lucile, Reville & Rossiter and Victor Stiebel. International couturiers are represented by creations from Balenciaga, Balmain, Chanel, Doucet, Fortuny, Lanvin, LeLong, Molyneux, Poiret, Pucci and Schiaparelli. The collection of men's clothes is relatively weak, but there is a large collection of children's clothes from 1800 onwards.

Simple everyday and working clothes have not been collected until very recently, and this is an aspect of the collection which the museum plans to develop. There is also a collection of occupational clothing and uniform relating to London, for example traffic wardens' uniforms and those of London Transport staff.

The unique collection of Royal clothing includes baby, child, adult and ceremonial clothing of the British royal family from the time of Charles I almost to the present day. The Museum recently held a fascinating exhibition of Royal wedding dresses ranging from that of Princess Charlotte to Norman Hartnell's design for Princess Margaret (1966).

The museum has a modest collection of fashion plates and designs in the Department of Prints & Drawings, and the library has an expanding collection of trade catalogues and magazines as well as archive material relating to London businesses and retail outlets. Photography is very much a growth area in the museum's collecting policy and a start has been made on recording both past and present fashions.

The Museum has not been long at its new home at London Wall, and the Costume & Textile Department is still in the process of completing the behind-the-scenes work caused by the move. For this reason there is restricted access to reserve material. Enquiries should be addressed to the Curator.

In 1980 the Costume Department founded The Friends of Fashion to support its work and aims. The main aim of the Friends is to help provide a special extension where the collection can be seen properly by the public. The Friends also brings together people interested in all aspects of clothing. Members range from those interested in observing fashion from the sidelines to those who are deeply involved in it professionally, as well as many dress historians. Applications for membership should be sent to The Friends of Fashion at the above address.

LONDON

Museum of Local History, Old Vestry House

Vestry Road, Walthamstow, London E17 9NH
Telephone: 527 5544 ext. 391
Opening hours: Daily, except Sundays, 10.00 am–5.30 pm.
Closed: Sundays and all Public and Bank Holidays.

This museum is concerned with the local history of the Waltham Forest area. Its costume holdings are sizeable for a small museum, most of the material having been donated by local people. There are about sixty women's dresses, including both day and evening dresses, the majority dating from the 1920s and 1930s although the range of styles does extend up until the 1960s. A considerable collection of women's and children's underwear from the late nineteenth century to the 1930s covers everything from divided drawers to camisoles and petticoats. The museum is also building up a small collection of children's clothes, mostly babies' gowns, capes and caps, but with some toddler's clothes, shoes and accessories.

Men's clothes are not well represented, although there are civic and military uniforms, and material from the local fire brigade. In particular, there is one gentlemen's dress suit and accessories made and worn by a local tailor, complemented by a small collection of tailoring tools.

The costume displays change from time to time and generally include some twentieth-century material. Although catalogue details are very basic, any enquiries about the collection are welcome. An appointment is, however, required to view the material which is not on display.

The museum has some fascinating ancillary material in the form of a large collection of photographs dating from the 1860s onwards. These include a number of albums devoted to the staff outings of Achille Serre, the dry-cleaning firm. The Borough Archive, also housed at Vestry House, holds a certain number of catalogues and other materials relating to firms that manufactured or marketed garments in the area.

LONDON

Victoria & Albert Museum

South Kensington, London SW7 2RL
Telephone: (01) 589 6371
Opening hours: Weekdays, 10.00 am–5.50 pm, Sundays, 2.30 pm–5.50 pm.
Closed: Fridays, New Year's Day, May Day, Christmas Eve, Christmas and Boxing Day.

The rich holdings of twentieth-century fashionable dress at the Victoria & Albert Museum are based on two major collections, one, part of Miss Heather Firbank's wardrobe dating from 1906–1921, and an outstanding and wide-ranging couture collection assembled especially for the museum by the late Sir Cecil Beaton. Together with the other holdings these collections represent the work of most of the leading European and American couturiers of the century. In the early decades the collection provides particularly good examples of Worth, Callot Soeurs, Paquin, Redfern, Lucile, Reville & Rossiter, Fortuny and, most notably, Poiret. The list of couturiers continues after 1920 with the Beaton collection, becoming even more comprehensive and featuring work by Adrian, Balenciaga, Cardin, Chanel, Courrèges, Dior, Givenchy, Charles James, Mainbocher, Missoni, Molyneux, Pucci, Saint Laurent, Schiaparelli, Mila Schön, Ungaro and Vionnet. The range of clothes covers informal day wear and outdoor clothes as well as ball gowns and unique, avant-garde items such as a sequined trouser suit of 1937–38 by Chanel. Apart from such *haute couture* there are also examples of informal clothing from both World Wars, those from the First World War showing the introduction of new freedom-giving lines and thus reflecting the idea that women should work; from the Second World War there is a collection of thirty Utility garments designed by the Incorporated Society of London Fashion Designers and given to the museum in 1942 by the Board of Trade.

From more recent years the collection of European designers has been supplemented with a wide range of examples from British houses, beginning with Norman Hartnell and Hardy Amies, and continuing with work by Mary Quant, John Bates, Gina Fratini, Bill Gibb, Jean Muir, Thea Porter and Zandra Rhodes, who is represented by, among other things, a punk rock evening dress. This part of the collection is kept constantly up-to-date with many donations from new, young designers.

The library at the museum offers a major, accessible study resource for students of fashion history. The holdings relevant to fashion (which can be easily located in the subject index) include comprehensive collections of books published in the United Kingdom, America and Europe, a complete run of the *Gazette du Bon Ton*, French *Vogue* from the 1920s up to 1975 and English *Vogue* from 1932, as well as runs of *Harper's Bazaar*, *The Queen* and *L'Officiel*. Also at the library are the Worth and Paquin archives, which can be studied on special request.

The Costume Gallery, closed over recent years for repair and renovation, is currently expected to reopen in the late Spring of 1983. The reserve collections may be seen by appointment made well in advance – contact the General Office of the Department of Textiles and Dress.

LUTON

The Luton Museum

Wardown Park, Luton LU2 7HA, Telephone: 0582 36941
Opening hours: Daily, except Tuesday, 10.00 am–6.00 pm.
Sundays, 2.00 pm–6.00 pm.
October–March, as above with the earlier closing time of 5.00 pm.
Closed: Tuesdays, New Year's Day, Christmas & Boxing Day.

The Luton Museum holds an extensive collection of historical costume, of which about 20% is from the twentieth century. This is mostly ready-to-wear and High Street fashion and includes dresses, suits, trouser suits, evening wear and lingerie. A touch of high fashion is introduced with a group of evening dresses donated by the late Lady Zia Wernher, dating from the late 1920s and including one gold lamé Molyneux model. A considerable number of modern items are added to the collection each year.

Because Luton was and is a hat-making town, the collection is particularly strong in head wear; notably straw hats, in which the local factory workshops specialized, obtaining their supplies of plaited straw from the surrounding villages.

The costume gallery usually has a display of costume of the 1920s and 1930s, and the 'Luton Life' Gallery is partially devoted to the manufacture of hats and hat styles.

MANCHESTER

Gallery of English Costume

Platt Hall, Rusholme, Manchester M14 5LL
Telephone: 061 224 5217
Opening hours: Tuesday–Friday, 10.00 am–6.00 pm.
Closed: The museum is completely closed from October–March. During the Spring and Summer closing days are Mondays and Weekends.

The Gallery of English Costume is the largest British collection of costume outside London. Founded in 1947 with the purchase of the Cunnington Collection, the stated aim of the museum is to collect a complete cross-section, where possible, of the costume worn in England. The collecting policy extends to highly fashionable and expensive items, because of their importance as pieces of social history: in contrast the other two major British museums of costume, the Victoria & Albert Museum in London and the Museum of Costume at Bath, see fashion in the context of the decorative arts.

The twentieth-century holdings of the museum present the major changes in fashion from 1900 to the present day. There are over 700 women's dresses and suits and these items are accompanied by a group of 75 wedding dresses, hats, coats, mantles and jackets, shoes and boots, not to mention sportswear, uniforms, handbags, fans and other accessories. Many items come from small provincial shops and individual dressmakers, but there is a good range of both British and international designers' work included in the collection. *Haute couture* is represented by Hardy Amies, Balenciaga, Balmain, Cardin, John Cavanagh, Creed, Bill Gibb, Jacques Griffe, Hartnell, Lanvin, Molyneux, Patou, Poiret, Schiaparelli, Victor Stiebel and Worth. Labelled dresses and outfits come from Burberry, Harrods, Jaeger, Liberty, Mattli and Susan Small. The era of 'Swinging London' and the 1960s is represented in outfits from Biba, Bus Stop, Ossie Clark and Mary Quant. Many of the designer dresses are model gowns, presented to the Gallery in the 1950s by the Cotton Board. These are documented with photographs of the dresses as modelled. There is a particularly good group of beautiful millinery from such distinguished names as Otto Lucas, Aage Thaarup and Madame Vernier.

Men's wear includes suits and coats together with accessories, uniforms and underwear, and there is a small group of children's and babies' clothes.

The library at the Gallery of English Costume is probably one of the finest devoted to fashion. As well as all the major textbooks, there are comprehensive editions of French, American and English *Vogue*, *Harper's Bazaar*, *Queen*, *The Lady*, *The Gentlewoman*, *19*, *Tailor & Cutter* and others. An assortment of patterns, pattern books, trade catalogues, knitting patterns and fashion plates, together with an important collection of over 8,000 photographs from 1840 to the present day, makes the library an invaluable resource for students. There is also a study collection of original garments for students to handle and view at close quarters.

Priority for study facilities is given to professional designers, historians and students in higher education. All visits to the library and study collection are by appointment, and students using the reserve collection are asked to bring a letter of reference as a security measure. As these study facilities are highly specialized, any enquiries should be as specific as possible, and it is a good idea to seek access only to material which is not generally available elsewhere. For these reasons, and since staff and time are limited, it is not always possible to open the reserve collection to the private collector. However, those researching for publication are of course welcome.

NEWCASTLE UPON TYNE

Laing Art Gallery
Higham Place, Newcastle upon Tyne NE1 8AG
Telephone: Newcastle 327734
Opening hours: Monday–Saturday, 10.00 am–5.30 pm.
Sundays, 2.30 pm–5.30 pm.
Closed: Good Friday, Christmas & Boxing Day.

The costume collection at the Laing Art Gallery is a sizable one, with items ranging from the eighteenth century to the present. The holdings of twentieth-century fashion have expanded considerably in recent years and there is an active policy of acquiring contemporary items – for instance, the museum has an impressive two-piece suit in chestnut leather, designed by Bill Gibb. There is also a printed silk chiffon dress by Molyneux c 1930.

The museum has in the past had very little exhibition space, but it is now expanding: as more room becomes available a greater proportion of the collection will be put on display. Exhibits will be changed every nine months. Reserve items can also be seen, by prior arrangement.

In addition to the costumes themselves there is a small group of shoes ranging from the eighteenth century to 1960, and a good selection of lingerie.

NORWICH

Strangers' Hall Museum
Charing Cross, Norwich, Telephone: Norwich 611277 ext. 275
Opening hours: Monday–Saturday, 10.00 am–5.00 pm.
Closed: New Year's Day, Christmas Eve, Christmas & Boxing Day.

Norfolk Museums have a large and fairly representative collection of dresses, accessories and underwear dating from 1900–1970. These are mainly middle class in origin, but there are examples of court dress as well as some working class costume. There is a fairly good group of children's and infant's costume, and some men's wear, but the range is more limited.

In addition, there are collections of occupational dress and uniforms, sportswear and other specialized costume like wedding dresses. The museum has also been acquiring a fascinating range of ecclesiastical, religious and clerical dress.

There is only one room at Strangers' Hall fitted for costume display and here the exhibits are changed annually. Exhibitions are generally devoted to a theme or period and are closely related to social background. Costume accessories are periodically displayed elsewhere in the museum. Most of the collection is in reserve, but will be made available to students by appointment. The museum is happy to assist with identification, and offer advice on the care and conservation of costume and textiles, again by appointment.

NORTHAMPTON

Abington Museum
Abington Park, Northampton, Telephone: 0604 31454
Opening hours:
Monday–Saturday, 10.00 am–12.30 pm, 2.00 pm–6.00 pm.
Sundays, April – September only, 2.30 pm–5.00 pm.
Closed: Good Friday, Christmas Eve, Christmas & Boxing Day.

Northampton's costume collection is housed at the Abington Museum. It is very much a local collection containing mostly women's costume dating from 1780 to 1940. There is little high fashion, but the holdings do offer the 'Sunday Best' of a working population. Unfortunately, none of the collection is on view, but it may be seen by appointment. Enquiries should be addressed to the Keeper at the above address. There is also a small collection of underclothes and accessories.

NORTHAMPTON

Central Museum
Guildhall Road, Northampton NN1 1DP
Telephone: 0604 34881 ext. 392
Opening hours: Monday–Saturday, 10.00 am–6.00 pm.
Closed: Sundays, Good Friday, Christmas Eve, Christmas Day & Boxing Day.

This museum specializes in historic footwear, and has what is probably the largest collection of shoes in the world. There is a considerable quantity of twentieth-century footwear, of all ranges from high fashion to working wear, sports shoes and footwear for special purposes – for example, over 300 pairs of army boots. The majority of the shoes are for women, but there are 900 pairs of men's footwear and 300 pairs of children's shoes and sandals. There is also a collection of jewelled heels, buckles and bows etc.

A very small proportion of the collection is on show, but the remainder may be seen by appointment. There is an extensive library devoted to all aspects of footwear.

NOTTINGHAM

Museum of Costume & Textiles
51 Castlegate, Nottingham NG1 6AF
Telephone: 0602 411881 ext. 28
Opening hours: Daily, 10.00 am –12.00 am, 1.00 pm–5.00 pm.
Closed: Christmas Day.

This museum houses the City of Nottingham's Costume & Textile collections. The twentieth-century part of the collections is fairly extensive – approximately 200 dresses, and innumerable other items of clothing and accessories. Emphasis has been laid on collecting dated specimens and items that have been made or worn locally. There are a few couture garments, but most are good quality store or dressmaker-made dresses. The museum has reasonably representative groups of hats, shoes, handbags, coats and underclothes. Christening robes and baby clothes from the early 1900s form part of the selection of children's costume, which also includes dresses and suits, underclothes, hats and shoes.

The museum has a series of period rooms which are intended to show off costume dating from before the twentieth-century, although it is planned to extend these to come up to c 1960. There are also separate displays devoted to hats, lingerie and shoes showing the changes that have emerged in style over 200 years. There is an excellent display of handmade and machine-made lace dating from the sixteenth century to the present day, stressing Nottingham's importance as the centre of machine-made lace from the eighteenth century onwards.

Appointments should be made at least two weeks in advance in order to see the reserve collections.

PETERBOROUGH

City Museum and Art Gallery
Priestgate, Peterborough PE1 1LF
Telephone: Peterborough 43329

Opening hours:
November–May: Tuesday–Saturday, 12.00 am–5.00 pm.
June–October: Tuesday–Saturday, 10.00 am–5.00 pm.
Closed: Sundays & Mondays, Christmas & Boxing Day.

This is a small collection, mainly confined to the period 1900–25. The costumes are entirely women's clothing, the majority of which have been acquired locally, although there is one black chiffon creation by Doucet c 1902–4. There is no active collecting policy for fashion items, and additions to the collection are principally by donation.

There is always some costume on display at the museum and the reserve collection, dating from the eighteenth century, is available for study on written application.

PRESTON

Harris Museum and Art Gallery

Market Square, Preston PR1 2PP, Lancashire.
Telephone: Preston 58248/9
Opening hours: Daily, 10.00 am–5.00 pm.
Closed: Sundays, all Bank Holidays.

The period 1810–1910 is the one most strongly represented in the collections of Preston's museum. However, acquisitions in the past ten years have added considerably to the twentieth-century holdings. The range of the collections is wide: a group of country occupational dress – striped wool skirts, sun bonnets and shawls from the turn of the century, and cotton dresses and overalls from the 1920s and 1940s; several fine Edwardian wedding dresses; beaded dresses from the 1920s; a collection of 'Utility' nightwear and underclothes. Particular items of local interest are the children's fancy dress worn at the Preston Guild Fancy Dress Balls in 1902 and 1922.

Recently-added display space means that there are usually some costume and fashion plates on view. Appointments should be made well in advance to see the reserve collections, which include accessories and a number of nineteenth- and twentieth-century fashion magazines.

READING

Reading Museum and Art Gallery

Blagrave Street, Reading RG1 1QL, Telephone: 0734 55911
Opening hours: Weekdays, 10.00 am–5.30 pm.
Saturdays, 10.00 am–5.00 pm.
Closed: Sundays, all Bank Holidays.

Reading's holding of twentieth-century costumes is very small and consists of some Edwardian costume, plus a few beaded and sequined dresses from the 1920s, together with accessories such as shoes, ostrich feather fans and hair ornaments. In addition there are a few examples of dresses from the 1940s and 1950s. It is hoped to enlarge the existing collection and add some men's wear. There is no costume on display, but it is hoped to make the collection available for study. Enquiries should be addressed to the Assistant Keeper of Archaeology.

TOTNES

Devonshire Collection of Period Costume

10a High Street, Totnes, Devon, Telephone: Totnes 862423
Opening hours: Spring Bank holiday–1 October:
Monday–Friday, 11.00 am–5.00 pm.
Sundays, 2.00 pm–5.00 pm.
Admission charge.

The Devonshire Collection of Period Costume was formed in 1967 by three people interested in the subject, who had each put together small collections of their own. In the early stages the costumes were shown in carefully mounted parades in aid of charity. In 1972 the collection became widely known after its inclusion in BBC Television's series, *Collector's World*. As a result, many interesting and valuable costumes were donated to the collection. In 1974 an exhibition gallery was opened and this space has since been added to. Exhibitions are mounted every summer.

The twentieth-century holdings include a good range of middle class women's clothing from 1900–20: evening, day and outdoor clothes plus underwear, shoes, hats, gloves, parasols etc. The period 1920 to 1940 has a similar range of fashions, but has fewer outer garments. There are a number of good printed silks and beaded dresses. From 1940 to 1970 there are fewer items, but the collection is always being added to.

Storage space is very limited, but given fourteen days' notice and a description of the date and type of garment of interest, it can be arranged for a few items to be made available for private study. A small fee will be charged.

This collection is an outstanding example of what can be achieved by the private collector, and is a monument to what can be built up from a small beginning.

WARWICK

St John's House

Coten End, Warwick, Telephone: (0926) 493431, ext. 2021
Opening hours:
Weekdays, except Mondays, 10.00 am–12.30 pm, 1.30 pm–5.30 pm.
Sundays (May–September only), 2.30 pm–5.00 pm.
Closed: Mondays.

St John's House is a seventeenth-century mansion originally built by the Stoughton family and now a branch of the Warwickshire County Museum. It houses the Social History collection, which includes domestic items, craft and agricultural tools, toys and furniture, as well as costume.

The costume holdings include a good range of twentieth-century women's clothes. They concentrate on everyday wear, though there is a group of high fashion evening dresses dating from the 1930s, once in the wardrobe of the late Lady Beryl Graeme Thomson. In the main the collection tries to reflect the trends in popular fashion, and it is interesting to note that, apart from donations, the museum's main sources are Oxfam shops and local jumble sales.

The museum generally has some costume on display, although this may or may not be twentieth-century. There are also small displays of accessories. The reserve collection of costume is available to students and to those with a serious interest in the subject, and can be seen by appointment with the Keeper of Social History.

WESTON-SUPER-MARE

Woodspring Museum

Burlington Street, Weston-super-Mare, Avon BS23 1PR
Telephone: Weston-super-Mare 21028
Opening hours:
Monday–Saturday, 10.00 am–1.00 pm, 2.00 pm–5.00 pm.
July and August: Monday–Saturday, 10.00 am–6.00 pm.
Saturdays, 10.00am–5.00 pm.
Closed: Sundays, Good Friday, Christmas & Boxing Day, New Year's Day.

Most of the costume in this collection is nineteenth century, but there is a small group of twentieth-century fashion, mostly local in origin, dating from 1900 to 1960. Many of the dresses, typically made of crêpe-de-Chine, chiffon, voile, georgette and artificial silk, are from the 1920s and 1930s, and there is a 1940s 'siren suit'. Other items include overcoats, hats, a range of twenty-five pairs of shoes together with stockings, underclothes and nightwear. There is also a small group of wedding dresses – one of cream satin with its original cream silk stockings, 1903, two 1920s examples, one with a dipped hemline from 1928 and a cream lace and net 1930s creation. Appointments should be made to see the reserve collection.

WEYBRIDGE

Weybridge Museum
Church Street, Weybridge, Surrey KT13 8DE
Telephone: Weybridge 43573
Opening hours:
Monday–Saturday, 10.00 am–1.00 pm, 2.00 pm–5.00 pm.
Closed: Sundays, all Bank Holidays.

The costume collection in Weybridge Museum consists of clothes collected from the towns and villages of Surrey, principally from the Walton and Weybridge area. These are the clothes of ordinary people, labourers, artisans, professional men and their families. While some items date back to the late eighteenth century, a good half of the collection is twentieth-century material. The museum tries to collect contemporary fashion as it goes out of date. There are babies' and children's clothes, dresses from the 1940s and 1950s, day and evening dresses, uniforms, underwear, shoes and accessories. The museum has a fine group of wedding dresses worn by local brides from 1824 to 1955. In addition they are now amassing a photographic archive of local people of all ages and occupations.

Weybridge is in the process of helping to set up a new industrial archaeological museum covering the history of aviation – the local industry – called the Brooklands Museum of Aviation. There is already a collection of related costume – Royal Flying Corps uniforms, Royal Air Force and WAAF uniforms, general early flying kit and fashionable clothes worn to aviation events at Brooklands. Many women worked in the local aircraft factories during both world wars and the museum is endeavouring to collect, or at least record, the clothes they wore to work. The collection of photographs is extensive, but has yet to be properly catalogued. It is hoped that it will soon be available as reference material at the Brooklands Museum of Aviation.

Such display space as there is, is devoted to special exhibitions. The bulk of the collection is in store and is widely used by researchers and students. As space is limited an appointment should be made in advance.

A charming restrained wedding outfit worn in the early 1950s.

WINCHESTER

Hampshire County Museum Service

Chilcomb House
Chilcomb Lane, Bar End, Winchester, SO23 8RD
Telephone: Winchester 66242/3
Opening hours: not open to the public.

Red House Museum
Quai Road, Christchurch, Dorset, Telephone: 0202 482860
Opening hours:
Tuesday–Saturday, 10.00 am–1.00 pm, 2.00 pm–5.00 pm.
Sundays, 2.00 pm–5.00 pm.
Admission charge.

Twentieth-century costume at Chilcomb House, the headquarters of the County Museum Service, occupies about one third of the County's collection. All periods up to the 1970s are represented. The Edwardian pieces include both day and evening dresses and many wedding dresses; there is also a fine collection of hats and other accessories. The 1920s evening dresses are mainly beaded and include a Chanel model and one by Louise Boulanger. Later clothes in the collection include, amongst others, short evening dresses of the 1960s, a 1960s Hardy Amies coat, sportswear and jeans. Children's wear and babies' clothes are also well represented. There are a few men's suits up to the 1970s, including a 1945 'demob' suit. The collection also holds women's lingerie, accessories, maids' and servants' dresses.

The collection at the Red House Museum, though smaller, has some sixty to seventy dresses ranging through the period – Edwardian, 1920s and 1930s, especially evening dresses and coats, and a Mary Quant purple moiré trouser suit. Babies' and children's clothes are well represented up to the 1920s. The collection also includes accessories and underwear and some occupational dress.

There are no displays at Chilcomb House and the small displays at the Red House Museum do not at present include twentieth-century material. The reference collections are accessible to students and those doing research, however, by arrangement with the Keeper of Costume & Textiles at Chilcomb House.

WORTHING

Worthing Museum & Art Gallery
Chapel Road, Worthing, Sussex BN1 1HD
Telephone: Worthing 204229
Opening hours:
October–March: Monday–Saturday 10.00 am–5.00 pm.
April–September: Monday–Saturday 10.00 am–6.00 pm.
Closed: Sundays

The costume collection at Worthing comprises approximately 12,000 items of costume covering the period from the mid-eighteenth-century to the present day. There are about 500 women's dresses, 1900–70, some men's suits and infants' and children's clothes. There is a fairly good collection of costume accessories including women's shoes, handbags and hats. The amount of *haute couture* in the collection is negligible, although there is a black velvet dress by Worth c 1925 and an Edwardian cape by Redfern. The majority of the collection would have been made by a local dressmaker or purchased in London or Worthing. There is a group of men's and women's 'Utility' clothing and a small uniform collection from the Sussex regiments.

The costume collection is displayed in a purpose-designed

gallery and features a display of Edwardian ball gowns and a scene showing 1920s day and evening dresses. Access may be had to the collection in store and the museum's library contains fashion magazines, dress and knitting patterns and photographs.

YORK

The Castle Museum

York, YO1 1RY, Telephone: 0904 53611
Opening hours:
April–September: Monday–Saturday 9.30 am–6.00 pm.
Sundays, 10.00 am–6.00 pm.
October–March: Monday–Saturday 9.30 am–4.30 pm.
Sundays, 10.00 am–4.30 pm.
Closed: New Year's Day, Christmas Day & Boxing Day.
Admission charge.

This museum is the Folk Museum of Yorkshire Life. The textile collection is vast, containing hundreds of garments and even more accessories. The earliest pieces date from the sixteenth century and the largest part of the collection is devoted to the development of nineteenth-century styles and accessories.

Twentieth-century fashion is mainly formal wear with a large proportion of dresses from the 1920s onwards. The collection stops around the mid-1960s but future plans incorporate collecting select items up to the present day. The majority of the styles in the collection represent middle-of-the-road fashion and bear ready-to-wear labels such as Horrockses, Cresta etc.

One important part of the holdings is the wardrobe of one woman, born just before World War I, which contains her garments from babyhood to the present day. These items not only illustrate the pattern of radical changes in style, but also the development of personal taste in relation to contemporary fashion. The museum hopes to pursue this idea in collecting dress assembled in this way rather than acquiring random selections from a variety of sources. This fascinating idea might make a solid base for your own collection, which, well documented, might prove an invaluable resource for a museum in later years.

The reserve collection is available for study purposes by appointment, as is the library. The latter contains a large number of contemporary books, fashion magazines and illustrations. An excellent bibliography can be supplied on request.

Finally, the textile department is willing to advise on the cleaning and storage of textile items, but it is unable to undertake actual work on behalf of clients. Enquiries of this nature should be addressed to the Assistant Keeper of Textiles.

NORTH AMERICA

BOSTON, MA.

The Museum of Fine Arts

465 Huntington Avenue, Boston, Massachusetts 02115
Telephone: (617) 267 9300
Opening hours: Tuesdays, 10.00 am–9.00 pm.
Wednesday–Sunday, 10.00 am–5.00 pm.
Closed: Mondays, New Year's Day, July 4th, Thanksgiving and Christmas Day.

The Museum of Fine Arts holds an extensive collection of costume covering the period from the eighteenth century to the twentieth century, and is especially strong in accessories such as footwear and hosiery. The holdings of twentieth-century costume consist almost exclusively of high fashion, both day and evening wear, from 1900 to the 1970s; there are over 200 garments from this period, mostly drawn from America and France though there are examples of work from other European countries and South America. There are also over fifty examples of footwear and forty hats, which give a good cross-section from the period. The best group of accessories is the Arthur Warren Rayner Hosiery Collection, consisting of over 551 items dating from between 1900 and 1940 and collected by a hosiery salesman; thus many have never been worn and display their original markings. Most of this group comes from either America or Germany.

The museum tries to display part of the costume collection in small exhibitions about two or three times each year, but lack of space pending renovations makes this difficult. Items not on view are available for study between 10.00 am and 4.30 pm by prior arrangement. The staff are also available for consultation.

CHICAGO, ILL.

The Art Institute of Chicago

Michigan Avenue at Adams Street, Chicago, Illinois 60603
Telephone: (312) 443 3600
Opening hours:
Monday–Wednesday & Friday–Saturday, 10.00 am–5.00 pm.
Thursdays, 10.00 am–8.30 pm.
Sundays & holidays, 1.00 pm–6.00 pm.
Closed: Christmas Day.

The Art Institute has what is primarily a textile collection, though this does include some costume accessories, and items such as black work, some embroidered waistcoats and salesmen's samples. The collection is exhibited in rotation, each display centred around some particular theme or topic and on view for up to three months. All the pieces not on view are kept in storage, and due to restrictions of space and staff time, an appointment should be made well in advance to see any particular item. There are no full dresses or gowns in this collection.

CHICAGO, ILL.

Chicago Historical Society

Clark Street at North Avenue, Chicago, Illinois 60614
Telephone: (312) 642 4600
Opening hours: Monday–Saturday, 9.30 am–4.30 pm
Sundays, 12 noon–5.00 pm.
Closed: Thanksgiving, Christmas & New Year's Day.

The Chicago Historical Society has an extensive collection of twentieth-century fashion, numbering over 10,000 pieces and focusing on Chicago history. The range of designers represented is very wide and includes Adrian, Callot Soeurs, Dior, Elizabeth Hawes, Charles James, McCardell, Zandra Rhodes, Vionnet

'Picasso' hat designs from Bes-Ben (1957).

An early 1960s fantastic floral hat by Bes-Ben.

and Worth as well as numerous local Chicago designers. In addition to high fashion the collection has examples of sports clothes, children's clothes, servants' and nursing school uniforms, and costume relating to the two Chicago World Fairs (1893 and 1933). There are many articles of clothing made by Chicago dressmakers, tailors and milliners.

The library, which is open to the public, has very good research facilities, including a designers' file (which includes Chicago stores and manufacturers) and a collection of catalogues from local shops such as Marshall Field and Carson Pirie Scott. Parts of the collection are displayed in turn in new costume galleries, and there are occasional special exhibitions such as the one in 1976 concentrating on Benjamin Benedict Green-Field, Chicago's 'Mad Hatter' who has been creating sensational hats for his firm, Bes-Ben, since the 1920s. The majority of the collection is in store, but can be seen by appointment. There is also a study collection of pieces which may be handled.

CLEVELAND, OHIO

The Costume Wing, Western Reserve Historical Society
10825 East Boulevard, Cleveland, Ohio 44106
Telephone: (216) 721 5722
Opening hours: Tuesday–Saturday, 10.00 am–5.00 pm.
Sundays, 12 noon–4.45 pm.
Closed: Mondays and major holidays.

This collection of women's and children's costume and accessories numbers some 6,500 articles of clothing. Of this nearly half is twentieth-century costume. The collection focuses on Cleveland, but also includes the Western Reserve (the north-eastern area of Ohio). In addition to high fashion items, the holdings include housedresses, sportswear, servants' uniforms, bathing suits and lingerie. Most major designers are represented, with an especially notable group of some twenty-five dresses and two hats by Lucile, and a large collection of Cardin. There is an enormous collection of fans (between 2,500 to 3,000). The group of hats is also very large, comprising some 700 pieces dating from 1890 onwards.

The Costume Wing has an exhibition of about fifty mannequins on display at any one time. This exhibition is changed

every six months and is usually thematic and instructive rather than chronological. The collection is available by appointment for study and the extensive library is open without appointment.

DALLAS, TEXAS

Dallas Museum of Fashion
North Texas State University, Denton, Texas
Telephone: (817) 788 2855
Opening hours: September–May: by appointment.

This is a respectably large collection, and practically the only one in this area of America. It has pieces by most major Seventh Avenue designers, and some very nice examples of work by Adrian, Bonnie Cashin, Chanel, Galanos, McCardell, and a superb group by Balenciaga. It is primarily a research and study facility and does not have specific costume galleries, though there are occasional exhibitions through the Art Department and Historical Museum, as well as in local department stores. Library facilities are also available and can be used by appointment.

DETROIT, MICHIGAN

Detroit Historical Museum
5401 Woodward Avenue, Detroit, Michigan 48202
Telephone: (313) 833 1805
Opening hours: Tuesday–Saturday, 9.30 am–5.00 pm.
N.B. the office hours are somewhat different from the gallery hours and telephone calls should be made between 8.00 am and 4.30 pm, Monday to Friday.
Closed: Sundays, Mondays and major holidays.

This collection of some 20,000 costumes and accessories for men, women and children is focused on Detroit and the life of the city. The holdings come up to 1980 and include high fashion, workaday dress and sportswear. The groups of children's clothing and wedding dresses are especially good.

There is a permanent exhibition of costume which is changed every four to six months. At the moment the reserve collections are not available for study as new storage is being planned and built. Once this programme is complete it is hoped to offer study facilities. Further information can be obtained by telephoning or writing to the address above. The museum has a large reference library, which is open by appointment.

HARTFORD, CONN.

Wadsworth Atheneum
Hartford, Connecticut 06103, Telephone: (203) 278 2670
Opening hours: Daily, 11.00 am–5.00 pm.
Closed: Mondays, New Year's Day & Christmas Day.

The Wadsworth Atheneum has a broad collection of twentieth-century fashion, and new acquisitions have been added to the collection regularly over the past ten years, building up a holding which illustrates the history of both American and European fashion. Among the American designers represented are Bill Blass, Lilly Dache, Charles James, Claire McCardell, Vera Maxwell and Pauline Trigère: the European couturiers include a few English examples – Norman Hartnell, for instance – and the Italian designers, but most of this side of the collection is devoted to Paris: Cardin, Dior, Courrèges, and Paquin. There are also a few pieces by Balenciaga.

The museum is in the middle of a renovation programme, as a result of which only a very few items are on exhibition at any one time, and it is difficult for museum staff to see items in storage. It is suggested that those interested should write ahead to make enquiries.

INDIANAPOLIS

Indianapolis Museum of Art

1200 West Thirty-Eighth Street, Indianapolis 46208
Telephone: (317) 923 1331
Opening hours: Krannert Pavilion (Main Building):
Tuesday–Sunday, 11.00 am–5.00 pm.
Lilly Pavilion (Textile Collection):
Tuesday–Sunday, 1.00 pm–4.00 pm.
(The Lilly Pavilion is closed on major holidays.)

The Indianapolis Museum is presently expanding an exsting collection of twentieth-century costume, which numbers some 200 pieces. Forty-five of these were worn by one Indianapolis lady between 1905 and 1927, while forty others were designed by Girolamo Giuseffi of St Louis; the remaining costumes in the collection are mixed designer examples from America and Europe. This basic collection is now being added to, with particular concentration on couturiers who were born in Indiana; in 1980 the Indiana Fashion Design Collection was established with the aim of acquiring works by Norman Norell, Bill Blass and Halston, in preparation for a major inaugural exhibition to be held in Spring 1985. It is envisaged that the Collection will be backed up by archive material containing information about other public collections which exhibit the work of these designers, with as complete a listing as possible of the holdings of those institutions and the people responsible for them. The 1985 exhibition will be accompanied by a major catalogue, with monographs on the three Indiana-born designers and a historical overview of the period and place they worked in.

LOS ANGELES, CA.

Los Angeles County Museum of Art

5905 Wilshire Boulevard, Los Angeles, California 90036
Telephone: (213) 937 4250
Opening hours: Tuesday–Friday, 10.00 am–5.00 pm.
Saturday & Sunday, 10.00 am–6.00 pm.
Closed: Mondays.
Admission charge, except for the second Tuesday of every month.

The Costume & Textile Department has the biggest holdings of all the departments at the Los Angeles County Museum, and is the leading collection of its kind on the West Coast. The holdings are notable for their range, including Renaissance costumes, a collection of English eighteenth-century dress,

A beige stencilled silk caftan coat designed by Mariano Fortuny c 1920s.

Victorian styles, and twentieth-century fashion. The early twentieth-century collection contains a number of dresses by Lucile, some of which can be seen in original photographs at the Fashion Institute of Technology in New York. The designer collection includes dresses by Callot Soeurs, Vionnet and Worth, and suits and dresses by Balenciaga, Chanel, Dior and American designers Galanos, Gernreich and Norell. Apart from these the holdings also include one of the most comprehensive collections of swimwear (1920–50) by Jansen, Cole of California and many others; many of these were worn by Janet Gaynor, Greer Garson and other celebrities. The museum recently acquired the designer wardrobe of the late Rosalind Russell and looks forward in the near future to receiving a collection of Bonnie Cashin designs. A representative collection of children's clothes includes shoes and accessories from the mid-eighteenth century to the present day.

There is an excellent research library containing a sizeable collection of designers' sketches from film and fashion, as well as numerous volumes on fashion from 1586 to the present, most notably in twentieth-century a complete set of the *Gazette du Bon Ton* (1912–25), as well as a nearly complete run of *Godeys Ladies Book* and *Peterson's Magazine*. The library is open to the public, and items in the fashion collection not on view are available for study by appointment.

NEW YORK

The Brooklyn Museum

Eastern Parkway, Brooklyn, New York 11238
Telephone: (212) 638 5000
Opening hours: Wednesday–Saturday, 10.00 am–5.00 pm.
Sundays, 12.00 am–5.00 pm.
Holidays, 1.00 pm–5.00 pm.

The Brooklyn Museum has an extensive collection of several thousand twentieth-century women's costumes and accessories, together with a smaller selection of men's and children's clothes. Both American and European collectors are well represented: Balenciaga, Chanel, Dior, Doucet, Galanos, Givenchy, Hawes and Norell, among others. Of particular note are the collections of work by Schiaparelli, Claire McCardell and Charles James, the latter two accompanied by designer drawings. Charles James was the subject of a major exhibition held at the museum (October 1982–January 1983), accompanied by a very well documented catalogue, *The Genius of Charles James*. The collection is displayed in rotation in a costume gallery on the fourth floor of the museum, while in the Costume Theatre there is a permanent display which contains some twentieth-century items. The Art Reference Library, open Wednesday to Friday between 1.00 pm and 5.00 pm, has publications relating to fashion as well as additional sketches for fashion and film and theatre costume. The Textile Department also holds swatches of couturier material, and the study collection can be seen at the Design Laboratory of the Fashion Institute of Technology, also in New York.

NEW YORK

Costume Institute, Metropolitan Museum Of Art

Fifth Avenue at 82nd Street, New York, NY 10028
Telephone: (212) 879 5500, ext. 3908/3909
Opening hours: Office, Library and Archives: by prior appointment only.
Gallery hours: Tuesdays, 10.00 am–8.45 pm.
Wednesday–Saturday, 10.00 am–4.45 pm.
Sundays, 11.00 am–4.45 pm.
Closed: Mondays.

The Costume Institute has the most comprehensive collection of costume in the Western Hemisphere, with examples of most of the leading twentieth-century couturiers. The wealth of this collection reflects not only a very active acquisitions policy at the museum, but also the great appreciation for *haute couture* which Americans have displayed since its inception in the latter part of the nineteenth century. Most of the items were brought to the country by Americans who travelled to Europe. Thus in the European holdings French designers predominate. Couturiers represented include, among many others, Balenciaga, Cardin (including men's clothes), Chanel, Callot Soeurs, Dior, Fath, Grès, Lanvin, Paco Rabanne, Ungaro, Worth and so on. Poiret and Vionnet are both particularly well represented. Most of the important American designers are included, with particularly large groups of Claire McCardell and Bonnie Cashin; a fine Adrian group including the Coty award dresses; numerous pieces by Charles James; Lucile and Fortuny, including both pleated and stamped velvets and crêpes; Mainbocher from his early Paris days (before 1939) onwards, including the Duchess of Windsor's wedding dress. There are many examples of Norell's work from throughout his career, including his famous sailor dress, the mermaid sequined gowns, many tailored suits, several gowns from the 1930s when he was at Hattie Carnegie's, and a few subway suits – short beaded dresses worn under black coats when wartime petrol rationing sent high society down the subway. Designs from the 'Swinging Sixties', when English designers began to establish a wider reputation, can also be found in the collection. Included in this area are Jean Muir, Molyneux, Thea Porter, Mary Quant and Zandra Rhodes. The collection does not stop here, but continues with a particularly good collection of shoes, including fine examples of the work of Yantorny, Herbert Levine and Roger Vivier when he was working for Dior.

This material is all catalogued in a designer file, which includes manufacturer's and store labels. Further reference material is available at the Irene Lewisohn Reference Library (closed on Mondays and at weekends) which can be visited by appointment with the Librarian. It contains some 65,000 items including books, bound periodicals, swatch books, clippings and photo material, boasting such rarities as the journals *Art, Goût, Beauté, Gazette du Bon Ton, Le Bon Genre* and *L'Homme Elegant* as well as all the Mainbocher drawings from 1940–c1970. Finally, the bookshop at the museum is a very useful source for recently published books or magazines which are not easy to find elsewhere.

NEW YORK

The Edward C. Blum Design Laboratory, The Fashion Institute of Technology
227 West 27th Street, New York, NY 10001
Telephone: (212) 760 7708
Opening hours: Wednesday–Saturday, 10.00 am–5.00 pm.
Tuesdays, 10.00 am–9.00 pm.
Closed: Sundays and Mondays.

The Edward C. Blum Design Laboratory was originally set up during the First World War to give New York designers the opportunity of studying and handling pieces from the great European fashion houses, whose work it was then very difficult to import. Now sited on Seventh Avenue, and part of the Fashion Institute in the heart of New York's 'Rag Trade', this magnificent reference collection has been kept constantly up to date and now has some 100,000 garments from the twentieth century alone. The items in the collection have been acquired by style of trim, detail and construction, rather than on an historical or chronological basis. It includes both *haute couture* and ready-to-wear, with a nearly equal representation of European and American designers. The collection has a marvellous group of Adrians including his 1930s designs for the films of Garbo, Joan Crawford and Norma Shearer, etc. Other strong points in the collection include Poiret (they have an example of his 'Sorbet' dress), Charles James and numerous Norells and McCardells.

The collection is available for study by appointment, but is only open to serious scholars, by membership to designers, and for reference to FIT students. There are tours available of the storage areas, for a fee and usually for groups: you should call the telephone number above to enquire further. There are three exhibition galleries, with one major exhibit presented each year on a particular theme. This is usually all or partly twentieth-century fashion. For example the exhibition in 1982 was a retrospective devoted to Hubert de Givenchy, and in 1982/83 a major exhibition entitled *The Undercover Story* featured intimate apparel from 1780 to 1980.

NEW YORK

Museum of the City of New York
Fifth Avenue at 103rd Street, New York, NY 10029
Telephone: (212) 534 1672
Opening hours: Tuesday–Saturday, 10.00 am–5.00 pm.
Sundays, 1.00 pm–5.00 pm.
Closed: Mondays.

All the costumes in this museum have either been made in New York or purchased by New Yorkers in various parts of the world. It is, however, a large collection, numbering some 20,000 pieces of men's, women's and children's clothing and accessories spanning three centuries of New York's history. The twentieth-century holdings contain many examples of Paris *haute couture*, with an excellent Poiret collection, and Seventh Avenue is well represented. The early twentieth-century is particularly illustrated by the work of small New York dressmakers. The museum had a unique file of these dressmakers.

The costume is displayed in a special Costume Gallery which has changing exhibitions; these concentrate on American designers such as Vera Maxwell, one of the innovators of casual clothing in the 1930s and French couturiers such as Worth, both of whom have had special exhibitions devoted to their work. Limitations of space and staff make it difficult to arrange for visitors to study pieces which are not on display, and they are advised to write ahead to make arrangements.

OAKLAND, CA.

The Oakland Museum
1000 Oak Street, Oakland, California 94607
Telephone: (415) 273 3842
Opening hours: Wednesday–Saturday, 10.00 am–5.00 pm.
Sundays, 12 noon–7.00 pm.
Closed: Mondays, Tuesdays and major holidays.

A regional museum with a focus on California, the land and the people, the Oakland Museum has a basically western collection of costume with primarily American material. This includes some high fashion but concentrates on everyday clothes. The collection also has a good group of uniforms – men's and women's – military, some sports uniforms and partially complete uniforms for the civil services (e.g. firemen, police, Red Cross and Scouts).

There is a permanent costume gallery which has some seven to eleven costumes on show including one mannequin dressed in theatrical costume. In general at least one third of the exhibition is twentieth-century fashion. The exhibits are changed every three to six months. In addition to costume the museum collects accessories: they have exceptionally good holdings of twentieth-century shoes and hats and a wide variety of baby things. The reserve collection is available for study by appointment.

PHOENIX, ARIZONA

The Arizona Costume Institute
The Phoenix Art Museum, 1625 North Central Avenue, Phoenix, Arizona 85004
Telephone: (602) 257 1222
Opening hours: Tuesday–Saturday, 10.00 am–5.00 pm.
Wednesdays, 10.00 am–9.00 pm.
Sundays, 12.00 am–5.00 pm.
Closed: Mondays.

The Arizona Costume Institute was organized at the Phoenix Art Museum in 1966 to collect and preserve clothing and textiles of historic and aesthetic interest. At present its growing collection numbers 6,500 articles of dress and accessories dating from 1690 to the present day. Most of these items have been given by donors in Arizona and throughout the rest of the country, so the collection as a whole has a rich variety; there are particularly good groups of Adrian, Balenciaga, Balmain, Chanel, Dior, Irene and Bonnie Cashin. Exhibits are changed every six weeks, and usually number about seven items, with major exhibitions occurring every two years. Recent exhibits have included 'Pierre Balmain', 'The Debutante' and 'The Japanese'. Future exhibitions are planned on 'Southwest Influences', 'Motoring Costume' and 'Chanel'. The collection is catalogued, and there is a designer file, study collection and an excellent library available for research purposes.

PHILADELPHIA, PA.

Philadelphia Museum of Art
Benjamin Franklin Parkway, Box 7646, Philadelphia, Pennsylvania 19101
Telephone: (215) 763 8100
Opening hours: Wednesday–Sunday, 10.00 am–5.00 pm.
Closed: Mondays and Tuesdays (except by prior, special arrangement); New Year's Day, Martin Luther King's Birthday, Lincoln's Birthday, Washington's Birthday, Good Friday, Memorial Day, Flag Day, Independence Day, Labor Day, Columbus Day, Election Day, Veteran's Day, Thanksgiving and Christmas Day.
Admission charge.
Library hours: Wednesday–Friday, 10.00 am–4 pm.
Admission charge.

The Philadelphia Museum of Art has an important collection of twentieth-century fashionable clothing and accessories, concentrating on the major fashion trends in Europe and America as well as the local fashion scene in and around Philadelphia. Most major twentieth-century couturiers are represented, with an especially notable group of Schiaparellis, donated by the designer. At present the collection is not exhibited, and access to pieces in it is limited. There is no published catalogue or designer file as yet, though one is in preparation. Visitors are advised to write ahead for further information.

The Museum's library can be used on payment of a fee.

RICHMOND, VA.

Valentine Museum
1015 East Clay, Richmond, Virginia 23219
Telephone: (804) 649 0711
Opening hours: Tuesday–Saturday, 10.00 am–5.00 pm.
Sundays, 1.00 pm–5.00 pm.
Closed: Mondays and major holidays.

The Valentine Museum has a very large collection of costume, containing over 8,000 items of twentieth-century fashion. This includes examples of the work of most of the major designers of this century, featuring pieces by Adrian, Chanel, Fortuny, McCardell, Poiret, Schiaparelli and Worth (including the only known Worth christening robe, dating from the 1920s). These items are well catalogued in a designer file, and other research resources include a large picture library with photographic material specifically from the South. The museum also holds a large textile embroidery and lace collection, as well as a group of wedding dresses. There is only space to display a small part of this holding, though it is open by appointment for study.

The museum has a design file and a large picture library which includes period photographs specifically from the Southern States. The library also includes a range of fashion magazines.

ST LOUIS, MI.

Missouri Historical Society
Jefferson Memorial Building, Forest Park, St Louis, Missouri 63112
Telephone: (314) 361 1424
Opening hours: Daily, 9.30 am–4.45 pm.
Closed: Mondays.

The Society's collection of costume ranks sixth in size in the United States and has large holdings ranging from a few eighteenth-century pieces to present day styles. The collection's greatest strength lies in the six decades from 1870 to 1930. One important group in the collection is the clothes donated by St Louis fashion designer, Alice Topp-Lee, which includes such outstanding American and European couture names as Balenciaga, Cardin, Chanel, Dior, Grès, Charles James, LeLong and Mainbocher. The Society's holdings are mainly formal clothes – party and ball gowns – rather than everyday and working clothes, and the collection is backed up with excellent documentary material.

Although fewer in number, there are examples of men's wear and children's clothes. There is a particularly good collection of shoes, reflecting the fact that St Louis has been a centre for the design and manufacture of footwear. The collection is very well catalogued and is presently exhibited in rotation in a gallery of period tableau displays. Items in the reserve collection can be seen by appointment.

SAN FRANCISCO, CA.

M. H. de Young Memorial Museum
The Fine Art Museums of San Francisco, Golden Gate Park, San Francisco 94118
Telephone: (415) 558 2887
Opening hours: Wednesday–Sunday, 10.00 am–5.00 pm.
Closed: Mondays and Tuesdays.

The M. H. de Young Museum (which, together with the Palace

of the Legion of Honor, forms the Fine Art Museums of San Francisco) has collected costumes, mostly by donation, since it was founded in 1895. There is a historical collection covering the period from the eighteenth century to 1900, with particular emphasis on the end of the nineteenth century. The twentieth-century collection is smaller, numbering some fifty items, but includes the work of several leading international couturiers: Cardin, several pieces of Callot Soeurs, Balenciaga, Dior and seven pieces by Fortuny. The historical value of these holdings is recognized and the museums hope in the future to make them available as a study resource. Since this is not possible at the present time, because of limited study space and museum personnel, visitors wishing to see the collection should inquire before going to the museum.

SEATTLE, WASHINGTON

Historic Costume and Textile Collection

Drama-TV, room 45 & 51, DL–10, University of Washington, Seattle, Washington 98195
Telephone: (206) 543 1739
Opening hours: By appointment: Monday–Friday, 8.00 am–5.00 pm.
Hours are subject to change in the summer months; visitors should make inquiries in advance.

The Costume and Textile Study Center is a collection of 14,000 artefacts representing textile arts and costume from all over the world. There is a growing collection of twentieth-century fashion with examples of work by Christian Dior, Norman Norell, Oscar de la Renta, Bill Blass, Geoffrey Beene, and a collection of pieces by Bonnie Cashin complete with paper patterns, sample books and other promotional material produced by the Sills Company. The collection is complete with a library of textile and costume related books and magazines. The pieces are available for study by appointment, by writing to the Curator, stating the intended area of research.

WASHINGTON DC

The National Museum of American History

Smithsonian Institution, Constitution Ave. between 12th & 14th Streets, NW, Washington DC 20560
Telephone (202) 357 3185
Opening hours: Daily, 10.00 am–5.30 pm.
Closed: Christmas Day.

The Division of Costume at the National Museum holds one of the major collections in America: it focuses on civilian everyday costume from all walks of life, but also includes most of the major twentieth-century fashion designers and high fashion items as well. Many of the costumes are important in terms of their historical documentation. There are no specific costume galleries or permanent exhibits, but at irregular intervals items from the costume collection are shown in major exhibitions. A unique feature at the museum is a collection of ball dresses donated by former First Ladies, and usually worn by them at Inaugural Balls; these are exhibited in the Political History Division of the Museum. Access to the library is by appointment only, as is access to items not on display.

CANADA, MONTREAL

McCord Museum

690 Sherbrooke Street West, Montreal H3A 1E9
Telephone: 392 4778

Opening hours: Wednesday–Sunday, 11.00 am–5.00pm.
Closed: Christmas Day.

The costume collection here was started in 1957 and is intended to reflect changing society in Canada, with rare seventeeth- and eighteenth-century clothes through to present-day fashion. The only collection of its kind in Quebec, it is one of the very few in Canada and has a representative collection of everything from shoes and corsets to overcoats and hat pins. There are many examples of the work of both European, American and Canadian designers including Courrèges, Chanel, Hattie Carnegie, Dior, Bill Blass, Balenciaga, Balmain, Fontana, Jacques Fath, Givenchy, Jacques Heim, Hartnell, Lanvin, Saint Laurent, Molyneux, Patou, Poiret and Schiaparelli.

There is a permanent Costume Gallery, where exhibits are changed every six months: if an appointment is made well in advance, items in the reserve collection can also be seen. There is an excellent reference library including publications on twentieth-century fashion as well as some fashion magazines.

OTTAWA, ONT.

National Museum of Man, National Museums of Canada

Metcalfe & Mcleod Streets, Ottawa, Ontario K1A OM8
Telephone: (613) 992 3497
Opening hours:
Winter: Tuesday–Sunday, 10.00 am–5.00 pm.
Summer: Daily, 10.00 am–5.00 pm.
Closed: Christmas Day.

The History Divison of this museum collects clothes drawn solely from Canadian sources. As well as day wear for adults and children, there are comprehensive holdings of evening and wedding clothes since the beginning of the century, with particular emphasis on the evening wear of the 1930s. This collection is very well documented, and cross-indexed by item, date, region of use, original owner, and by trade mark, designer and retailer. Although the majority of the collection is held in storage, arrangements to view it by appointment can be made by writing to the Curator c/o the History Division, National Museum of Man, Ottawa KIA OM8.

SAINT JOHN, NEW BRUNSWICK

The New Brunswick Museum

277 Douglas Avenue, Saint John, New Brunswick E2K 1E5
Telephone: (506) 693 1196
Opening hours:
June–September: Daily, 10.00 am–9.00 pm.
October–May: Daily, 2.00 pm–5.00 pm.
Admission charge.

This museum has a very large collection of nineteenth-century costume, and its particular strength lies in Canadian chintz dresses made before 1830, of which it has one of the largest and best holdings of any Canadian museum. The collection of twentieth-century fashion is not as large or comprehensive, but attempts are being made to add contemporary clothes in all areas; as is generally the case, this is proving to be far easier in the area of women's clothes than men's. There are some excellent dresses from the 1920s, especially of the short beaded type, and good examples of lingerie and accessories from the first three decades of the century. Shoes and hats are represented up to the present day. Similarly in the area of men's and children's clothes the collection is strongest in the early decades of the century, and there is very little dating from after 1930. The holdings are kept in storage, but they can be seen at any time simply by making an appointment in advance.

TORONTO, ONT.

Royal Ontario Museum

100 Queen's Park, Toronto, Ontario M5S 2C6
Telephone: (416) 978 3655
Opening hours:
Monday–Saturday, 10.00 am–5.00 pm.
Sunday, 1.00 pm–9.00 pm.
Closed: Christmas Day.
Admission charge.

The Royal Ontario Museum has a very impressive collection of fashion dating from the eighteenth century to recent years, including pieces produced by the best-known designers in Canada, the USA and Europe. The collection of twentieth-century fashion since 1971 represents about 50% of the acquisitions made by the costume department; it is computer-indexed, stored in drawers in acid-free tissue paper and displayed on a four-monthly rotating basis under glass in controlled lighting.

The range covered by the holdings is very wide, extending from sport and work clothes to court and ceremonial dress. However the most impressive section is that of modern designer clothes, in some cases acquired immediately after their first appearance in the press or at fashion shows. These are particularly significant as prototypes for mass-produced commercial adaptations, and the emphasis of the acquisitions policy as a whole is on design for manufacturers and boutique clothing. The number of designers represented in the collection is very large, including most of the major French couturiers and British designers such as Hardy Amies, Ossie Clarke, Sybil Connolly, Norman Hartnell, Lucile, Jean Muir, Zandra Rhodes, Victor Stiebel and Mary Quant. American fashion is featured with work by Geoffrey Beene, Hattie Carnegie, Galanos, Charles James, Mainbocher, Claire McCardell, Norman Norell, Oscar de la Renta, Nettie Rosenstein and Pauline Trigère. Finally, Canadian design is represented by the work of Angelina, Louis Berai, Cornelia (Toronto), Meme Dysthe, Claire Haddad, Olivia of Hamilton, Marie Paule (Montreal), Maggy Reeves, John Warden.

Pieces from the collection are loaned to other museums with exhibition facilities meeting the necessary standards of the Conservation Department. Museum staff will identify costume and other textile material by appointment on Wednesday afternoons between 2.00 pm and 4.00 pm.

Cowl-neck tunic dress designed by Katherine Grinyer (1974).

THE REST OF THE WORLD

Fashion in New Zealand

We are extremely grateful to Ms Jennifer A. Quérée, Curator of the Early Colonial Department of Canterbury Museum, Christchurch, for supplying the following description of modern fashion history in her country. Her account mirrors the uniformity of taste and style throughout Europe, which was described in the chapters on accessories, such as fans. It is quite likely that the same pattern of imitation, importation, and local manufacture applies to other colonial territories, but at the time of going to press we had, regrettably, not received such information from Australia, or South Africa, or other areas in the East. The people who could supply such information are themselves involved in the day-to-day running of museums, and did not have the time they needed to prepare such information for us. However, it is sincerely hoped that this omission will be remedied in future editions, and any information supplied will be greatly appreciated.

'The settlers who poured into New Zealand, from the 1840s onward, adhered to the fashions prevailing in their homeland, unsuited though these were to the often harsh conditions of a pioneering life. These largely English modes continued to influence New Zealand clothing for well over a century.

Amongst the emigrants were many tailors, dressmakers, milliners and drapers. By 1900 the small businesses which they had founded were flourishing, and the larger towns and cities could boast numerous substantial tailoring and dressmaking establishments, as well as department stores, providing for the clothing needs of all classes of people from the humblest home-dressmakers to the fashionable élite. The same businesses also provided a mail-order service for materials and bespoke and ready-made clothing.

Even country drapers imported stock directly from England, while many of the larger firms had London houses, and buyers who ensured that the latest "novelties" in London and Paris appeared almost simultaneously in New Zealand. However the local woollen industry was also of considerable importance, having expanded rapidly from the early 1870s. Some of the mills, in addition to producing their wool and carrying out all the processing and finishing, ran clothing factories and retail stores throughout the country. The value of quality woollen fabrics and garments continues to be stressed: the New Zealand Wool Board, through the International Wool Secretariat (of which New Zealand was a founder member in 1937), promotes research and production, and young designers are encouraged with an annual award scheme.

Despite the availability of bespoke and ready-made clothes, home-dressmaking was, and is, wide-spread. The arrival of every ship brought the latest copies of *The Queen* or *The Englishwoman's Domestic Magazine*, and during the twentieth century the market has been inundated with all the popular British, American, Continental, and Australian fashion publications, as well as local magazines such as *Academy Fashion News* (begun in the early 1940s), and the long-running *New Zealand Woman's Weekly*. Paper patterns such as Butterick's, McCall's, Simplicity, and Vogue have always been available, and were more popular than their New Zealand rivals.

The production of clothing is one of New Zealand's most important manufacturing industries. Because of its flexibility and ability to produce small, high-quality runs, it has now acquired a multi-million dollar export market, throughout the Pacific, Australia and America. Fashion manufacturers draw their inspiration mostly from the top international designers, but there is a growing number of New Zealand designers – such as Isabel Harris, Marilyn Sainty, Miranda Joel, and Trish Gregory – producing original garments. These cater for small, fashion-conscious groups within New Zealand, but some have also been successful on the European, New York and Middle East markets – an encouraging omen for a New Zealand-designed-and-manufactured industry.'

Designs for the New Zealand Wool Board.

AUSTRALIA, SYDNEY

Museum of Applied Arts & Sciences
659–695 Harris Street, Ultimo, Sydney, NSW 2007
Telephone: (02) 211 3911
Opening hours: Daily, 10.00 am–5.00 pm.

This museum and its collections are in the process of redevelopment and expansion. The first stage of the redevelopment has been completed and the conversion of a large powerhouse is being actively planned. There is now a small exhibition area, with the major space devoted to workshops and storage. The Textiles and Costume Department has excellent storage there and it is anticipated that the public will have access to the collections in storage.

The collections include fashionable and workaday costume for men, women and children, with a wide range of accessories and lace, textiles, needlework and jewellery, drawn from many cultures. Twentieth-century fashion is receiving particular attention, and major displays are planned. It is hoped the collections will eventually include examples of the work of prominent designers from Europe, America and, naturally, Australia.

JAPAN, KYOTO

Kyoto Costume Institute
Wacaol Corporation, 29 Nakajimacho Kisshoin, Minami-ku, Kyoto 601, Telephone: 075 681 1171

Founded in 1978, the Kyoto Costume Institute is the first Japanese museum of Western fashion, and is based in a city traditionally associated with the crafts of weaving, dyeing and the design of the Kimono, Japan's national costume. However, nowadays Western clothing is worn everywhere in Japan as being 'practical and efficient wear', the design being mostly a matter of imitation, copies and imports. The inspiration behind

the development of the Kyoto Costume Institute was to provide a source of Western dress for study so that the Japanese could consider it, its origins and history, with a view to creating their own modern clothing based on Japanese culture, needs, habits and body shapes. The Institute is presently housed on one floor of the Wacaol Corporation, its parent organization and one of Japan's leading manufacturers of lingerie, and it has been helped through its early years in matters of acquisitions and conservation policy by a number of museums in Europe and America, particularly the Costume Institute at the Metropolitan Museum in New York. By the beginning of 1981 the collection numbered 3,635 costumes dating from the sixteenth to the twentieth century, and a library of 1,614 books had been built up. Expansion continues, and by 1984 it is hoped to have a separate building for the Institute. In the meantime a number of exhibitions are in preparation, designed for showing in New York and Kyoto, and an educational programme is being developed for Japanese students.

KYOTO

Nishijin Textile Museum
Imadegawa, Kamigyoku, Kyoto, Telephone: (075) 432 6131
Opening hours: Daily, 9.00 am–5.00 pm.
Closed: 1 January, 31 December.

Although this museum falls outside the strict limits of this book, any collectors of fashion who visit Japan would find it very interesting. Nishijin textile is a traditional Japanese silk cloth, and all the items in the collection are made out of it. Thus the holdings have a conservative, ethnic character, and contain no pieces which approach western styles. The collections are constantly being added to by new work which reflects the continuing vitality of these Japanese ethnic traditions.

NEW ZEALAND, AUCKLAND

Museum of Transport and Technology
Great North Road, Western Springs, Auckland 2
Telephone: 860 198
Opening hours: Daily, 9.00 am–5.00 pm.
Closed: Christmas Day.

This must be one of the largest New Zealand museums, incorporating as it does a thirty-four acre replica of a World War II airfield. Most of the clothes in the collection are kept at the seven-acre Western Springs site. They include some early pioneering fashions, in a Pioneer Village setting, and many of the uniforms connected with the other exhibits, both military and civil, such as tramway, airline and bus service uniforms. Some World War II uniforms, army and air force, are in the airfield display. These holdings obviously take second place to the aeroplanes, steam rollers, double decker buses and working tramway at the museum, which are used very distinctively: every weekend members of the museum, dressed in suitable costume, participate in events designed to recreate the world of early technology.

CHRISTCHURCH

Canterbury Museum
Rolleston Avenue, Christchurch 1
Telephone: Christchurch 68 379
Opening hours: Monday–Saturday, 10.00 am–4.30 pm.
Sundays, 2.30 pm–4.30 pm.
Closed: Good Friday, Anzac Day (April 25), Christmas Day.

A pretty display of early twentieth-century underclothing.

This museum has a major holding of costumes and fashion items, mainly acquired from local donors, and housed in the Colonial History Department. The earlier, and larger, parts of the collection are devoted to seventeenth- and eighteenth-century (pre-colonial) and nineteenth-century (colonial) items, some of which were brought from Britain by the settlers. The twentieth-century holdings include over 1400 items of women's fashion, mostly from the earlier part of the century, though the years since 1945 are also covered. This collection is very comprehensive, and contains complete dresses (evening, day, casual, wedding etc.), a large range of lingerie, outerwear such as shawls, scarves, cloaks and capes, and a wide variety of accessories. This material is backed up where possible by documentary information, with details of the history of each item and its wearer. Due to the difficulties involved in bringing pieces out of storage, visitors wishing to see parts of the collection not on view should make arrangements well in advance.

DUNEDIN

Otago Museum
Great King Street, Dunedin, Telephone: 772 372
Opening hours: Monday–Friday, 10.00 am–5.00 pm.
Saturdays, 1.00 pm–5.00 pm.
Sundays; 2.00 pm–5.00 pm.
Closed: Good Friday, Labour Day, Christmas Day.

This museum houses one of the larger New Zealand collections of fashion items, which has been drawn totally from local sources, and relies on donations from Dunedin inhabitants in order to expand. The years covered by the collection are from the earliest European settlements at Dunedin (1844) to the early 1950s; gradually as new donations come in the holdings will be brought more up to date. The clothes were either brought to New Zealand by immigrants or made by them according to foreign patterns; there are no examples of designer work in the collection. In the near future it is hoped to restore a wing of the museum in order to house a new store room, conservation laboratory and display area, but until this project is complete it is advisable to get in touch with the Anthropology curator so that fashion items in storage may be seen.

INVERCARGILL

Southland Museum and Art Gallery
Victoria Avenue, Invercargill, Telephone: 89 753
Opening hours: Weekdays, 10.00 am–4.30 pm

Saturdays, 1.00 pm–5.00 pm.
Sundays & Public holidays, 2.00 pm–5.00 pm.
Closed: Good Friday & Christmas Day.

This museum has a collection of twentieth-century clothing in its holdings, which, while it is not very specialized, covers a wide range dating from Edwardian times through the fashions of the 'flappers' in the 1920s to the mini-skirts of the 1960s. There is also a large selection of accessories including ties, hats, shoes, gloves, shawls, handbags and even spectacles. As well as this there is a great variety of underclothing, nightwear and children's clothes. Much of the collection is not as yet properly catalogued and is in storage, but it is all available for study.

NELSON

Nelson Provincial Museum
P.O. Box 2069, Stoke, Nelson, Telephone: 79 740
Opening hours: Tuesday–Friday, 10.00 am–4.00 pm.
Weekends, 2.00 pm–4.00 pm.
Closed Mondays.

The collection at the Nelson Provincial Museum covers the years from the mid-nineteenth century up to the 1930s, and is all drawn from local sources. It thus illustrates the local fashions in the years before New Zealand developed a large clothing industry of its own. The clothes on view reflect on the one hand the influence of European fashion, through clothes brought to New Zealand from Britain, and on the other the influence of a rough pioneering world on clothes designed for working in.

The museum also houses a very large photographic collection, which represents an important resource for anyone researching clothing and fashion. The fashion holdings are displayed from time to time, but it is advisable to contact the museum to make sure that it is possible to see the collection.

NORTHLAND

The Otamatea Kauri & Pioneer Museum
Matakohe, Northland, Telephone: 153 Paparoa
Opening hours: Daily, 9.00 am–4.30 pm.
Closed: Christmas Day.
Admission charge.

Pioneering settlers were attracted to Matakohe and Paparoa by the timber industry based on the kauri tree, and the museum at Matakohe aims to record the way of life enjoyed by these early bushmen. Although some of the clothes in the collection reflect the rough working conditions of the life of the early settlers, many are drawn from the more affluent homes of the area. These start off with the sort of clothes which the pioneers would have brought with them when Matakohe was settled in 1862, and concentrate on the years between the 1880s and 1920s. There is a range of women's, children's and servants' clothes, varying from nightgowns and underwear to formal 'Sunday Best'. The clothes are displayed in rotation in charming contemporary settings.

SOUTH AFRICA, CAPE TOWN

South African Cultural History Museum
49 Adderley Street, Cape Town, Telephone: (41) 1051
Opening hours: Monday–Saturday, 10.00 am–5.00 pm.
Sundays, 2.00 pm–5.00 pm.

This museum has a collection of women's costumes dating from between 1800 and 1982, supplemented by a range of lingerie and accessories. Apart from this there are examples of children's clothes, men's clothes and uniforms. Although all these items are presently in storage, it is hoped in the future to have facilities for a textile museum in which they could be displayed.

DURBAN

Local History Museum

Old Court House, Aliwal Street, Durban, Telephone: 328694
Opening hours: Daily, 9.30 am–5.00 pm.
Wednesdays, 9.30 am–2.00 pm. Sundays, 2.30 pm–5.00 pm.
Closed: Good Friday and Christmas Day.

The costume collection is one of the most important collections at this museum. All the clothes are in some way connected with Natal, being either made there or brought there in early years by settlers as family heirlooms. In this century there is a comprehensive collection of fashion items up to the 1940s, consisting mainly of women's clothes but including all sorts of garments and accessories such as fans, bags and jewellery, as well as shoes, stockings and hats. The underwear section in the collection is particularly comprehensive. The museum also has a certain amount of research material in the form of photographs, fashion plates, patterns and pattern books.

EAST LONDON

East London Museum

319 Oxford Street, East London 5201
Telephone: (0431) 22623
Opening hours: Monday–Friday, 9.30 am–5.00 pm.
Saturdays, 9.30 am–12.00 am.
Sundays, 9.30 am–12.30 pm, 2.30 pm–4.30 pm.

This general museum has a number of collections drawn from local sources which cover natural history, ethnography and cultural history. The ethnography collection contains a wide range of African tribal costumes and jewellery, while European fashion is displayed as part of the cultural history collection. New acquisitions are often made to this collection, with the aim of establishing as representative a holding as possible with special emphasis on garments and accessories of local interest. The collection concentrates on the decades between the 1920s and 1960s, and is comprehensive and well balanced, containing men's, women's and children's clothes and including everything from formal wear to bathing suits. There are many accessories, including dressing cases and other bedroom accessories which are used to recreate period interiors.

GRAHAMSTOWN

Albany Museum

Somerset Street, Grahamstown 6140, Telephone: (0461) 2243
Opening hours:
Monday–Friday, 8.30 am–12.45 pm, 2.00 pm–5.00 pm.
Saturdays, 8.30 am–12.45 pm.
Closed: Sundays and public holidays.
Admission charge.

This museum, which incorporates the Natural History Museum and the 1820 Settlers Memorial Museum, has a very large collection of fashion and costume which embraces masonic uniforms, sportswear, court dress, christening robes and wedding dresses as well as very comprehensive holdings of everyday dress dating from the 1890s to the 1930s. These include ladies' dresses and skirts, children's wear and men's clothes, underwear and both men's and women's accessories.

The collection was put together from local sources and is very well documented, with details, wherever possible, of where the items were made, who owned them and where they were worn. Although most of the twentieth-century holdings are in store, the collector will find the museum well worth a visit, and should contact the assistant curator in order to see items not on display.

JOHANNESBURG

Bernberg Museum of Costume

1 Duncombe Road, Forest Town, Johannesburg 2193
Telephone: 836 8482
Opening hours:
Monday–Saturday, 9.00 am–1.00 pm, 2.00 pm–4.30 pm.
Sundays & holidays, 2.00 pm–4.30 pm.

The Bernberg Museum of Costume is administered as a branch of the Afrikana Museum, and is based in a converted private house. Unfortunately this house is rather small, and it is not possible for the museum to keep all of its holdings on display; a lot of the twentieth-century section is kept in storage, so serious students who wish to study particular items are advised to make arrangements with the Custodian of Costume at the Afrikana Museum, at the above telephone number.

The collection is fairly comprehensive, with the slight exception of holdings of hats, evening dresses and lingerie up to the 1920s: equally men's and children's clothes are as so often, under-represented. However there is a very complete range of infants' clothes and household linen.

PRETORIA

National Cultural History & Open Air Museum

Boom Street 0002, Pretoria 0001, Telephone: 33120/8/9
Opening hours: Daily, 10.30 am–5.00 pm.
Sundays, 2.00 pm–5.00pm.
Admission charge.

The collection of clothes held by this museum dates from the early part of this century and all derive from Britain and Europe. Most of the items are women's clothes, and the holdings include accessories, such as handbags and walking sticks. The majority of the collection is held in store and advance notice should be given by visitors wishing to see it. Visits to the storage departments can only be made during normal office hours – 7.30 am–4.00 pm, Monday to Friday.

STELLENBOSCH

Stellenbosch Village Museum

18 Ryneveld Street, Stellenbosch, Telephone: (02231) 72937
Opening hours: Monday–Saturday, 9.30 am–5.00 pm.
Sundays & Religious holidays, 2.00 pm–5.00 pm.
Closed: on Good Friday and Christmas Day.

Costume does not form a major part of this museum's collections, and most of the items at the museum date from previous centuries. However the twentieth-century pieces in the collection are of high quality. They are all women's clothes, and feature six attractive evening dresses of the 1920s and a group of day frocks dating from about 1944. Though none of these is presently on display, they are all available for study by appointment by bona fide research students.

Stellenbosch Museum consists of several sections situated in various parts of the village. Stellenbosch Village Museum is one of these and this is where the costume collection is housed and displayed. Correspondence should be addressed to Stellenbosch Museum, Private Bag X5048, Stellenbosch.

USEFUL ADDRESSES

In this necessarily short section, we have tried to supply a range of useful addresses of auction rooms, dealers, street markets and specialist societies. Obviously this list is not comprehensive, lack of space prevents that, but we hope that the addresses supplied do at least provide a starting point for your search for rare, beautiful or interesting items for your collection.

Great Britain

Inevitably this list concentrates on London where the major auction houses, street markets etc. are to be found. However, we feel certain that your own local area is bound to repay investigation and reveal all kinds of sources for antique clothing, second-hand clothes, accessories, books or what to some is just junk. Happy hunting!

Auctions

The four major London auction houses all have costume and textile departments which hold sales of twentieth-century fashion. They are: BONHAM'S (Eric Knowles), Montpelier Galleries, Montpelier Street, SW7 (584 9161); CHRISTIE'S SOUTH KENSINGTON (Susan Mayor), 85 Old Brompton Road, SW7 (581 2231); PHILLIPS (Ann-Marie Benson), Blenstock House, Blenheim Street, W1 (629 6602); SOTHEBY'S (Meg Andrews), 34–35 New Bond Street, W1 (493 8080).

In all cases collectors should apply to the departments for information about sales dates and subscription forms for sales catalogues.

Outside London there are many auctions and, more promisingly, antique fairs. Over and above the local papers, the best source of information is the ANTIQUES TRADE GAZETTE, 116 Long Acre, London WC2, a weekly newspaper sold by subscription only at an annual charge of £22.50 (240 5753).

Societies

The COSTUME SOCIETY. Honorary Secretary: Naomi Tarrant, The Royal Scottish Museum, Chambers Street, Edinburgh EH1 1JS (031-225 7534). A large society with local branches throughout the country, which organise lectures and other activities.

The COSTUME SOCIETY OF SCOTLAND. Honorary Secretary: Miss Margaret Fraser, 4 Glencairn Crescent, Edinburgh EH12 5BS (031-225 5908). Active from October to May, the Society organises monthly meetings and lectures as well as putting together exhibitions; there is a Bulletin with book reviews, etc.

The FAN CIRCLE INTERNATIONAL. Honorary Secretary: Mrs Jacqueline Morris, 24 Asmuns Hill, London NW11 6ET (458 1033). A society with a country-wide membership which organises a wide range of activities from museum visits to an annual dinner with the Worshipful Company of Fan Makers; there is also a Bulletin.

The FRIENDS OF FASHION, Museum of London, London Wall, EC2Y 5HN (600 3699 ext. 240/280). This society was established in 1980, and has now developed an active timetable of lectures and meetings for a growing membership. One great advantage for the Friends is that their activities can be centred on the Museum of London's own fine collection of twentieth-century fashion.

London Dealers

ALFIES ANTIQUE MARKET, 13 Church Street, NW8 (723 0449; opposite Melody Sachs and the Topfloor Gallery, see below) has a number of interesting stands. AUDREY FIELD deals in lace and caters both for the serious collector and the novice, with a stock ranging from valuable sixteenth-century lace to Victorian and Edwardian work and examples of machine-made and chemical lace. Closed on Mondays and Wednesdays.

ANTIQUARIUS, 135/141 King's Road, SW3 (351 5353) and the CHENIL GALLERIES, 181/183 King's Road, (352 2123) have about a dozen likely stands between them, covering both antique and modern clothing as well as jewellery and accessories of all periods.

The ANTIQUE TEXTILE COMPANY, 100 Portland Road, W11 (221 7730) mostly deals in items over 100 years old, though occasionally good examples by designers such as Fortuny can be found.

BUTTERFLY, 28a Ponsonby Place, SW1 (821 5309) & 3 Lower Richmond Road, SW15 (788 8304). The two branches of this shop deal in nearly new clothes, a fair proportion of which are by well known designers. Also furs, costume jewellery and other accessories.

The BUTTON BOX, 44 Bedford Street, Covent Garden, WC2 (240 2716). Deals in wood, glass, pearl, casein, horn and metal buttons from the 1920s to the present day. Sales can be made by mail order; for further information send sae.

The BUTTON QUEEN, 19 Marylebone Lane, W1 (935 1505), has buttons from Victorian times to the post-war period, with good examples of Art Deco and early plastic. Cufflinks, brooches, etc. are also stocked.

JOHN CONNOR (450 7936) collects fashion dating from 1900 to 1960. Although not primarily a dealer, simple limitations of space force him to part with certain items from his collection; serious collectors might benefit from contacting him.

CORNUCOPIA, 12 Tachbrook Street, SW1 (828 5752). This shop deals in costume jewellery and accessories from the 1920s to the 1950s, with occasional pieces from the 1960s.

The DRESS POUND, 125 Notting Hill Gate, W11 (229 3311) and The FROCK EXCHANGE, 450 Fulham Road, SW6 (381 2937), both deal in nearly new fashionable clothes with many designers such as Bill Gibb and Zandra Rhodes represented.

DODO, 185 Westbourne Grove, W11 (229 3132). This shop has dresses (particularly silks and crêpes) dating back to the 1940s. Closed on Mondays, Thursdays and Sundays and open on the other days of the week from 12.00 to 6.00 pm.

EAT YOUR HEART OUT, 360 King's Road, SW3 (352 3392). This shop has a range of old clothes and accessories designed to appeal to the changing tastes of King's Road. While occasional 'names' may appear, collectors are likely to find the less expensive items here.

The GIMMICK, 117–119 Harwood Road, SW6 (corner of New King's Road) has a wide range of clothes stretching back to the 1930s. Not many designers, but fascinating and often eccentric.

GRAY'S ANTIQUE MARKET, 58 Davies Street, W1 (629 7034) and GRAY'S MEWS, 1–7 Davies Mews W1 (493 7861) (closed on Saturdays) have a number of likely stands, including the BUTTON LADY (499 4340) and RITVA WESTENIUS, (408 0053) who deals in old lace and linen, christening robes and 1920s beaded dresses.

ALAN & VANESSA HOPKINS, 96 Streathbourne Road, Tooting Bec, SW17 (672 5140) both have a professional background in fashion design and costume, as well as being keen collectors. They specialise in everyday and working clothes from the nineteenth century to the 1960s.

JOHN JESSE & IRINA LASKI LTD, 160 Kensington Church Street, W8 (229 0312), deal in Art Nouveau and Art Deco, though they often have items extending up to the 1950s. They deal in fashion accessories in general, though specialising in jewellery made out of anything from Bakelite to gold; also handbags, scarves, belts and other accessories.

LUNN ANTIQUES, 86 New King's Road, SW6 (736 4638) specialises in 'whites' with examples up to the 1930s.

The PURPLE SHOP, 15 Flood Street, SW3 (352 1127) deals in fine antique jewellery from the Georgian period to the 1930s.

TOPFLOOR GALLERY, 14 Church Street, NW8 (723 9981) deals in a wide range of costume and accessories up to the 1920s, as well as 'whites', children's clothes, lace and textiles. Next door MELODY SACHS (12 Church Street; 262 1370) deals in evening and day dresses from the 1920s to the 1950s.

Street Markets

PORTOBELLO (Notting Hill Gate underground station) is active on Saturdays from 8.30 am to 5.30 pm, though it is worthwhile going earlier. For clothes as for antiques it is the two ends of the market which are important; two dealers to note at the Ladbroke Grove underground station end are MRS BURNETT, 290 Portobello Road, and SUNSET BOULEVARD, 306 Portobello Road, which specialises in the 1930s and 1940s.

BERMONDSEY (at the intersection of Long Lane, Tower Bridge Road and Bermondsey Street SE1; London Bridge or Borough underground stations), operates on Fridays from sunrise to sunset. Serious business is over by 8.00 or 9.00 in the morning. Although a dealers market, it is well worth trying, particularly as the stall-holders move on to Portobello Road with what they haven't sold.

There are also smaller weekend markets: CAMDEN LOCK (off the Chalk Farm Road, NW1; nearest underground station Chalk Farm); and nearby INVERNESS STREET (opposite Camden Town underground station).

Further information can be found in *A Guide to London Street Markets* by Mel Lewis and Andrea Soole (Harvill Press, London, 1983).

Charity Shops
OXFAM are the best known; there are 36 listed in the London Telephone Directory and information about country shops can be got from Oxfam, 274 Banbury Road, Oxford OX2 7DZ (Oxford 56777).

WAR ON WANT have four shops in London: 1 The Green, W5; 245 Westbourne Grove, W11; 129 Churchfield Road, W3; 301 Finchley Road, NW3. There are a further 22 in England and Wales; information from the Shops Development Officer, War on Want, 467 Caledonian Road, London N7; tel: 609 0211. Their shops also hire out costume.

Other shops in London include: CHILDREN AND YOUTH ALIYAH, 57 Upper Montague Street, W1; HELPING HAND GIFT SHOPS, 32 Dover Street, W1 and 67 Moorgate, EC2; and HELP THE AGED, 124 Muswell Hill Broadway, N10.

Bookshops
COSTUME AND FASHION BOOKSHOP (Lesley Hodges), Queen's Elm Parade, Old Church Street, SW3 (352 1176). This shop has old and new books on historical and national costume, costume accessories, tailoring, textiles and related embroidery, needlework and lace, twentieth-century fashion and fashion photography, beauty culture and social and industrial histories. Also fashion magazines, fashion plates, water-colours and prints.

R. D. FRANKS, Kent House, 1 Market Place, Oxford Circus, W1 (636 1244). Very much a trade bookshop, selling new and second-hand books dealing with practical aspects of costume design and production; as such it is likely to be of interest to students and designers. However serious collectors may find trade manuals dating from the 1950s, for instance, interesting.

DAPHNE LUCAS, 28 Addison Way, NW11 (455 3110) deals in books, old and new, on costume, accessories and textiles. Chiefly a mail order business, she issues regular catalogues and also searches for specific titles required by customers on the above subjects.

Out of London
The presence of fashion collections in museums such as those at Bath or Brighton seems to have generated a serious interest in antique clothes there, attracting both dealers and collectors. The best source of local information is in fact the costume and textiles department in such a museum. This list will, however, give some interesting starting points for the collector outside London

Alresford, Hampshire
MARGARET SMITH, Beresford House Museum, Pound Hill, Alresford, Hampshire (Alresford 2869). As well as running a museum with her husband Vernon, in which her costume collection spanning the years 1770–1940 is exhibited, Margaret Smith has a shop which specialises in textiles and clothes, particularly the twentieth century. A serious collector herself, she generally sells to people who can be trusted not to wear the clothes. Open 9.00 am to 5.30 pm every day except Sunday, and at other times by appointment.

Bath
There are two street markets, the GREAT WESTERN ANTIQUES MARKET at Bartlett Street, and the ANTIQUES MARKET at Guinea Lane, where dresses and accessories are sold on Wednesdays. SHEILA SMITH, 10a Queen Street, (Bath 60568) deals in needlework, tools and accessories, as well as specialising in fans. Her shop is open by appointment in the morning and from 1.30 to 6.00 pm.

Edinburgh
HAND IN HAND, 3 North West Circus Place, Edinburgh EH3 6ST (031-556 8897). Mrs Hand has been in business for twelve years, dealing in costume up to the 1950s.

Epsom, Surrey
STEPHEN FURNISS, 10 Kingsdown Road, Epsom, Surrey (Epsom 22085), started collecting fashion dating from 1918–1946 when he was head of the Collector's Department at Bonhams, where he added the costume and textile department. He deals from home, and occasionally exhibits at Sunday antique fairs held in London hotels – for further information contact the above address.

Manchester
BUTTERLANE ANTIQUE MARKET, King Street West, Manchester 2 (061-834 1809). About ten stands deal in period clothes, most notably ROSALIND ROSENVELT, who specialises in clothes from the 1920s to the 1960s and often has fine examples of beaded dresses in stock.

CAMISOLE, All Saints, Oxford Road, Manchester 10, stocks second-hand clothes which appeal to current fashionable taste, with an eye to the students from the nearby university.

Sawbridgeworth, Herts.
HERTS & ESSEX ANTIQUES CENTRE, The Maltings, Station Road, Sawbridgeworth, Herts (0279 725809). A group of about twenty antique shops whose stock tends to vary but generally includes lace, linen, textiles and costume; specialist weekend fairs take place about four times a year – further information from the Antiques Centre.

AMERICA

Auctions
Of the New York auction houses, only Christie's East holds costume sales on a regular basis. CHRISTIE'S EAST (Julie Collier), 219 East 67th Street, NY 10021 (212-570-4141). Christie's accepts articles on consignment at their branches around the country, but auctions are held only in New York. They also offer an appraisal service. For subscription to catalogues on costume call 212-784-1480; the fee is $35.00 per year. It is also possible to subscribe to Christie's South Kensington through Christie's East.

Two trade papers which offer advertisements for more auctions, antique centers, shops and flea markets than anyone could possibly go to are: JOEL SATER'S ANTIQUES & AUCTION NEWS, available free from many dealers, or by subscription at $12.00 per year – 26 issues. Write: Box B, Marietta Pa 17547 (717-426-1956). Published every other Friday; NEWTOWN BEE ANTIQUE & ARTS WEEKLY, published weekly, the subscription is $22.50 per year. Write: Newtown Bee, 5 Church Hill Road, Newtown, Connecticut 06470 (203-426-3141).

Periodicals
In New York, the Sunday *New York Times* has listings of estate sales, which sometimes include clothes. Local papers, especially the very local weekly papers, list auction sales and 'house' sales – these can range from the entire contents of a house to items someone doesn't want to take with them when they move. Occasional finds include costume jewelry and baby clothes. Vintage clothing is often, alas, thrown out first, but old magazines are sometimes left, and usually go for nothing.

ANTIQUES MAGAZINE usually lists some auctions, flea markets and antique shows. While costume is not yet a mainstream topic for these magazines, it is certainly worth looking through glossy magazines such as ART & ANTIQUES and CONNOISSEUR as they do occasionally carry articles of interest to the collector of vintage clothing and fashion.

Societies
THE COSTUME SOCIETY OF AMERICA (212-563-5552), 330 West 42nd Street, Suite 1702, NY 10036. This would appear to be the only major society dealing with the study and further understanding of costume and fashion in America. Recently moved to this address and with a professional office staff for the first time, it is hoped to extend their range of activities in the future. They organise lectures and conferences, circulate a newsletter and journal, and also have a publications programme. The Society provides a consultation service for the identification and conservation of costumes. Individual subscription is currently $30.00 per year (students $10.00).

Dealers
If you are collecting couture clothes, using a good dealer is definitely a

good idea. Dealers have done the work of finding the item, cleaning it and, in most cases, mending any little snags etc. Although using a dealer is more expensive than finding a piece yourself, dealers do have more resources and most will look for specific things for you.

CORA GINSBURG 815 Madison Avenue (near 77th St.), NY 10021 (212-744-1342). A widely known dealer whose great love is the eighteenth century. She also has fine twentieth-century dresses and accessories and a large collection of lace and quilts. Mrs Ginsburg does do appraisals of pieces, but you should always call ahead.

GENE LONDON 106 East 19th Street, NY 10003 (212-533-4105). By appointment. Deals in 1900 – c 1960 in both couture and everyday costume. Does a lot of rental for TV and film and occasionally hires to private clients (e.g. for a wedding or costume ball). Large business in wearables. He will search for specific items and concentrate on *you*.

HARRIET LOVE 412 West Broadway (in SoHo), NY (212-966-2280). Specializes in trendy clothing in good condition, e.g. Hawaiian shirts or a good 1940s skirt, i.e. wearables rather than couture.

MARLENE 185 East 79th Street (Lexington to 3rd), NY (212-737-7671). Tiny, charming shop, with lots of lacy Edwardian lingerie blouses. They also sell quilts.

TENDER BUTTONS 143 East 62nd Street, NY. The owner, Diana Epstein, is the author of *Buttons: A History of Buttons and Button Collecting*. The store carries a number of antique buttons as well as lots of current ones.

TROUVÉ 1200 Lexington Avenue (near 81st St.) NY 10028 (212-744-4409). Wearables; a mixed bag with everything from everyday to dressmaker clothes, mostly 1930s to 1960s with the occasional couture item.

MARK WALSH 78 Wendover Road, Yonkers, NY, 10705 (914-963-1694). By appointment. Depending on where you are located, he will occasionally bring specific items to New York City. Well known as a specialist in Fortuny, Mark Walsh is a good source for important twentieth-century couture and accessories. While expensive, he has a talent for turning up pieces by Schiaparelli, Vionnet etc., which are *extremely* hard to find on your own. Does appraisals and will look for specific items.

Antique Clothes Shops

In New York these shops tend to be grouped in certain areas, for example, on Columbus Avenue, between about 72nd and 77th Streets, with a few shops further up to 86th Street, as what one newspaper calls 'gentrification' continues! Antique clothes shops are also spreading west to Amsterdam, notably LUNATIQUE (at 79th Street). This is a mind-blowing experience; do not go there if you are the slightest bit claustrophobic. SCREAMING MIMI on 83rd Street off Columbus Avenue carries 1940s and 1950s wearables. Another locale is St Mark's Place, which is what 8th Street becomes between Second and Third Avenues. This has a number of shops specializing mostly in the punk look and the 1950s – everyday and mixable wearables for the most part. The largest shop is TRASH AND VAUDEVILLE at 4 St Mark's Place (212-982-3590), which occasionally has the odd 1930s gown as well as the current punk look. Nearby is CHEAP JACK'S, at 167 First Avenue and 151 First Avenue, both very popular with theatrical designers because of their large stocks of men's suits, shirts etc. from the 1930s to 1950s (with a few earlier pieces). Mostly everyday clothing rather than high fashion; they do sometimes have shoes in stock. SOHO CANAL STREET FLEA MARKET at 369 Canal Street, NY 10013. This is a three-storey building which houses a number of clothing dealers, mostly twentieth century, not very expensive, and wearables, although YESTERDAY'S DREAM (second floor) sometimes has couture pieces. Everyone seems to open at different hours, and Monday is generally to be avoided. UNIQUE CLOTHING WAREHOUSE 718 Broadway (in the Village below 8th Street), NY (212-674-1767). This is a huge store offering very mixed, but affordable everyday clothing. The women's clothes are mostly 1940s and 1950s, but there is an enormous selection of men's uniforms: army, navy, some foreign (very few), waiters' white jackets, dinner jackets and tails, pea jackets. They also carry articles like thermal underwear and British Raj-style men's shorts.

Army-Navy Stores, which are listed in Yellow Pages all over the States, should provide clothing along the same lines as the Unique Clothing Warehouse. The following is a short list of the sort of stores

you can expect to find:

Atlanta OLD SARGE ARMY NAVY SURPLUS 5316 Buford HWy Drive (451 6031).

Chicago UNCLE DAN'S LTD 2440 N. Lincoln Avenue (312-477 1918).

Los Angeles ARMY NAVY STORE 131 East 6th Street (213-623 3142). CAMP BEVERLY HILLS 9640 Santa Monica Blvd. (213-274 8317).

New Orleans WESTSIDE ARMY SURPLUS 522 Lafayette Gretna (504-361 1215).

San Francisco CALIFORNIA SURPLUS SALES 1393 Haight (415-861 0404).

Seattle LIGHTHOUSE UNIFORM CO. 1532 15th W. (206-282 5600).

As far as other dealers and antique clothes shops outside New York are concerned, we have set out below a tiny proportion of those that can be found from coast to coast. Unfortunately clothing dealers are rarely listed conveniently in the Yellow Pages under Antique Clothes; sometimes they are, but you should also look under Resale Clothing, Vintage Clothing, Second Hand Clothing or Antique Stores. In extremis, ask at a local antique store, since dealers usually know one another.

Atlanta, Georgia SWEET EMALINE P O Box 8526, Atlanta, Georgia 30306 (Owner: Deborah Garey Barrett). Does appraisals as well as dealing in clothes and accessories.

Hartford, Conn. GRACE DYAR 20 Vernon Street, Hartford, Conn. 06106. This dealer also does clothing appraisals.

Montclair, New Jersey BOOMERANG 416 Bloomfield Avenue, Montclair, NJ. A large, beautiful store dealing in clothing and accessories. MEMORIES 415 Bloomfield Avenue, Montclair, NJ. Art Deco *objets*, clothing and shoes from the 1930s to 1950s. Moderately priced; wearables, not couture.

New Orleans, Louisiana THE YOU BOUTIQUE 8131 Hampson, New Orleans (504-866-9666). Highly recommended for hats, including new ones which the owner will make to order from a mammoth stock of antique trims.

San Diego, California ONCE UPON A TIME 2454 Heritage Park Row, San Diego (714-692-1189). Beautiful antique clothes in excellent condition.

Washington, D. C. BROADWAY BABY 1641 Wisconsin Avenue, Georgetown Men's and women's clothes mostly from the 1920s, including shoes.

This list must seem pitifully brief, but to begin to be comprehensive would have taken another book. Happily, one book already exists which should prove invaluable in supplying addresses of good antique clothes stores. This is Catherine Houck's *The Fashion Encyclopedia* (St Martin's Press, New York, 1982).

Resale Shops

Merchandise in resale shops is accepted on consignment from the owner to be sold, with the store manager taking a percentage. Most shops have the clothes dry cleaned before putting them on sale, so they are generally in good condition. These shops are good sources for more recent designers such as Sonia Rykiel, but it is not unheard of to discover a 1950s or 1960s Norell hanging on the rails. Two good New York stores are: ENCORE 1132 Madison Avenue (at 84th St.) (212-879-2850). They occasionally get unsold broken lots from department stores; MICHAEL'S 1041 Madison Avenue (near 78th St.) (212-737-7273). Catherine Houck's book again lists a wide range of resale shops.

Thrift Shops

For those truly dedicated to the spirit of the chase, there are the thrift shops. They are charity-related, accepting donations to be sold and the money going to specific charities. The variety and condition of the merchandise on offer can be bewildering. The prices can be outrageous, depending on who prices the garments and what she likes, but almost all the shops hold sales and you can bargain with varying success. Most shops are open 10.00 am – 4.30 pm, some Tuesday–Saturday, and some Monday–Friday, and almost all close in August. The best sales are always just before they close for August. On the other hand, the selection is richest in January, because so many people donate to charity at the end of the year in order to receive the tax deduction. Most charities have links with thrift shops, and you can call them to find out which ones; for example, B'nai B'rith always have several. Usually listed in the Yellow Pages under 'Thrift Shops', in New York they are mostly to be found on Third Avenue between about 75th and 90th Streets, and also on Ninth Avenue in the 50s. The Salvation Army shops are spread all around the city. The Junior League runs some 111 shops across the country and other thrift shops which have been recommended to us include THE BLUE BIRD CIRCLE in Houston, Texas, THE TRADING POST RUMMAGE SHOP in Lake Forest, Illinois and THE NEXT-TO-NEW SHOP in San Francisco

Flea Markets

The challenge of finding fashion in flea markets is a good one, as apart from anything else, they can move around a lot. In addition to regular flea markets the keen hunter of fashion should consider 'block parties' in New York and the fairs which are held more or less regularly annually on the big Avenues, for example, the Third Avenue Festival, which occurs in late Spring, and occupies two successive weekends, all of which attract a multitude of clothing dealers. They are announced by posters and listed in The Weekend Guide of the *New York Times*. Bargaining is the rule, and it's better to have cash – you can usually get things for less. For all fairs and flea markets there are 'best times' to go – early in the morning when the selection is best, and just before the whole thing shuts up (roughly 6.00 pm) because dealers would often rather sell than cart everything home again.

In New York THE CANAL STREET FLEA MARKET is held in a parking lot on Canal Street, two blocks east of the SoHo Canal Street Flea Market building, on Saturday and Sunday, Spring to late Fall. It has a fair number of clothing dealers and items range from junk to a Stavropoulos cocktail dress once found by our American editor there.

ROOSEVELT RACEWAY FLEA MARKET (in Westbury, Long Island, NY) on Sundays – lots of new clothing; try for old magazines and costume jewelry.

THE 26TH STREET FLEA MARKET on Sixth Avenue, in what is normally a parking lot. Held every Sunday between May and October, although it has been known to continue through November, depending on weather conditions. Open from 10.00 am – 7.00 pm, there is $1.00 admission charge. There is a wild and wonderful variety here, with quite a lot of clothing on offer, anything from the 1850s to modern polyester, though rarely anything of museum quality.

JOEL SATER'S ANTIQUES & AUCTION NEWS, mentioned before, lists lots and lots of flea markets, mainly in Pennsylvania and New Jersey and elsewhere in the country. One of the largest and oldest in New England is the NORTON FLEA MARKET SALE – on Route 140 between Norton and Mansfield in Massachusetts. This is held every Sunday (and Monday holidays), April – October. The gate opens at 5.30 am; admission 50¢. (617-339-8554). A couple of others to note are the FLEA MARKET, ENGLISHTOWN, NEW JERSEY, which is huge and open on Saturdays, Spring to Fall. It includes every kind of item and should be reached at crack of dawn. The BRIMFIELD, MASSACHUSETTS, FLEA MARKET is held three times a year, in May, July and September, for five days (a moveable feast – check the dates with NEWTOWN BEE). The best things tend to turn up at the Spring sale (dealers have been collecting all winter).

Book Dealers

Any dealer in old and secondhand books may have old books on costume and/or magazines. Valuable old books on costume can be found at HACKER ART BOOKS 54 West 57th Street, NY, and RIZZOLI 712 Fifth Avenue, NY, has one of the largest international selections of current costume books and magazines. Museum book shops, such as those at the Metropolitan Museum of Art in New York, the Philadelphia Museum of Art, or the Smithsonian Institute in Washington, can offer a good selection, particularly of their own exhibition catalogues. Since exhibition catalogues are usually printed in limited numbers it is always worthwhile to buy them while you can. Two mail order businesses which have lists of costume, lace and textile books are: LACIS (which also sells antique lace, textiles, tools and equipment for conservation and making lace) 2990 Adeline Street, Berkeley, California 94703. Send $1.00 for the catalogue (and invest in a magnifying glass to read it!). The catalogue includes old pattern books for knitting, crochet etc. and a selection of period patterns for those who prefer to make their own antique clothing.

THE TEXTILE BOOKLIST Subscription $11.00 per year (USA, Mexico and Canada), overseas $14.00 (airmail). Write: Box C-20, Lopez, Wyoming 98261. They publish reviews, lists of new books – some of

which may be ordered through them – and a chatty newsletter about various costume shows.

BIBLIOGRAPHY

Adburgham, Alison *Shops & Shopping 1800–1914* (Allen & Unwin, London, 1964); *View of Fashion* (Allen & Unwin, London, 1966).

Amies, Hardy *Just So Far* (Collins, London, 1954)

Anthony, P. and Arnold, J. *Costume: A General Bibliography* (Costume Society, London, 2nd ed. 1974).

Arnold, Janet *A Handbook of Costume* (Macmillan, London, 1973)

Baker, Lillian *100 Years of Collectible Jewelry* (Collector Books, Kentucky, 1978).

Balmain, Pierre *My Years and Seasons* (Cassell, London, 1964)

Beaton, C. *The Glass of Fashion* (Weidenfeld & Nicolson, London, 1954).

Becker, Vivienne *Antique and 20th Century Jewellery* (N.A.G. Press, London, 1980).

Bernard, Barbara *Fashion in The 60's* (Academy Editions, London; St Martin's Press, New York, 1978).

Bender, M. *The Beautiful People* (Coward, McCann, New York, 1967).

Bertin, Celia *Paris à la Mode* (Harper & Row, New York, 1957).

Battersby, Martin *The Decorative Twenties* (Studio Vista, London, 1969); *The Decorative Thirties* (Studio Vista, London, 1971).

Baynes, Ken & Kate, eds. *The Shoe Show: British Shoes Since 1790* (Crafts Council, London, 1979).

Byrde, Penelope *The Male Image: Men's Fashions in Britain 1300–1970* (Batsford, London, 1977).

Carter, Ernestine *The Changing World of Fashion* (Weidenfeld & Nicolson, London, 1977).

Chambers, B. *Fashion Fundamentals* (Prentice-Hall, New York, 1947).

Charles-Roux, Edmonde *Chanel and Her World* (Weidenfeld & Nicolson, London, 1981).

Crawford, M. D. C. *The Ways of Fashion* (Putnam, New York, 1941).

Daché, Lilly *Talking Through My Hats* (John Gifford, London, 1946).

Davenport, M. *The Book of Costume* (Crown, New York, 1948, 2 vols.).

Daves, Jessica *Ready-Made Miracle: The American Story of Fashion for the Millions* (Putnam, New York, 1967).

De Graw, Imelda G. *25 Years/25 Couturiers* (Denver Art Museum, Denver, 1975).

De Marly, Diana *The History of Haute Couture 1850–1950* (Holmes & Meier, New York, 1980).

De Osma, Guillermo *Fortuny – Mariano Fortuny: His Life and Work* (Aurum Press, London, 1980).

Dior, Christian *Christian Dior and I* (E. P. Dutton, New York, 1957); *Talking About Fashion* (Putnam, New York, 1954)

Dorner, Jane *Fashion in the Forties and Fifties* (Ian Allen, London, 1975).

Earnshaw, Patricia *The Identification of Lace* (Shire Publications, Bucks, 1980); *The Dictionary of Lace* (Shire Publications, Bucks, 1982).

Epstein, Diana *Buttons* (Studio Vista, London, 1966).

Ewing, Elizabeth *Dress and Undress, A History of Women's Underwear* (Batsford, London, 1978).

History of Children's Costume (Batsford, London, 1977)

Ferragamo, Salvatore *Shoemaker of Dreams* (Harrap, London, 1957).

Finch, K. and Putnam, G. *Caring For Textiles* (Barrie & Jenkins, London, 1977).

Foster, Vanda *Bags and Purses* (Batsford, London, 1982).

Garland, Madge *The Changing Form of Fashion* (Praeger, New York, 1970); *The Decisive Decade* (Macdonald, London 1968).

Gernsheim, A. *Fashion and Reality 1840–1914* (Faber, London, 1963).

Ginsburg, Madeleine *Fashion: An Anthology by Cecil Beaton* (Victoria & Albert Museum, London, 1971).

Glynn, Prudence and Ginsburg, Madeleine *In Fashion: Dress in the 20th Century* (Allen & Unwin, London, 1978).

Guppy, Alice *Children's Clothes 1939–70*; *The Advent of Fashion* (Blandford Press, Poole, 1978).

Halliday, L. *The Makers of Our Clothes* (Zenith Books, London, 1966).

Hartnell, Norman *Silver and Gold* (Evans Bros, London, 1955).

Hawes, Elizabeth *Fashion is Spinach* (Random House, New York, 1938).

Hollander, A. *Seeing Through Clothes* (Avon Books, New York, 1980).

Houart, V. *Buttons: A Collector's Guide* (Souvenir Press, London, 1977).

Howell, Georgina *In Vogue: Sixty Years of International Celebrities and Fashion from British Vogue* (Penguin Books, London, 1978).

Hughes, T. *Edwardiana for Collectors* (G. Bell & Sons, London, 1977).

Jarnow, Jeanette, and Judelle, Beatrice *Inside the Fashion Business* (Wiley, New York, 1974).

Jefferys, James *Retail Trading in Britain 1850–1950* (Cambridge University Press, Cambridge, 1964).

Keenan, Brigid *Dior in Vogue* (Harmony Books, New York; Octopus, London, 1981).

Kidwell, Claudia, and Christman, Margaret C. *Suiting Everyone: The Democratisation of Clothing in America* (Smithsonian Institute, Washington, 1974).

Lambert, Eleanor *The World of Fashion: People, Places, Resources* (R & R Bowker, New York, 1976).

Latour, A. *Kings of Fashion* (Weidenfeld & Nicolson, London, 1958).

Laver, James *Taste and Fashion* (Harrap, London, revised ed., 1945); *Modesty in Dress* (Heinemann, London, 1969).

Levin, Phyllis Lee *The Wheels of Fashion* (Doubleday, New York, 1965).

Levine, Louis *The Women's Garment Workers* (B. W. Huebsch, New York, 1924).

Leese, Elizabeth *Costume Design in The Movies* (Bow Publications, London, 1976).

Ley, Sandra *Fashion for Everyone: The Story of Ready-To-Wear 1870s to 1970s* (Scribner, New York, 1975).

Lowes, Mrs E. L. *Chats on Old Lace and Needlework* (T. Fisher Unwin, London, 1908).

Luscombe, S. *The Encyclopedia of Buttons* (Bonanza Books, New York, 1967).

Lynam, Ruth *Paris Fashion* (Michael Joseph, London, 1972).

Mansfield, Alan, and Cunnington, Phyllis *Handbook of English Costume in the Twentieth Century 1900–1950* (Faber, London, 1973).

Mulassano Adriana, and Custaldi, Alfa *The Who's Who of Italian Fashion* (G. Spineldi, Florence, 1979).

Picken, M. B. *Dressmakers of France* (Harper & Row, New York, 1957).

Poiret, Paul *My First Fifty Years* tr. Stephen Haden Guest (Gollancz, London, 1931).

Pond, G. *An Introduction to Lace* (Garnstone Press, London, 1973).

Pope, Jesse *The Clothing Industry in New York* (Burth Franklin, New York, 1970).

Richards, Florence *The Ready-to-Wear Industry 1900–1950* (Fairchild, New York, 1950).

Riley, R. and Vecchio, W. *The Fashion Makers* (Crown, New York, 1967).

Robinson, Julian *Fashion in the 30s* (Oresko Books, London, 1978); *Fashion in the 40s* (Academy Aditions, London; St Martin's Press, New York, 1976).

Roshco, Bernard *The Rag Race* (Funk & Wagnalls, New York, 1963).

Rubin, L. *The World of Fashion* (Canfield Press, San Francisco, 1976).

Sallee, Lynn *Old Costume Jewelry 1870–1945* (Books Americana, Alabama, 1979).

Saunders, Edith *The Age of Worth* (Indiana University Press, Bloomington, 1955).

Simeon, Margaret *A History of Lace* (Stainer & Bell, London, 1979)

Smith, Lillian, and Kent, Albert & Katherine, *The Complete Button Book* (World's Work, Surrey, 1952).

Stein, Leon *Out of the Sweatshop* (Quadrangle, New York, 1977).

Stevenson, Pauline *Edwardian Fashion* (Ian Allen, London, 1980).

Swann, June *Shoes* (Batsford, London, 1982).

Thaarup, Aage *Heads and Tales* (Cassell, London, 1956).

Tomerlin, S. L. ed. *American Fashion* (FIT/Quadrangle, New York, 1975).

Watson, G. G. *Collecting Tomorrow's Antiques* (Kaye & Ward, London, 1977).

Waugh, Norah *The Cut of Men's Clothes 1600–1914* (Batsford, London, 1964); *Corsets and Crinolines* (Batsford, London, 1965).

Wilcox, R. Turner *The Mode in Hats and Headdresses* (Scribner, New York, 1959); *The Dictionary of Costume* (Scribner, New York, 1969).

Willet, C. and Cunnington, Phyllis *The History of Underclothes* (Faber, London, revised edn., 1981).

Wilson, Eunice *The History of Shoe Fashion* (Theatre Arts Books, New York, 1969).

Worth, J. P. *A Century of Fashion* (Little, Brown, Boston, 1928).

ACKNOWLEDGEMENTS

Anyone writing about collecting starts out with a great advantage. Collectors are born enthusiasts, and the author is able to learn from a large number of generous people, who are only too free with their time and happy to share their pleasure in collecting. Their kindness does not go unappreciated, and I am deeply grateful to the following people, who gave me their confidence and spared me their valuable time; with the faith that I would make good use of their far superior taste and experience. To the following I owe gratitude and respect, and I hope that this book will repay their kindness':

Mrs Hélène Alexander of the Fan Circle, London, who showed me her lovely collection and trusted me with her books; Penelope Byrde, Curator of the Museum of Costume, Bath; Anne Marie Benson, of Phillips Son & Neale, who gave me much useful information, besides further names and addresses; Francesca Bianco of Saks Fifth Avenue, New York; Julie Collier of Christie's East, New York; Linda Donahue of Trouvé, New York; Jean Drussedow of the Metropolitan Museum, New York (who satisfied my long-standing ambition to see some Schiaparelli evening jackets in the pink); Audrey Field, lace dealer, London; Karen Finch of the Textile Conservation Centre at Hampton Court Palace, who made free with all her writings on the subject; Philippe Garner of Sotheby's Belgravia, who also helped most generously with the illustrations; Lesley Hodges, who runs a fashion bookshop in London; Harriet Love, who sat me in her boutique in SoHo and helped me see what fashion style really means in perspective; Avril Hart of the Victoria and Albert Museum, London, and Betty Kirke of the Conservation Department of New York's Fashion Institute of Technology, both of whom described the pitfalls of conservation with great patience and clarity; Phyllis Magidson of the Museum of the City of New York, who also gave me many handy tips on clothes care; Mrs Jaqueline Morris, of the Fan Circle, London, who showed me many fine examples from her own collection; Mrs Jean Pendle, who gave up a day, and unearthed practically her whole collection of lace on my behalf, and in so doing transformed my appreciation for the subject; Robert Pusilo, who even in a brief meeting, inspired me with the essence of collecting fashion; Caroline Reynolds of Sotheby's, who did her best to make me like Charles James; Robert Riley of the F.I.T., who disapproved of the whole venture but who nevertheless opened all the doors wide with humour and kindness; Shannon Rogers, who in spite of heavy schedules and weightier matters, showed me endless wonderful treasures from his own collection, besides telling me some memorable stories; Judy Straeton, my American editor, whose interest and hard work added immeasurably to the book; June Swann, Curator of the Shoe Museum, Northampton, who filled in some academic research with first-hand experience; Dorothy Tricarico, in charge of fabrics at F.I.T., who revealed drawers full of fascinating samples; and Stan Weaver, of Spence Chapin, who found me in the store and gave me an impromptu lecture on couture and, in particular, Norell, in the most entertaining way. Lastly to Lorraine Wieberg of the F.I.T. Library; the efficiency and accessibility of which makes me long to emigrate.

A few people I wish to thank more personally, because the book would have been impossible to write without them. Madeleine Ginsburg of the Victoria and Albert Museum, who has always given me wholehearted advice and support; Ruth Lynam, with whom I worked on a beautiful book, *Paris Fashion*, and who gave me an appreciation of fashion I have never lost; Peggy Kelly, who helped support me in my studies in New York, in many friendly ways; Frank Riess, who taught me to study in the first place, and stepped in to cope with the family while I was away; Bettina Tayleur, my publisher, whose courage and determination made the book possible, and Thaddeus O'Sullivan, without whom the book might have been written, but missing half the pride and confidence.

Picture Credits

Illustrations for this book appear by courtesy of the people, collections and organisations listed below. The letters indicating the position of the illustrations on the page give the order, running down column by column, in which the left-hand edges of the pictures appear.

American Vogue (Angelo Hornak) 34/35, 66b, 71b & d, 76/77, 79b, 135b, 160b & c, 162a, 170a, 188c; Hardy Amies 77b & c, 100b, 107b, 151b; Giorgio Armani: foto Karim 120/121; Asprey, London 158/159c, 178c; BBC Hulton Picture Library 12, 19c, 22a & b, 23c, 31a, 36a & b, 46b, 48b, 60b, 67a & d, 68a, 70a, 70/71, 72a, 77a, *88/89*, *89b*, 90b, 127c & d, 128a & b, 128/129a & b, 129c, e, f, 130/131, 131c & d, 133a, 136b, 149c, *161b*, 166b, 169a & b, 170/171, 171b, *172a*, 175, 179d, 180e, 184/185, 187c, 188d, 194a, 195d, 198b & c, 200/201, 202a, 203c, 204g; Cecil Beaton Photograph: Courtesy Sotheby's Belgravia 44/45, 58a, 59a, 94/95, 96b, 167a & b; Bethnal Green Museum (Angelo Hornak) 127a, *129d*, *132b*, 207b, 232; Biba 103c; Bildarchiv Preussischer Kulturbesitz, Berlin 19a, 35b & c, 39b, 42c, 49a, 55, 64, 166a; The Bridgeman Art Library *21*, *29*, *32a*, *56b*, *60a*, *145a & d* (The Button Queen); The British Library (Ray Gardner) 63a & b, 206b & c, 207a; The Button Box, London WC2 (P. J. Gates) 148c, e, f, *148/149*, *149b*, 150/151, 158/159a; Camera Press, London 79c, 82a, 84c, 119b Camera Press: Giancarlo Botti 105d; Loomis Dean 110a; Terence Donovan/Queen 181a; David Montgomery/Queen 100c; Helmut Newton/Queen 98/99; David Steen 103a; Canterbury Museum, Christchurch, N.Z. 246; Centraal Museum, Utrecht 222; Centre d'Enseignement et de Documentation du Costume, Paris 45, *57d*, 58c, 167c; Cerruti 1881 205f; Chelmsford & Essex Museums 227; Chicago Historical Society 238, 239; The Costume & Lace Museum, Brussels 208c; The Costume Institute Library: Metropolitan Museum of Art 17b, 26b, 27; David Cripps *53*, *116b*, *116/117*; Elliott/McCorkells Sidaway & Wright Ltd *192a, b, c, 193b*; ET Archive *37b*; Mary Evans Picture Library *45*, *165b & c*, 197b, 202b, 202/203b; Focal Point *196a, b, c*; John French Picture Library 74b, 81, 86b, 92b & c, 92/93, 93b, 100a, 103c, 104b, 106b, 171c, 172b, 195e; Philippe Garner 122b, *125b*, 161a; Cecil Gee 204/205, 205a; Tom Gilbey 204d, 205b & c; Bill Gibb 114/115, 115b, *117b*; Photo Toby Glanville *104/105*; Harper's Bazaar 60c, 61b, 65a & b, 66a, 67b & c, *68b*, 69b, 73a & c, 83a, 84a, 90c, 172c, 198d, 199a, 201d; Harper's Bazaar (USA) 42a, 47b, 79a; Angelo Hornak Library *25a & c*, *141b*, *153b*, *153c* (Dan Klein), *156/157* (John Jesse), *157c* (Dan Klein), *160a* (Martins Forest), *177d*; Bevis Hillier 54a, 72/73, 80a, 83b, 86/87, 159c (Anton & Susan Marsh), 178d, 204b; William Hollins & Co. 136a; Il Vittoriale 221; Georg Jensen, Copenhagen 153d; John Jesse & Irina Laski Ltd 154a & b, 157b, 158b, 159d, 176b, *176c*, 178a & b, 179a, b, c, 180a & b; Keystone Press Agency 89a, 97b, 101a; Calvin Klein 122a; The Kobal Collection 42a, 71c, *84b*, 133c, 187a, 195a, 199c, 200d, 202/203a, 203a & c, 204a, c, e; Krizia: photo Tony McGee 121b; Photo Gunnar Larsen, Paris 107a; Ralph Lauren 112/113; Philippa Lewis 126, 127b, 134a; Los Angeles County Museum of Art: Gift of Mrs Henry P. Russell 30a; Gift of The Fashion Group of Los Angeles 108/109; Gift of Mrs Harry d'Arrast 240; Lotherton Hall, Leeds 231; The Mansell Collection 13, 17c, 18, 19b, 20a, b, c, 26a, 37a, 38a, 62a, 131e, 197a & d, 198a; The Metropolitan Museum of Art: The Costume Institute Collection – Gift of Irene Castle (Mrs George Enzinger) 31b; Gift of Joseph F. Simms *80b*; Missoni 118/119; Mothercare 135a; Jean Muir 113c; Musée de la Chaussure, Romans – Collection Jourdan 188b, 190c; Collection UNIC 187d; Musée des Arts Decoratifs, Paris 152; Museen der Stadt Wien 176/177, 177c, 218; The Museum of Costume, Bath 14c, 16, 26c, 39a, 51b, 56c, 57b, 59b & c, 99c, 101c, 131b, 135c, 157d, 164b, *180c*, 183, 184a & c, 186c, 191c, 194 b, c, d, 207c, 224; Courtesy, Museum of Fine Arts, Boston: Gift of Mrs Frank K. Idell 200a, b, c; The Museum of London 208b; New Zealand Wool Board 245a & b; Northampton Museums & Art Gallery 184d, 185b, c, d, e, 186a, b, d, 187b & e, 189a & b; Norsk Folkemuseum, Oslo 223; Tommy Nutter 205d; Phillips Fine Art

Auctioneers *title page*, 188e, 207f; Popperfoto 111b, 155, 173a, 179e, 195c, 199e; Mary Quant Ltd 99b; Janet Reger 199a; Zandra Rhodes (Grant Mudford) *116a*; Rijksmuseum, Amsterdam 139a; Courtesy of Royal Ontario Museum, Toronto, Canada: Gift of Miss Minnota Grinyer 244; Sonia Rykiel 118a; Photo Seeberger, Paris 34, 47c, 62b, 74a, 168; David Shilling 174a, b, c; Clive Shilton *180d*, *181b*, *193a*; Stern (Peter Knapp) *124/125*; Syndication International *97a*; The Tailor & Cutter 202c, 204f; Jane Thistlethwaite *140/141a*; Time-Life Inc. *101*; John Topham Picture Library 86a, 110/111, 122/123, 182, 188a, 190a, 201b; Gianni Versace 205e; Victoria & Albert Museum 14a & b, 15b, c, d, e, 23a & b, 24/25, 25b, 26d, 30b, *32/33*, *33b*, 33a, 35a, 40a, 40/41, 41a, 42/43, 46a, 47a, 48a, 50a, 50/51, 54c, 57c, *69a*, 130a, 133b, 139b, 140a, *140/141b*, 148d, 162a, 164c & d, *165a*, 166c & d, 176a, 191b, 197c, 206/207a, 207e, 208a, 208/209a, b, c; Weidenfeld & Nicolson Archive 17a, 54b, 58b, 106a, 113b & d, 164a, 184b, 191a, 199b, 200e, 201c; Westminster City Library Archive: Liberty, London (Godfrey New) *56a*, *60/61*, 61c, *132a*, *196d*; Weybridge Museum 237; The White House, London (P. J. Gates) *41b*, 206a; The Wool Bureau, New York 105b; The Worshipful Company of Goldsmiths 161c; Württembergisches Landesmuseum Stuttgart 220.